LORDSHIP IN FOUR REALMS

MANCHESTER MEDIEVAL STUDIES

SERIES EDITOR Professor S. H. Rigby

The study of medieval Europe is being transformed as old orthodoxies are challenged, new methods embraced and fresh fields of enquiry opened up. The adoption of interdisciplinary perspectives and the challenge of economic, social and cultural theory are forcing medievalists to ask new questions and to see familiar topics in a fresh light.

The aim of this series is to combine the scholarship traditionally associated with medieval studies with an awareness of more recent issues and approaches in a form accessible to the non-specialist reader.

ALREADY PUBLISHED IN THE SERIES

Peacemaking in the middle ages: Principles and practice
Jenny Benham

Money in the medieval English economy: 973-1489
James Bolton

Reform and the papacy in the eleventh century
Kathleen G. Cushing

Picturing women in late medieval and Renaissance art
Christa Grössinger

The Vikings in England
D. M. Hadley

A sacred city: consecrating churches and reforming society in eleventh-century Italy
Louis I. Hamilton

The politics of carnival
Christopher Humphrey

Holy motherhood
Elizabeth L'Estrange

Music, scholasticism and reform: Salian Germany 1024-1125
T.J.H. McCarthy

Medieval law in context
Anthony Musson

The expansion of Europe, 1250-1500
Michael North

Medieval maidens
Kim M. Phillips

Gentry culture in late medieval England
Raluca Radulescu and Alison Truelove (eds)

Chaucer in context
S. H. Rigby

The life cycle in Western Europe, c.1300–c.1500
Deborah Youngs

MANCHESTER MEDIEVAL STUDIES

LORDSHIP IN FOUR REALMS
THE LACY FAMILY, 1166-1241

Colin Veach

Manchester University Press

Copyright © Colin Veach 2014

The right of Colin Veach to be identified as the author of this work has been asserted by him in accordance with the Copyright, Designs and Patents Act 1988.

Published by Manchester University Press
Altrincham Street, Manchester M1 7JA, UK
www.manchesteruniversitypress.co.uk

British Library Cataloguing-in-Publication Data is available

Library of Congress Cataloging-in-Publication Data is available

ISBN 978 1 7849 9117 3 *paperback*

First published by Manchester University Press in hardback 2014

This paperback edition first published 2015

The publisher has no responsibility for the persistence or accuracy of URLs for any external or third-party internet websites referred to in this book, and does not guarantee that any content on such websites is, or will remain, accurate or appropriate.

Printed by Lightning Source

For Freya, Owen and Dylan

CONTENTS

List of maps, figures and tables   viii
Acknowledgements   ix
List of abbreviations   x
Maps   xiii

Introduction   1

I: Hugh de Lacy

1   A transnational magnate: 1166–74   21
2   'Lord of the Foreigners of Ireland': 1177–86   47

II: Walter de Lacy

3   Divided allegiance: 1189–99   77
4   Factionalism: 1199–1206   101
5   Royal v. aristocratic lordship: 1206–16   130
6   Sheriff of Herefordshire: 1216–22   167
7   The dangers of transnational lordship: 1222–41   191

III: Lordship

8   Lordship in four realms   237

Conclusion   279

Appendix 1: Family trees   287
Appendix 2: Tables   289
Appendix 3: Charter of Walter de Lacy   307
Select bibliography   310
Index   323

LIST OF MAPS, FIGURES AND TABLES

Maps

1	Lacy lands in England and Wales	*page* xiii
2	Lacy lands in Normandy	xiv
3	Lacy lands in Ireland	xv

Figures

7.1	Trim Castle	204
8.1	Walter de Lacy's charter to Craswall Priory (Herefordshire) (*Copyright Mappa Mundi Trust and Dean and Chapter of Hereford Cathedral*)	250
8.2	Hugh de Lacy from Gerald of Wales's *Expugnatio Hibernica* (*Courtesy of the National Library of Ireland*)	265

Tables

1	Tenants of Hugh de Lacy in England	289
2	Tenants of Walter de Lacy in England	293
3	The subinfeudation of Meath	301
4	Assorted Lacy knights and officials	302
5	Most frequent witnesses to Lacy acta	304

ACKNOWLEDGEMENTS

This book was researched and written with the help of many. Professors Seán Duffy and Robin Frame inspired this project's scope through their impressive oeuvres, and helped to guide its direction as supervisors of my doctoral thesis at Trinity College Dublin. Since then, I have benefited tremendously from the kindness shown to me by Professor David Crouch, who not only shared his vast collection of unpublished seigniorial acta, but also offered very detailed (and very critical) feedback on the entire draft manuscript. Professor Nicholas Vincent likewise generously allowed me access to his unpublished acta of the Angevin kings, sent me various Lacy deeds and commented on the draft manuscript throughout. The series editor, Professor Stephen Rigby, also read and offered advice on the entire manuscript. All three of these readers saved me from a great many errors (though, stubbornly, I have not heeded all of their warnings). In addition, Professor David Carpenter, Dr Katharine Simms, Dr Peter Crooks and Dr Freya Verstraten Veach have read portions of the text, adding their individual insights. Professor Marie Therese Flanagan, Dr Brendan Smith and Professor Daniel Power have informed my research through their helpful, often timely, guidance. Dr David Ditchburn, and the staff and students of Trinity College Dublin's History Department and Medieval History Research Centre, provided a scholarly platform to shape and test my ideas. Lately, my colleagues at the University of Hull have provided an accommodating environment in which to bring this project to fruition. I have often relied upon the patience of archival staff, though special thanks must go to those of the National Library of Ireland and Hereford Cathedral Archives for permission to reproduce copyrighted material. I would also like to acknowledge the efforts of the staff of Manchester University Press. Finally, my greatest debts are to my wife, Freya, and children, Owen and Dylan, without whose support and forbearance this book would not have been possible.

Hull
15 March 2013

LIST OF ABBREVIATIONS

AC	Annála Connacht. The Annals of Connacht (A.D. 1224-1544), ed. A. M. Freeman (Dublin, 1944).
AFM	Annála Ríoghachta Éireann: Annals of the Kingdom of Ireland by the Four Masters, From the Earliest Period to the Year 1616, ed. and trans. John O'Donovan, 7 vols (Dublin, 1848-51).
AI	The Annals of Inisfallen (MS, Rawlinson B. 503), ed. and trans. Seán Mac Airt (Dublin, 1951).
ALC	The Annals of Loch Cé. A Chronicle of Irish affairs from A.D. 1014 to A.D. 1590, ed. and trans. William M. Hennessy, 2 vols (Oxford, 1871).
Ann. Clon.	The Annals of Clonmacnoise: Being the Annals of Ireland from the Earliest Period to A.D. 1408, ed. D. Murphy (Dublin, 1896).
AU	Annála Uladh. Annals of Ulster, Otherwise Annála Senait, Annals of Senat; a Chronicle of Irish Affairs A.D. 431-1131: 1155-1541, ed. and trans. Bartholomew Mac Carthy, 4 vols (Dublin, 1893).
BL	British Library
BM	Bibliothèque Municipale
CFR	Calendar of the Fine Rolls of the Reign of Henry III available both on the Henry III Fine Rolls Project's website (www.finerollshenry3.org.uk) and within Calendar of the Fine Rolls of the Reign of Henry III [1216-1224, 1224-1234, 1234-1242], eds Paul Dryburgh and Beth Hartland (Woodbridge, 2007, 2008, 2009).
CR	Close Rolls of the Reign of Henry III, Preserved in the Public Record Office, [A.D. 1227-1231, 1231-1234, 1234-1237, 1237-1242] (London, 1902, 1905, 1908, 1911).

LIST OF ABBREVIATIONS

Deeds	The Deeds of the Normans in Ireland. La Geste des Engleis en Yrlande, ed. and trans. Evelyn Mullally (Dublin, 2002).
Expugnatio Hibernica	Expugnatio Hibernica: The Conquest of Ireland by Giraldus Cambrensis, eds A. B. Scott and F. X. Martin (Dublin, 1978).
Flores Historiarum	Rogeri de Wendover Liber Qui Dictur Flores Historiarum ab Anno Domini MCLIV annoque Henrici Anglorum Regis Secundi Primo, ed. H. G. Hewlett, 3 vols (London, 1886–89).
HCA	Hereford Cathedral Archives.
Howden, Chronica	Chronica Magistri Rogeri de Hovedene, ed. William Stubbs, 4 vols (London, 1868–71).
Howden, Gesta	Gesta Regis Henrici Secundi Benedicti Abbatis. The Chronicle of the Reigns of Henry II and Richard I, AD 1169–1192, Known Commonly Under the Name of Benedict of Peterborough, ed. William Stubbs, 2 vols (London, 1867).
Irish Llanthony	The Irish Cartularies of Llanthony Prima & Secunda, ed. E. St J. Brooks (Dublin, 1953).
Irish Pipe Roll 14 John	Davies, Oliver and Quinn, David B., 'The Irish Pipe Roll of 14 John, 1211–1212', Ulster Journal of Archaeology, 4, Supplement (1941).
MCB	Mac Carthaigh's Book in Miscellaneous Irish Annals (A.D. 1114–1437), ed. Séamus Ó hInnse (Dublin, 1947).
NHI, ii	A New History of Ireland, ii: Medieval Ireland 1169–1534, ed. Art Cosgrove (Oxford, 1987).
Orpen, Normans	Orpen, G. H., Ireland Under the Normans, 4 vols (Oxford, 1912–20).
PR	Patent Rolls of the Reign of Henry III Preserved in the Public Record Office, [A.D. 1216–1225, 1225–1232] (London, 1901, 1903).
RBE	The Red Book of the Exchequer, ed. Hubert Hall, 3 vols (London, 1896).
Royal Letters	Royal and Other Historical Letters Illustrative of the Reign of Henry III from the Originals in the Public Record Office, ed. W. W. Shirley, 2 vols (London, 1862–88).
Song	The Song of Dermot and the Earl: An Old French

LIST OF ABBREVIATIONS

	Poem. From the Carew Manuscript no. 596 in the Archiepiscopal Library at Lambeth Palace, ed. G. H. Orpen (Oxford, 1892).
TNA	The National Archives.

MAPS

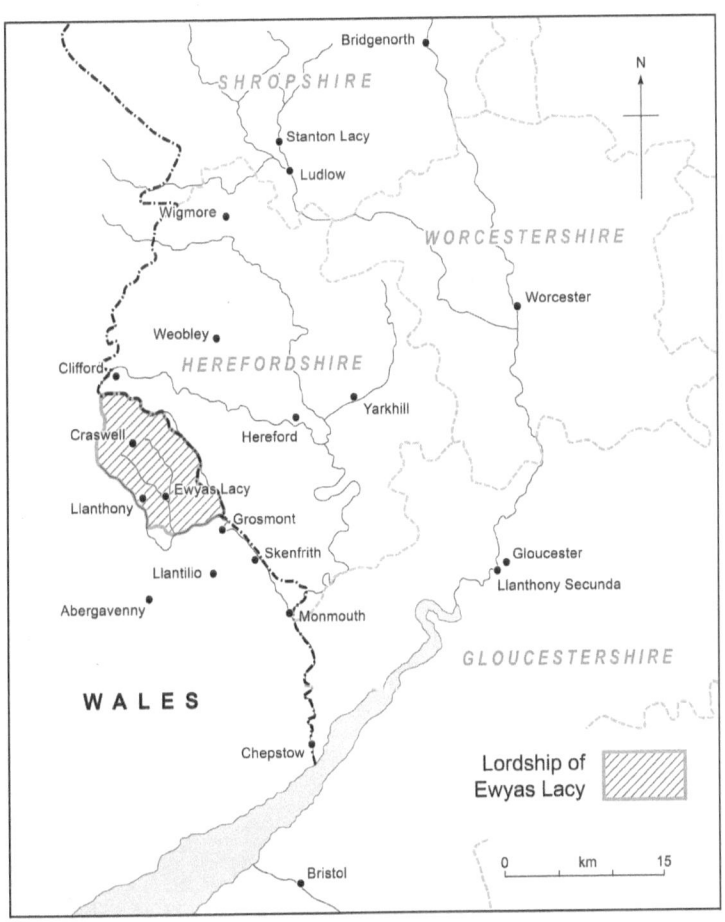

1 Lacy lands in England and Wales

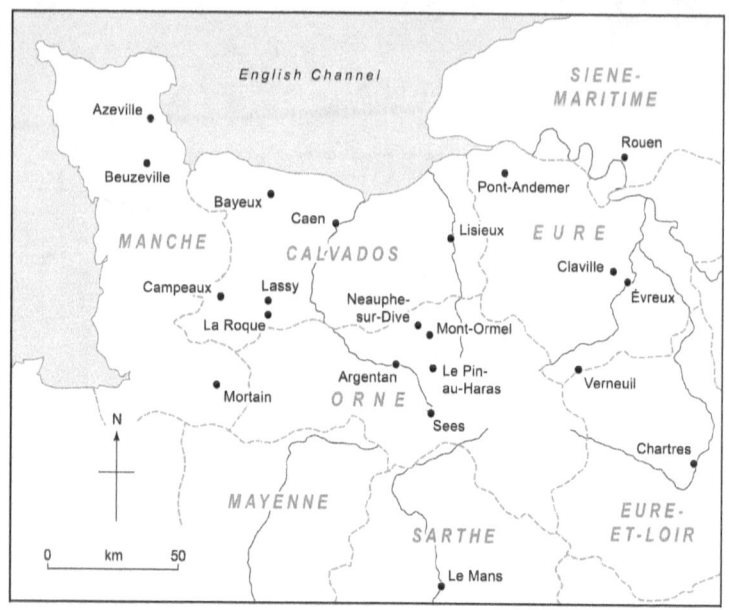

2 Lacy lands in Normandy

3 Lacy lands in Ireland

Introduction

Transnational aristocracy

In the twelfth and thirteenth centuries, a complex network of lordship transcended traditional national boundaries. The cross-border connections of the men involved were invaluable to those at the top, such as the king of England, who could thus harness their service across several provinces. The aristocratic communities of north-western Europe were knit together in this way. The forces involved were not all to the king's advantage, however. Bonds of allegiance could often lose focus for those holding lands in several realms. For those whose lands included significant frontier components, profiles could be raised, fortunes made and rebellion contemplated.

The field of medieval British history is currently led by historians who, eschewing to a greater or lesser extent traditional national boundaries, situate their studies within the interconnected histories of north-western Europe. Most full-length works of this genre tend to have rather broad scope, charting general themes over centuries of interaction. For instance, Rees Davies's *Domination and Conquest: The Experience of Ireland, Scotland and Wales, 1100–1300* (Cambridge, 1990) and *The First English Empire: Power and Identities in the British Isles 1093–1343* (Oxford, 2000) are unrivalled in their adroit handling of the complex history of the British Isles. Likewise, his final book *Lords & Lordship in the British Isles in the Late Middle Ages* (Oxford, 2009), though dealing with a later period, has a pertinence which transcends its chronological bookends. Robin Frame's *The Political Development of the British Isles, 1100–1400* (Oxford, 1995) perfectly complements Davies's oeuvre by bringing the Irish dimension into sharper focus. David Carpenter's *The Struggle for Mastery: Britain*

1066–1284 (London, 2003) is a detailed and unified narrative of the medieval British Isles over two centuries.[1]

In addition, studies of frontier regions are becoming increasingly popular, owing to the intensity of research they afford their authors. For instance, Max Lieberman's *The Medieval March of Wales: The Creation and Perception of a Frontier, 1066–1283* (Cambridge, 2010) and Brock Holden's *Lords of the Central Marches: English Aristocracy and Frontier Society 1087–1265* (Oxford, 2008) use individual border counties, Shropshire and Herefordshire respectively, to examine the intricate interrelationships of those living on the militarised border between England and Wales. Daniel Power's *The Norman Frontier in the Twelfth and Early Thirteenth Centuries* (Cambridge, 2004) is a painstaking assessment of the Norman frontier, and Brendan Smith's *Colonisation and Conquest in Medieval Ireland. The English in Louth, 1170–1330* (Cambridge, 1999) adroitly highlights the political imperatives facing the colonial community north of Dublin. Such case studies are important, because, in addition to providing painstaking analyses of their particular bailiwicks, their authors' depth of inquiry allows them to offer great insight into the general texture of medieval political society.

Yet the focus can be narrowed further, and on to the way individuals exploited the potential of this complex world. David Crouch's *The Beaumont Twins: The Roots and Branches of Power in the Twelfth Century* (Cambridge, 1986) offered a groundbreaking analysis of transnational lordship as it pertained to two brothers, Count Waleran of Meulan and Earl Robert of Leicester, in England, Normandy and Capetian France. It is perhaps banal to state that the only way to understand a society is by also studying the individuals of whom it was comprised, yet, apart from Crouch's work, the intense study of individuals in the twelfth and early thirteenth centuries has been relatively neglected in favour of broader examinations. When these focus on particular arenas such as the Welsh marches, the Irish Sea region or even the British Isles, their authors place their own artificial restrictions on their assessments of the men and women under investigation. This risks misinterpreting the actions of those whose interests may have stretched far beyond the arenas in question. So for instance, Crouch's assessment of the career of William Marshal, original though it is, suffers by its focus on the Marshal as courtier, so missing the nuances of the relationship of Marshal with King John generated out of their mutual rivalry in Ireland.

It is essential that these individuals – and their particular interests, outlooks and ambitions – do not become subsumed within the groups into which historians sort them. For instance, Hugh and Walter de Lacy were recognised by their contemporaries as Welsh marchers, but they were also English and Norman magnates whose efforts often went to extending their position in Ireland. To lose sight of all these factors is to take them out of context. As Sidney Painter observed in his biography of the (decidedly atypical) 'feudal baron', William Marshal: 'to know a typical feudal baron is to have a fuller comprehension of feudal society as a whole'.[2] A view from below often uncovers characteristics not immediately apparent from above. Consequently, the Middle Ages can be better understood through studies of the interplay between individuals, regions and the kingdom. This book aims to achieve greater familiarity with the nature of transnational lordship and the interaction between king and magnate through a focused study of the fortunes of the Lacy family from 1166 to 1241. It may not answer all the questions raised within, but it is a case-study of individuals who consciously acted in a far wider landscape than one court and one kingdom, and who happily exploited the unparalleled opportunities their situation presented.

The case of the Lacys is an interesting one, ideally suited to close examination. Because their rise to prominence from the late twelfth century was to last only two generations, the study of the family at the height of its power may be focused more intensely upon the political careers of Hugh de Lacy (d. 1186) and his son, Walter (d. 1241), in England, Ireland, Wales and Normandy. What is more, because of their pertinence to certain aspects of British and (especially) Irish history, an assumption of familiarity has grown up around these men (about whom we in fact know comparatively little), which seems to have deflected any previous in-depth analyses of their careers. The 1966 study of the Lacy family by W. E. Wightman is chiefly concerned with the formation and management of the Lacys' English and (to a lesser extent) Norman honors. It says very little about Hugh, and almost nothing about Walter.[3] It fails to unpick the complexity of the Norman evidence and also ignores Ireland, a decision which, though clear in the title, is questionable given Ireland's importance to the family from 1177 (if not 1172). In shorter studies, Robert Bartlett situates Hugh de Lacy within the general aristocratic diaspora of the twelfth century by comparing his career in Ireland to those of his contemporaries on the German frontier,[4] and Joe Hillaby provides a brief narrative of Walter's political career in Ireland to 1224, and an insightful analysis of his debt thereafter.[5]

The Lacys feature as one of five baronial families in Brock Holden's study of Herefordshire and the central Welsh march, providing a welcome glimpse of the family's network within that region. However, the limitations of a regionalised approach are apparent in that the Lacys' Norman and Irish interests are dealt with only cursorily by Holden. What is more, his focus on Herefordshire means that the family's other English interests (which included important components in Shropshire, Wiltshire, Oxfordshire and Gloucestershire) are all but ignored. This approach led Holden to misinterpret several of the Lacys' actions, which were taken for reasons weightier than the concerns of the local marcher community. In similar vein, Holden's fellow border historian, Max Lieberman, chose not to include the Lacys among the Shropshire barons of his own study. Hugh and Walter de Lacy make several appearances in Lieberman's work, but they are always identified as 'lords of Weobley and of Meath' and presented in terms of their Herefordshire holdings.[6] Like Holden, Lieberman provides a case-study based on a handful of baronial families. He may have left the Lacys out to avoid encroaching upon Holden's work, but, by failing to acknowledge the Lacys' major Shropshire interests centred on Stanton Lacy and Ludlow (which, as will be seen, was the administrative centre of Walter's English stewards),[7] Lieberman also misses important local connections.

This highlights a very real problem for the study of the Lacy family in this period. In order to give due attention to their activities in England, Ireland, Wales and Normandy, a familiarity with the histories of each region is required. English historians have become adept at incorporating Normandy into their studies, but Ireland remains surprisingly foreign to the large majority. Irish historians traditionally have been much better at incorporating English history (as it pertained to Ireland) into their work, but few would presume actually to *write* English history itself.[8] This study of the Lacy family has been obliged to span several historiographical traditions. Such breadth of research is an asset in producing a more focused conclusion. By involving the histories of several realms, this book is able to provide an enticing glimpse of the bonds that stretched between them. Differences in the nature of lordship, and the demands of allegiance, were very real considerations for cross-border aristocrats. So too were local conditions, which could vary widely between, for instance, Calvados and Bréifne. The degree to which these 'were taken in their stride'[9] was a major determinant of a magnate's success or failure. In Ireland and the Welsh march, private warfare was often a way of life. Hugh de Lacy was established in Meath with the understanding that he would conquer the territory himself. Likewise, his son Walter could intrude into native Irish succession disputes, using military force to ensure that his preferred candidate was the victor. Such tactics could not be contemplated in England or Normandy by this period, where conflict was acted out at court or within judicial tribunals. The theme of regional adaptability is therefore central to this study.

Hugh and Walter de Lacy were not alone in transcending national and regional boundaries. The English king's hegemony was so far-reaching that several aristocratic families were able to cultivate interests spanning his several realms, and sometimes even step outside them, into France, Flanders and Scotland. Aristocratic and royal interests interacted in different theatres of operation. Consequently, disputes might flare up in one, only to be played out in another. A magnate might overstep his bounds in Ireland, only to see the king take retributory action on his more accessible English lands. Similarly, political disaffection in Normandy might ignite rebellion in the Welsh marches as happened in Stephen's reign. This mobility of conflicts has obscured a full understanding of some of the more significant events examined in this book, and it is hoped that they have benefited from a transnational approach.

While focusing on the aristocracy, this book also has much also to say about English kingship. The political fortunes of Hugh and Walter de Lacy were inextricably linked to their relationship with the king of England, their ultimate overlord in Normandy, Wales and Ireland. Throughout this book, the bestowal and removal of royal favour are charted and analysed, hopefully allowing a better understanding of the political and diplomatic forces at work on events. This process involves the examination of royal practice during four reigns, which proves all the more revealing because the aristocratic family involved remains constant. Kings were themselves individuals. King Henry II and King John could relate to their greatest barons in ways which are loosely comparable, but at others they might differ in their tactics. When assessing their rule, it is a matter of some significance when one can show that the two kings treated the same family in different ways. In this instance, for example, both kings were forced to confront a growing intractability on the part of the lord of Meath in Ireland. Their reactions were quite dissimilar and say much about the nature of their rule. Of particular interest is the degree to which the nature of Crown–magnate relations changed during the minority of Henry III. The extent to which those who ruled in Henry III's name retained or departed from the practices of the preceding three reigns is an important indicator not only of their own interests (which could be transformed into royal initiatives) but also of whether and how their policies were shaped by the royal authority they were briefly handed.

This study of transnational aristocracy in action has resulted in a 'thickened' narrative in which sections of concentrated analysis are held together by a narrative account of the Lacys' careers. In this way, the temporal contexts of the Lacys' actions are retained and the two sub-themes of royal power and transnational lordship can be addressed where appropriate. To use David Carpenter's metaphor, 'a more analytical approach to the period would bring familiarity with the individual bricks but give little idea of their place in the construction of the building'.[10] The book closes with a thematic chapter on lordship, which provides an anatomy of the Lacys' aristocratic enterprise across four realms.

Lordship

'Lordship' is complicated. Being derived from the medieval concept of *dominium* (or *seigneurie*) it carries considerable historiographical baggage. In the Middle Ages, *dominium* could describe a multitude of relationships, including those between lord and vassal, husband and wife, and God and humanity. *Dominium* was a theoretical concept as well as a social reality, meditated upon in intellectual treatises, celebrated in *chansons de geste*, documented in charters and judged in local courts. A word so ubiquitous does not lend itself to precision in definition, and 'lordship' (or *seigneurie*, *Herrschaft*) has acquired a plurality of meanings in modern studies. To the influential German sociologist Max Weber (d. 1920), *Herrschaft* was a subset of power. '"Power" (*Macht*) is the probability that one actor within a social relationship will be in a position to carry out his own will despite resistance, regardless of the basis upon which this probability rests. *Herrschaft* is the probability that a command with a given specific content will be obeyed by a given group of persons.' He later elaborates:

> *Herrschaft* will thus mean the situation in which the manifested will (command) of the ruler or rulers is meant to influence the conduct of one or more others (the ruled) and actually does influence it in such a way that their conduct to a socially relevant degree occurs as if the ruled had made the content of the commend the maxim of their conduct for its very own sake. Looked upon from the other end, this situation will be called 'obedience' (*Gehorsam*).[11]

Weber also described three types of legitimate *Herrshaft*: (1) legal *Herrschaft* derived from known principles and applied administratively or judicially; (2) traditional *Herrschaft*, which was inherited; and

(3) charismatic *Herrschaft* based upon the unique qualities of the lord which drew personal devotion to him.[12] Weber devised this definition to provide a neutral, scientific concept of *Herrschaft* to be used in his own work, divorced from its previously negative portrayals born of Enlightenment ideals.[13]

In France, *seigneurie* is conceived of as an expression of aristocratic privilege, and was for a long time closely related to the concept of the *ban*. A father of the *Annales* school of history, Marc Bloch, explained the *ban* in terms of the exactions a *seigneur* imposed upon his tenants. The *ban* was 'the lord's acknowledged power to give orders', 'the right of coercion' and the 'power to give orders and to punish'.[14] The *ban* was a legitimate power to be delegated by legitimate rulers. In this way, it resembles Weber's definition of a 'state' as an association which 'successfully claims the monopoly of the legitimate use of physical force within a given territory'.[15] According to Bloch, the *ban* was devolved by legitimate *seigneurs* on to their officials, 'petty local potentates', who used it to impose exactions – termed by him (but not by contemporaries) *banalités* – upon their tenants. Bloch's thesis of transformation was reinforced and refined as to chronology by George Duby, who through his study of the medieval Mâconnais region of France posited a transformation in society occurring around the year 1000, a *mutation féodale*, which included (among other things) the diffusion of the *ban* amongst *seigneurs* of lower social standing.[16] This theory, which charted the dissolution of the old Carolingian order and the gradual reformation of public authority in the form of the thirteenth-century French nation-state, served as the dominant meta-narrative of French medieval history from the 1960s until the late 1990s. However, more recent scholarship has undercut the theory of millennial transformation by stressing continuity rather than change. The theory's main assailant, Dominique Barthélemy, suggests that the transformation apparent in the sources was actually down to a change in the sources themselves – a *mutation documentaire*.[17] He also criticises historians' contrasting of 'private jurisdiction' and 'public order' as anachronistic, based on 'statist' assumptions that their medieval subjects did not share. Instead of the privilege of the *ban*, Barthélemy places the focus on socio-economic domination.[18]

The American medievalist Thomas Bisson was a strong proponent of the French mutationist theory in the 1990s, highlighting the horror of violence inflicted upon the medieval European populace by those upon whom the *ban* descended.[19] He has since cooled on the theory of a firmly datable millennial mutation, but has maintained the mutationists' focus on the violent and anarchical character of privatised lordship. In 2008, Bisson suggested a twelfth-century revolution, in which private affective lordship was superseded by public lordship (which he terms 'government').[20] To Bisson, legitimacy of power resided in a concern for the common weal, with strong centralised power almost always preferred over diffused. In the eleventh century, the profusion of knights and castellans pretending to noble powers and status led to a society filled with men whose ambitions outstripped their capacities, and who, consequently, were predisposed to violence to achieve the lifestyle they craved. 'Men fought for lordship, or for shares in it, and they learned to despise the peasants they felt compelled to exploit. Incipient nobility could be pitiless – and precarious.'[21]

Bisson's view of the nature of lordship contrasts with that held by Rees Davies. Both Bisson and Davies argue that medieval conceptions of power were tied into the experience of lordship, and, like Barthélemy, regard the historiographical focus on the medieval 'state' as anachronistic and unhelpful.[22] However, while Bisson posits a mid-twelfth-century crisis of lordship, after which the process of state formation began, Davies recognises no such watershed. Instead, he calls for an end to teleological and Rankean searches for the origins of modern states in medieval Europe. In place of the state, Davies offers lordship, which he uses to legitimise the use of power in the periphery as well as the core throughout the Middle Ages. Davies derives his definition of lordship from the mutationists' more pragmatic French contemporary, Robert Boutruche, who writes simply that '*seigneurie* [lordship] is a power of command, constraint and exploitation. It is also the right to exercise such power.'[23] This definition closely resembles the concept of the *ban*, but, crucially, Davies in his treatment casts aside the idea that the aristocracy obtained their lordship from some 'legitimate' centralised authority. '[Lordship] is a word which respects the continuum of power, rather than necessarily privileging one particular form of power, and seeing other manifestations of power as derogations from, or aspirations towards this privileged power.'[24] To Davies, royal lordship was merely one form of lordship, which, once it had reached a dominant position in medieval society, constructed the theory that it was the only 'public' lordship, and that all others were 'private' and derivative.[25] Davies argues that medieval lordship had social, judicial, economic, ideological and political aspects, and its nature could be distinguished between 'intensive lordship', involving a lord in direct control of his tenants, and 'tributary lordship', based upon a loose acknowledgement of superior status. He stresses the importance of studying the multifarious structures and substructures of aristocratic lordship, which run counter to the statist view of royal lordship constructed on the surviving products of Crown administration. Being purpose-built for the transnational aristocratic study I follow here, Davies's conception of mobile lordship is the one most consistent with what I find to be the experiences of Hugh and Walter de Lacy from 1166 to 1241. Consequently, it is the one adhered to in this book.

This conception of lordship may be popular, but it has not yet carried all before it. David Crouch, for one, has mounted a vigorous challenge to its portrayal as the sole operating principle behind medieval society. In a review article, Crouch summarises the historiography, attacks a few sacred cows and laments the lack of progress in medieval history.[26] One point that Crouch deplores is a tendency towards over-simplification in writing on lordship, and he has a point. Many modern definitions of medieval lordship are structuralist, aiming to articulate the underlying rules that governed medieval behaviour, and almost all are reductionist, distilling complex processes into a simple principle. This combination is dangerous unless it is recognised and allowed for. Reductionism is useful as a conceptual tool, but its conclusions cannot be permitted to replace the phenomena they describe in historical analysis. The present study of the Lacy family uncovers many complexities previously hidden from historiographical scrutiny by over-simplified pronouncements on royal policy or aristocratic behaviour. In some cases, these details have been enough to overturn long-held theories. Synthesis in light of historical models is vitally important to the progress of history, but not more so than detailed analysis. As Martin Aurell declares, 'C'est la source qui fait l'historien!'[27]

Medieval people often thought in terms of lordship, or, to put it another way, they often meditated on the relationship with their lord, which was key to their worldly success. This does not mean that lordship was the *single* organising principle of their society. Historians would be remiss to ignore other social realities (e.g. ethnic identity, gender construction or religious community) simply because they were not clearly appreciated or articulated by medieval writers.[28] However, lordship *was* real. Its ubiquity in medieval life and modern historiography does not preclude its effective use to help explain the (two-way) bonds of dependence that it maintained and described. Its broad contemporary usage is especially useful in this regard, because it provides a means of comparison between otherwise dissimilar local structures. Hugh and Walter de Lacy did not deal with their lands in Herefordshire as they did those in Meath, where they were forced to adapt to pre-existing Celtic conditions, or even Normandy, which had its own unique power structure. Lordship (as used in this book) was present in all three. It can be used to describe to describe the Lacys' experience as sub-tenants in Normandy, tenants-in-chief in England, marcher lords in Wales and magnate-administrators in Ireland. It even allows the question to be posed of whether they thought of their lordship in Ireland as kingship on the Celtic model. The ability to accommodate these experiences under one blanket is what encourages me to use lordship as the key concept behind this study.

Sources

The materials available for an investigation of the Lacy family are much the same as those for any other magnate family of the period. They were not blessed with contemporary biographies and were not sufficiently high in the royal government for their correspondence to have been preserved. The Lacys' position as lords of Meath brought them to the attention of the Irish annalists, whose work stands as a most welcome addition to the record of their careers. But this is not a particular disadvantage. In many ways the strength of this study of the Lacys lies in its replicability. There were many other families like them. From the commencement of the great series of chancery enrolments during King John's reign, there exists a vast body of data, which, when combined with baronial acta and contemporary narratives, provides sufficient raw material upon which to base comprehensive analyses of the careers of specific men and particular families.

Seigniorial acta
A brief thirteenth-century 'charter roll' of Lacy deeds exists at the Hereford Cathedral Archives that preserves several deeds regarding the family's grants in Herefordshire, Shropshire and the Welsh march. The late-fourteenth-century register book of the lords of Gormanston (Co. Meath) also contains a number of useful Lacy charters regarding Ireland.[29] Compiled by Sir Christopher Preston from the contents of his family's muniment chest, the register contains a number of charters for this period, both those granted and those received. These can be supplemented by the contents of several ecclesiastical cartularies, including those of the priories of Llanthony Prima (Gwent) and Secunda (Gloucestershire), the priory of St Guthlac (Hereford), Hereford Cathedral, St Thomas's Abbey (Dublin), St Mary's Abbey (Dublin), the hospital of St John the Baptist (Dublin) and Haughmond Abbey (Shropshire).[30] Isolated original deeds and later copies of charters now lost are also scattered among the archival collections of England, Ireland and France with little more than chance ensuring their survival.

Record sources

The output of the English royal administration is – as has been said – of great use to the study of medieval individuals. However, it must be kept in mind that these sources provide a one-sided view of the period: the overlord's view. What is more, the nature of transnational landholding in some ways confounds the royal chancery, which did not or could not always penetrate the great marcher liberties. The existence of multiple administrations (English, Irish and Norman) also complicates matters. Tragically, the records of the medieval Irish administration were lost in the fire that destroyed the Irish Public Record Office in 1922, obscuring one perspective. For England, the great enrolments of the English exchequer, the pipe rolls, survive from the outset of the period under consideration. A number of Norman pipe rolls also survive, as well as two rolls and numerous extracts from Ireland (all in transcription).[31] From the end of the twelfth century, the study of medieval individuals is greatly aided by further enrolments of the English administration. The Plea Rolls of the king's justices (1194), Charter Rolls (1199), *Oblata* and Fine Rolls (1199), *Liberate* and Close Rolls (1200) and Patent Rolls (1201) were all systematic enrolments of the activities of the English royal government, and provide a new and detailed perspective on the later period of this book.[32] From the reign of Henry III, the great *corpus* of ancient correspondence and petitions (TNA SC 1, TNA SC 8) enters this study. Being an artificial collection of letters once in the Tower of London, the ancient correspondence comprises letters from many different sources. Many letters of note have been published by Shirley,[33] and those concerning Wales calendared by J. G. Edwards,[34] but more remain unpublished.

Narrative sources

The grant of Meath brought the Lacys to the attention of contemporary Anglo-Norman writers, and narrative works have been utilised alongside the record sources throughout this book.[35] If monastic chroniclers or secular lyricists are not always the most reliable sources for the bare facts of the events they describe, they are at least helpful barometers of opinion and retailers or rumour, which can sometimes be as important as more factual records of events. If, for instance, the Augustinian prior Richard de Morins, author of the Dunstable annals, believed that there was a conspiracy afoot in 1210 to replace King John with Simon de Montfort, a sentiment which would not have found its way into the record sources, then this at least reveals a great deal about the conditions of the time. As it turns out, there may have been something to the rumour, and certain of King John's actions in 1210 perhaps should be viewed in that light.[36] By far the most important commentators on Hugh de Lacy are Gerald of Wales and Roger of Howden.[37] On the whole, the testimony of the well-positioned court chronicler Roger of Howden is to be preferred to Gerald or almost any other contemporary narrative source (except when Gerald accompanied John's court to Ireland in 1185). However, Roger of Howden was not universally attendant upon the English king, and John Gillingham has shown that his presentation of events of which he had no direct knowledge can be flawed.[38] Gerald of Wales provides invaluable commentary on the early years of the English colony in Ireland, though his perspective is largely that of his Geraldine cousins and their fellow colonists.[39] The St Albans chroniclers, Roger of Wendover and Matthew Paris, are important for the first half of the thirteenth century, though both had their own agendas and have to be treated with caution.

Another source of great utility is the poem often called *The Song of Dermot and the Earl*.[40] The *Song* provides details of the invasion of Ireland, and the subinfeudation of Meath and Leinster, which would not otherwise survive. Probably composed in the last decade of the twelfth century, the poem is contemporary with Gerald's work, and shares much of its bias. However, while Gerald is willing to chastise those Englishmen who might oppose his family, the *Song* is almost universally supportive of the invaders and their initial patron, Diarmait Mac Murchada, king of Leinster. The Irish are presented as traitors in so far as they did not support the English. One significant problem with the *Song* is its chronology. The author never mentions the year in which an event occurred, and events are sometimes grouped thematically rather than chronologically. The obvious risks of using a laudatory poem as a historical source must be kept firmly in mind while utilising the *Song's* unique insight.[41] Another such poem, the near contemporary *History of William Marshal*,[42] contains important information regarding Walter de Lacy, and is an unparalleled source on noble conduct and the exercise of lordship in this period.

Gaelic sources

King Henry II's grant of Meath brought the Lacys to the attention of Irish commentators. The annals are the most useful Gaelic sources for this study. The main problems in using the annals concern their chronology and bias.[43] The annalists' method of compilation meant that events that occurred at a distance or were not immediately pertinent for their audience could be placed at the end of a given year, or even in the next. Thus, the most important events in the eyes of the annalist (such as notable deaths or battles) might be grouped at the beginning of a year, while seemingly unimportant or distant events placed at the end. This bias could also have an editorial quality, so that events particularly humiliating to local powers might be ignored (though this was not always the case), and victories made to sound more momentous than they were. For those annals, such as the Annals of the Four Masters, which were later compilations, the danger of chronology is compounded by their conglomerate nature. The obvious additional problem of scribal error is common to almost all of the sources under consideration.

Orthography and terminology

This book has sought to use a uniform orthography and terminology across several historiographical traditions and seventy-five years of history, challenging ambition though that is. Regarding toponyms, I follow John le Patourel's sound practice:

> 'Surnames' that are identifiable place-names are given as other place-names, with the particle in the appropriate language – thus, 'Henry of Winchester' but 'William de Rouen'. This cannot be done wholly consistently, since to speak of 'William de Varenne' rather than 'William de Warenne' for example, would only introduce obscurity.[44]

So, for instance, 'Hugh de Lacy' is preferred to 'Hugh de Lassy', or any of its antiquarian variant forms. In difficult cases such as Briouze/Braose (where 'Briouze' represents the modern place-name and 'Braose' is favoured in Irish historiography), the form used in the *Oxford Dictionary of National Biography* has been followed (so, 'Briouze').

The period 1172 to 1241 witnessed a formalisation of Irish spelling from Middle to Classical Irish. Assuming that it is preferable to be somewhat traditional rather than anachronistic, Irish names have been rendered in Middle Irish. Scottish names are in their generally recognised (largely anglicised) forms, while Manxmen and Islesmen have been given their Norse names (following the practice in *A New History of the Isle of Man*)[45] with their Gaelic forms in parentheses where pertinent.

After a period of myriad hyphenated alternatives, the current consensus among historians of medieval Britain and Ireland is that the men who inhabited England, and who then invaded Ireland, ought to be called English. This is a sensible approach, which reflects both the contemporary state of acculturation within England[46] and the way in which the invaders thought of themselves in Ireland.[47] Indeed, before they reverted to the general term *gall* (foreigner), the Irish annals referred to the first invaders from the English king's dominions as *Sasanach* (Saxon).[48] That having been said, calling Hugh and Walter de Lacy 'English' would have run counter to the aims of this study by begging the question of their negotiable identities. Before 1204, the Lacys seem to have been as much Norman as they were English, and as likely to have been in Normandy as England. These international aristocrats were English Normans who devoted much time and energy to their lands in Ireland and Wales.

Finally, the use of 'realms' in the title, and throughout the course of this book, to indicate England, Ireland, Wales and Normandy, should perhaps be justified. 'Realm' is used as a translation of the Latin *'regnum'* and Middle French 'realme' or 'reame', which was commonly used to denote a political unit, not necessarily a kingdom. England and Ireland were quite clearly *regna*, as royal lordships. Each had a king (or high king in the case of Ireland), and they were frequently referred to as *regna* in contemporary sources. For instance, in 1177, King Henry II considered appointing his youngest son John 'king of Ireland', and in the coming years secured a crown fashioned in the shape of peacock feathers from the pope.[49] What is more, in a letter written just before King John's Irish expedition of 1210, Gerald of Wales urged John to conquer Ireland so that he might elevate his two sons to royal status in two *regna*: England and Ireland.[50] Indeed, three years later, in 1213, King John surrendered 'the entire *regnum* of England and the entire *regnum* of Ireland' to Pope Innocent III.[51]

Wales was also a *regnum*.[52] The *monarchia Britonum* (i.e. kingship of the Welsh) is mentioned in the narration of Bishop Herwald of Llandaff's election in 1059 as being then held by Gruffudd ap Llywelyn, which may come ultimately from a contemporary Llandaff chronicle copied in the 1120s.[53] Gruffudd is also called *rex Britonum* in the *Annales Cambriae* under 1063.[54] The Welsh lawyers who put together the Laws of Hywel Dda in the late twelfth century perceived him as ruling a *regnum*.[55] Peter of Blois in a letter to Archbishop Walter of Palermo refers to Henry II acquiring the *ducatūs* of Normandy, Brittany and Aquitaine, and the *regna* of England, Scotland, Wales and Ireland. This shows a twelfth-century perception of the French regions as principalities under a king, but that the British nations were *regna* worthy of their own king.[56] The *regnum* of the Welsh was a contemporary ideal even if it was not a geographical reality. It was on the back of that ideal that the dynasty of Gwynedd exalted itself in the thirteenth century to a principality of Wales.

Despite Peter of Blois's classification, there are also numerous references to the *regnum* of Normandy. The *Recueil des actes des ducs de Normandie* contains eight instances of *regnum* applied to Normandy (and also one to Aquitaine) from 968 onwards. The most interesting is the preamble of an act of Robert I (dated 1030) which talks of his temporal realm (*temporale regnum*) of which he is the '*dux et rector*' and which he rules.[57] This respects the Isidorean definition found in Book IX of his *Etymologia*, which offered the medieval writer a rationale for his choice of Latin title to adorn a particular individual and define his power. So a king (*rex*) got his name from ruling (*regere*), and if he failed to govern righteously (*recte*) then he lost his right to rule, as all had long acknowledged.[58] By this definition anyone ruling (*regere*) might claim to exert power over a *regnum*. So in my view, from 1166 to 1241, the Lacys participated in the political lives of, and expressed their lordship in, four distinct 'realms': England, Ireland, Wales and Normandy.

Notes

1 See also Robert Bartlett, *England Under the Norman and Angevin kings 1075–1225* (Oxford, 2000); J. A. Green, *The Aristocracy of Norman England* (Cambridge, 1997).
2 Sidney Painter, *William Marshal: Knight-Errant, Baron, and Regent of England* (Baltimore, 1933), p. viii.
3 William E. Wightman, *The Lacy Family in England and Normandy 1066–1194* (Oxford, 1966).
4 Robert Bartlett, 'Colonial aristocracies of the high middle ages', in Robert Bartlett and A. MacKay (eds), *Medieval Frontier Societies* (Oxford, 1989), pp. 23–47.
5 Joe Hillaby, 'Colonisation, Crisis-Management and Debt: Walter de Lacy and the Lordship of Meath, 1189–1241', *Ríocht Na Mídhe*, 8/4 (1992–93), pp. 1–50.
6 Lieberman, *The Medieval March of Wales: The Creation and Perception of a Frontier, 1066–1283* (Cambridge, 2010), pp. 83, 85, 87, 98, 191.
7 See Chapter 8.
8 Robin Frame, 'The "Failure" of the First English Conquest of Ireland', in Frame (ed.), *Ireland and Britain, 1170–1450* (London and Rio Grande, 1998), pp. 1–13.
9 Robin Frame, *The Political Development of the British Isles, 1100–1400* (Oxford, 1995), p. 70.
10 David Carpenter, *The Minority of Henry III* (London, 1990), p. 4.
11 Max Weber, *Economy and Society*, ed. Guenther Roth and Claus Wittich, 2 vols. (Berkeley, 1979), pp. 53, 946.
12 *Ibid.*, pp. 215–16.
13 For a history of the concept of *Herrschaft*, see Melvin Richter, *The History of Political and Social Concepts: A Critical Introduction* (Oxford, 1995), pp. 58–78.
14 Marc Bloch, *Feudal Society*, trans. L. A. Manyon, 2 vols (2nd edn, London, 1965), i, p. 251.
15 Max Weber, 'Politics as vocation', in H. H. Gerth and C. W. Mills (eds and trans.), *From Max Weber: Essays in Sociology* (London, 1947), pp. 77–128, at p. 78.

16 Published as George Duby, *La société aux XIe et XIIe siècles dans la région mâconnaise* (Paris, 1953).
17 Dominique Barthélemy, 'La mutation féodale a-t-elle eu lieu? (Note critique)', *Annales: Économies, sociétés, civilisations*, 47 (1992), pp. 767–77.
18 Dominique Barthélemy, *The Serf, the Knight, and the Historian*, trans. G. R. Edwards (Ithaca, 2009). The historiography is also discussed in David Crouch, *The Birth of Nobility: Constructing Aristocracy in England and France, 950–1300* (Harlow, 2005), pp. 191–8.
19 Witness the lively debate: Thomas Bisson, 'The "feudal revolution"', *Past & Present*, 142 (1994), pp. 6–42; Dominique Barthélemy, 'Debate: the "feudal revolution" I', trans. J. Birrell, *Past & Present*, 152 (1996), pp. 196–205; Stephen White, 'Debate: the "Feudal Revolution" II', *ibid.*, pp. 205–23; Timothy Reuter, 'Debate: the "Feudal Revolution" III', *ibid.*, no. 155 (1997), pp. 177–95; Chris Wickham, 'Debate: the "Feudal Revolution" IV', *ibid.*, pp. 197–208; Thomas Bisson, 'Debate: the "Feudal Revolution" Reply', *ibid.*, pp. 208–34.
20 Thomas Bisson, *The Crisis of the Twelfth Century: Power, Lordship, and the Origins of European Government* (Princeton, 2008).
21 Bisson, *Crisis*, p. 7.
22 Thomas Bisson, 'Medieval lordship', *Speculum*, 70/4 (Oct. 1995), pp. 743–59, at pp. 744–6; Bisson, *Crisis*, pp. 12–13; R. R. Davies, 'The medieval state: the tyranny of a concept?', *Journal of Historical Sociology*, 16/2 (June 2003), pp. 280–300 (quote at p. 295).
23 Davies, 'Medieval state', p. 295; R. R. Davies, *Lords & Lordship in the British Isles in the Late Middle Ages*, ed. Brendan Smith (Oxford, 2009), p. 2 (quoting Robert Boutruche, *Seigneurie et feodalité*, 2 vols, (Paris, 1959–70), ii, p. 80).
24 Davies, 'Medieval state', p. 295.
25 *Ibid.*, pp. 295–6.
26 David Crouch, 'Captives in the head of Montesquieu, some recent work on medieval nobility', *Virtus*, 19 (2012), pp. 185–9. My thanks to Professor David Crouch for an advanced copy of his article, and for many informal discussions on the topic.
27 Martin Aurell, *L'empire des Plantagenêt* (Perrin, 2003), p. 21.
28 See for instance Susan Reynolds, 'There were states in medieval Europe: a response to Rees Davies', *Journal of Historical Sociology*, 16/4 (Dec. 2003), pp. 550–5, at p. 553.
29 National Library of Ireland MS 1646; *Calendar of the Gormanston Register, [c. 1175–1397]*, eds James Mills and M. J. McEnery (Dublin, 1916).
30 TNA C 115/75, C 115/77 (Cartulary of Llanthony Priory); Bodleian Library MS Rawlinson B 498 (Cartulary of St John the Baptist, Dublin); Bodleian Library MS Rawlinson B 329 (Hereford Cartulary); Balliol College Oxford MS 271 (Cartulary of St Guthlac, Hereford); *The Irish Cartularies of Llanthony Prima & Secunda*, ed. Eric St John Brooks (Dublin, 1953); *Register of the Abbey of St. Thomas, Dublin*, ed. John Thomas Gilbert (Rolls Series, London, 1889); *Chartularies of St Mary's Abbey, Dublin; With the Register of Its House at Dunbrody, and Annals of Ireland*, ed. J. T. Gilbert, 2 vols (London, 1884); *Register of the Hospital of S. John*

the Baptist Without the New Gate, Dublin, ed. Eric St John Brooks (Dublin, 1936); *The Cartulary of Haughmond Abbey*, ed. Una Rees (Cardiff, 1985).
31 Irish Pipe Roll of 14 John (see abbreviations for full reference).
32 See Michael Clanchy, *From Memory to Written Record, England 1066–1307* (3rd edn, Oxford, 2012); Philomena Connolly, *Medieval Record Sources* (Dublin, 2002).
33 *Royal Letters* (see abbreviations).
34 *Calendar of Ancient Correspondence Concerning Wales*, ed. J. G. Edwards (Cardiff, 1935).
35 See Antonia Gransden, *Historical Writing in England, c.550–c.1307* (London, 1974).
36 See Chapter 5.
37 *Expugnatio Hibernica*; Howden, *Gesta*; Howden, *Chronica* (see abbreviations).
38 John Gillingham, 'The travels of Roger of Howden and his views of the Irish, Scots and Welsh', in Christopher Harper-Bill (ed.), *Anglo-Norman Studies XX* (Woodbridge, 1997), pp. 151–69, at p. 166.
39 For Gerald see Robert Bartlett, *Gerald of Wales: A Voice of the Middle Ages* (Stroud, 2006).
40 *Song*; *Deeds* (see abbreviations).
41 J. F. O'Doherty, 'Historical criticism of the Song of Dermot and the Earl', *Irish Historical Studies*, 1 (1938–39), 4–20; *Deeds*, introduction.
42 *History of William Marshal*, eds A. J. Holden and David Crouch, trans. Stewart Gregory, 3 vols, Anglo-Norman Text Society, Occasional Series, 4–6 (London, 2002–7).
43 For Gaelic sources see Katharine Simms, *Medieval Gaelic Sources* (Dublin, 2009); D. P. McCarthy, *The Irish Annals: Their Genesis, Evolution and History* (Dublin, 2008).
44 John le Patourel, *The Norman Empire* (Oxford, 1976), p. vi.
45 Seán Duffy (ed.), *A New History of the Isle of Man: Volume 3* (Liverpool, forthcoming).
46 Hugh M. Thomas, *The English and the Normans. Ethnic Hostility, Assimilation, and Identity 1066–c.1220* (Oxford, 2003), pp. 3–4.
47 John Gillingham, 'The foundations of a disunited kingdom', in Gillingham (ed.), *The English in the Twelfth Century: Imperialism, National Identity and Political Values* (Woodbridge, 2000), pp. 93–109, at p. 99.
48 Freya Verstraten [Veach], 'The anglicisation of the Irish nobility c.1169 – c.1366', PhD (University of Dublin, 2008), p. 11. The Irish word 'Gall' originally referred to the Gauls, but by this period had been applied to non-Irish peoples (especially the Vikings) for centuries.
49 See Chapter 2. Stephen Church argues that John's eventual style, *dominus Hiberniae* (lord of Ireland), mirrored the contemporary English practice of calling the king-designate *dominus Angliae* as he awaited coronation. Stephen Church, 'Succession and Interregnum in the Kingdom of England and the Kingdom of Ireland in the Twelfth and Thirteenth Centuries' (forthcoming).
50 *Expugnatio Hibernica*, pp. 260–4.
51 'Totum regnum Angliae et totum regnum Hiberniae', *Foedera, Conventiones,*

Litterae, et Cujuscunque Generis Acta Publica, inter Reges Angliae et Alios Quosvis Imperatores, Reges, Pontifices, Principes, vel Communitates, ed. Thomas Rymer, 4 vols (London, 1816–25), I, i, pp. 111–12. And see Chapter 5, p. x.

52 Cf. Ifor Rowlands, 'King John and Wales', in S.D. Church (ed.), *King John: New Interpretations* (Woodbridge, 1999), pp. 273–87, where the author argues against a Welsh *regnum*. However, the fact that the Welsh were called and called themselves *Britones* until the end of the twelfth century somewhat undermines his approach.
53 *The Text of the Book of Llan Dâv*, ed. John Rhys (Oxford, 1893), p. 266.
54 *Annales Cambriae*, ed. John Williams ab Ithel (London, 1860), p. 25, *s.a.* 1063.
55 *The Law of Hywel Dda*, trans. D. Jenkins (Llandysul, 1986).
56 Jacques-Paul Migne (ed.), *Patrologia Latina*, 221 vols (1844–55 and 1862–65), ccvii, col. 201, Ep. 66.
57 Marie Fauroux (ed.), *Recueil des actes des ducs de Normandie de 911 à 1066* (Caen, 1961), no 61.
58 *The Etymologies of Isidore of Seville*, eds S. A. Barney, W. J. Lewis, J. A. Beach and O. Berghof (Cambridge, 2006), pp. 199–206.

I

Hugh de Lacy

1

A transnational magnate: 1166–74

The Lacys took their name from the Norman town of Lassy (Calvados, cant. Condé-sur-Noireau), where they held a subtenancy under the bishop of Bayeux. Two brothers, Ilbert (d. 1093) and Walter (d. 1085), accompanied William the Conqueror to England in 1066, and were rewarded for their service with substantial grants there. The elder brother, Ilbert, was granted a northern barony centred on Pontefract (Yorkshire). The younger brother, Walter, was established in the west midlands and along the Welsh march, centred on his fee at Weobley (Herefordshire). The Norman territories of the family were shared by the two brothers, so that from 1066 both branches of the Lacy family controlled territories either side of the English Channel. However, the Herefordshire branch was to extend itself even further. From the outset, the Herefordshire Lacys sought to control lands in Wales, being lords of Ewyas Lacy in the Welsh march. In 1172, however, King Henry II granted them the ancient Irish kingdom of Mide (henceforth known as the lordship of Meath). This meant that the Herefordshire Lacys' territorial portfolio extended by then into four realms: England, Ireland, Wales and Normandy.

This chapter explores the early career of Hugh de Lacy, who utilised his service to King Henry II in England, Normandy and Wales to embark upon a spectacular Irish endeavour. The Lacy lordship of Meath is writ large in Irish historiography, but its contemporary importance to Hugh in 1172 has yet to be fully investigated. Hugh was already then a transnational aristocrat, with lands in three other realms. In a period when seigniorial administration was in its infancy, any attention that Hugh paid to Meath was attention diverted from his other interests. Another issue yet to be explored is the English king's motivation in making the Irish grant. King Henry had gone to Ireland to curb the ambitions of another magnate,

Strongbow, who succeeded to the kingship of Leinster in 1171, yet as he left he delivered Meath and Dublin to Hugh.

The early years: 1155-66

Hugh was the second son of Gilbert de Lacy, a man who had won control of most of his family's inheritance during the civil war of King Stephen's reign.[1] Because Hugh was not his father's heir, traces of his early life are difficult to assemble. Hugh's first datable appearance comes on 25 July 1155, when he appears with the territorial identifier 'of Colemere' (a village in north-western Shropshire) in William fitz Alan's grant to Haughmond Abbey (Shropshire).[2] The two families of Fitz Alan and Lacy maintained a close connection throughout this period, with Hugh's daughter eventually marrying William's son (also named William).[3] The Lacys also shared a close connection with the Mortimers, and there is evidence of Hugh finding service with the family about this time. In the period immediately preceding 1155, the canons of Shobdon (Herefordshire) were allowed to migrate to Aymestery (Herefordshire) by Hugh de Mortimer (d. c.1181).

> Soon after, the friends of Sir Hugh de Mortimer, and especially Sir Hugh de Lacy, saw the church which the canons had built at Aymestery, and they came to Sir Hugh de Mortimer, exhorting and counselling him not to tolerate the completion of this enterprise at the entrance to his land in case his enemies should make inroads into his territory, and find there a refuge and stronghold in spite of him to the detriment of the whole region ... And he acted on their advice and made the canons move to the vill of Wigmore [Herefordshire].[4]

The Fitz Alans were predominantly Shropshire barons, and the Mortimers, predominantly Herefordshire. The Lacys' English interests spanned both shires, and included components in Gloucestershire, Oxfordshire, Worcestershire, Wiltshire and Staffordshire.[5] The surviving records are too problematical to allow for an accurate economic assessment of the Lacys' territories in this period, but two royal inquests reveal their level of obligation in England: the 1165-6 *cartae baronum*, an audit of military tenure, and the 1242-3 inquest into landholding (see Appendix 2). The *cartae baronum* returns detailed the number of English knights' fees owed to all tenants-in-chief. The Lacy honor was revealed to be owed 52¼ fees (although 3½ were unacknowledged by their holders) of old enfeoffment, and 5½ of new enfeoffment (the distinction being for fees created before and after the death of Henry I in 1135).[6] This was a respectable fee, but nowhere near the size of those belonging to members of the upper echelon of the aristocracy, such as the great earldoms of Gloucester (289⅓), Cornwall (215¾) and Norfolk (125).[7] Unlike the *cartae baronum*, the 1242-3 inquest was conducted hundred by hundred throughout England. Consequently, while the Lacys' 1166 return comprised a single statement of service owed, the 1242 inquest broke it down by shire. In 1242, the English Lacy honor was owed just over 27½ knights' fees in Herefordshire, 2½ in Oxfordshire, 10¾ in Shropshire and 1 in Staffordshire.[8] Unfortunately, the 1242 returns for Gloucestershire have not survived, but the transcribers of the *Book of Fees* have included a statement as to the levy of the scutage for Gascony in the bailiwick of Cirencester, which shows that the Lacys were owed 4½ fees there.[9] The late twelfth-century *Hereford Domesday* also provides a useful indication of landholding around the time of the *cartae baronum*. When all three sources are taken together (as they are in Appendix 2), they show that, although the fees were considerably less concentrated in 1242 than they had been in 1166, the service owed to the Lacys remained fairly constant during the three-quarters of a century under investigation. In fact, the progressive fragmentation of knightly tenures broadened the family's tenurial base in England. The family also held the Welsh marcher lordship of Ewyas Lacy (in the south-western corner of modern Herefordshire), which was excused scutage and is generally absent from Exchequer reckoning.

Hugh was preceded in his lordship over the Lacys' English lands by his elder brother Robert, who had succeeded their father Gilbert by 1160,[10] but was associated with the seigniorial administration for some time prior to his succession. In an undated charter, Gilbert and Robert together granted 'Arnold our dapifer' (steward) land in Droitwich (Worcestershire).[11] In a royal confirmatory charter dating from 1154-5, 'Gilbert de Lacy and Robert his son' are listed together as benefactors of the Augustinian priory of Llanthony Prima (Monmouthshire), which had been founded in about 1103 by Hugh de Lacy (d. *c*.1115) amongst others. Their gifts included churches in the Lacys' main demesne manors in England: Weobley (Herefordshire) and Stanton Lacy (Shropshire), and another, St Clydawg's, in the vicinity of their Welsh marcher castle of Ewyas Lacy.[12] Before then, in 1150 or 1151, the two had been involved in a complaint made to the bishop of Hereford, Gilbert Foliot, against Roger, earl of Hereford.[13] The earl violated the custom of sanctuary by capturing one of Robert de Lacy's knights, Richard le Bret, in a churchyard and holding him to ransom, and Gilbert lodged the complaint on his son's behalf.[14] Around 1160, Gilbert became a Knight Templar, and bestowed his English inheritance upon Robert before setting off for the Holy Land where he died around 1163.[15]

While Robert is principally associated with the English inheritance, there is evidence to suggest that Hugh obtained a share of it: notably the family's Welsh marcher lordship of Ewyas Lacy. At some point between 1155 and 1158, King Henry II addressed a writ to Hugh and the sheriff of Herefordshire, ordering them to ensure that the monks of Gloucester were able to enjoy in peace their territory of Leghe (now in Herefordshire, but then in Ewyas Lacy).[16] This mandate may have been prompted by Hugh's attempts to impose his authority over the Gloucester monks of Ewyas Lacy, a common practice by those new to lordship. The mandate is preserved in the Gloucester Cartulary, where it is preceded by the initial grant of the lands by Sybil de Lacy, as well as confirmations by Hugh's father Gilbert de Lacy and Hugh himself (but not Robert).[17] The order, and its preservation among the Lacy confirmatory charters, implies that, in addition to holding Colemere in northern Shropshire, Hugh exercised lordship over the family's strategic marcher lordship in the late 1150s.

The situation in Normandy is less clear, though there was undoubtedly a division there too. Gilbert de Lacy had been associated with the administration of the family's Norman sub-tenancy at Lassy and Campeaux from as early as 1133.[18] However, an analysis of several Évreux charters shows that Gilbert also held one knight's fee in the Évreçin at Claville (Eure, cant. Évreux-Ouest), where he was a tenant of the Montfort counts of Évreux.[19] In about 1150, Gilbert witnessed a charter of Simon III de Montfort, count of Évreux (d. 1181) to the abbey of Jumièges.[20] 'Hugh de Lacy and Amaury his brother', then appear in two of Count Simon's charters just before, or at around the time of Gilbert's son Hugh's eventual entry into the family's English inheritance (discussed below).[21] Amaury de Lacy (whose name may indicate that Count Simon's father, Count Amaury (d. c.1137), had been his godfather) was a prominent knight in the county of Évreux.[22] The mention of his son Gilbert in his grant to the chapter at Évreux makes it clear that he is the same Amaury de Lacy (d. c.1186) who is later found holding lands of Hugh de Lacy at Cressage and Harnage (Shropshire) and Castle Frome (Herefordshire) in England.[23] This same charter, datable to between 1170 and 1180 and concerning his church in Claville, proves that Amaury, not his elder brother Hugh, received the Lacys' Évreux subtenancy.[24]

In light of this evidence it appears that Gilbert de Lacy divided his inheritance among his three sons, giving Robert the larger part of the English honor (held *in capite*); Hugh the Welsh marcher lordship and (perhaps) ancestral fee at Lassy and Campeaux; and Amaury the Évreux subtenancy. Such a division was in keeping with the Norman practice of partible inheritance, and is paralleled somewhat in the situation following the death of Hugh de Lacy in 1186.[25] Had it continued, the separation of the Lacys' English and Norman fees would have critically diminished their strategic importance, not to mention their prestige as lords in three realms. However, it did not endure. Although the survival of Amaury's heir Gilbert meant that the Évreux interest was permanently alienated from the main line (which nevertheless remained mindful of its connections to the Évreçin and the Montfort counts of Évreux), Hugh de Lacy soon succeeded his brother Robert, reuniting the family's English, Welsh and Norman patrimonies.

Robert de Lacy's tenure in England and the Welsh march was to be short lived. Although the reasons for his supersession are unknown (he may have died or perhaps followed his father on crusade), Hugh had replaced him by the time of the *cartae baronum* in 1166. Hugh received a royal confirmatory charter after his succession, but unfortunately no copy survives. Its erstwhile existence is proved by its description in the Mortimer Cartulary as 'the Charter which King Henry made to Sir Hugh de Lacy of the manors of *Stauntone Lacy* [Stanton Lacy, Shropshire], *Lodelowe* [Ludlow, Shropshire], *Webbeley* [Weobley, Herefordshire], *Ewyas* [Ewyas Lacy], *and Yarkhulle* [Yarkhill, Herefordshire]'.[26] The timing of the confirmation charter is impossible to determine. Hugh may have received it immediately, but it is just as possible that it was granted in relation to service in one of King Henry's Welsh campaigns of the mid-1160s, or as part and parcel of the king's definition of lordship within the *cartae baronum* audit of knights' fees. Whatever the precise dating of the charter, Hugh was in clear possession of the Lacys' English honor by 1166.

Having succeeded to his English inheritance, Hugh sought to make his lordship effective. Hugh at once disputed the service he owed the see of Hereford for the manor of Holme Lacy (Herefordshire).[27] Bishop Gilbert Foliot, recently transferred to London, heard about the dispute, whereupon he declared that, while bishop of Hereford, he was accustomed to receive the service of two knights from both Gilbert and Robert de Lacy, freely and without contradiction.[28] However, Hugh defended his position until finally forced to acquiesce to the new bishop's demands in 1177, the timing of which, as will be seen, corresponded with a drastic change in Hugh's priorities.[29] In the interim, Hugh was fined for making illegal assarts in Herefordshire and Wiltshire.[30] All of these actions are typical of a baron's drive to extend his lordship locally.

The grant of Meath: 1172

Hugh's aspirations to local dominance in England, Normandy and (to a lesser extent) Wales were constrained by those of his fellow lords and the centralising administration of King Henry II. However, the king soon provided Hugh with an outlet for his ambitions on the new European frontier in Ireland. The history of the English invasion of Ireland has been dealt with extensively, and need not be reproduced here.[31] Suffice to say that King Henry II and Richard fitz Gilbert (nicknamed 'Strongbow') were not on the best of terms in 1168 when the king granted the latter's request that he be allowed to journey to Ireland in aid of the exiled king of Leinster, Diarmait Mac Murchada. Strongbow's successes in Ireland, which included his marriage to Diarmait's daughter, Aífe, in 1169, and eventual succession to the kingdom of Leinster in 1170, drove Henry to open negotiations with Strongbow and to plan an expedition to Ireland to assert his authority over the new lord of Leinster. Strongbow ultimately decided to return himself in 1171 to England (or, more likely, Wales), where he was reconciled with Henry and surrendered Dublin, the coastal cities and all of his castles to the Crown.[32]

King Henry II nevertheless proceeded with his voyage to Ireland, which took on the character of a tour of his new acquisitions. Hugh de Lacy had much to recommend him for the expedition, not least because he was married to Strongbow's cousin, Rose of Monmouth.[33] Rose was the daughter of Baderon of Monmouth and Rose de Clare,[34] daughter of Gilbert de Clare (d. 1115?). Rose de Clare's brother was the earl of Pembroke, Gilbert fitz Gilbert (d. 1148), father of Strongbow (Richard fitz Gilbert de Clare). Through his marriage, Hugh was not only related to the new lord of Leinster but also connected to the southern Welsh marcher nexus that supplied so many of the first adventurers in Ireland. Henry may have recruited Hugh while the two were in Normandy earlier that year, and Hugh was with the royal army as it departed Pembroke.[35]

While in Ireland Henry received the submission not only of Leinster but also of the majority of Irish kings. The most notable exception was the king of Connacht, and high king of Ireland, Ruaidrí Ua Conchobair, who had driven Diarmait Mac Murchada to seek assistance in England, and who was unprepared to admit the legitimacy of the resulting English conquests in Ireland.[36] It is unclear what the English king had in mind for the kingdom of Mide (the future lordship of Meath), but the timing of its grant to Hugh, immediately prior to Henry's hasty departure on 17 April, does not bespeak a first choice of scheme. It is plausible that, because he received the submission of the king of Bréifne, Tigernán Ua Ruairc, for Mide,[37] Henry was waiting on the king of Connacht's submission to reinstate the partition of Mide carried out in 1169, which saw Ua Ruairc and Ua Conchobair take one half each.[38] This would have kept to Henry's policy of confirming the *status quo* in Ireland, taking only the former Norse cities as royal demesne. However, that scenario would seem at odds with what is known of Henry II's military and strategical expertise. It assumes that he was not aware of the power and influence an English Meath would gain him. Roger of Howden, who was in Ireland with Henry at the time, claims that Henry planned to lead an expedition against Ruaidrí Ua Conchobair for his intransigence.[39] As he sat wintering in Dublin at the head of an impressive army, Henry was most likely waiting for his chance to pacify the kingdoms of Mide and Connacht himself. However, his priorities took him elsewhere.

From his arrival in Ireland, Henry II had received no word from his vast continental dominions. While this isolation may have at first been a welcome relief from the load of cares which he had purposely left behind him, it eventually became a source of anxiety. On 1 March 1172, Henry left Dublin for Wexford in the hopes that a ship might sail safely through the inclement weather to bring word to him there. None came until after Mid-Lent (26 March). They brought news from England that papal legates awaited his arrival in Normandy to negotiate a settlement to the Becket scandal. The king's reputation had been tarnished by the murder of Archbishop Thomas Becket at the hands of four of Henry's own knights a year earlier. Escape from the political furore created by the murder is frequently cited as a reason for Henry's Irish expedition, but, as he was an anointed king, absolution for his crime was essential.[40] He dared not tarry. Henry gave a clue to his feelings on the matter when he reportedly exclaimed in exasperation during the ensuing negotiations that he would return to Ireland where he had pressing matters.[41] Henry therefore likely granted Mide to Hugh de Lacy as a last resort, aimed at securing the rich but vulnerable midland territory in his absence.[42]

Hugh was also appointed *custos* (keeper) of Dublin, with the power to enfeoff his followers in Dublin's hinterlands for service rendered in the city. Through his grant of Meath and appointment of Hugh as Dublin's *custos*, Henry hoped to preserve the most important, and vulnerable, of his newly acquired demesne cities in Ireland. Henry had shown his appreciation of Dublin's commercial significance that winter when he had attempted to entice inhabitants to the evacuated city by granting it to his men of Bristol.[43] Henry was also well aware of Dublin's strategic importance. Seven years earlier, in 1165, he had used the fleet of Dublin on his unsuccessful expedition to Wales.[44] Now that the old Norse kingdom was his, Wales was surrounded, its princes contained. His hold on Dublin elevated Henry to a position of *de facto* master of the Irish Sea region. The sea itself became, in the words of Robin Frame, 'a second Angevin lake'.[45]

Henry II's hegemonic claims to Ireland also hung on his retention of Dublin. His use of a temporary palace in the city as a setting for the submissions of Irish kings bespeaks an appreciation of Irish custom, and a willingness to engage the Irish on their own terms.[46] Consequently, the status of Dublin relative to the high kingship of Ireland could not have been unknown him. Over the course of the past two centuries, control of Dublin had gradually come to symbolise control of the high kingship.[47] Henry II's retention of Dublin consequently lent symbolic import to the submissions he had received. For his part, Gerald of Wales refers to Dublin as *'regni caput'* ('head of the kingdom') in his *Expugnatio Hibernica*, and, given Dublin's many international links, his designation would almost certainly have reflected the prevailing view of the English community.[48]

Dublin's significance meant that its security trumped all other concerns. With the king's attention elsewhere, only a magnate could muster the forces necessary for the city's defence. Rather than entrenching his forces within the city, Hugh de Lacy pushed the bounds of his speculative grant to their furthest extremities and took the fight to the Irish. Henry harnessed Hugh's localised power to his royal authority, increasing the effectiveness of both. This was to be a pattern in the relationship between the Lacys and the English Crown: the roots of the Lacys' power were often found in the inability of the English king to exercise his own lordship effectively in his absence. Consequently, a number of the Lacys' greatest personal triumphs came while they were ostensibly instruments of the royal administration.

One of Hugh's first acts upon being granted Meath, even before subinfeudating his lordship among military tenants, was to make grants in Meath to the Lacy monastic foundation of Llanthony Priory.[49] It is interesting to note that Hugh did not found a new monastery in his new Irish lordship. Instead, in the early days of Meath's conquest, the Welsh priory of Llanthony constituted the main focus of ecclesiastical patronage among the colonial community of Hugh's new Irish lordship. It was only after this religious patronage that Hugh set about installing his military tenants in Meath. The near-contemporary *Song of Dermot and the Earl* provides a description of how Hugh 'planted' his new lordship with vassals.[50]

However, its presentation of the subinfeudation of Meath gives the impression that the process was more or less completed in 1172. This it certainly was not. For instance, the second grant that the *Song* mentions, to William le Petit, is one of the few for which a charter survives. Because William's service was to be rendered at the castle of Killare (Co. Westmeath), the grant is datable to after 1182 or 1184 – not 1172.[51] The subinfeudation of Meath was a process without a master plan. It is also very important to note that in 1172 the conquest of Meath was not Hugh's only (or even primary) concern. With this in mind, it is unsurprising that only a few grants in Meath were to Hugh's tenants or retained knights, as listed in his 1166 *cartae baronum* return. Any speculative grants in Meath would have removed experienced fighting men from his service in England, Wales or Normandy. What is more, Hugh's priority was more likely to have been to extend his affinity through outside recruitment to match his new eminence.

One household knight who did receive a grant in Meath was Adam de Feipo, whom Hugh granted Skreen (Co. Meath), Clontarf (Co. Dublin) and Santry (Co. Dublin). This placed a proven soldier in a position to protect Hugh's new lordship of Meath and the royal city of Dublin. Adam may have been an experienced household knight, but he lacked the resources to realise his Irish grant. Consequently, Hugh built Adam a castle at Skreen, but demanded that Adam provide the heavy service of twenty-one knights (twenty for Skreen and one split between Clontarf and Santry).[52] Hugh provided the start-up capital for Adam's Irish enterprise, and obtained vital military service and lucrative tax from twenty-one fees in return for his investment.[53] Adam, in turn, subinfeudated his grant, but first he founded a chapel in his castle at Skreen and assigned to it the tithes of all his lands there before 1175. Adam then granted the chapel and tithes to his brother, Thomas de Feipo, who was presented to the chapel by the bishop of Clonard (in whose diocese Skreen lay). When, about a decade later, Thomas became a monk of St Mary's Abbey, Dublin, he brought the chapel, tithes and church of Skreen under the abbey's control, as well as the land his brother had granted him (which was henceforth known as 'the grange' or Monktown). Consequently, the cartulary of St Mary's includes a list of Adam de Feipo's tenants at Skreen from about 1185, whose lands all owed tithes to the abbey.[54] So before 1185, Adam de Feipo enfeoffed Geoffrey de Cusack (who held Killeen),[55] Amaury de Feipo the elder (who held Athlumney), Amaury the younger, Maurice de Beaufussel, Robert d'Aveny (who held Danestown – perhaps originally 'Avenystown'), Geoffrey, John, Ranulf and Walter Duff (who held Dowdstown – originally 'Duffstown'). In about 1201, the tenants of the honor were listed by the bishop, which added the names of William Garbe (who held Garbestown), Alan Beg, Richard Talbot[56] (who held Talbotstown), Walter de Folleville (who held Follistown), Stephen of Kent, Ralph, Robert the cook and Walter the squire (*lescuier*).[57] This is but one example of the way the web of lordship entangled all sorts of men as Hugh de Lacy transplanted a retained knight (with a Norman surname)[58] from the Welsh border to Ireland.

The only pre-1172 Lacy tenant listed in the *Song of Dermot and the Earl* as benefiting from the subinfeudation of Meath was Hugh Tyrell, 'whom [Hugh] loved greatly', who was granted Castleknock (Co. Dublin) and placed in charge of Meath's defences in Hugh's absence.[59] Another 1166 tenant, Richard de Escotot, was not mentioned in the initial subinfeudation, but eventually held lands at Donaghmore (bar. Ratoath, Co. Meath) and Trevet (bar. Skreen, Co. Meath).[60] That said, Richard's first datable appearance, in the witness list of Walter de Lacy's 1194 charter of liberties to Drogheda, came after Walter granted these demesne lands to his brother, Hugh de Lacy the younger.[61] It may be that it was this Hugh, rather than his father, who enfeoffed Richard. Finally, Hugh granted the land of Rathwire (Co. Meath) to Robert de Lacy (whose relationship to Hugh is impossible to determine on the basis of existing evidence). Nevertheless, the grant of Rathwire introduced another line of Lacys into Meath.[62]

For the most part, Meath was divided among men drawn to Hugh's service, rather than split between his existing tenants. For instance, Jocelin and Gilbert de Angulo, to whom Hugh granted the territories of Navan, Ardbraccan and Morgallion (Co. Meath), were from a Pembrokeshire family and likely came to Ireland in Strongbow's service.[63] Hugh also attracted Meiler fitz Henry, one of the first adventurers from Wales to enter Ireland. Meiler was a grandson of King Henry I, and therefore Henry II's cousin. He was also the nephew of Robert fitz Stephen, and a member of a prominent colonial family, the Geraldines.[64] Meiler had already been heavily enfeoffed in north-western Leinster by Strongbow,[65] but in the 1180s Hugh made him a grant of the neighbouring territory of Ardnurcher (Co. Westmeath), built a castle for him on his Leinster lands at Timahoe (Co. Laois) and gave him his niece as a wife.[66] Similarly, when Hugh granted Gilbert de Nugent the territory of Delvin (Co. Westmeath) for the service of five knights, he built a castle for him there and gave him his sister, Rose de Lacy, in marriage.[67] As will be explored in more detail below, even William le Petit seems to have been an outsider before he was granted lands in Meath.[68]

Barriers to conquest

Hugh's main opponent in the early days of his conquest and settlement of Meath was the king of the neighbouring Irish kingdom of Bréifne, Tigernán Ua Ruairc. Tigernán harboured a strong claim to the kingship of Mide from several pre-invasion partitions of the midland kingdom, and had submitted to Henry II in 1171 as its king. However, Bréifne was an exposed buffer kingdom, and Tigernán's loyalty was as variable as it needed to be for his survival.[69] When Henry granted Hugh de Lacy a territory already claimed by the equally aggressive Tigernán Ua Ruairc, he must have known what he was doing. Their peaceful coexistence in the disputed territory was highly unlikely, and, because Ua Ruairc was the most immediate threat to both Dublin and Meath, his elimination may have been implicit in Hugh's grant. The situation quickly came to a head as Hugh set about realising his grant in the summer of 1172. His forces had advanced as far as Fore (Co. Westmeath)[70] when the two men agreed to parley at the hill of Tlachtgha (Hill of Ward), near Athboy (Co. Westmeath). Gerald of Wales writes that, after brief entreaties by proxy, each brought a skeleton force picked from their entourage to the meeting. An act of treachery was then committed which ended in Ua Ruairc's decapitation. Gerald claims that Ua Ruairc's death was in retaliation for his own attempted assassination of Hugh de Lacy, while the Irish 'Mac Carthaigh's Book' contends that Hugh's forces treacherously set upon Ua Ruairc as he approached the meeting place.[71] Whichever the case, there could not have been a better result for Hugh de Lacy or Henry II. Tigernán Ua Ruairc's death opened up vast stretches of Meath to colonisation, and, more importantly for the English king, removed a very persistent thorn from Dublin's side. Hugh celebrated his accomplishment by having Ua Ruairc's body mangled and gibbeted upside-down to the north of Dublin, and his head set above the gate of Dublin Castle, before ultimately sending it to Henry II.[72] This elaborate spectacle, with Dublin as its centre, was stage-managed to display Hugh's military dominance, an essential aspect of his lordship on the frontier. The macabre piece of theatre would hardly have been undertaken for the death of a man to whose fate the royal government was indifferent. If Hugh de Lacy was set against Ua Ruairc in Meath, he did his job well. Conquest could continue.

There is an interesting correlation between the activities of 1172 and those that precipitated English intervention in Ireland in 1169. In 1166, an army comprising Tigernán Ua Ruairc, Diarmait Ua Máel Sechlainn of Meath, Domnall Mac Gilla Pátraic, king of Osraige, Murchad Ua Brain, king of Uí Fáeláin (in northern Leinster) and the Hiberno-Norse of Dublin marched against the provincial king of Leinster, Diarmait Mac Murchada. This was a rebellion against the hegemony of Diarmait's dynasty of Uí Chennselaig, one aided (perhaps instigated) by his bitter rival, Tigernán Ua Ruairc. The rebels drove Diarmait from Ireland, and, when he returned, it was at the head of the English fighting force.[73] Over the next few years, the leaders of the 1166 rebellion either submitted to Diarmait or died. In 1169, Mac Gilla Pátraic submitted to Diarmait and his new son-in-law Strongbow,[74] while Diarmait Ua Máel Sechlainn fell in a dynastic struggle in Mide.[75] When Áskell Ragavalsson (Ascall mac Ragnaill mic Turcaill), the leader of the Dublin Norse, was captured in a failed attempt to recover Dublin after the death of Mac Murchada in 1171, he was brought into the city, paraded before the court and beheaded.[76] Later that year, Strongbow's forces captured Ua Brain. The *Song of Dermot and the Earl* states that, 'Because this rebel had betrayed / Diarmait, his rightful lord, / the earl had him beheaded / and his body thrown to the dogs.'[77] These public executions are comparable with the treatment of the remains of the conspirator, Ua Ruairc the following year. As a direct result of his visit to Ireland, Henry II acquired Dublin and Uí Fáeláin as royal demesne[78] and had granted away the midland kingdom of Mide to one of his barons. The assassination of Tigernán Ua Ruairc meant that the last of the unrepentant offenders of 1166 was eliminated. Diarmait Mac Murchada was almost avenged.

Next on the list of Mac Murchada's former enemies was the high king of Ireland, Ruaidrí Ua Conchobair. Ruaidrí had been an ally of Ua Ruairc in the struggle leading up to Diarmait's expulsion, and played his part in the attack of 1166. He was inaugurated as king of Dublin earlier that year, and had the men of Dublin in his army as he toured Ireland securing recognition of his status as high king.[79] The Hiberno-Norse contingent would not have been in the army against Uí Chennselaig without his consent. Ruaidrí's unwavering opposition to the English presence in Ireland is well known, and his failure to capitulate while the English king was in Ireland made Ua Conchobair a very real threat to Henry II's overlordship. The reverse was also true. The growing English colony in the east of Ireland was an even more obvious threat to Ruaidrí's high kingship, and the settlers showed little sign of being content with the previous role of foreigners in Ireland: to stay on the coast. They had refused Ruaidrí's offer of the Hiberno-Norse cities of Dublin, Waterford and Wexford at the siege of Dublin in 1171,[80] and were expanding from Leinster at an alarming rate. Hugh de Lacy's presence in Meath and his treatment of Ruaidrí's ally, Tigernán Ua Ruairc, must have been particularly troubling to Ua Conchobair, especially since Hugh de Lacy's eyes were unmistakably fixed westward upon Ruaidrí's own territory.

Hugh de Lacy was thus faced with strong native opposition from the very outset of his grant, yet the prevailing view amongst historians has been that Hugh de Lacy was placed in Meath act as a counterbalance to Strongbow in Leinster.[81] This theory assumes that, in granting Meath to Hugh, Henry II was playing off one baron against the other, thereby assuring that neither grew too powerful. 'His object was not peace for its own sake but a system of checks and counter-checks to prevent any one man, particularly an Anglo-Norman baron, becoming dominant. For this reason he set up Hugh de Lacy to counterbalance Strongbow.'[82] This begs, instead of addressing, the question as to whether Hugh had the ability to muster the forces necessary to act as an effective counterbalance to Strongbow during the early years of his tenure in Meath. In fact, from the moment he received his grant, Hugh de Lacy was at a considerable disadvantage against Strongbow in Ireland. The lord of Leinster had been campaigning and consolidating his position, albeit in the name of Diarmait Mac Murchada, for some time, while Meath remained merely a parchment lordship. There was always bound to be some internal resistance to the accession of Strongbow in Leinster, but this was nothing compared to the task facing Hugh in the summer of 1172. Previous to the grant, Mide had been the stage for almost constant warfare since the death of Murchad Ua Máel Sechlainn in 1153.[83] More recently, in 1169, Ruaidrí Ua Conchobair and Tigernán Ua Ruairc divided the kingdom between themselves.[84] The following year, Diarmait Mac Murchada, accompanied by Strongbow, invaded and took control.[85] Underlying all of this were the Uí Máel Sechlainn and the regional kings within Meath. Consequently, it would be some time before Meath could become productive and provide the support necessary to oppose Strongbow.

All of the evidence suggests that, if anything, the lords of Meath and Leinster were expected to help each other in Ireland, not to be rivals for dominance. They already shared a connection through Hugh's marriage to Strongbow's cousin, Rose of Monmouth. While a familial connection does not necessarily signify amiable relations, it makes it far less likely that Henry II would have expected Hugh de Lacy to combat Strongbow at a time when he was turning the family fortunes around, or that Hugh would himself consent to such an arrangement. Once the grant was made, none of the players, Hugh, Strongbow or Henry II, acted in a way indicative of rivalry.

The revolt of 1173-4

With his southern border secured by his wife's cousin, Hugh de Lacy was able to push north and westwards in 1172. However, his conquest was cut short by an episode of military service in Normandy in 1173. King Henry II's eldest son, the Young King Henry, had been crowned king of England in 1170 in order to secure his inheritance. Despite his coronation and sobriquet, there was little that was regal in the Young King's responsibilities. The ambitious young man chafed under his father's bridle, and, in an alliance with King Louis VII of France in 1173, threatened to depose Henry II and grasp the reins of power for himself.[86] Both Hugh de Lacy and Strongbow were called upon to defend Henry's position in Normandy. Hugh had returned to England after the end of the campaigning season in 1172, and was at Canterbury for a ceremony in honour of the second anniversary of Becket's martyrdom on 29 December 1172, where, according to Gerald of Wales, he rebuked an overzealous Archbishop Richard for his bombast.[87]

Upon the outbreak of rebellion in Normandy, Hugh de Lacy and Hugh de Beauchamp were placed in charge of the Norman frontier town of Verneuil-sur-Avre (Eure). On or around 9 July 1173, King Louis VII besieged the town. Lacy and Beauchamp held firm, but, with supplies running low after almost a month, the defenders agreed to a three-day truce to determine whether help was near, and if it was not, to surrender. King Louis broke the truce, however, and, when Henry II's army (which included Strongbow) arrived on the third day (9 August), they found that the French king had fired a section of the town known as 'the great bourg'. Henry was too late to save the houses, but pursued the fleeing French forces, inflicting heavy losses upon Louis's army. The citadel had not been breached, and, when Henry returned from his pursuit, he gave orders for the town's refortification.[88]

As Hugh and Strongbow fought for Henry in Normandy, the Irish colony suffered. Gerald of Wales reports that 'all the princes of that country [were] in open revolt against the king'.[89] Gerald's testimony may be coloured by his disdain for William fitz Audelin, who was justiciar in the interim, but King Henry nevertheless sent the seasoned veteran Strongbow back to Ireland as justiciar that autumn in order to secure the colony and act as recruiting agent for the war abroad.[90] The *Song of Dermot and the Earl* makes it seem as though Hugh de Lacy returned with him. After recounting Strongbow's voyage and listing those who were dispatched to Henry II's, it states, 'But Hugh de Lacy, who was so fierce, / Set out for Meath / With many renowned vassals / To plant his territory.'⁹¹ However, this is an isolated mention of Hugh, and, given the source's notoriously unreliable chronology, it seems far more likely that Hugh remained in Normandy as governor of Verneuil.

While Hugh was in Normandy, Strongbow set about expanding his own lordship in Ireland. In the early months of 1174, the lord of Leinster planned a campaign against the south-western kingdoms of Munster.⁹² Ruaidrí Ua Conchobair, in his capacity as high king, dispatched men south from Connacht to aid the destruction of the English force. Learning of this, Strongbow sent to Dublin for reinforcements. The Dublin contingent, comprising Norse soldiers under the command of English knights, hastened to Cashel, where Strongbow's men awaited their arrival. They did not make it. Instead, the Dublin force was attacked by the Irish as they camped near Thurles (Co. Tipperary), and was completely destroyed. The slaughter served as a signal to those opposed to the English that the time was ripe for concerted resistance. Strongbow was forced to retreat first to Waterford, where he found that the English garrison had been slaughtered, and thence to shelter on Little Island in the river Suir, east of Waterford, for the next two months.⁹³

With the defeat of the Dublin contingent at Thurles, the displacement of the Irish justiciar and in the continued absence of the *custos* of Dublin, Hugh de Lacy, Ruaidrí Ua Conchobair led the combined forces of Leth Cuinn (the northern half of Ireland) through Meath to Dublin. The *Song of Dermot and the Earl* claims that the expedition was in retaliation for Hugh de Lacy's construction of a castle at his seigniorial caput of Trim.

> But when the man
> Who was king of Connacht at this time
> Heard that Hugh had fortified a castle,
> He was angered by the news.
> He summoned his army:
> He would go and attack the castle.⁹⁴

However, this timing of events does not make sense. Hugh had advanced to Fore before his parley with Ua Ruairc in 1172. Thereafter that same year, he raided in the region of Angaile (Co. Longford) with Domnall Ua Ruairc.⁹⁵ It is unlikely that Hugh would have advanced so far west without first securing his supply lines by fortifying the strategic crossing of the river Boyne at Trim. Furthermore, the events of early 1174 suggest that Hugh was in Normandy, not Ireland, before Ruaidrí's expedition. Trim Castle may have been a target, but its construction two years earlier cannot have been the catalyst for the Irish campaign. Instead, Ruaidrí's target was almost certainly the royal city of Dublin, with all of its economic and symbolic import for the high kingship. Ruaidrí even recruited Islesmen to his army, whose expertise and long association with the coastal city would have been much more useful at Dublin than Trim.[96] Trim was merely (and purposefully) situated on the route to Dublin at a ford on the river Boyne.

Faced with such an impressive army, Hugh's custodian of Trim, Hugh Tyrell, dispatched a messenger to Strongbow on Little Island and fled without a fight.[97] Finding no resistance at Trim, and not wanting to leave an abandoned English castle at his back, Ruaidrí razed it to the ground and continued on. Meanwhile, upon receiving word from Hugh Tyrell, Strongbow gathered his forces and raced north. He arrived too late to save anything but the city of Dublin itself, which at least one set of Irish annals (with the benefit of hindsight) claims was his objective from the start.[98] The lordship of Meath therefore served its purpose even in Hugh's absence. For two years it kept the Irish away from Dublin. The invasion route from Connacht to Dublin ran the entire length of the lordship, and the passage of any army would have been slowed by Meath's fortifications, abandoned or otherwise. What is more, without the advanced warning of Hugh Tyrell at Trim, Strongbow might not have arrived in time to save the depleted garrison at Dublin.

Of course, Meath might have been saved in 1174 had it simply been granted to Strongbow in the first place. But, for all of the trust he was to later show the lord of Leinster, this concession was plainly beyond the intention of Henry II. The English king had gone to Ireland with the expressed purpose of curbing the ambitions of his wayward magnate, and curb them he would. Strongbow could not be left to his own devices in the strategic midland kingdom, for he had already become a large enough threat to prompt Henry's Irish expedition without positioning himself on what amounted to the fulcrum of the high kingship. Hugh, consequently, was inserted in Meath to provide a northern limit to Strongbow's ambitions, thereby forcing both magnates to move westward. Their familial tie fortified the boundary more effectively than combative positioning could have, making it all but impossible for Strongbow to obtain what he had been denied. Had Meath been granted to an Irish beneficiary, Strongbow's aspirations would have had no such bounds. Instead of pushing into Munster, his attention might have been drawn to Meath, with all of its economic, political and military advantages. Furthermore, Dublin would have had very little warning of an Irish attack, and the dispersed English forces an equally short amount of time to come to the city's aid should the

Irish decide to shrug off their oaths. In granting Meath to Hugh de Lacy, Henry II was therefore insulating the important royal city of Dublin, while denying the strategic midland kingdom to any of the established powers in Ireland.[99]

Aftermath

Although these Irish offensives were not part of the wider Plantagenet civil war, their outcome was a direct result of the colony's military depletion in aid of the war abroad. The precarious position of the English enclave convinced Henry II to come to terms with the high king of Ireland, Ruaidrí Ua Conchobair. The resultant Treaty of Windsor, agreed in October 1175, was just one of the treaties in which the English king sought to assert his relationship with native rulers within his hegemony, but, nevertheless, its significance should not be underestimated.[100] It was a treaty negotiated entirely by proxy. Henry II needed emissaries to the Irish king, and none was more suited than his trusted administrator, William fitz Audelin, and the colony's prop against Connacht, Hugh de Lacy. Gerald of Wales mentions a meeting between these two men and Ruaidrí Ua Conchobair in the context of the 1172 submissions to Henry at Dublin: 'but Ruaidrí of Connacht met royal emissaries, Hugh de Lacy and William Fitz Audelin, towards the river Shannon, which separates Meath and Connacht. He likewise obtained the English king's peace, became dependent for the tenure of his kingdom on the king as overlord, and bound himself in alliance with the king by the strongest ties of fealty and submission.'[101] Gerald's dating of the meeting is almost certainly incorrect, because it is clear that Henry left Ireland in 1172 without Ruaidrí's submission. Marie Therese Flanagan characterises the meeting as preliminary to the Treaty of Windsor, which seems likely, and speculates that the meeting occurred in 1173.[102] As Hugh was absent from Ireland for the duration of that year, a meeting after the devastating campaigns of 1174 is more probable.

Ruaidrí's summer offensive would have required Hugh to return to Ireland in order to re-establish his personal lordship in Meath, but he was still busy in Normandy. At some point before the end of 1175, Hugh purchased the entire honor of Le Pin-au-Haras in Normandy from Count Robert of Meulan. The price was 200 *livres* Angevin, and it was to be held as a sub-tenancy of Count Robert for the service of two knights.[103] The honor included Le Pin-au-Haras, Neauphe-sur-Dive and Mont-Ormel (Orne) just north of Sées, as well as Azeville and Beuzeville (Manche) in the Cotentin. This wide territorial spread of a middling honor was not unusual in Normandy, nor was its grant out as a sub-tenancy. Count Robert's great-uncle, Earl Henry of Warwick (d. 1119), was lord of Neubourg (Eure) and Pouppeville (Manche), possessions separated by entire provinces,[104] while the Tosny, Bertrand and Goz families similarly held honors with far-flung components in the Cotentin.[105] Hugh is unlikely to have purchased the honor of Le Pin-au-Haras during the open warfare from April 1173 to October 1174, when Count Robert was out of Normandy and he and Hugh were on opposite sides. An early date is possible, but the period after the cessation of hostilities in October 1174, as Count Robert raised money to cover his wartime expenses, suggests itself. Hugh witnessed royal acta in Normandy datable to late 1174 or 1175, which makes this scenario more probable.[106] After buying the Norman honor, Hugh granted his new tenant Durand du Pin the fee of Neauphe-sur-Dive (Orne) for 25½ *livres* a year, with instalments at Easter and the feast of St Rémi (1 October). As usual, Durand had to pay for the grant: 120 *livres* and a further 10 *livres* from his account at Hugh's mill at Azeville (Manche).[107] By this single grant, Hugh's monetary outlay for the honor of Le Pin-au-Haras would have been recouped within three years. This highlights the financial nature of Norman lordship in this period, in which rents and milling rights were often used to ensure tenants' fidelity.[108] The Lacys also acquired two knights' fees in the count of Meulan's honor of Pont-Audemer (Eure) at some point before 1204, when Walter de Lacy's lands there are listed in King Philip Augustus's survey of *Feoda Normanniae*.[109] Hugh de Lacy was with King Henry at Pont-Audemer during this stay in Normandy, which may suggest a point of sale.[110]

Hugh must have hurried to Ireland shortly after the purchase of Le Pin-au-Haras, because his grant to Durand du Pin was made in Dublin.[111] Hugh then set to work reasserting his lordship in Meath. Under 1175, the Irish annals record the sort of heavy-handed response that his return would have heralded. 'Durrow, and the whole of Meath, from Athlone to Drogheda, was laid waste by the Foreigners.'[112] Several local Irish chieftains were eliminated. The Irish king of east Meath, Magnus Ua Máel Sechlainn, 'was hanged by the English, after they had acted treacherously towards him at Trim'. Lacy's forces also plundered the seat of the bishop of eastern Meath at Clonard (Co. Meath) as well as the territories of Muinter Sercacháin (Co. Westmeath?) and Muinter Mailshinna (bar. Kilkenny West, Co. Westmeath).[113] In the extreme south-west of Meath (near Durrow), the king of Fir Cell (baronies Ballycowan, Ballyboy and Eglish, Co. Offaly), Gilla Colum Ua Máel Muaid, was 'treacherously' killed by Ruaidrí mac Conchobair Mac Cochláin, king of Delbna Ethra (bar.

Garrycastle, Co. Offaly), who seems to have been acting at Hugh de Lacy's behest.[114] In northern Leinster, Fergal Ua Brain of Uí Fáeláin was 'killed by the Foreigners of Trim'.[115]

By the end 1175, Hugh de Lacy had almost doubled his landed wealth (at least on parchment), received royal commissions as *custos* of Dublin and governor of Verneuil, proved his loyalty during the revolt of 1173-4, endured an Irish assault upon his lordship of Meath and served as royal emissary to deflect the leader of that assault. Hugh travelled to England by October 1175, when he appeared alongside Strongbow and William fitz Audelin witnessing royal charters at Feckenham (Worcestershire) and Woodstock (Oxfordshire).[116] Interestingly, this means that the three most powerful men in colonial Ireland were in England when the Treaty of Windsor was concluded, yet none attested it.[117] The Treaty of Windsor, while beneficial to Henry II and Ruaidrí Ua Conchobair, circumscribed the ambitions of the settler community in Ireland. Not only did the treaty theoretically halt conquest by limiting English power in colonial Ireland to Meath, Leinster and parts of Munster, it also recognised the settlers' most ardent opponent, Ruaidrí Ua Conchobair, in his position as high king. The treaty even ensured Ruaidrí royal military support. It should not be forgotten that only a year before contingents from Connacht helped to slaughter the Dubliners at Thurles, and that Ua Conchobair had razed Meath in his march to Dublin. In early 1175, Hugh de Lacy had found it necessary to waste all of Meath from Athlone to Drogheda in order to re-establish his lordship. For those still recovering from Ua Conchobair's activities of 1174, Henry II's regularisation of relations with the king of Connacht may have been a bitter pill to swallow. For the next two years, Hugh de Lacy's activities are obscured through a general silence of the sources, though it is clear through what evidence remains that he did not return to Ireland. Instead, Hugh appears only in England, where his lordship had been relatively neglected during his Irish and Norman adventures.[118]

Conclusion

Hugh de Lacy's father Gilbert maintained a larger network of lordship than has previously been realised. Although Gilbert's Évreux sub-tenancy descended through a cadet branch under his younger son, Amaury, the ultimate heir to the main inheritance, Hugh, maintained a connection by acting as lord to his brother in Herefordshire. Having lost one Norman sub-tenancy at Claville, Hugh compensated himself by buying another and larger one at Le Pin-au-Haras. Buying the honor from the cash-strapped Count Robert of Meulan was an unofficial reward Hugh reaped for his royal service in the revolt of 1173-4. It also puts the grant of Meath into perspective. Transnational though they may have been, Anglo-Norman lords such as Hugh de Lacy continued to identify strongly with Normandy. The importance of Normandy is highlighted for the Lacys, as with others, in their active interest in the proliferation of landed interest in the duchy. Acquiring lands across the duchy allowed Hugh greater freedom of action within Normandy and a stronger voice at the ducal court. His actions in the duchy also ran counter to the trend of regionalisation in the Anglo-Norman nobility, which had begun in the wars of succession which divided England and Normandy following the death of William the Conqueror (1087), but which gained new impetus in the unification of the Anglo-Norman realm under Henry II. Instead of divesting his Norman interests in order to focus on England and the Welsh march, or vice versa, Hugh expanded on all fronts, as Waleran of Meulan had earlier done in Stephen's reign. Hugh's purchase of Le Pinau-Haras came shortly after he had been given a speculative grant of the vast lordship of Meath in Ireland. Hugh also maintained a connection to the Évreçin through his patronage of the monastery of Saint-Taurin d'Évreux.[119] Hugh granted the monks of Saint-Taurin the churches and tithes of Fore in Meath, along with a nearby wood and mill of St Fechin.[120] Despite his new western acquisition, or perhaps because of it, Hugh de Lacy reasserted his status as a *Norman* magnate by cultivating and expanding his interests in Normandy. Hugh spent very little time in Ireland in this period, for the most part trusting his tenants to carry forward the lordship's consolidation in his absence. Whatever his importance to Irish history, at this point Hugh de Lacy was still first and foremost an Anglo-Norman magnate.

If Meath was not Hugh's top priority, nor was Hugh Henry's first choice as lord of Meath. Henry's grant of Meath has previously been characterised as an attempt to counterbalance Strongbow in Leinster, but it seems rather more likely that Henry had planned to conquer Meath (along with Connacht) himself. Being recalled from Ireland to settle the fallout from Becket's murder, Henry's grant to Hugh was a last-minute measure to secure the royal city of Dublin, key to the control of Ireland and the Irish Sea region. This revised rationale for King Henry's grant of Meath to Hugh de Lacy characterises the relationship between the king of England and the lords of Meath and Leinster as amicable, rather than combative. One manifestation of this dynamic – Henry II's complicity in the assassination of the king of Bréifne – is also one of the earliest instances of royally imposed, or at the very least condoned, factionalism among those bound to the English king in Ireland.

Strongbow died in 1176.[121] Colonial Ireland was now without a royal official to guide its administration, and William fitz Audelin was sent as the king's chief agent, to the apparent chagrin of a number of English settlers.[122] Hugh, perhaps a more obvious choice as replacement for Strongbow, remained in England for the time being. From May 1177, however, that was to change. Thereafter, the focus of Hugh's lordship and the balance of his time were to be invested in Ireland, with secondary attention paid to his English and Norman estates. While he had always given it a certain amount of consideration, from 1177 Ireland was Hugh de Lacy's primary concern.

Notes

1 Wightman, *Lacy*, pp. 187–8.
2 *The Cartulary of Haughmond Abbey*, ed. Una Rees (Cardiff, 1985), p. 137.
3 *Rotuli Hundredorum Temp. Hen. III et Edw. I in Turr. Lond. et in Curia Receptae Scaccarii West. Asservati*, eds W. Illingworth and J. Caley, 2 vols (London, 1812–18), ii, pp. 69b, 76, 80.
4 J. C. Dickinson and P. T. Ricketts, 'The Anglo-Norman chronicle of Wigmore abbey', *Transactions of the Woolhope Naturalists' Field Club*, 39/3 (1969), pp. 413–46, at p. 431.
5 Wightman, *Lacy*, pp. 117–66.
6 *Liber Niger Scaccarii*, ed. Thomas Hearne, 2 vols (London, 1774), i, pp. 153–5; *RBE*, i, pp. 281–3. The *cartae baronum* in the Red Book of the Exchequer was copied from that in the *Liber Niger*, and incorrectly states that Robert de Baskerville owed the service of eight knights (instead of five).
7 *RBE*, i, pp. 189–90, 288–91, 261–2, 395–7.
8 *Liber Feodorum: The Book of Fees Commonly Called Testa de Nevill*, 3 vols (London, 1920), ii, pp. 741, 797–818, 964, 967.
9 *Liber Feodorum*, ii, pp. 818–19.
10 *Pipe Roll 6 Henry II*, p. 30; *Pipe Roll 2–4 Henry II*, pp. 144, 169, 170.
11 Bodleian Library MS Ashmole 833, p. 13.
12 TNA C 115/75, fo. 228. A Robert de Lacy also witnessed a grant of Henry II's brother William to Robert Mantel 1154 × 64, BL MS Cotton Vitellius F VIII, fo. 24r.
13 R. H. C. Davis, 'Treaty between William Earl of Gloucester and Roger Earl of Hereford', in P. M. Barnes and C. F. Slade (eds), *A Medieval Miscellany Presented to Doris Mary Stenton* (London, 1960), pp. 139–46.
14 *The Letters and Charters of Gilbert Foliot*, eds Adrian Morey and C. N. L. Brooke (Cambridge, 1967), no. 94.
15 *Pipe Rolls 2, 3, 4 Henry II*, pp. 144, 169, 170; *Recueil des actes de Henri II, roi*

d'Angleterre et duc de Normandie, concernant les provinces françaises et les affaires de France, eds Léopold Delisle and Élie Berger, 4 vols (Paris, 1906-27), i, p. 253; Wightman, *Lacy*, p. 189.
16. Gloucester Cathedral Library, Register A, fo. 154r. It can be dated by the appearance of 'chancellor' Thomas Becket as a witness at Woodstock.
17. Gloucester Cathedral Library, Register A, fo. 154r.
18. *Recueil des historiens des Gaules et de la France*, eds M. Bouquet, et al., 24 vols (Paris, 1864-1904), xxiii, pp. 700(k)-701(a).
19. Archives Départementales [AD] de l'Eure G 122, p. 47; *Recueil historiens*, xxiii, p. 712b.
20. *Chartes de l'abbaye de Jumièges*, ed. J.-J. Vernier, 2 vols (Rouen, 1916), i, pp. 176-7.
21. 'Hugone de Laceio. Amalrico fratre eius', AD Eure G 122, pp. 37-8 (1160 × 1165), 42 (1141 × 1165).
22. See Power, *Norman Frontier*, p. 292.
23. Cressage: *Pipe Roll 24 Henry II*, p. 85; *Pipe Roll 31 Henry II*, p. 128; *Pipe Roll 32 Henry II*, p. 57; Harnage: *Monasticon Anglicanum: A History of the Abbies and Other Monasteries, Hospitals, Frieries, and Cathedral and Collegiate Churches, with Their Dependencies, in England and Wales*, eds William Dugdale, et al. (new edn, London, 1823), v, p. 356; Eyton, *Shropshire*, vi, pp. 74-5); Castle Frome: *Pipe Roll 32 Henry II*, p. 32; *Pipe Roll 33 Henry II*, p. 133. For this Gilbert in Normandy, *Recueil des actes de Philippe Auguste Roi de France*, ed. H. Delaborde, et al., 4 vols (Paris, 1916-79), ii, no. 754.
24. AD Eure, G 122 p. 47. Amaury appears in another Count Simon charter, *Le Grand Cartulaire de Conches et sa copie*, ed. Claire de Haas (Le Mesnil-sur-l'Estree, 2005), pp. 152-3.
25. See Chapter 8.
26. BL Additional MS 6041.
27. *Liber Niger*, i, p. 150. The Red Book of the Exchequer incorrectly states that Hugh denied only one-half of a knight's fee. *RBE*, i, p. 279.
28. *Registrum Ricardi de Swinfield, Episcopi Herefordensis, 1283-1317*, ed. W. W. Capes (London, 1909), p. 477.
29. See Chapters 2 and 8.
30. *Pipe Roll 16 Henry II*, pp. 59, 64.
31. The best account is in: M. T. Flanagan, *Irish Society, Anglo-Norman Settlers, Angevin Kingship: Interactions in Ireland in the Late Twelfth Century* (Oxford, 1989).
32. *Expugnatio Hibernica*, pp. 70, 88.
33. *Reg. St Thomas*, pp. 13, 420.
34. *Monasticon Anglicanum*, iv, pp. 596-7.
35. *Recueil Henri II*, i, nos 403, 431, 440; *Calendar of the Charter Rolls Preserved in the Public Record Office, vol I., Henry III, A.D. 1226-1257* (London, 1903), pp. 258-9.
36. Flanagan, *Irish Society*, pp. 167-228, 308-11. For what follows see Colin Veach, 'Henry II's grant of Meath to Hugh de Lacy in 1172: a reassessment', *Ríocht na Mídhe*, 18 (2007), pp. 67-94.

37 See below, p. 31.
38 This was the latest of several partitionings of Mide in the pre-Anglo-Norman period.
39 *Gesta Henrici*, ii, pp. 29–30.
40 Kate Norgate, *England Under the Angevin Kings*, 2 vols (London, 1887), ii, pp. 116–17. For Becket see Anne Duggan, *Thomas Becket* (London, 2004); Barlow, *Thomas Becket*. For several miracles of St Thomas reflecting Henry II's Irish expedition see Marcus Bull, 'Criticism of Henry II's Expedition to Ireland in William of Canterbury's Miracles of St Thomas Becket', *Journal of Medieval History*, 33 (2007), pp. 107–29.
41 '"Redeo," inquit, "in Hiberniam, ubi multa mihi incumbent"', *Materials for the History of Thomas Becket, Archbishop of Canterbury*, ed. J. C. Robertson, 7 vols (London, 1875–85), vii, p. 514.
42 *Gormanston Register*, p. 177.
43 Seán Duffy, 'Town and crown: the kings of England and their city of Dublin', in Michael Prestwich, Robin Frame, and Richard Britnell (eds), *Thirteenth Century England X* (Woodbridge, 2005), pp. 95–117, at pp. 100–2.
44 Paul Latimer, 'Henry II's campaign against the Welsh in 1165', *Welsh History Review*, 14/4 (1989), pp. 523–52, at p. 537.
45 Frame, *British Isles*, p. 37.
46 See Flanagan, *Irish Society*, pp. 167–228.
47 For Dublin's significance see Seán Duffy, 'Irishmen and Islesmen in the kingdoms of Dublin and Man, 1052–1171', *Ériu*, xliii (1992), pp. 93–133; Seán Duffy, 'Ireland's Hastings: the Anglo-Norman conquest of Dublin', in Christopher Harper-Bill (ed.), *Anglo-Norman Studies XX* (Woodbridge, 1997), pp. 69–86; Duffy, 'Town and crown', pp. 95–117.
48 *Expugnatio Hibernica*, p. 88.
49 *Irish Llanthony*, p. 83; Arlene Hogan, *The Priory of Llanthony Prima and Secunda in Ireland, 1172–1541: Lands, Patronage and Politics* (Dublin, 2008), p. 49. Many of these early grants are simply to 'Llanthony', so it is difficult to determine whether Llanthony Prima (in Ewyas Lacy) or the later foundation of Llanthony Secunda (next to Gloucester) is intended.
50 *Song*, lines 3129–207; *Deeds*, lines 3127–205.
51 *Song*, p. 301 and see Chapter 2.
52 *Chart. St Mary's*, ii, p. 21; *Song*, lines 3156–7 and p. 314; *Deeds*, lines 3154–5; Orpen, *Normans*, ii, p. 85. This compares with the twenty knights demanded by Hugh for Robert le Fleming's grant of Slane (Co. Meath), (*Song*, lines 3174–201; *Deeds*, lines 3174–99) and twenty knights demanded by Strongbow for Walter de Riddlesford's grant of Uí Muiredaig (*Song*, lines 3096–9, p. 305; *Deeds*, lines 3094–7).
53 Adam also held Rathconnell (Co. Westmeath), the tithes of which he granted to Llanthony Priory at some point between 1174 and 1184. *Irish Llanthony*, p. 239.
54 *Chart. St Mary's*, i, pp. 1–3, 96, 101–4, 156–7; ii, pp. 21–2; See also A. J. Otway-Ruthven, 'Parochial development in the rural deanery of Skreen', *Journal of the Royal Society of Antiquaries of Ireland*, 94/2 (1964), pp. 111–22, at pp. 117–19.

55 Geoffrey granted of the tithes of 40 acres in Killeen (Co. Meath) to Llanthony Priory, the grant being made for the souls of his wife, Matilda, and lord, Adam de Feipo. *Irish Llanthony*, p. 94.
56 The Talbots and Lacys were related. During the civil war in Stephen's reign, Hugh de Lacy's father, Gilbert, fought alongside his cousin (*cognatus*), Geoffrey Talbot. *Gesta Stephani*, eds K. R. Potter and R. H. C. Davis (2nd edn, Oxford, 1976), pp. 58-9. Geoffrey was the son of Gilbert's aunt, Agnes de Lacy, wife of Geoffrey Talbot the elder.
57 *Chart. St Mary's*, i, p. 157.
58 Feipo ('*Futipo*' in the *cartae baronum*) refers to Flipou (Eure), which was written *Futipou* in 1184, *Foutipou* in 1221, *Foutipou* in 1467 and *Faipou* in 1469. François de Beaurepaire, *Les noms des communes et anciennes paroisses de l'Eure* (Paris, 1981), p. 110. Interestingly, another of the Lacys' tenant families in Herefordshire, the Gamacheses, held lands in Flipou, about 17 miles west of Gamaches-en-Vexin (Eure). L. C. Loyd, *The Origins of Some Anglo-Norman Families* (Leeds, 1951), p. 45.
59 'K'il tant amat', *Song*, lines 3132-3; *Deeds*, lines 3130-1.
60 Bartlett, 'Colonial aristocracies', pp. 38-41.
61 *Na Buirgéisí, xii-xv aois*, ed. Gearóid Mac Niocaill, 2 vols (Dublin, 1964), i, pp. 172-3. Also see Chapter 3.
62 Robert's descendants, Hugh and Walter de Lacy, were expelled from Ireland in 1317 for aiding Edward Bruce's invasion from Scotland. *The Annals of Ireland by Friar John Clyn [Clyn's Annals]*, ed. Bernadette Williams (Dublin, 2007), p. 167; Otway-Ruthven, *Medieval Ireland*, p. 233.
63 Orpen, *Normans*, ii, p. 84.
64 *Ibid.*, i, p. 145.
65 *Ibid.*, i, pp. 378, 381-2.
66 See Chapter 2.
67 *Song*, lines 3138-60; *Deeds*, lines 3136-58; *Expugnatio Hibernica*, p. 194. It is unclear whether Gilbert and his brother, Richard de Capella (*Irish Llanthony*, p. 85), were related to the former bishop of Hereford, Richard de Capella (d. 1127).
68 See Chapter 2.
69 Veach, 'Henry II's grant of Meath', pp. 75-7.
70 *Annals of Tigernach*, ed. Whitley Stokes, 2 vols (Llanerch, 1993), ii, *s.a.* 1172.
71 *Expugnatio Hibernica*, p. 115; *MCB*, p. 58, *s.a.* 1173.
72 *Ann. Tig.*, ii, p. 430, *s.a.* 1172; *AU*, ii, p. 172, *s.a.* 1172; *AI*, p. 304, *s.a.* 1172; *MCB*, p. 58, *s.a.* 1173; *Expugnatio Hibernica*, p. 114.
73 M. A. Freeman, 'The annals in Cotton MS Titus A. XXV', *Revue Celtique*, 41 (1924), pp. 301-30; 42 (1925), pp. 281-305; 43 (1926), pp. 358-84; 44 (1927), pp. 336-61, *s.a.* 1166; *AFM*, ii, pp. 1160-2, *s.a.* 1166; *AI*, p. 300, *s.a.* 1166; *MCB*, p. 46, *s.a.* 1165 [*recte* 1166].
74 *MCB*, p. 50, *s.a.* 1167 [*recte* 1169].
75 *AI*, p. 302, *s.a.* 1169.
76 *Expugnatio Hibernica*, pp. 76-8; *Song*, lines 2255-492; *Deeds*, lines 2253-490.

77 *Deeds*, lines 2167-72.
78 See M. T. Flanagan, 'Henry II and the kingdom of Uí Fáeláin', in John Bradley (ed.), *Settlement and Society in Medieval Ireland: Studies Presented to F. X. Martin, O.S.A.* (Kilkenny, 1988), pp. 312-24.
79 Duffy, 'Irishmen and Islesmen', p. 132.
80 *Song*, line 1849; *Deeds*, line 1847.
81 Orpen, *Normans*, vol. i, p. 279; Duffy, *Ireland*, pp. 86-7; Warren, *Henry II*, pp. 200-1; Otway-Ruthven, *Medieval Ireland*, p. 58; F. X. Martin, 'Allies and an overlord, 1169-72', in *NHI, ii*, p. 96, among others. For what follows see Veach, 'Henry II's grant of Meath', pp. 79-86.
82 F. X. Martin, 'Overlord becomes feudal lord', in *NHI, ii*, pp. 98-126, at p. 98.
83 *AFM*, ii, pp. 1104-72.
84 *Ibid.*, p. 1172, s.a. 1169.
85 *Ibid.*, p. 1178, s.a. 1170.
86 See Warren, *Henry II*, pp. 111-42.
87 *Giraldi Cambrensis Opera*, eds J. S. Brewer, J. F. Dimock and G. F. Warner, 8 vols. (London, 1861-91), vii, p. 69.
88 Warren, *Henry II*, pp. 127-8.
89 *Expugnatio Hibernica*, p. 135.
90 *Song*, lines 2898-939; *Deeds*, lines 2896-937; Orpen, *Normans*, i, pp. 326-7.
91 *Deeds*, lines 2938-42.
92 Orpen, *Normans*, i, p. 332.
93 *Expugnatio Hibernica*, p. 138; *Song*, lines 3232-341; *Deeds*, lines 3220-339. See also *AFM*, iii, pp. 14-18, s.a. 1174; *AI*, p. 306, s.a. 1174; *MCB*, pp. 60-2, s.a. 1175 [*recte* 1174]; Freeman, 'Cottonian Annals', s.a. 1174.
94 *Deeds*, lines 3230-5.
95 *Ann. Tig.*, ii, s.a. 1172; *AU*, ii, p. 172, s.a. 1172. For Angaile see Freya Verstraten Veach, 'The Ó Fearghail lordship of Anghaile', in Martin Morris and Fergus O'Ferrall (eds), *Longford: History and Society* (Dublin, 2010), pp. 51-74.
96 Seán Duffy, 'The prehistory of the galloglass', in idem (ed.), *The World of the Galloglass: Kings, Warlords and Warriors in Ireland and Scotland, 1200-1600*, (Dublin, 2007), pp. 1-23, at pp. 7-8.
97 *Expugnatio Hibernica*, p. 138.
98 *MCB*, p. 60, s.a. 1175 [*recte* 1174].
99 Frame, *British Isles*, p. 35.
100 See Flanagan, *Irish Society*, pp. 229-72.
101 *Expugnatio Hibernica*, p. 94.
102 Flanagan, 'Household favourites', p. 360.
103 BM Rouen Y201, fos 43v, 61v.
104 Crouch, *Beaumont Twins*, p. 157n.
105 David Bates, *Normandy Before 1066* (London, 1982), p. 103.
106 *Recueil Henri II*, ii, nos 476, 478, 484, 518, 521, 524, 526-7. Nicholas Vincent dates Henry II's confirmation of the sale to before Henry's return to England in May 1175, *Acta of Henry II*, ed. Nicholas Vincent (forthcoming), no. 1441.
107 BM Rouen Y201, fos 61r-v.

108 Power, 'Henry, Duke of the Normans', pp. 96–7; And see Chapter 8.
109 *Recueil historiens*, xxiii, p. 711a.
110 *Recueil Henri II*, ii, no. 478.
111 BM Rouen Y201, fo. 43v.
112 *Ann. Tig.*, ii, *s.a.* 1175 (quote); *AU*, ii, p. 182, *s.a.* 1175.
113 *AFM*, iii, p. 18, *s.a.* 1175 (quote); *AU*, ii, p. 182, *s.a.* 1175; *Ann. Tig.*, ii, *s.a.* 1175.
114 *Ann. Tig.*, ii, *s.a.* 1175; *AU*, ii, p. 182, *s.a.* 1175.
115 'Fergal Ua Braín do marbad do Gallaib Atha Truim.' *Ann. Tig.*, ii, *s.a.* 1175.
116 *Chart. St Mary's*, i, pp. 79–81; Maurice Sheehy, 'The registrum novum, a manuscript of Holy Trinity cathedral: the medieval charters', *Reportorium Novum. Dublin Diocesan Historical Record*, 3/2 (1964), pp. 249–81, at p. 253; Flanagan, *Irish Society*, p. 233.
117 Howden, *Gesta*, i, 102–3
118 *The Manuscripts of His Grace the Duke of Rutland, K.G., Preserved at Belvoir Castle*, 4 vols (London, 1888–1905), iv, p. 22 (Brewood); *Cart. Haughmond*, pp. 23–4 (Shrewsbury), 98 (Shrewsbury), 109 (Shrewsbury), 149 (Feckenham), 251 appendix C (Shrewsbury); *Acta Henry II*, no. 1786 (Reading).
119 An unidentified Robert de Lacy received 13 *livres* from the farm of the honor in 1198, *Mag. Rot. Normanniae*, ii, p. 462.
120 *Calendar of Documents Preserved in France, Illustrative of the History of Great Britain and Ireland, A.D. 918–1206*, ed. J. H. Round (London, 1889), nos 302, 314–15.
121 Orpen, *Normans*, i, pp. 356–7.
122 *Expugnatio Hibernica*, pp. 166–72.

2

'Lord of the Foreigners of Ireland': 1177–86

The year 1177 marks a turning point in the career of Hugh de Lacy; the year's events had a profound effect on the strength and character of his lordship in England, Ireland, Wales and Normandy. The change is evident in the highly symbolic resolution to Hugh de Lacy's dispute with the bishop of Hereford over one knight's fee at Holme Lacy. This was a very local, English, dispute between two of the most powerful landholders in Herefordshire, and had rumbled on for over a decade. However, on 3 June 1177, Hugh relented.[1] The bishop claimed that Hugh owed him the service of two knights and *hundredse* (a hundred fine) for his lands in Holme Lacy (Herefordshire), while Hugh claimed that he owed only the service of one knight, plus another at the muster, and nothing for *hundredse*. Hugh was finally forced to admit to a large assembly (*in magna audientia*) that he owed the full two knights and the *hundredse* whenever it was due from the six geldable hides in Holme Lacy. He then paid the arrears of the relief for the two knights' fees and of the *hundredse* at the chapterhouse at Hereford when the decision was made. It was further decided, contrary to Hugh's wishes, that he, not a certain knight named William, was to pay the yearly rent of 20s. for the manor of Onibury (Shropshire). At the same time, land at Onibury was taken from William of Stokes's prebend and given to Hugh.[2] The issue was quite clearly not the performance of military service, but rather the financial obligations involved, a point one would never understand only by reading the 1166 *cartae baronum* return. The survival of a text of this written settlement is more than fortuitous. It was preserved in a psalter, because, as the bishop's scribe writes: 'in order to prevent lawsuits being revived after having once been settled, out of forgetfulness or through someone's ill-will, it is necessary to commit their end to writing'.[3]

Hugh was willing to back down in Herefordshire that June, because by then his priorities lay elsewhere. The previous month Hugh had been appointed royal governor of one-third of colonial Ireland, where he was about to journey and (apart from a few short recalls) spend the rest of his life. Henceforth, Ireland was to be the focus of the Lacy family enterprise. Henry II's choice of Hugh as royal administrator ran counter to his practice of promoting lesser men to positions of influence within the localities in his other realms. The reasons for Henry's break in Ireland with his former policy say much about Angevin rule there, and the adaptability of Henry's kingship. So too does his reaction to Hugh's rapid rise to pre-eminence across the Irish Sea. Henry had to balance his desire for a stable Ireland with his need to control the colony, and his handling of Hugh de Lacy's new prominence set the tone for Crown involvement in Ireland for many years to come. However much Henry laid the foundation for Hugh's achievements in Ireland, a royal commission was no guarantee of success. Hugh's eventual position was bought with a great deal of effort and ingenuity on his own part. His methods take us to the very heart of frontier lordship in the late twelfth century.

A new direction in Ireland: 1177

In May 1177, King Henry II held a council at Oxford which sought to reaffirm royal lordship in Ireland. Since Strongbow's death the previous year, the failure of William fitz Audelin as an omni-competent royal governor of colonial Ireland had become obvious. In the absence of both Strongbow and Hugh de Lacy, the career administrator was unable to exert effective control over the unruly colonial barons who remained. In February 1177, John de Courcy, who had accompanied William fitz Audelin to Ireland, marched north with 22 knights and three hundred others and conquered the northern Irish kingdom of Ulaid.[4] When Ruaidrí Ua Conchobair made a royal circuit of western Connacht later that year, another member of the Dublin garrison, Miles de Cogan, raided eastern Connacht in alliance with Ruaidrí's disaffected son, Murchad.[5] Both expeditions were direct contraventions of the Treaty of Windsor, which had in theory limited colonial activities to Meath, Leinster and the south-east corner of Munster, and had assured Ruaidrí Ua Conchobair of the support of the English government. The Geraldines, the only settlers over whom William fitz Audelin was apparently able to exert firm control, chafed at their restraints, and their spokesman, Gerald of Wales, complained bitterly of William's maladministration.[6] Henry II was forced to rethink his strategy for Ireland, or risk losing control of it.

At Oxford, Henry decreed that his ten-year-old son, John, would be king of Ireland, and had the barons of Ireland, whom he had assembled for the council, do John homage for their lands there. However, for all of the constitutional importance this designation was to assume, in 1177 the more pertinent result of the Oxford council was the reorganisation of the political and administrative map of colonial Ireland. The Irish Tigernach annalist, who had access to intelligence reports reaching the court of the king of Connacht, Ruaidrí Ua Conchobair, records for 1177 that 'Three fleets of Englishmen arrived in Ireland, to wit, the fleet of Hugh de Lacy, and the fleet of William Fitz Audelin, and the fleet of Philip de Briouze. Hugh's to Dublin; William's to Wexford; Philip's to Waterford'.[7] Roger of Howden explains that Henry made a tripartite division of the Irish government.[8] William fitz Audelin was effectively demoted from his position as the king's principal agent in Ireland to custodian of Wexford and a much diminished Leinster during the minority of its heir. Portions of western Leinster, including the whole of Osraige, were attached to the royal demesne of Waterford, which itself was extended west to the river Blackwater, and administered by Robert le Poer. Hugh de Lacy was re-granted Meath for the service of one hundred knights (probably reflecting his expanded territorial responsibilities) and given custody of Dublin, with the north-Leinster territories of Uí Fáeláin, Uí Failge, Kildare, and Wicklow, along with their appurtenances.[9]

This partition of Strongbow's former lordship corresponded to the pre-English division of Leinster into northern (Laigin Tuathgabair) and southern (Laigin Desgabair) halves along the Gabair, or Liffey and Slaney watershed, and the exclusion of Osraige from Leinster proper.[10] The diocesan structure of Leinster reflects this division. The geographical extent of Laigin Tuathgabair was preserved in the dioceses of Dublin, Glendalough and Kildare, while Laigin Desgabair encompassed the dioceses of Leighlin and Ferns. From 738 until 1042 the provincial kingship of Leinster had lain in the northern half of Leinster, in the hands of the Uí Dúnlainge sub-dynasties of Uí Dúnchada (centred on Liamain – on the Dublin/Kildare border), Uí Fáeláin (centred on Naas – eastern Liffey plain) and Uí Muiredaig (centred on Maistiu – South Kildare). Under Diarmait mac Murchada's ancestor, Diarmait mac Máel na mBó (d. 1072), the southern kingdom of Uí Chennselaig grasped the provincial kingship. Diarmait mac Máel na mBó was able also to control Dublin, making his son Murchad mac Diarmada mic Maíl na mBó (eponymous ancestor of the Meic Murchada) its king, and even harboured designs on the kingdom of Mide.[11] Therefore, although Diarmait Mac Murchada's southern kingdom of Uí Chennselaig was ascendant immediately preceding English intervention in Ireland in 1168, its claims to provincial pre-eminence were relatively recent and were bitterly opposed by the kings of north Leinster. In 1161, Ruaidrí Ua Conchobair had unsuccessfully attempted to dislodge Uí Dúnlainge from Leinster. He was aided in this enterprise by the kings of Uí Fáeláin and Uí Failge, from whom he took hostages as a sign of submission.[12] Later, in 1166, those same Leinster kings did homage to Ruaidrí, a direct assault upon Diarmait's provincial kingship. As mentioned above, the Uí Dúnlainge then marched along with Tigernán Ua Ruairc, Diarmait Ua Máel Sechlainn of Mide and the Dublin Norse against Mac Murchada, driving him from Ireland to seek assistance from Henry II.[13]

It is little surprise, therefore, that, once that aid was obtained, Diarmait and his new English allies turned their attention towards securing northern Leinster, Dublin and eventually Mide. They were pursuing the same road as Diarmait, with the man himself as their guide. Consequently, by 1171, Strongbow held a reunited Leinster, the Norse city of Dublin, and exercised strong claims to Mide. As seen above, Henry II made a point of separating Dublin and Mide from Strongbow's lordship. He may also initially have divorced the northern kingdoms of Laigin Tuathgabair from Leinster, reserving the troublesome territories as royal demesne. Although the cases of the other sub-kingdoms are not certain, Henry II undeniably exercised direct lordship over Uí Fáeláin for a period in 1171–2 when he granted Robert fitz Stephen lands therein. The territory was ultimately restored to Strongbow upon his return to Ireland in 1173 as a reward for his faithful service in Normandy that summer. Marie Therese Flanagan speculates that Uí Failge was also royal demesne in 1172, and that further Leinster lands had been reserved in 1171 or 1172 only to be restored in 1173.[14] Unfortunately, limited evidence renders it difficult to determine the exact situation. However, it is interesting for the division of Leinster in 1177 that over the winter of 1171–2 the Uí Dúnlainge kings of Uí Fáeláin, Uí Muiredaig and Uí Dunchada, along with the kings of Uí Felmeda and Osraige, submitted directly to Henry II.[15] It has been suggested that, by the terms of their submission, the Meic Gilla Mo Cholmóc kings of Uí Dunchada were to hold their lands directly of Henry II, a distinction Henry marked by granting away their lands in north Dublin to men of his choosing.[16] It is not clear whether or not a similar direct relationship was established with the other Leinster kings who submitted to Henry II, but their territories' restoration to Strongbow in 1173 suggests that one may have been. These arguments are relevant to the grant of Meath to Hugh de Lacy. In both instances the submissions of Irish kings meant little to the English king in the face of strategic concerns and political expediency. The fact that the lands of northern Leinster were separated in 1177 from the portion of Leinster administered by William fitz Audelin certainly suggests that they were acknowledged as being separate from Strongbow's inherited powerbase in Uí Chennselaig and southern Leinster.

Interestingly, at least two of the northern territories had also been the scene of disputes between William fitz Audelin and prominent Geraldines in 1176, during the immediate build-up to the restructuring of the royal administration in Ireland. Gerald of Wales complained that William cheated the sons of Maurice fitz Gerald out of their rightful possession of Wicklow Castle upon Maurice's death.[17] Gerald also claimed that William deprived Raymond le Gros of his lands in the vale of Dublin, along with those adjacent to Wexford, and had refused to act upon a royal order to restore a cantred in Uí Fáeláin to Robert fitz Stephen.[18] It would seem that, in light of the circumstances surrounding their tenure in 1171-2 and the complaints against his principal agent in Ireland, Henry II decided to utilise the minority of the boy Gilbert, Strongbow's heir, to exploit the historical division of Leinster, once again reserving the northern territories of Laigin Tuathgabair for the Crown. These were handed to Hugh de Lacy to differentiate them from Laigin Desgabair, held by William fitz Audelin, while also demoting the career royal administrator and removing him from areas of contention. The end result was that, despite Gerald of Wales's claim that Hugh de Lacy was made *procurator generalis*, none of the principal Angevin administrators, Hugh de Lacy, Robert le Poer or William fitz Audelin held a superior position in Ireland. This was all part of a more general strategy by Henry II throughout his dominions to curtail baronial influence at the local level, and restructure royal custodianships. In 1176, Roger of Howden states that the king took every English castle into his hand, removed their seigniorial castellans, and put in his own custodians.[19] The following year, in 1177 (the year of the council of Oxford), he even changed these around, removing his officials from one castle to another in an attempt to curb any feelings of entitlement a castellan might harbour towards a particular castle. Consequently, when Henry granted Hugh de Lacy his Irish custodies, he had seized Hugh's strategic castle of Ludlow (Shropshire), limiting Hugh's lordship in England.[20]

Conquest and consolidation in Ireland: 1177-8

If Henry had been seeking to limit Hugh de Lacy's activities to Ireland, he succeeded. Hugh settled his affairs in England (including his long-running dispute with the bishop of Hereford), and returned to an Ireland ripe for conquest. Since his last visit in 1175, the Cenél nEógain of northern Ireland had been harassing Meath, burning Slane in 1176. This activity had kept the northern frontier of Meath well south of the lordship's theoretical boundary. However, John de Courcy's conquest of Ulaid in early 1177 marked a turning point. With an ambitious Anglo-Norman baron on their very doorstep, the Cenél nEógain had more immediate concerns than the settlers' activities in Meath. The expansion of Meath could begin in earnest. Hugh thereafter mounted a concerted effort to exploit and enhance his stature in Ireland through a pragmatic combination of diplomacy, conquest and settlement.

The initial conquest of Meath had forced many of the Irish to flee the new colonial lordship. However, Hugh's territory was useless without a local labour force. There is no evidence to suggest that Hugh was capable of attracting enough immigrant labour to make his lordship profitable. In 1175, the Treaty of Windsor addressed this problem directly. It stated that the Irish who had fled were to be permitted to return to the lands of the English barons, either paying tribute or performing to the barons the service that they had previously performed for their lands (whichever their new lords preferred). Ruaidrí Ua Conchobair was to compel any of the Irish who refused to repopulate the colony in this way.[21] Whether or not such a drastic step was required, Hugh was in the end especially successful in his efforts to establish his lordship over the Irish of Meath. The colonial partisan, Gerald of Wales, writes:

> Hugh went to great trouble to conciliate those [i.e. the Irish] who had been conquered by others and forcibly ejected from their lands, and thus he restored the countryside to its rightful cultivators and brought back cattle to pastures which had formerly been deserted. So when he had won their support, he enticed them to his side still further by his mild rule and by making agreements on which they could rely, and finally, when they had been hemmed in by castles and gradually subdued, he compelled them to obey the laws.[22]

Although Gerald is clearly juxtaposing Hugh's 'mild rule' and 'reliable agreements' to highlight what he saw (by contrast) as incompetent royal officials and oath-breaking Irishmen (common figures in his works), his testimony is corroborated not only by the early success of Hugh's lordship in Meath but also by the pragmatically inclusive nature of the Lacys' tributary lordship in Ireland.[23]

From 1177, Hugh also controlled the provisioning of Dublin. The pipe rolls record his agents conveying grain for the royal *familia* (household troops and officers) from England to Dublin.[24] A significant component of conquest and settlement on the Irish frontier was encastellation, and here Hugh was regarded as something of an expert. Gerald of Wales records his construction of many castles throughout the lordship of Meath in this period, and also mentions that Hugh travelled outside his bailiwick to reconstruct the castle at Leighlin (Ballyknockan, Co. Laois), which Gerald claims had been abandoned by the royal governor of Waterford and Osraige, Robert le Poer.

The government's over-reliance upon Hugh caused Gerald to complain bitterly of the lack of military acumen in the likes of Robert le Poer and William fitz Audelin, declaring at the end of a diatribe that 'it amazes me that a prince who was himself so noble and courageous should have made a practice of appointing to command remote border areas men who were so lacking in courage and nobility'.[25] Gerald was biased, but his comment cut to the heart of the problems of frontier administration. As much as King Henry wanted to use experienced administrators to oversee the Angevin empire's western fringe, he needed powerful military men like Hugh de Lacy on the ground to sustain his authority. If Gerald is to be believed, Hugh appointed his own custodian of Leighlin Castle,[26] thereby assuming military responsibility for much of colonial Ireland. Being employed thus by the king, Hugh used his office to extend his own influence. His town and castle of Drogheda guarded a bridge over the river Boyne, the main crossing from Dublin, through the northern kingdom of Airgialla, to the new Courcy lordship of Ulster. The security of Drogheda and communication with Ulster required that Airgialla be pacified. In 1178, contingents from Dublin, to whom Hugh must have given direction as *custos*, made forays into Airgialla, attacking Lugmad (Louth, Co. Louth) and Machaire Conaill (bar. Upper Dundalk, Co. Louth).[27] The Irish of Airgialla would have to heed their new neighbour.

Next, Hugh turned to Connacht. A confrontation with Ruaidrí Ua Conchobair was perhaps inevitable from the grant of Meath in 1172, but the situation did not come to a head until Hugh took up permanent residence in Ireland. Before then, much of the work of conquest and settlement had been entrusted to his local representatives. But this progressed only so far. In 1178, Hugh expanded his effective lordship beyond the line of English settlement by adopting the Irish practice of promoting his favoured candidate for the kingship of a neighbouring territory. Exploiting the disputed succession for the Ua Máel Sechlainn kingship of Westmeath, Hugh allied himself with the Leinster Irish of Uí Failge and supported Art Ua Máel Sechlainn against the rival claimant Máel Sechlainn Beg, and his supporters from the Meath territories of Delbna Ethra (Co. Offaly) and Tethba (Cos Longford and Westmeath).[28] Hugh's involvement in the struggle was clear to contemporaries, with the lord (*tigerna*) of Tethba, In Sinnach ('the fox') Ua Catharnaig possibly blaming Hugh personally for the death of his son in battle.[29]

By playing kingmaker to the as-yet-unconquered (or only partially subjugated) Irish of western Meath, Hugh was intruding into Ruaidrí Ua Conchobair's hegemony, and indeed deliberately challenging it. The king of Connacht held a claim over western Meath, put forward in its 1169 partition.[30] Although Ruaidrí ostensibly had renounced this sphere of influence when he agreed to the Treaty of Windsor, the reality was very different.[31] Ruaidrí was keen to exercise the prerogatives inherent in the formal recognition of his high kingship within the treaty, which included the power to invade, annex and intrigue in the territories of the other Irish kings.[32] This is exactly what he attempted. Under Ruaidrí's protection, a 'vibrant Irish web of social interaction woven together by alliance and kinship' persisted in the Irish midlands.[33] The Uí Conchobair benefactions to Clonmacnoise (Co. Offaly), on the eastern bank of the Shannon were an instance, and assurance, of Connacht's continuing presence in the region. Clonmacnoise was heavily patronised by the royal house of Connacht, and was the site of their ancestral burial ground. Clonmacnoise was first associated with the Uí Conchobair in the time of Áed Ua Conchobair, (d. 1067).[34] The former high king, Toirdelbach Ua Conchobair, did much to further this affiliation, and was himself buried there in 1156. He also established a mint at Clonmacnoise, which was still coining money in the 1170s.[35] The foundation continued to serve as burial place for the Uí Conchobair, and Ruaidrí himself was eventually buried there in 1198.[36] Just like Hugh's town of Drogheda, in order for Clonmacnoise to be secure, its surrounding territories had to be on good terms with the king of Connacht.

The importance of Clonmacnoise to Ruaidrí's influence in western Meath made it the perfect target for Hugh. In 1178 the Irish annals record that 'The constable of the king of England in Dublin and east Meath (namely, Hugh) marched with his forces to Clonmacnoise, and plundered all the town, except the churches and the bishop's houses'.[37] The annals' designation of Hugh as the constable of Dublin and *east* Meath is a good barometer of the extent of Hugh's effective lordship in 1178, and may be a further indication that Hugh's supersession of Connacht's supremacy in western Meath had not been recognised by the Irish. By attacking Clonmacnoise, Hugh showed that he could reach the river Shannon, and the border of Connacht. Burning the settlement was a very personal attack on the Uí Conchobair, and Ruaidrí's sense of outrage can be imagined.

Conflict with Connacht: 1179

Roger of Howden records that a delegation of Irishmen complained to Henry II in January 1179 of the harsh and unjust rule of his representatives in Ireland, William fitz Audelin and Hugh de Lacy.[38] However, the Irishmen seem to have been sent not by the Irish communities of Meath or Leinster (over whom Hugh and William exercised their royal authority) but by the king of Connacht. The Treaty of Windsor gave Ruaidrí Ua Conchobair recourse to appeal to Henry II for aid, and the colonists' assault upon the Connacht hegemony in western Meath (especially Clonmacnoise) provided his motive. The passage of Archbishops Lorcán Ua Tuathail of Dublin and Cadla Ua Dubthaig of Tuam through England on their way to the Third Lateran Council in Rome, and their presence at court, is noted by Roger of Howden and corroborated by an entry on the pipe roll of that year for the cost of their passage.[39] Given that they were present at court at the time when, according to Howden, the complaints against Hugh de Lacy and William fitz Audelin were made, it was most likely they who complained. Both the archbishops of Dublin and Tuam are known to have served as representatives of the king of Connacht around this time. In 1175, the Treaty of Windsor was concluded in the presence of Archbishop Lorcán Ua Tuathail, which may or may not indicate his prominence in the negotiations, while Archbishop Cadla Ua Dubthaig was explicitly named within the document as one of Ruaidrí's negotiators. What is more, Lorcán Ua Tuathail was to act as emissary of the king of Connacht to Henry II when a quarrel arose between the two in the early months of 1180.[40] Seán Duffy further speculates that the two archbishops may have acted on Ua Conchobair's behalf while in Rome, resisting the English king's request for a crown for his son John as king of Ireland (as decreed at Oxford in 1177), a political realignment which would have displaced Ruaidrí as high king.[41] Their contemporary service to Ruaidrí, coupled with the nature and targets of Hugh de Lacy's activities since 1177, makes it more than likely that the archbishops were the emissaries acting on Ua Conchobair's behalf at the English court in January 1179.

Though Howden records that William fitz Audelin and Hugh de Lacy thereafter incurred the displeasure of the king of England and were consequently removed from office, there is little concrete evidence to corroborate his testimony.[42] If Henry took action against Hugh, it is unlikely to have been for long. For all of the risks involved, William fitz Audelin's ineffectual tenure as justiciar had proved that a strong local presence was required for the maintenance and extension of the English enclave in Ireland. Indeed, far from being curtailed after the Irish delegation to Henry II, Hugh's activities intensified. He suffered several reverses that year, most of which occurred beyond the boundaries of Meath.[43] The timing of Hugh's offensive was problematic for Ruaidrí Ua Conchobair, because he was facing internal opposition to his rule in Connacht.[44] Ruaidrí should have been able to call upon the assistance of Henry II under the terms of the Treaty of Windsor, but, if requested, no aid was forthcoming. What is more, the *custos* of Dublin would in theory have been responsible for rendering that aid, and Hugh de Lacy was one of Ruaidrí's more persistent opponents. The situation for Ruaidrí was daunting. On the other hand, for Hugh, the king of Connacht had so far proved himself to be a wily opponent. By complaining to Henry II of Hugh's actions as royal administrator, Ua Conchobair was attempting to undermine Hugh's position. Henry II had shown in Wales that he was willing to promote the interests of a native ruler over those of his own magnates. For instance, in 1171 Henry II made the native 'Lord' Rhys of Deheubarth his justiciar in south Wales, while confiscating the castles of several marcher lords. Hugh would have himself been present when Rhys's pre-eminence was confirmed at the council of Oxford in 1177 (the same council that dealt with Ireland), at which point Dafydd of Gwynedd was confirmed as overlord of north Wales and terms similar to the Treaty of Windsor were agreed with both Welsh princes.[45] Two years on, in Ireland, the profitable solution to Hugh and Ruaidrí's mutual aggression proved to be an alliance.

Marriage alliance with Connacht: 1179–81

Under the year 1180, the so-called 'Dublin annals of Inisfallen' record: 'Rois, the daughter of Ruaidrí Ua Conchobair, married Hugh de Lacy.'[46] References to marriages in contemporary Gaelic annals are rare; indeed, an explicit statement such as this is almost unprecedented. Completed in 1765, the 'Dublin annals of Inisfallen' is a compilation of many sources, with apparently little attention paid to their historical merit. It is also the sole authority for dating the marriage to 1180. In fact, two marriages are recorded for 1180, the other being that of John de Courcy to Affrica Guðrøðardóttír, daughter of Guðrøðr Óláfsson (Gofraid mac Amlaíb), king of Man. This makes their dating appear like an act of organisational convenience, but the timing of the Lacy/Ua Conchobair marriage seems plausible. It must have taken place after the conflicts of 1179, but before the first evidence of political fallout from the alliance: a hasty journey to the royal court by Archbishop Lorcán Ua Tuathail by February 1180. After complaining to Henry II of Hugh de Lacy's activities in January 1179, Ua Tuathail continued on to Rome, where he attended the Third Lateran Council that March.[47] He did not leave Rome until after 13 May, when the second of two papal bulls of protection was issued to him.[48] Ua Tuathail, now with legatine powers, made his way through Henry II's lands, and was back in Dublin by the end of the summer. He wasted little time in convening a synod at Clonfert (Co. Galway) aimed at further reforming the Irish church. From Clonfert, the archbishop hurried through Connacht to Armagh, where he consecrated Ruaidrí Ua Conchobair's nephew, Tomaltach, as archbishop of Armagh in the winter of 1179-80.[49]

It is at this point that his near-contemporary *Vita* states that Ua Tuathail crossed the Irish Sea in order to negotiate on behalf of Ruaidrí Ua Conchobair in a 'sudden and violent quarrel' which had arisen between the kings of Connacht and England, and to deliver Ruaidrí's son as a hostage.[50] Ua Tuathail was therefore in Ireland only a few months before he was once again called upon to act as Ruaidrí's emissary to Henry II. Following Roger of Howden's testimony that the delivery of Ruaidrí's son as a hostage was associated with the tribute stipulated in the Treaty of Windsor,[51] historians have generally cited the terms of the Treaty of Windsor as the point of contention between Henry and Ruaidrí. This may be so, but if it were, the catalyst for the difficulties may have been the Lacy-Connacht marriage alliance. Given what is known of Henry II's reaction to Strongbow and Aífe's marriage in 1169, it is difficult to imagine a more likely cause of a 'sudden and violent quarrel' than a marriage alliance between the king of Connacht and the lord of Meath. Indeed, in light of Howden's testimony, it is perhaps significant that the Annals of Loch Cé report upon the death of Hugh de Lacy in 1186 that, in addition to holding the kingship of Meath, Bréifne and Airgialla, 'it was to him the tribute of Connacht was paid'. They also claim that in the previous year, 1185, Henry's son, John, was to return to England from his Irish expedition complaining of Hugh de Lacy because 'he did not permit the men of

Ireland to give tribute or hostages to him [John]'.⁵² As *custos* of Dublin and its associated royal custodies in north Leinster, Hugh de Lacy was the obvious agent for the collection of Ruaidrí's royal tribute. In 1185, their marriage alliance clearly caused an uncomfortable situation in the collection of this tribute. It is possible, therefore, that the marriage of Hugh and Ruaidrí's daughter prompted Henry's demand in 1180 for security regarding the payment of the tribute of Connacht, lest it go directly into the coffers of Ruaidrí's new and powerful son-in-law, Hugh de Lacy.

Henry needed to assert his authority over the new partnership, but could not afford to alienate either partner. Hugh de Lacy and Ruaidrí Ua Conchobair were the two most conspicuous instruments of Henry's rule in Ireland, instruments which were at the time irreplaceable. Once again, the need to ensure stability won out, and Henry was forced to favour obstinacy over action. For much of the following year, Archbishop Lorcán Ua Tuathail attempted to negotiate a settlement with Henry II on behalf of the king of Connacht, only to be frustrated time and again. The archbishop eventually died on 14 November 1180, his mission unfulfilled.⁵³ The problem with the preceding explanation is that there is no evidence of Henry's anger at Hugh de Lacy in early 1180. This would not of itself be a problem (the sources are silent on many such matters), but Roger of Howden explicitly stated that Hugh was recalled to the English court the following year, 1181, owing to his 'unlicensed' marriage.⁵⁴ There is reason, however, to question Howden's testimony. Henry's relationship with Ruaidrí was mended by Archbishop Lorcán's successor as legate, Alexis, shortly after the death of Ua Tuathail.⁵⁵ There exists no evidence of contention between Ruaidrí and Henry in 1181. Moreover, Ua Tuathail's death set in motion a sequence of events which could offer an alternative explanation for Hugh's recall.

Roger of Howden records that in 1181 King Henry sent his cleric, Geoffrey de Haye, and the papal legate, Guido, to Ireland to take possession of the temporalities of the see of Dublin for the Crown. Along with them were sent John de Lacy, constable of Chester (of the Pontefract Lacys), and Richard de Pec, who were to replace Hugh de Lacy as *custos* of Dublin. Howden then posits the marriage as the reason for Hugh's recall. However, John Gillingham has made a convincing case, based upon the content of Howden's writing, for the chronicler's absence from Henry's court for much of 1179 and 1180, arguing that he accompanied the Irish prelates to the Third Lateran Council in 1179 (perhaps as their minder) and that he served as emissary of Henry II to King William of Scotland in 1180.⁵⁶ If the marriage occurred before 1181, Howden would not have been well placed to know anything of King Henry II's reaction to it. Consequently, the marriage may have occurred prior to the 'sudden and violent quarrel' between Ruaidrí and King Henry, only for Howden to conceive it as the cause of Hugh's later recall once he finally returned to regular court attendance from July 1181.[57] The marriage certainly would have contributed to the king's unease over his magnate's growing power, but Howden is alone in suggesting it to be the direct cause of the king's ire, and Hugh's recall.[58] Nor would this have been an isolated error on his part. Howden is known to have misdated King Richard's demand for a three-hundred-knight army to 1198, although it actually occurred in early 1197, when Howden was absent from England.[59] Furthermore, as Flanagan has pointed out, the dispatch of the new custodians of Dublin was clearly linked to royal control of the vacant see of Dublin, as the two parties were sent and travelled together.[60] It seems then that, wary of Hugh's growing stature in Ireland and unwilling to allow him to exert his influence over the temporalities associated with the archiepiscopal see, Henry recalled him to England to allow for the smooth establishment of his candidate John Cumin in Dublin.

Hugh's actions that summer make sense only if his replacement by others was a matter of little inconvenience, as if it were a brief substitution for administrative efficiency. They certainly are not those of an overmighty subject called to account for a grievous offence. Gerald of Wales dates the arrival of John de Lacy and Richard de Pec to around 1 May 1181.[61] He then writes that Hugh joined with his replacements in building a great number of castles in Leinster, 'for hitherto very many castles had been built in Meath, but few in Leinster'. Those castles included Fotharta Uí Núalláin (Castlemore Mote, near Tullow, Co. Carlow) for Raymond le Gros, another, possibly Knocktopher (Co. Kilkenny), for Raymond's brother Griffin fitz William, Kilkea (Co. Kildare) for Walter de Ridelesford, another on the river Barrow near Leighlin for John de Clahull, and *Collacht* (probably Tullow, Co. Carlow) for John of Hereford. The three men also provided for the defence of the Irish midlands by convincing the 'true son of Mars' Meiler fitz Henry to trade his territory in the cantred of Conall in Uí Fáeláin (bar. Connell, Co. Kildare), which had been given him by Strongbow, for the border territory of Laigis (Co. Laois). These efforts took the entire summer, and John de Lacy and Richard de Pec returned to England that winter.[62] It was only after his programme of castle construction that Hugh also returned to England, so his 'recall' may actually have coincided with that of his replacements. William fitz Audelin also journeyed to England that winter.[63] The fact that all of these men left Ireland around the same time suggests that Howden got it wrong. Hugh's stay in England would have afforded him the opportunity to oversee personally his English and Welsh estates, which he may not have visited in the four years since his Irish appointment in 1177. Hugh returned to Ireland the following year as sole royal representative – a veritable promotion.

In Ireland, the alliance was beneficial to both Hugh and Ruaidrí. Hugh's bride was probably Ruaidrí's daughter by Dub Coblaid (d. 1181), who was herself the daughter of Tigernán Ua Ruairc, king of Bréifne, and Derbforgaill, daughter of Murchad Ua Máel Sechlainn, king of Mide. Hugh de Lacy's men had killed Tigernán in 1172, after which he began to intrude into the politics of the strategic, and neighbouring, kingdom of Bréifne. Derbforgaill's father, Murchad Ua Máel Sechlainn, was Hugh's Irish *antecessor* in Meath, so that through the marriage Hugh gained a further association with two territories, Meath and Bréifne, that he sought to control.[64] Intermarriage was not absolutely necessary to justify lordship over conquered territories, but none the less gave Hugh and his contemporaries, Strongbow and William de Burgh, an even closer association with their Irish lordships.[65] On the more concrete level, the marriage gave Hugh a free hand in western Meath, and allowed Ruaidrí to face Connacht's internal struggles unmolested from the east. As seen above, Ruaidrí even extended his influence by presenting his nephew to the primatial see of Armagh that winter (1179–80).[66] The succession, though realised by the efforts of Archbishop Lorcán Ua Tuathail, remained an unprecedented show of political might from the king of Connacht. The birth of William de Lacy to Hugh and his Ua Conchobair wife strengthened the alliance and ushered in an extended period of peace between Connacht and Meath. Such was the impact of the marriage in Ireland.

However, Hugh de Lacy was a transnational aristocrat, with extensive interests in England, Wales and Normandy. For him, the impact of the marriage at King Henry's distant court was just as significant. The problem with it for Henry II was that it recalled his fears for Ireland in 1171 when Strongbow's succession to Leinster had led to Henry's Irish expedition. In 1176, Henry also recalled Raymond le Gros when rumours of a similar sort reached him.[67] Henry II would have been very suspicious of a similar merger between the houses of Ua Conchobair and Lacy a few years later. While Diarmait had been an ousted king in search of a reversal of fortunes, and Strongbow a disgraced English magnate possessed of 'a great name rather than great prospects',[68] Ruaidrí was the high king of Ireland, while the lord of Meath, Hugh de Lacy, was Henry's supposed counterweight against him in Ireland. The alliance of these two men, and Hugh's consequent succession to Connacht (unlikely though it might have been), was considered possible by contemporaries. Gerald of Wales writes that 'The net result [of Hugh's dealings with the Irish] was that he was strongly suspected of wanting to throw off his allegiance and usurp the government of the kingdom, and with it the crown and sceptre'.[69] However, Hugh de Lacy's importance to the colony saved him once again (as Strongbow's and Raymond's had saved them before). Henceforth, Hugh was left to cut a splendid figure for himself in Ireland, while incurring the suspicion, if not outright ire, of the English king.

Pre-eminent in Ireland: 1182-4

Once John de Lacy and Richard de Pec left Ireland, Gerald of Wales reports that 'Hugh once more enjoyed the king's confidence and was entrusted for a second time with the administration of the country'.[70] Like his non-official activities the previous summer, Hugh's 1182 commission was focused on the colony's security. Gerald writes that Hugh embarked upon an intense programme of castle construction, both without and within his by-now thriving lordship of Meath. He was assisted in this role by the royal clerk, Robert of Shrewsbury, who also was charged with keeping a watchful eye on him. Hugh began in 1182 where he left off in 1181, by constructing the castle of Timahoe (bar. Cullenagh, Co. Laois) for Meiler fitz Henry in his new territory of Laigis. Hugh also gave his niece in marriage to Meiler, and granted him the cantred of Ardnurcher (bar. Moycashel, Co. Westmeath) in Meath.[71] These acts may have formed part of the compensatory package for Meiler's exchange of lands in Uí Fáeláin, but they also harnessed the energy of the veteran campaigner. Hugh further secured the Leinster midlands by constructing castles for Robert de Bigarz in Uí Buide (bar. Mallyadams, Co. Laois), for Thomas of Flanders just across the river Barrow at Ardree (bar. Kinkea and Moone, Co. Kildare) in Uí Muiredaig, and for Robert fitz Richard at Norrach (now Narraghmore, bar. Narrach and Reban, Co. Kildare).[72]

In Meath, Hugh built castles for his tenants Adam de Feipo at Skreen (Co. Meath), Gilbert de Nugent at Castletown Delvin (bar. Delvin, Co. Westmeath), 'and many others which it would be tedious to enumerate individually'.[73] Hugh also erected demesne castles at the symbolic sites of Clonard (bar. Upper Moyfenrath, Co. Meath) and Killare (bar. Rathconrath, Co. Westmeath). Clonard was the seat of the most powerful bishop in Meath, Echthigern mac Máel Chiaráin (Eugenius), bishop of Clonard. It was also the dividing point used in several partitions of the

Irish kingdom of Mide. By fortifying Clonard, Hugh positioned himself to influence the ecclesiastical life of his lordship, while asserting his dominance over all of Meath. Despite Gerald's testimony regarding 1182, historians generally date the construction of Killare to 1184, when the Irish annals report the erection of a castle there.[74] However, although Gerald's prose is fairly laconic at this point, there is little reason to doubt his chronology. The following year, 1183, Gerald journeyed to Ireland to visit his brother Philip of Barry, and stayed for about a year.[75] Consequently, he was well placed to know whether Hugh, a minor hero of Gerald's history, had already built a castle at Killare. What is more, the annals of Loch Cé imply that the 1184 castle was a replacement for an earlier one, because they record that 'another castle was destroyed there' by an Ua Máel Sechlainn and Conchobar Máenmaige Ua Conchobair, with many of 'the foreigners' being killed.[76] The annals are silent on the vast majority of castles constructed by the colonists, and the 1184 construction might not have attracted annalistic attention had it not been marked by a confluence of military and dynastic activity in the region (discussed below).

Whether built in 1182 or 1184, the Killare castle was built in the heartland of Ua Máel Sechlainn power, and within sight of the symbolic hill of Uisnech, which marked the meeting point of Ireland's five ancient provinces and served as a ceremonial site.[77] In his *History of the Kings of Britain*, composed around 1130, Geoffrey of Monmouth repeats a popular belief that the stones of Stonehenge were brought to England from Uisnech, which he calls 'the mountain of Killare' (*mons Killaraus*).[78] Gerald of Wales describes Uisnech in his *Topography of Ireland*, writing:

> at length five chieftains, who were also brothers ... landed in Ireland. Finding it empty, they divided it into five equal portions amongst themselves. The boundaries of these divisions come together at a stone in Meath near the castle of Killare (*Kilair*), which stone is called the navel of Ireland, placed as it were in the middle of the land. Consequently, that part of Ireland is called Meath (*Media*), because it is situated in the middle (*medio*) of the island.[79]

Medieval tradition placed a druidic fire ceremony at Uisnech, and a Middle Irish source likened Uisnech's importance for Ireland to that of an animal's kidney (the other kidney being the traditional seat of the high kingship at Tara, Co. Meath).[80] The psychological significance of the castle of Killare should not be underestimated. It commanded a militarily and culturally strategic position in western Meath. Its defence was provided for in a grant that Hugh made to William le Petit about this time. Hugh granted William Dunboyne and Rathkenny (Co. Meath), and lands in the baronies of Magheradernon (Co. Westmeath) and Shrule, (Co. Longford).[81] William's service was set at one knight for every thirty carucates, to be performed at the castle of Killare.[82] This stipulation dates William le Petit's entry into Hugh's service to the 1180s, which is also the rough timing of his first appearance in Ireland. William may have been a member of the Parvus family, formerly attached to the earls of Hereford.[83] If so, this would be evidence that Hugh de Lacy attracted to his service characters who had been cut adrift by the extinction of the powerful Hereford family connection in 1165. Strongbow had benefited from the break-up of the earldom of Hereford in expanding his lordship in Gwent in the 1160s and recruiting new blood for his Irish endeavour.[84] It would have made sense for Hugh to do likewise. Whatever William's provenance, only constant attention could keep the strategic castle of Killare secure. As argued above, it appears to have been destroyed and rebuilt in 1184, and once again was razed in 1187, within a year of Hugh de Lacy's death.[85]

In 1184 the strength of Hugh de Lacy's lordship was unmatched in Ireland. His old foe, and recent ally, Ruaidrí Ua Conchobar had relinquished the kingship of Connacht to his son Conchobair Máenmaige the previous year. This not only removed the experienced king from the political chessboard but also rendered the Treaty of Windsor void. The treaty had been a personal agreement between Henry II and Ruaidrí, with no mention of either's successors. Hereafter the theoretical designation of Munster, Connacht and Ulster as 'Gaelic Ireland', ignored though it might have been by those on both sides, no longer stood in the way of rapid conquest and settlement. What is more, the marriage alliance between Ruaidrí and Hugh does not seem to have translated into congenial relations between Hugh and the new king of Connacht (Hugh's brother-in-law). Rumours at the English court suggested that Hugh had designs on the succession to Connacht, or even the high kingship of Ireland. In 1184 he let his dissatisfaction with the reigning Ua Conchobair be known. Allied with Murchad Ua Cerbaill, king of Airgialla, he raided Armagh, burning thirty houses and replacing Archbishop Tommaltach Ua Conchobair with Máel Isu Ua Cerbaill.[86] Hugh then firmly stamped his authority on the former Connacht hegemony in western Meath. The reigning Irish king of western Meath, Art Ua Máel Sechlainn, was removed by Diarmait Ua Briain of Ormond, at Hugh's behest.[87] It is unclear whether it was Art, or his successor Máel Sechlainn Beg, who joined with Conchobair Máenmaige Ua Conchobair in burning the castle of Killare, but it was quickly rebuilt.[88]

Hugh de Lacy's stature in Ireland during these later years is evident from both English and Irish sources. His position at the head of the royal administration blended well with his hold on Meath, important diplomatic ties and aggressive forays into the frontiers of colonial domination, imbuing him with a viceregal status to his contemporaries. Under 1184, Mac Carthaigh's Book records a raid into Armagh by 'Murchad Ua Cerbaill, king of Airgialla, and Hugh de Lacy, lord of the Foreigners of Ireland (*tigearna Gall Eireann*)'.[89] In his obituary, the annals of Loch Cé remark that 'he was king of Mide, and Bréifne, and Airgialla, and it was to him the tribute of Connacht was paid; and he it was that won all Ireland for the Foreigners'. As impressive as this statement is, the same annals go so far as to afford him the title 'king of Ireland' (*ri Érenn*) when John 'son of the king of the English' (*mac ri Saxan*) journeyed to Ireland in 1185.[90]

Although the Irish annals constitute key evidence in determining the stature of Hugh de Lacy owing to their presentation of the workings of colonial society from without, English authors knew the dangers of Hugh's impressive display of lordship at the English court. For instance, while rehearsing Hugh de Lacy's career, William of Newburgh writes of the rumour that Hugh had acquired a royal crown for himself and that 'the king, on hearing those circumstances, sent for him, but he refused the summons, and by his disobedience proved the popular rumour'.[91]

The activities of 1184 combined to procure Hugh's recall about the beginning of that September. Philip of Worcester was sent to Ireland as *procurator* with forty knights: the same number of knights assigned to Dublin under Hugh de Lacy in 1172.[92] Replacing Hugh de Lacy was not a matter of simply overseeing the smooth administration of the English enclave, however. First, parts of Ireland had to be prised from Hugh's lordship. For instance, owing to an ambiguity in his grant of Meath, Hugh had seisin of lands around Dublin that the king was eager to recover. Gerald of Wales states that Philip was first required to wrench portions of the royal demesne, including the land of Ua Cathasaig in Saithne (bar. Balrothery West, Co. Dublin), from Hugh's firm grasp.[93] Early the following year, about the beginning of March 1185, Philip of Worcester marched north to Armagh and reversed Hugh's work. Máel Isu Ua Cerbaill was ousted and Tomaltach Ua Conchobair returned to his position of archbishop. A large tribute was also collected from the clergy there, perhaps as punishment for their connivance with Lacy and Ua Cerbaill the previous year.[94] But Hugh's power ran too deep to be so easily diverted. Although the archbishop of Dublin and Philip of Worcester had been sent to pave the way for the triumphant arrival of Henry's son John as king of Ireland,[95] Hugh de Lacy was none the less restored to head the Irish administration that same year (1185). For a second time Hugh seems to have been recalled to England not in disgrace but merely to facilitate a transfer of power. His absence lasted only the space of a winter. Hugh held the title of constable (*constabularius*) in six of the eight charters he witnessed for Henry's son John that year.[96]

Ruling Ireland: 1185-6

Much has been written of John's ill-fated 1185 expedition, with each historian's view of it mirroring their overall opinion of John.[97] John's crossing to Ireland must have been envisioned by Henry II as early as his designation as 'king of Ireland' at the council of Oxford in 1177. Arrangements were certainly under way in 1184, when Archbishop John Cumin and Philip of Worcester were sent to Ireland. John arrived in Ireland as 'lord of Ireland' (*dominus Hiberniae*), and was never crowned 'king of Ireland'. Instead, the lord of Ireland returned to England, destitute, less than eight months after his departure. Gerald of Wales, who was on the expedition, states that the trip was one which Henry II 'had prepared for with such care', and laments that, because of its failure, 'all his careful preparation and expenditure of money was wasted'.[98] John needed a scapegoat, and Hugh de Lacy proved a perfect target. As mentioned above, pretensions to regality had always jarred with Henry II. The old suspicions resurfaced, and Hugh's supposed ambitions were used as an excuse for John's failure. But was this justified?

Upon first glance, Hugh de Lacy seems to have kept to the strictures of feudal obligation, attending his lord's court and witnessing several grants. However, Hugh seems to have been present only to witness charters of the most benign nature: several grants to the church and a confirmation of Henry II's Dublin charter. At the very least, this suggests Hugh's opposition to the major new land-grants in Munster that John made to his supporters while in Ireland.[99] Hugh had made his own way in Ireland through a pragmatic mixture of conquest, diplomacy and coexistence, so his objection to the outright subjugation of the claims of the native Irish to the ambitions of John's new men might have been expected. In fact, when Hugh's constable of Meath, William le Petit, defeated an invading army from the northern-Irish kingdom of Tír Eógain that same year, he took the highly symbolic step of parading their severed heads through Dublin.[100] Hugh de Lacy's dominant lordship was on display in the *regni caput* while the young lord of Ireland frittered away his chances of coronation.

The following year, Hugh pushed the bounds of his lordship even further. The annals of Loch Cé report:

> Hugh de Lacy went to Durrow [Co. Offaly], to build a castle in it, having a countless number of foreigners along with him; for he was king of Mide, and Bréifne, and Airgialla, and it was to him the tribute of Connacht was paid; and he it was that won all Ireland for the Foreigners. Mide, from the Shannon to the sea, was full of castles and of foreigners. After the completion by him of this work, i.e. the erection of the castle of Durrow, he came out to look at the castle, having three foreigners along with him. There came towards him then a youth of the men of Mide, having his axe concealed, viz. Gilla gan-inathair ('the boy without bowels') Ua Miadaigh, the foster son of In Sinnach [('the Fox') Ua Catharnaig, lord (*tigerna*) of Tethba] himself; and he gave him [Hugh] one blow, so that he cut off his head, and he [Hugh] fell, both head and body, into the ditch of the castle.[101]

The Annals of the Four Masters add: 'Gilla gan-inathair fled, and, by his fleetness of foot, made his escape from the English and Irish to the wood of Kilclare [Co. Offaly]. He afterwards went to In Sinnach and Ua Braoin [of Lune, Co. Meath], at whose instigation he had killed the Earl [*sic*].'[102]

It will be remembered that In Sinnach had fought against Hugh in the dynastic struggles of 1178, and may have blamed Hugh for the death of his son in battle then. Orpen at least saw a connection between the two deaths, and it would have been appropriate for In Sinnach's foster son to have carried out the retribution.[103] However, such a grudge might not have been a necessary precursor to assassination. Durrow had once been within the kingdom of Tethba, and the church of Durrow (from which Hugh reportedly took stones to build his castle) was thought to have been dedicated to St Columcille by In Sinnach's ancestor approximately 640 years earlier.[104] Being some of the only stone structures in Ireland, such ecclesiastical foundations were often utilised as storehouses for their secular patrons. Consequently, they were military targets. Irish warfare could involve the systematic destruction of enemy churches, and an Irish king's death was frequently said to have been in reparation to the saints whose churches they had profaned. For instance, the Annals of Loch Cé report that Diarmait Mac Murchada died in 1171 'through the merits of Columcille, and Finan, and the other saints whose churches he had spoiled'.[105] In Hugh's case, the church of Columcille might have provided a ready source of stone for his new castle. The Annals of Ulster report that Hugh, 'destroyer [and] dissolver of the churches and sanctuaries of Ireland', was 'killed in reparation to Columcille, whilst building a castle in his church'.[106] The murder probably involved more than a lone assassin, because Lacy's men fled without taking his body with them. It took almost a decade, and the intervention of the archbishops of Cashel and Dublin before Hugh's heir, Walter, was able to recover his remains from the Irish in 1195. Hugh's body then was transmitted for burial near Trim in Bective Abbey (Co. Meath), and his head was buried alongside his first wife, Rose of Monmouth, in the abbey of St Thomas, Dublin.[107]

English sources also notice Hugh's death. The dean of St Paul's Cathedral, London, Ralph of Diss, relates: 'In Ireland, Hugh de Lacy, lord of the province of Meath, was killed by the hands of the lowest man, the evil Ua Miadaigh (*Miadaich*), on 25 July.'[108] The fact that this London-based chronicler is so specific about the date of Hugh's death, and correctly names the assassin (rather than simply calling him 'an Irishman') proves the significance of Hugh's death to those in England. William of Newburgh includes a detailed account of the murder, claiming treachery on the part of Hugh's Irish allies:

> just as [Hugh's] fortunes were rivalling those of the king of England, he died a victim of the expert treachery of a young household servant recruited from his Irish allies. For when he went out from his castle to wander in the countryside, and was barely a stone's throw away from his servants, by chance he bent down – I do not know what he planned. Rejoicing, the traitor, who had long looked for an opportunity, struck Hugh forcefully on the head with an axe. After he had made his cut, and as Hugh's attendants ran up in vain to take revenge, the youth escaped unscathed due to the convenient proximity of a forest and his own agility. News of these matters, reached the king of England in the most distant part of his realm, and it is said they infused him with great joy. Soon after, Irish affairs were to be undertaken more prudently by him.[109]

Roger of Howden agrees that upon hearing of Hugh's murder 'the lord king greatly rejoiced, because Hugh had done many things in Ireland against the king's will and command'.[110] However, Hugh's death also marked the end of an era in colonial Ireland, something which contemporaries realised. The importance to the colony of Hugh's vigorous personal lordship is summed up by one set of Latin annals, which simply remarks at his death: 'thereupon the conquest ceased'.[111]

Conclusion

Although Meath had been granted to him in 1172, it was not until 1177, when Henry II placed Hugh in charge of one-third of the English colony, that the conquest of Meath began in earnest. From 1177, Hugh combined the administrative power vested in him with a pragmatic blend of war and diplomacy which spanned the cultural divide to imprint his lordship upon the Irish midlands. His progress shows that the conquest was not simply a case of native versus newcomer, and that aristocratic lordship was not exclusively based upon overt violence and intimidation. Hugh was praised for his treatment of the indigenous Irish of Meath, whom he invited back to their lands in the midst of his consolidation of power. He also intrigued in local dynastic disputes and sought alliances with neighbouring Irish kings where he could not extend his direct lordship effectively. His marriage to the daughter of the high king of Ireland, Ruaidrí Ua Conchobair is the most famous instance of Hugh's pragmatic approach to Irish politics. Through this alliance, Hugh enhanced his status as a key player on the Irish scene. Hugh's decision to focus on Ireland to the possible (though not entirely certain) detriment of his reputation at court harked back to Strongbow's early years in Ireland, and stoked once more the fears of over-mighty independent baronial lordship which had spurred Henry II to mount his Irish expedition in 1171. It also anticipated the regional specialisation which was increasingly to characterise aristocratic lordship in the British Isles from the later thirteenth century. For several years Hugh was too effective to be replaced, but in 1185 Henry sent his son John to Ireland as *dominus Hiberniae* to be crowned its king and to introduce stable centralised authority. In this Henry failed. Hugh and his fellow settlers were able to stare down the uncrowned king of Ireland, and send him home in disgrace. Hugh was assassinated the following year, before King Henry could respond to John's complaints.

Notes

1. The bishop's account of the dispute is edited in H. M. Colvin, 'Holme Lacy: an episcopal manor and its tenants in the 12th and 13th centuries', in V. Ruffer and A. J. Taylor (eds), *Medieval Studies Presented to Rose Graham* (Oxford, 1950), pp. 15-40, at pp. 36-7.
2. *English Episcopal Acta VII: Hereford 1079-1234*, ed. Julia Barrow (Oxford, 1993), no. 159.
3. 'Ne lites semel terminate iterum ex malignitate alicujus seu oblivione resuscitentur earum finem scripto commendare est necessarium.' Colvin, 'Holme Lacy', pp. 36-7.

4   Seán Duffy, 'The first Ulster plantation: John de Courcy and the men of Cumbria', in T. B. Barry, Robin Frame and Katharine Simms (eds), *Colony and Frontier in Medieval Ireland. Essays Presented to J. F. Lydon* (London and Rio Grande, 1995), pp. 1-27.
5   Helen Perros [Walton], 'Crossing the Shannon frontier: Connacht and the Anglo-Normans, 1170-1224', in T. B. Barry, Robin Frame and Katharine Simms (eds), *Colony and Frontier in Medieval Ireland. Essays Presented to J. F. Lydon* (London and Rio Grande, 1995), pp. 117-38, at p. 121.
6   *Expugnatio Hibernica*, pp. 166-72; Flanagan, 'Household favourites', p. 366.
7   *Ann. Tig.*, s.a. 1177. Philip de Briouze had been granted the honor of Limerick in Munster at the council of Oxford.
8   Howden, *Gesta*, ii, pp. 162, 164.
9   Howden, *Chronica*, ii, p. 135.
10 For pre-Anglo-Norman Leinster see: A. P. Smyth, *Celtic Leinster: Towards an Historical Geography of Early Irish Civilization, A.D. 500-1600* (Blackrock, 1982); F. J. Byrne, *Irish Kings and High-Kings* (Dublin, 2001), pp. 130-64; M. T. Flanagan, 'Strategies of lordship in pre-Norman and post-Norman Leinster', in Christopher Harper-Bill (ed.), *Anglo-Norman Studies XX* (Woodbridge, 1997), pp. 107-26, among others.
11 See Duffy, 'Irishmen and Islesmen', pp. 94-101.
12 Emmett O'Byrne, *War, Politics and the Irish of Leinster, 1156-1606* (Dublin, 2003), p. 7.
13 *Ann. Tig.*, s.a. 1166; *AFM*, ii, pp. 1160-2, s.a. 1166; *AI*, p. 300, s.a. 1166.
14 M. T. Flanagan, 'Henry II and the kingdom of Uí Fáeláin', in John Bradley (ed.), *Settlement and Society in Medieval Ireland: Studies Presented to F. X. Martin, O. S. A.* (Kilkenny, 1988) pp. 229-39.
15 *Expugnatio Hibernica*, p. 94.
16 O'Byrne, *Leinster*, p. 21.
17 *Expugnatio Hibernica*, p. 170.
18 *Ibid.*, p. 172. This was the cantred that Henry originally granted to Robert in 1171-2, but was regranted by Strongbow to Adam de Hereford, in 1173.
19 Howden, *Gesta*, p. 141.
20 A royal custodian accounts for Ludlow for a quarter of a year. *Pipe Roll 23 Henry II*, p. 52.
21 Howden, *Gesta*, i, p. 103.
22 *Expugnatio Hibernica*, p. 190.
23 See Chapter 8.
24 *Pipe Roll 23 Henry II*, p. 36; *Pipe Roll 24 Henry II*, pp. 38, 56; *Pipe Roll 25 Henry II*, pp. 67, 88.
25 *Expugnatio Hibernica*, p. 190.
26 *Ibid.*, p. 192.
27 *MCB*, p. 66, s.a. 1178.
28 *AFM*, iii, p. 44, s.a. 1178.
29 Orpen, *Normans*, ii, p. 53.
30 See Chapter 1.

31 Flanagan, *Irish Society*, pp. 312-13.
32 Duffy, *Ireland*, pp. 90-1.
33 O'Byrne, *Leinster*, p. 16.
34 Seán Duffy, 'Ua Conchobair, Áed (d. 1067)', *Oxford Dictionary of National Biography* (Oxford, 2004).
35 *AFM*, ii, p. 1118, *s.a.* 1156; *Ann. Tig.*, *s.a.* 1156; Perros [Walton], 'Shannon frontier', p. 117.
36 *AFM*, iii, pp. 112-14, *s.a.* 1198. Other Uí Conchobair kings buried there: *ALC*, i, p. 162, *s.a.* 1181.
37 *AFM*, iii, p. 42, *s.a.* 1178 (quote); M. A. Freeman, 'The annals in Cotton MS Titus A. XXV', *Revue Celtique*, 41 (1924), pp. 301-30; 42 (1925), pp. 281-305; 43 (1926), pp. 358-84; 44 (1927), pp. 336-61, *s.a.* 1178.
38 Howden, *Gesta*, i, p. 221.
39 *Ibid.*, i, p. 221; *Pipe Roll 25 Henry II*, pp. 35, 120.
40 See below, p. 57.
41 Duffy, *Ireland*, p. 92.
42 Howden, *Gesta*, i, p. 221.
43 *MCB*, p. 68, *s.a.* 1179.
44 *AFM*, iii, p. 50, *s.a.* 1179.
45 Warren, *Henry II*, p. 202.
46 'Rois ingean Rughruidhe h Conchubhair do posad do Hugo de Lacy', Trinity College Dublin MS 1281, *s.a.* 1180. For the misappellation of 'Rois', see Colin Veach, 'A question of timing: Walter de Lacy's seisin of Meath 1189-94', *Proceedings of the Royal Irish Academy, Section C*, 109 (2009), pp. 165-94, at p. 166n.
47 J. F. O'Doherty, 'St. Laurence O Toole and the Anglo-Norman invasion', *Irish Ecclesiastical Record, 5th Series*, 50 (1937), pp. 449-77, 600-25; 51 (1938), pp. 131-46, at p. 141.
48 Aubrey Gwynn, 'Saint Lawrence O'Toole as legate in Ireland (1179-1180)', *Analecta Bollandiana*, 68 (1950), pp. 223-40, at p. 227.
49 *Ibid.*, pp. 228-9.
50 *Ibid.*, p. 237; Charles Plummer, 'Vie et miracles de S. Laurent, archeveque de Dublin', *Analecta Bollandiana*, 33 (1914), pp. 121-86, at p. 152; Howden, *Gesta*, i, p. 270.
51 Howden, *Gesta*, i, p. 270; Howden, *Chronica*, ii, p. 253.
52 *ALC*, i, p. 172, *s.a.* 1186, p. 170, *s.a.* 1185; See also *AFM*, iii, p. 71, *s.a.* 1186.
53 Gwynn, 'St. Lawrence', pp. 239-40; Martin, 'Overlord', p. 120; Flanagan, *Irish Society*, pp. 261-3.
54 Howden, *Gesta*, i, p. 270.
55 Flanagan, *Irish Society*, p. 262.
56 Gillingham, 'Travels of Roger of Howden', pp. 160, 165.
57 *Ibid.*, p. 160.
58 Gerald of Wales and William of Newburgh record Henry's fear of a possible Lacy *regnum*. *Expugnatio Hibernica*, pp. 190-4; William of Newburgh, 'Historia rerum Anglicarum', in R. Howlett (ed.), *Chronicles of the Reigns of Stephen, Henry II and Richard* (London, 1884-89), ii, pp. 239-40.

59 Gillingham, 'Travels of Roger of Howden', p. 166.
60 Flanagan, 'Household favourites', p. 368.
61 *Expugnatio Hibernica*, pp. 182-4.
62 *Ibid.*, p. 195.
63 Flanagan, 'Household favourites', p. 367.
64 Colin Veach and Freya Verstraten Veach, 'William *Gorm* de Lacy "Chiefest Champion in These Parts of Europe"', in Seán Duffy (ed.), *Princes, Prelates and Poets in Medieval Ireland: Essays in Honour of Katharine Simms* (Dublin, 2013), pp. 63-84.
65 Robin Frame, '"Les Engleys nées en Irlande": the English political identity in medieval Ireland', *Transactions of the Royal Historical Society, 6th series, 3* (1993), pp. 83-103, at pp. 84-5
66 Gwynn, 'St. Lawrence', pp. 229, 234-5; Aubrey Gwynn, 'Tomaltach Ua Conchobair, coarb of Patrick (1181-1201)', *Seanchas Ardmacha*, 8 (1975-77), pp. 231-74, at pp. 239-50.
67 *Expugnatio Hibernica*, pp. 158-60.
68 *Ibid.*, p. 54.
69 *Ibid.*, p. 190.
70 *Ibid.*, p. 194.
71 *Ibid.*, p. 194; *Song*, lines 3138-41; *Deeds*, lines 3136-9.
72 *Expugnatio Hibernica*, p. 194.
73 *Ibid.*, p. 194. See also G. H. Orpen, 'Motes and Norman castles in Ireland', *English Historical Review*, 22 (1907), pp. 228-54 and 440-67, at pp. 233-54.
74 For example, Orpen, *Normans*, ii, pp. 66n, 80-1; *Expugnatio Hibernica*, p. 341.
75 *Expugnatio Hibernica*, pp. xiv, 189.
76 *ALC*, i, p. 166, *s.a.* 1184; *AU*, ii, p. 202, *s.a.* 1184; *AFM*, iii, p. 62, *s.a.* 1184.
77 Orpen, *Normans*, vol. ii, p. 80.
78 Geoffrey of Monmouth, *The History of the Kings of Britain*, ed. M. D. Reeve, trans. Neil Wright (Woodbridge, 2007), pp. 170-3 (Book VIII, chapters 10-11).
79 'tandem quinque duces, et hi germani fraters ... in Hibernia applicuerunt. Et eam vacuam invenientes, in quinque portiones aequales inter se diviserunt: quarum capita in lapide quodam conveniunt apud Mediam juxta castrum de Kilair; qui lapis et umbilicus Hiberniae dicitur, quasi in medio et meditullio terre positus. Unde et Media pars illa Hiberniae vocatur, quia in medio est insulae sita.' *Giraldi Cambrensis Opera*, eds J. S. Brewer, J. F. Dimock and G. F. Warner, 8 vols. (London, 1861-91), v, p. 144.
80 Byrne, *Irish Kings*, p. 58. Tlachtgha (Hill of Ward, where Lacy's men had killed Ua Ruairc) and Tailtiu (Telltown, Co. Meath) were also linked to Uisnech and Tara.
81 *Song*, lines 3135-7; *Deeds*, lines 3133-5.
82 *Song*, p. 310.
83 David Walker, 'Charters of the Earldom of Hereford, 1095-1201', *Camden Miscellany*, 22 (London, 1964), pp. 1-75.
84 David Crouch, 'The transformation of medieval Gwent', in R. A. Griffiths, Tony Hopkins and Ray Howell (eds), *The Gwent County History, Volume 2, The Age of the Marcher Lords, c. 1070-1536* (Cardiff, 2008), pp. 1-45, at pp. 29-30.

85 *AFM*, iii, p. 78, *s.a.* 1187.
86 *MCB*, p. 72, *s.a.* 1184; *ALC*, i, p. 166, *s.a.* 1184; *AU*, ii, p. 202, *s.a.* 1184; Martin, 'Overlord', p 120.
87 *ALC*, i, p. 166, *s.a.* 1184; *AFM*, iii, p. 62, *s.a.* 1184.
88 See above, p. 54.
89 *MCB*, p. 72, *s.a.* 1184.
90 *ALC*, i, p. 172, *s.a.* 1186, p. 170, *s.a.*1185; *AFM*, iii, pp. 66-8, *s.a.* 1186. 'King of Airgialla' may be explained by Murchad Ua Cerbaill's submission to Hugh. Smith, *Colonisation and Conquest*, p. 23.
91 'Quibus regi nuntiatis, evocatus ab eo, mandatum contempsit, et per hanc inobedientiam fidem fecit praesumptionis vulgatae.' Newburgh, 'Historia rerum Anglicarum', p. 240.
92 *Expugnatio Hibernica*, p. 104.
93 *Ibid.*, p. 198. The kingdom of Mide had once included Saithne (John Brady, 'The kingdom and county of Meath', *Ríocht Na Mídhe*, 1/2 (1956), pp. 6-13, at p. 8), and Hugh's grant of Meath allowed him to grant lands in Dublin to maintain the city's garrison.
94 *Expugnatio Hibernica*, p. 198; *AU*, i, p. 204, *s.a.* 1185.
95 *Expugnatio Hibernica*, p. 198; the annals of Chester state that John sent Philip of Worcester, *Annales Cestrienses*, pp. 24-5.
96 See Seán Duffy, 'John and Ireland: the origins of England's Irish problem', in S. D. Church (ed.), *King John: New Interpretations* (Woodbridge, 1999), pp. 221-45, at p. 233.
97 For the historiography see *ibid.*, pp. 221-5.
98 *Expugnatio Hibernica*, p. 204.
99 Duffy, 'John and Ireland', p. 233.
100 *Expugnatio Hibernica*, p. 234.
101 *ALC*, i, pp. 172-4, *s.a.* 1186. 'In Sinnach' was the title given to the head of the Uí Catharnaig.
102 *AFM*, iii, pp. 70-6, *s.a.* 1186.
103 Orpen, *Normans*, ii, p. 53; and see above, p. x.
104 *AU*, ii, p. 208, *s.a.* 1186.
105 *ALC*, i, p. 144, *s.a.* 1171.
106 *AU*, ii, p. 208, *s.a.* 1186.
107 *Jacobi Grace, Kilkenniensis: Annales Hiberniae [Grace's Annals]*, ed. Richard Butler (Dublin, 1842), p. 18, *s.a.* 1195; *Chart. St Mary's*, ii, *s.a.* 1195; BL MS Additional 4792, fos 160r-2r, *s.a.* 1195.
108 'In Hybernia Hugo de Laceio, dominus provinciae quae Media vocatur, interfectus est a Malua Miadaich infimae manus homine viiivo kalendas Augusti.' *Radulfi de Diceto Decani Lundoniensis Opera Historica*, 2 vols (London, 1876), ii, p. 34.
109 'Verum post modicum, tanquam pro rege Anglorum aemulante fortuna, cujusdam ex foederatis Hiberniensibus familiaris et domestici juvenis perfidiam expertus, occubuit. Cum enim spatiandi gratia in agrum ex munitione egressus, avulsusque a satellitibus fere quantum jactus est lapidis, forte se inclinasset, ut nescio quid designaret in terra, perfidius ille diu quaesitam occasionem nactum

se gaudens, bipennem fortiter in caput ejus vibravit; quo absciso et satellitibus ad ulciscendum frustra concurrentibus, beneficio silvae proximae et pernicitatis propriae elapsus evasit. Hujus rei nuntius regem Anglorum in extremis regni finibus, ut dictum est, constitutum ingenti perfudit laetitia. Moxque res Hibernicae cautiorem ab eo ordinationem suscepere.' Newburgh, 'Historia rerum Anglicarum', p. 240.

110 'De cujus nece dominus rex plurimum gavisus est; quia ipse Hugo in multis agebat in Hibernia, contra voluntatem et praeceptum regis.' Howden, *Gesta*, i, p. 350.

111 'Ibi cessavit conquestus', *Chart. St Mary's*, ii, p. 305.

II

Walter de Lacy

3

Divided allegiance: 1189–99

A number of factors combine to deprive us of sources for the history of the Lacy family for the period following Hugh de Lacy's death. The minority of Hugh's son and heir, Walter, presents the first problem. It had taken quite some time and an ambitious venture in Ireland for contemporary writers to take notice of Hugh de Lacy, and, just when he had become a regular object of their attention, his unexpected death delivered his inheritance into wardship. The magisterial figure who could rival Ruaidrí Ua Conchobair, high king of Ireland, and even John, the Angevin dynasty's uncrowned king of Ireland, was replaced by an underage boy. King Richard's crusade and imprisonment, which disrupted the records of royal government (the normal framework for evidence of patronage or disfavour), meant that Walter's early career is even less well documented than might have been expected in other circumstances. Finally, many of the chroniclers who had paid attention to Hugh ceased writing in Walter's minority. Bereft of such sources, the early career of Walter de Lacy is a historical uncertainty.

All is not lost, however, for the Irish annals continued uninterrupted throughout this period and so provide the foundation of any analysis of the Lacy family in this period. However, their survival results in a decidedly Hibernocentric view of the early years of Walter de Lacy's career. What information survives suggests that this was a period of great contention for the young magnate, during which he faced multiple difficulties. There were initiatives by his immediate lord, whether king of England or lord of Ireland, to deny him seisin (formal delivery) of his lands. Walter also faced the possibility that his power was insufficient to meet the challenge of transnational lordship, including the indefinite allegiance that it could entail when forced to serve different overlords. In due course his name was writ large on the Irish scene, as the lord of Meath was once again deputed to advance royal policy in the island. Walter also spent a substantial, though less attested, amount of time in England, Wales and Normandy. Either on his own or in the train of the royal court, Walter must have used these periods to administer his territories. The early career of Walter de Lacy picks up where his father's ended, but, essentially, without the upward trajectory of power and influence. Hugh may have been too dominant a figure in Ireland for the royal government to hazard a direct challenge, but, as was very quickly made apparent, his son, the young Walter, had no such stature.

Gaining an inheritance

Immediately upon hearing of Hugh de Lacy's death in 1186, King Henry II issued orders to send his son John back to Ireland and began preparations for his coronation. Because John had complained of Hugh de Lacy as the cause of his failure the previous year, Hugh's assassination provided John with the perfect opportunity to start anew and finally be crowned king of Ireland. Hugh's removal also threatened the delicate balance of power between native and newcomer in Ireland. Roger of Howden reports that John's 1186 expedition was to take charge of Lacy's Irish lands and castles.[1] A lord was supposed to parade his lordship, and the symbolic import of John's triumphal entry into Meath as king of Ireland and lord of Meath (while in wardship) should not be underestimated. As it happened, the death of John's elder brother, Geoffrey, duke of Brittany, brought an abrupt end to these plans. John received the news, and his father's decision to cancel the Irish expedition, while waiting for a favourable wind at Chester. Henry sent Philip of Worcester in John's stead.[2]

The deaths of Hugh de Lacy and Duke Geoffrey roughly coincided with a shift in policy at the French court from one of pragmatic compromise to outright obstinacy in its dealings with the head of the Angevin empire.[3] Thereafter, Henry II found himself opposed at every turn by the machinations of the Capetian king, Philip Augustus, and those, such as Henry's own son Richard, duke of Aquitaine, who were periodically attached to Philip's cause. The wardship of the Lacy inheritance brought the Lacys' strategic possessions in England, Ireland, Wales and Normandy under royal control. All heirs succeeded on the nod of the king, and there is evidence that Henry may have moved to prolong his custody of the Lacy inheritance.

Walter was not in fact Hugh de Lacy's eldest son. In one undated charter in the cartulary of St Guthlac's, Hereford, Hugh made a grant with the assent of 'Robert de Lacy, my son and heir'. In another, he made a grant to the monks of St Mary, Monmouth, alongside his wife Rose and son Robert.[4] No record of Walter's birth exists which would show when he would have been expected to reach his majority (which was in any case not yet a fixed age in England), but he entered into his English inheritance in the summer of 1189, that is, at about the time of Henry II's death and Richard's accession. The pipe roll for 1188/9 records a custodian accounting for the Lacy honor for three-quarters of a year.[5] This would put the approximate date of Walter's seisin at the end of June 1189. King Henry died on 6 July. It is possible that Henry allowed Walter's succession just before he died, but the circumstances make that improbable. By the end of 1188, Henry's position was dire. A coalition including King Philip and Duke Richard was threatening to overwhelm the now ailing English king. What is more, the worse the situation became for the old king, the more willing his castellans and magnates were to defect to Richard as Henry's heir and their future lord. Trust was in short supply. He made great efforts to secure the allegiance of those around him, but baulked at making good his promises.[6] In these circumstances, the succession of Hugh de Lacy's heir – and the release of his inheritance from royal custody – might not have appealed to Henry.

However, upon Henry's death, his son Richard sought to draw a sharp distinction between his reign and that of his miserly father. Roger of Howden reports that many who had been disinherited under King Henry found immediate redress under his son Richard.[7] Famously, William Marshal received the heiress of Striguil and Leinster, whom he had long been promised by Henry, just after the old king's death. When members of Henry's household told Richard that Henry had given William the hand of Strongbow's daughter, Isabel de Clare, Richard reportedly replied: 'Oh! by God's legs, he did not! ... rather, he *promised* her to him.' Richard promptly bestowed the rich reward upon the Marshal himself.[8] This episode is preserved in the near-contemporary *History of William Marshal*, which asserts that Richard likewise delivered on his father's unrealised promises to several others.[9] It may not be a coincidence that Walter received his inheritance at the same time that Richard was making amends for his father's parsimony.

Besides the obvious need to emphasise his own break with the previous reign, Richard may have had a more immediate reason to allow Walter's seisin. As part of King Richard's preparations for departure on crusade, he established William Marshal in the southern Welsh march, giving him the hand of Isabel and making him sheriff of Gloucester with control of Gloucester castle and the forest of Dean. William was supposed to counterbalance Richard's brother John, who had rights to the earldom of Gloucester, the city of Bristol and the marcher lordships of Glamorgan and Wentloog.[10] The threat from native Wales was also a concern,[11] and another strong magnate in the vicinity would have been welcome to the departing king.

Walter de Lacy's grant to his Norman tenant, Durand du Pin, made some time between 15 September and 31 December 1189, proves that Walter was by then in possession of his Norman fees.[12] It also provides a tantalising connection between Walter and King Richard. The sole witness to the grant was Richard's chancellor, William Longchamp, a very influential man.[13] Longchamp's mother may have been a Lacy; at the very least, she brought a Herefordshire knight's fee held of the Lacys as part of her dowry.[14] What is more, Hugh de Lacy and William Longchamp's father, Henry Longchamp, appear together in several witness lists,[15] and Walter later, in 1201, granted William's brother, Stephen, the vill of Frome (Herefordshire).[16] Walter's connection to William Longchamp gave him a strong ally at the new king's court as he attempted to secure his inheritance.

Walter may have initially succeeded to all of his father's lands in Normandy, but he did not retain them all. Just as the Norman custom of partible inheritance led his grandfather, Gilbert de Lacy, to divide his Norman fees among his three sons (Robert, Hugh and Amaury), so Walter de Lacy soon shared his Norman inheritance with his brothers Hugh and Gilbert. Legislation asserting the indivisibility of fiefs had been enacted in Normandy before 1200,[17] which may be why the division involved the redistribution of entire fees. Walter held the Pont Audemer sub-tenancy in 1204, but this may have been his only stake in the duchy. In his 1189 grant to Durand du Pin, Walter states that it was for Durand's service to 'my father, my brother, and me'.[18] This suggests that the honor of Le Pin-au-Haras had formed an appanage for Walter's elder brother Robert before 1186 as their father, the elder Hugh de Lacy, associated Robert with the administration of the Lacy inheritance. After Walter's succession, the honor of Le Pin-au-Haras eventually provided for his younger brother Hugh.[19]

The family's patrimony at Lassy and Campeaux eventually came into the hands of a third brother, Gilbert de Lacy. That Gilbert was not merely Walter's seneschal is suggested by King Philip's grant of the whole holding (*tenementum*) that Gilbert held at Lassy and Campeaux, along with other substantial territories, to the mayor of Falaise, André Propensée, in 1204.[20] The previous year, 1203, King Philip granted to Richard de Garancières land that Richard had contested with Gilbert (but which Gilbert then held by agreement).[21] Given the relative insignificance of the Lacys' Norman patrimony when compared to their interests in Ireland, England and Wales, it is unsurprising that the former should descend to a third son. It had been split from the English inheritance between the exile of Roger de Lacy in 1096 and the accession of Henry II in 1154,[22] and possibly between the accession of Robert de Lacy in 1160 and that of his brother Hugh before 1166. While it is possible that Walter, Hugh and Gilbert de Lacy worked together in Normandy (just as Walter, Hugh and their half-brother William were to do in Ireland),[23] the partition of the Lacys' Norman lands would have restricted Walter's influence in the duchy.

William Longchamp's appearance as *'dominus Willelmus elect [us Eliensis] domini regis Anglie cancellarius'* in Walter's charter to Durand du Pin dates the charter and proves that it was issued in England, not Normandy.[24] This is significant. Just as John would have wanted to display his lordship over the Lacy lands in Ireland following the death of Hugh de Lacy in 1186, so Walter needed to parade himself before his men upon receiving seisin of his inheritance. But Walter could not be everywhere at once: he held lands in four realms, and they had to be prioritised. His family's lucrative and politically important English lands came first, with the nearby Welsh marcher lordship of Ewyas Lacy a convenient second. The Lacys' Norman lands were important for their status and history, but they were all sub-tenancies. Consequently, Walter remained in England for this Norman grant, before journeying to Ireland to secure his lordship of Meath.

The situation in Ireland was not as simple as that in England, Wales or Normandy. Henry II had exercised a great deal of control in Ireland, but he had also granted it to his son John in 1177.[25] Although the relationship between the Crown of England and the lordship of Ireland evolved throughout the Middle Ages, in 1189 Ireland lay outside King Richard's direct control. Realistically, Richard could expect to exert a degree of influence in Ireland thanks to its many ties to England, but the fact remained that in Ireland it was to John that homage was sworn and from him that seisin of lands derived. Henry's death freed John from parental oversight and finally gave him the chance to exercise independent lordship in Ireland. He was quick to flex his muscles. For instance, William Marshal acquired the lordship of Leinster through his marriage to Isabel de Clare that July. However, according to the *History of William Marshal*,

John refused to part with it, forcing William to petition King Richard for seisin that winter. In a well-known scene, Richard demanded that John rectify the situation, and after John put on a brief show of defiance William received Leinster.[26] So, although seisin had to come from John as lord of Ireland, in 1189 King Richard was able to influence his brother's rule in Ireland.

Although there is no evidence for a similar situation involving Walter de Lacy and Meath, it is likely that Richard would also have moved in Walter's favour. Walter certainly had seisin of Meath before Richard departed on crusade. At some point before 1191 (probably as early as 1189), Walter travelled to Ireland and granted lands in Meath to his younger brother, Hugh.[27] That it was Ireland and not Normandy that drew Walter's immediate attention should come as little surprise. Hugh de Lacy the elder had devoted a great deal of time and energy to Meath, spending the latter part of his life developing his lordship there. More than that, Meath was an integral part of the Lacys' tenurial nexus, as several of Meath's knightly families held lands of Walter in England or Wales.[28] This interconnectedness is why the majority of the Lacy inheritance had to descend to Walter intact, with no disruption by a sea crossing. As Robin Frame comments, 'the integrity of the main inheritance may have had as much to do with assumptions of post-Glanville man as with royal or baronial policy; its consequence was to maintain the closeness of the tenurial weave that bound Ireland to Wales and England'.[29] The Norman sub-tenancies shared fewer connections, and seem eventually to have been granted to Walter's younger brothers.[30] Walter's visit to Ireland allowed him to receive the homage of his tenants, personally oversee the administration of the lordship, settle disputes arising from the period of his wardship and generally assert his position as lord of Meath. As will be seen, John's conduct during Walter's minority made an early trip essential.

John and Meath: 1186–94

Irish politics had changed greatly in the three years since 1186. The power vacuum caused by Hugh de Lacy's death and Ruaidrí Ua Conchobair's removal from the Connacht kingship drew in others to tussle for their places.[31] Conchobar Máenmaige Ua Conchobair invaded western Meath, razing the castle of Killare for a second and final time in 1187.[32] The settler community of Meath showed itself cohesive and ambitious enough to join with two Uí Ruairc in plundering Drumcliff (bar. Carbury, Co. Sligo), near Ireland's Atlantic coast.[33] In that same year, the political situation was further disturbed by the death of the king of Man and the Isles, Guðrøðr Óláfsson, who was succeeded by his son Rǫgnvaldr Guðrøðarson (Ragnall mac Gofraid).[34] The eclipse of these established figures meant that the time was ripe for one who might wish to re-centre the balance of power in Ireland, a possibility which John was not slow to take up.

The cancellation of his mission to Ireland in 1186 had not stopped John from utilising Walter's minority to enhance his own position. He issued a general charter protecting the liberties and possessions of the priories of Llanthony Prima and Secunda, heavily supported by the Lacy family, in Ireland.[35] The cultivation of this seigniorial bond of patronage was an excellent way for John to assert his position as overlord of Meath, while also befriending two institutions with vast territorial wealth and prestige locally. However, there is evidence that John went further by permanently alienating Lacy lands. John issued charters confirming Hugh de Lacy's grants to Llanthony in Saithne and Drogheda, but two grants in Duleek (Co. Meath) and Ballybin (bar. Ratoath, Co. Meath) seem to have been new alienations.[36] There also may be evidence for John's alienation of Lacy lands to a secular lord. Between 1186 and 1191 Robert le Poer made grants in Ratoath and Dunshaughlin to the abbey of St Thomas, Dublin.[37] The elder Hugh de Lacy had already granted the ecclesiastical benefices in Ratoath and Dunshaughlin to St Thomas's in or before 1183, while his son Hugh was to do the same for Ratoath upon reception of the territory from his brother Walter before 1191.[38] Consequently, Robert le Poer seems to have been enfeoffed in Meath by John after 1186, only to have his seisin overturned by Walter upon his assumption of lordship. This is reminiscent of the situation in Leinster mentioned above. *The History of William Marshal* reports a discussion between John and King Richard, in which John agreed to allow the Marshal seisin of Leinster as long as his own alienations there remained intact. Richard angrily refused, and only the grants to Theobald Walter were allowed to stand (thereafter held of William Marshal).[39]

If King Richard's presence saved Leinster and Meath from John's acquisitiveness, Richard's departure on crusade left them exposed. Before leaving, Richard appointed Walter's ally William Longchamp as chief justiciar and chancellor of England in May 1190. Two months later, he thought better of his decision and appointed four co-justiciars to act as a check on Longchamp.[40] By early 1191, politics in England had turned violent in a political duel between John and William Longchamp, but the co-justiciars ultimately chose to support John against Richard's administrator. The distant King Richard agreed with his co-justiciars and removed

Longchamp from the justiciarship, installing Walter de Coutances, archbishop of Rouen, in his stead.[41] John was in the ascendency, and this placed Walter de Lacy in a very vulnerable position in Ireland. Walter's English and Norman estates remained relatively safe thanks to the co-justiciars' oversight, but Ireland was a different matter. The struggle for authority in England had kept John preoccupied, but its resolution left him free to rule his independent lordship of Ireland as he saw fit.

John was acknowledged heir-apparent to the English Crown, and set about turning this into real power. In February 1192, he attempted to intrigue against the absent king with Philip Augustus of France, and gave up only when his mother, Eleanor of Aquitaine, and the English justiciar threatened to confiscate all of his English and Norman lands if he went to France.[42] Just as was to happen after the fall of Normandy in 1204, John's failure in France translated into an interventionist approach to Ireland. On 13 May 1192, John granted the monks of Kells lands from the Lacy demesne at Durrow (the site of Hugh's assassination).[43] Two months later, on 21 July, John bestowed a carucate of land in Mag Cuillinn (Cooksborough, bar. Moycashel, Co. Westmeath?) and the sergeancy of County Dublin upon his own household sergeant, Henry Tyrell.[44] Both alienations were direct assaults upon Walter de Lacy's lordship in Meath.

John reordered the Irish administration, replacing the Irish justiciar, John de Courcy, with one of his Louth tenants-in-chief, Peter Pipard.[45] He then issued a fresh charter of liberties to Dublin, launched an offensive in Munster, and set about fortifying the colony.[46] In Meath, native and settler forces fought a battle at Rahugh (bar. Moycashel, Co. Westmeath).[47] Additionally, the castles of Ardnurcher (bar. Moycashel, Co. Westmeath) and Kilbixy (bar. Moygoish, Co. Westmeath) were constructed,[48] with Rathconrath (Co. Westmeath) having been built the previous year.[49] The land and castle of Kilbixy was another alienation that Walter had to put right after his full resumption of lordship, when he granted Kilbixy to Geoffrey de Costentin 'through the petition of John, count of Mortain' in 1195.[50] Leinster, the other of John's pre-1189 targets, may have been protected by William Marshal's position as co-justiciar in England, and his close relationship with John in this period.[51] However, if N. B. White is correct in his dating of John's grant to Theobald Walter of Tullach Chiaráin in Osraige and Tullach Ua Felmeda in Uí Felmeda, then Leinster may have felt John's grip in this later period as well.[52] Whatever relationship had existed regarding Ireland before Richard's departure, in the absence of the king and William Longchamp, John was exploiting his position as lord of Ireland in his own right.

On 11 December 1192 King Richard was captured by the duke of Austria near Vienna and spent over a year in captivity.[53] During that time John and King Philip orchestrated an unsuccessful revolt that led to the creation of a special roll of escheats in England to record lands forfeited during the conflict. Although identification is problematic, there appear to be several Lacy estates under the Herefordshire section of the roll. Frome (Herefordshire), Stanton Lacy (Shropshire) and Stanford (Worcestershire) were most likely part of Walter's demesne, while '*Maurðin*' may refer to a Lacy tenant estate, Marden (Herefordshire).[54] The first three estates were accounted for by the same man: John of *Maurðin*, which certainly implies a previous administrative unity. Ludlow castle, which had been in royal hands since 1177, with a brief break prior to Richard's crusade,[55] is curiously absent from both the roll of escheats and the pipe roll of that year. The official responsible for its upkeep continued to draw revenue from the lands given him to that end, and made a fine with the king to hold them independently, but the castle itself is not mentioned.[56] Unfortunately, the silence of the sources makes it unclear why any Lacy estates should have escheated to the Crown. Once King Richard returned, however, things began to change.

The lordship of Meath restored: 1194-5

Very little is known of Walter de Lacy during John's ascendancy in England, which perhaps indicates his political insignificance at the time. His obscurity ends, appropriately, with the return of the king. Richard was set free in February 1194, and arrived in England in mid-March.[57] Of all the strongholds that had declared for John, only Nottingham remained defiant, and Walter de Lacy was in the royal army that laid siege to it. Walter's mere presence is not that noteworthy as all but the most ardent of John's supporters flocked to King Richard to display their loyalty, steadfast or newly found. The shrewd courtier and erstwhile Johannite William Marshal left his brother's funeral cortege as soon as news of Richard's landing reached him.[58] Looming much larger in the pages of history, owing in part to his near contemporary biography, the Marshal provides a very useful reference point when analysing Walter de Lacy's career. For instance, the two magnates' actions after the siege of Nottingham imply much about their political dispositions.

Walter and William both joined their king on his triumphal march to crush the last vestiges of rebellion, and were both asked to render him homage for their Irish lands. This was a direct assault upon John's lordship in Ireland, and a much stronger statement of loyalty to Richard than their presence at the siege. William famously refused, insisting that he could not perform homage to Richard for lands that he held of John. Whether one believes the Marshal's biographer that this stance was greeted with great approval by the king and assembled barons, no such dilemma stayed Walter's hand.[59] His rights ignored by the lord of Ireland, Walter's strict adherence to the king must have appeared the best way to re-establish Lacy lordship in Meath. This crisis of allegiance was rendered moot by Richard's prompt sequestration of John's dominions, and, on 8 April, Richard rewarded Walter's homage with a confirmatory charter for Meath.[60] Walter would have to wait over a year for John to issue his own charter for Meath, on 15 June 1195,[61] during which time Walter was a principal agent of English royal control in Ireland.

Once he had Richard's charter, Walter wasted little time in crossing to Ireland, where, on 5 July 1194, he granted a charter of liberties to his town of Drogheda.[62] His position in Ireland was further strengthened by his royal commission as co-justiciar along with the lord of Ulster, John de Courcy. Marleburgh's chronicle reports that one of Walter's first official actions was the arrest of John's former justiciar, Peter Pipard.[63] This is one of the earliest discernible instances of royally sponsored factionalism within the colonial community in Ireland.[64] The English Crown had always recognised that the most cost-effective method in asserting its power within Ireland was to find magnates whose self-interest coincided with the interests of the Crown, and to invest them with the authority of a governmental commission. However, instead of being aimed at the native Irish like Hugh de Lacy had been,[65] the lords of Meath and Ulster were set against their fellow colonials: John's Munster feofees.

John's recent grant of the whole Irish kingdom of Connacht to William de Burgh (elder brother of John's chamberlain, and future justiciar of England, Hubert de Burgh), provided the kindling for the conflagration to follow.[66] The grant of Connacht rendered void an earlier grant by John of six cantreds of north Connacht to Walter de Lacy's brother Hugh,[67] and disinherited the most powerful native Irish dynasty, the Uí Conchobair. If Ireland had escaped the tumult of John's rebellion from 1193 to 1194, and if Richard's appointment of Walter de Lacy and John de Courcy had not already set the scene for factionalist politics, John's grant of Connacht was enough to sound a general call to arms throughout the island. William de Burgh had come to Ireland with John in 1185, when he had received lands in Munster.[68] By 1193, he had married a daughter of the king of Thomond (northern Munster), Domnall Mór Ua Briain, which greatly increased his stature in the region.[69] Domnall Mór's death the following year allowed William to intrigue in the ensuing succession dispute, during which the warring claimants gifted him the city of Limerick.[70] Combined with his grant of Connacht, William posed a real threat to Ireland's established powers.

The situation quickly came to a head as the king of Connacht, Cathal Crobderg Ua Conchobair (Ruaidrí's younger brother), himself married to a daughter of Domnall Mór Ua Briain, mounted an expedition against the settler community of Munster.[71] The annals of Inisfallen record that Cathal demolished many castles and raised hopes that he might drive out the English altogether. However, the castles were simply rebuilt and, although Ua Conchobair made arrangements for a return expedition, none materialised.[72] Cathal's failure to return may have been thanks to the intervention of King Richard's justiciars: Walter de Lacy and John de Courcy. The annals record that the two men made a circuit of Leinster and Munster in order to bring the settlers there to heel.[73] Seán Duffy concludes that the targets of these assaults were John's henchmen 'whose successes at land-grabbing in the south-west of Ireland were beginning to challenge the older ascendancy',[74] which, though correct, should not obscure the actions of Burgh and Ua Conchobair as their immediate cause.

Cathal Crobderg and Richard's justiciars had a common interest in seeing William de Burgh's grant of Connacht go unrealised, and were quick to grasp the advantages of an alliance. The three met at Athlone that same year (1195), where it seems a *modus vivendi* was reached. The annals of Loch Cé's description of the meeting includes the phrase 'and the nobles of the foreigners', which might indicate a form of common council present at the parley.[75] The two sides were thereafter able to focus their energies on mollifying the threat in Thomond in a way which would not lead to further destabilisation in the region.[76] Orpen speculates that the justiciars traded an official acknowledgement of Cathal Crobderg as king of Connacht for Cathal's promise to stay out of Munster, which, if correct, would certainly explain Cathal's failure to mount his return mission.[77] The meeting also paved the way for more cordial relations between Meath and Connacht, which may have aided Walter's recovery that same year of his father's body from the Irish of western Meath. The archbishop of Cashel, Muirgeas (Matthew) Ua hÉanna, who was also papal legate for Ireland, joined the archbishop of Dublin, John Cumin, in recovering Hugh's body, which had been retained by the Irish since his murder in 1186. The body was transmitted for burial in Bective Abbey (Co. Meath); the head was buried alongside Hugh's first wife, Rose of Monmouth, in the Abbey of St Thomas, Dublin.[78] Coming in the same year as Walter's efforts in Munster and at Athlone, the success of the mission may be indicative of his increased stature in Ireland.

The 1195 Athlone conference was probably the final instance of Richard's direct rule in Ireland. John was reconciled with the king, and soon began exercising his authority in Ireland once more. That same year, Philip of Worcester was once again sent to Ireland 'to reinforce the English of Munster'.[79] Philip's history of overseeing administrative change (as in 1184 and 1186) suggests that this meant supporting John's men against Richard's justiciars, while preparing for John's resumption of direct lordship over Ireland. As soon as he once again held the reins of power in Ireland, John replaced Walter de Lacy and John de Courcy as justiciars with his former custodian of Waterford, Hamo de Valognes.[80]

Reconciliation with John: 1195-7

Having handed Ireland back to John, King Richard ensured that John would not punish Walter for his role in Richard's administration of Ireland. According to a mandate John sent to his men in Ireland, King Richard compelled John to accept Walter's peaceful seisin of Meath:

> John, lord of Ireland and count of Mortain, to all his justices, barons and sworn men, English and Irish, greeting. Know that, at the request of King Richard, my brother, I have remitted to Walter de Lacy and all his heirs the animosity, anger and ill will I had conceived against them, and all the outrages which they have committed against me up to now. I have received the aforesaid Walter and all his men into favour, and have restored to the aforesaid Walter all his rights in Ireland for 2,500 marks, which Walter has given me for this reason. Wherefore I order that you regard him and all his men as my faithful men, and that you maintain, protect and defend them, and that you do no trouble or injury to them or theirs, nor suffer it be done; and if anyone does that [trouble or injury] to him or his in anything, you shall do it back to him [i.e. attack the offending party] without delay.[81]

It is fascinating to note that the restoration of Walter's rights in Ireland under John was accomplished only after a massive fine of 2,500 marks was agreed. By way of comparison, three years later Walter had to pay King Richard 3,100 marks for the restoration of his English and Norman lands after a period of sequestration.[82] Clearly Richard was willing to allow for the financial realities of feudal prerogative while dictating terms to his brother.

This settlement was a watershed in the relationship between Walter and the lord of Ireland. Walter's promised fine of 2,500 marks placed him in John's debt, a financial obligation to mirror his social and political dependence upon the lord of Ireland. From that point John seems to have genuinely softened his stance towards the Lacys and for the next decade acted as a courteous, if not overly beneficent, lord to Walter and his family. On 15 June 1195, the first step was taken when John issued his own charter for Meath,[83] which officially recognised Walter's lawful tenure, and John's authority over him. A reciprocal gesture seems to have been made by Walter, who (as mentioned above) granted Geoffrey de Costentin the land and castle of Kilbixy and the adjoining territory of Conmaicne for the service of twenty knights 'through the petition of John, count of Mortain'.[84] Conmaicne is roughly co-extensive with the modern diocese of Ardagh, which is 61 miles long, and from 5 to 18 miles broad.[85] If the entire territory was meant, then it was a generous (if speculative) grant. It seems likely that John had granted the lands and castle to Geoffrey in 1192, and that Walter's charter confirmed John's alienation while preserving Walter's lordship in Meath. The parallel with William Marshal's 1189 confirmation of Theobald Walter's Leinster lands is clear.[86] The conciliatory spirit was not lost on the primary target of Walter's 1195 Munster expedition, William de Burgh, who granted ten cantreds of Connacht to Walter's brother, Hugh de Lacy.[87] The grant amounted to a third of the province, incorporating and expanding upon John's earlier grant of six cantreds which William's 1194 grant of Connacht had superseded. Walter responded by granting Moymet (Co. Meath), Clonmore (bar. Lune, Co. Meath) and Clonfane (bar. Navan Upper, Co. Meath) to William and his brother Hubert.[88]

It may have been around this time that the Lacys formed an alliance with another of John's Irish grantees, the Verduns, through the marriage of Walter's brother, Hugh, to Lescelina, daughter of Bertram de Verdon (d. 1192) and sister of Thomas and Nicholas de Verdon. Bertram had accompanied John to Ireland in 1185, and was granted lands in the north of modern county Louth. Bertram was left in Ireland as seneschal once John returned to England, and was also granted custody of the castle of Drogheda after Hugh de Lacy the elder died in 1186.[89] Hugh's marriage to Bertram's daughter gained Hugh extensive lands north of Dundalk (Co. Louth) and on the Cooley peninsula (Co. Louth), which bordered John de Courcy's lordship of Ulster and introduced the Lacy family to Ireland's north-eastern maritime network. However, there may have been more to this marriage than Irish politics. Hugh's in-laws were also active in the

Évreçin, with Lescelina's brother Thomas enjoying a 20 *livres* money fief in the honor of Évreux.[90] Hugh's marriage may have been as much about looking back to the family's ancestral association with the Évreux tenancy at Claville as forward to its newest endeavour in Ireland.

The relationship between Walter and John was strengthened soon thereafter. Both the annals collected by James Ware and the so-called 'Dublin annals of Inisfallen' record under 1196 that Gilbert de Angulo disturbed the peace of Ireland to the extent that he was driven from Ireland and his lands confiscated by the Irish justiciar, Hamo de Valognes.[91] John bestowed these forfeited lands, which extended beyond the lake of Tír Briúin (Lough Oughter, Co. Cavan) into Bréifne, upon Gilbert's former lord, Walter de Lacy. While informing the justiciar of this grant, John also granted a messuage in the city of Limerick and three knights' fees in a neighbouring cantred to Walter.[92] These gifts can be dated to about the year 1197, when John established his lordship over the city and vicinity of Limerick, bestowing patronage upon his men there.[93] From the peace of Athlone in 1195 to the reorganisation of Limerick in 1197, a gradual process of reconciliation between John and Walter de Lacy unfolded.

The royal relationship tested: 1196-8

The dangers of a transnational inheritance and allegiance to two different lords were soon apparent, however, for, in focusing so much of his attention on Ireland, Walter neglected his relationship with King Richard. In 1195/6, Walter incurred a fine of 1,000 marks.[94] The reason for this substantial fine is not explicitly recorded, though its appearance under the accounts for that year's scutage for Normandy suggests that it arose from Richard's campaigns in the duchy. Furthermore, there is evidence that Walter's Norman lands had been confiscated about this time. An undated entry on the Norman memoranda rolls under Vaudreuil reads: 'The bailiff is to take into the king's hand all the lands of Walter de Lacy, and answer for them. And Geoffrey the Exchanger (*Cambitor*) is to answer for the profits of the same land from the previous year.'[95] W. E. Wightman suggests that the accounts referred to the fiscal years 1195/6 and 1196/7,[96] which would correspond well with the 1,000 mark fine of 1195/6.

This dating corresponds well to the progress of King Richard's war in Normandy. From 1194 to 1195, while Walter de Lacy served as co-justiciar and re-established himself in Ireland, Richard fought to restore his own position on the continent. In April 1196, Richard prepared for a new offensive.⁹⁷ However, the Welsh prince Rhys ap Gruffudd (Lord Rhys) had just been released from his imprisonment (which had resulted from a Deheubarth succession dispute), and the English government feared further escalation of violence in Wales.⁹⁸ Consequently, the Welsh marcher lords were instructed to fortify the march, despite the general call to arms in Normandy.⁹⁹ The fighting in Wales later that year proves that such concerns were warranted.¹⁰⁰ This episode shows the difficulties facing King Richard. The restoration of his continental inheritance was of paramount importance, but he also had to secure his kingdom. A similar dilemma may have faced Walter de Lacy. Walter was a Norman baron, as well as a Welsh marcher lord, and might have been expected to answer the king's call in either realm. However, he was also an Irish magnate and the flow of patronage in Ireland suggests that he was preoccupied with strengthening his relationship with his lord there, John. Whatever his other identities, the administrative heart of the Lacy inheritance lay in England, and it was here that the fine was recorded. The entire episode vividly illustrates the inherent dangers of exercising lordship across four realms.

Such a penalty is less surprising given the circumstances. The chancellor's roll for 1195/6 is awash with new entries, as the English justiciar strove to bring in old and new debts for the king.¹⁰¹ A similar situation occurred in December 1197, when the bishops of Lincoln and Salisbury refused to join Richard's continental campaign. The king ordered their lands to be confiscated immediately, though the political practicalities meant that only the bishop of Salisbury suffered and had to pay a heavy price for restoration.¹⁰² In 1196, Walter did nothing to pay off his debt, and it remained undiminished on the next year's pipe roll (1196/7). Sequestration was one of the few remedies available to the king for a defaulting baron, and Richard was not averse to the practice. Kate Norgate suggests that Richard's seizure of lands and castles as pledges for the repayment of debts may have lay behind the English barons' demand to King John on his accession that he 'restore to each of them his rights'.¹⁰³ In 1197, the year in which John granted him lands in Bréifne and Limerick, all of Walter's English and Norman lands were confiscated by King Richard for his failure to make any payment on his fine. The fact that Walter's Irish lands were not similarly sequestrated, and were instead augmented by John, displays the limits of Richard's hegemony by 1197. Walter's English lands certainly had been seized by Christmas 1197, when the *custos* of the Lacy castle of Ludlow was changed by the justiciar.¹⁰⁴ Confirmation that Walter's lands were in the king's hand appears in the corresponding

English pipe roll (1197/8).[105] In Normandy, the Norman pipe roll of 1197/8 records the proceeds from Walter's lands for the whole of the previous year, 759*l* 8*s* 5*d*, which means that Walter's Norman territories had also been in the king's hand since at least 1197.[106] On the same roll, under Vaudreuil, Stephen de Vaudreuil rendered his account of 58*l* 5*s* 2*d* for the land of 'Hugh' de Lacy,[107] which, given the entries under Vaudreuil on the Norman memoranda roll, was either a mistake for Walter de Lacy or named Walter's custodian.

Walter was with King Richard at Vaudreuil on 7 January 1198, where he witnessed a royal charter to Alan Basset.[108] However long Walter remained with the king, his presence must have involved negotiations over his fine and restoration. The entry on the pipe roll for that year (1197/8) gives the reason for the confiscation and the terms for restoration that Walter was able to negotiate with Richard. Under the third scutage of Normandy, which arose from the 1196 expedition mentioned above, Walter's fine of 1,000 marks remained. However, the account states that, in remission of that fine, Walter personally made a fine of 3,100 marks. The account for the 3,100 mark fine is made under the heading 'new offers', where it states that it was made 'so that he [Walter] might have the king's pleasure and seisin of his land'.[109] Thus, after their proceeds had filled Richard's coffers for at least a year, and upon the proffer of an enormous fine, Walter's English and Norman lands were restored to him; the debt that prompted their sequestration was cancelled, but only in return for a threefold augmentation. In Ireland, Count John was quick to ensure that his lordship over Walter did not suffer as a result of Walter's mishandling of the situation in Normandy. In December 1198, John confirmed the grant that Walter had made to his brother Hugh between 1189 and 1191 (discussed above), at once reasserting his bond with the lord of Meath and admitting the legitimacy of Walter's 1189 seisin.[110]

This sequence of events is at odds with what is normally claimed: that Walter de Lacy suffered both the abiding enmity of Count John and the sequestration of his inheritance for his actions in Ireland from 1194 to 1195. Although the fine for the return of Walter's lands is recorded on the pipe roll for 1197/8,[111] the obscurity into which Walter slips from about 1196 until 1198, or at least the inability to provide a definite date for his actions within the period, has led historians to pin its cause to his last firmly datable actions. Although this tendency predated him,[112] its longevity is largely down to the Lacys' modern biographer, W. E. Wightman. Wightman concluded that *all* of Walter's lands (not just those in England and Normandy) had been seized in 1197. He explains:

In that year [1198] Richard Silvain accounted for the lands of Walter II de Lacy for the twelve months before they were returned to him. The sum for which he answered to the exchequer at Caen was the enormous one of £759. 8s. 5d. The total annual yield of the English lands of the Herefordshire branch of the family during Walter's minority between 1186 and 1189 was £91. 6s. 0d.[113]

Wightman contends that so large a discrepancy between the average annual yield of Walter's English lands from 1186 to 1189 and the render at the Norman exchequer in 1198 proves that the total in 1198 would have had to include the lucrative Irish lordship of Meath. Wightman assumes Ireland's constitutional position, and that profits from Meath would have filled Richard's coffers in 1198. The question goes begging. Wightman's sum for the Lacys' English lands is invalid, because it includes both accounts for issues (what the land produced) and farms (a predetermined render). Furthermore, he overestimates the significance of the Norman total. In English sterling currency (worth roughly four times the *livre* Angevin) this would have been £189 17s 1d: a significant sum, but one based on an advanced financial system of lordship.[114] Wightman's errors, the relative independence of the Irish administration, and Count John's courting of Walter de Lacy after 1195 make it clear that Walter's Irish lands were not taken along with their English and Norman counterparts.

Two alternative explanations have been offered to reconcile Walter de Lacy's continued seisin of Meath and his forfeiture in the Anglo-Norman realm, both of which are included in his entry in the *Oxford Dictionary of National Biography*:

> It may be that John, as lord of Ireland, had persuaded King Richard to sequestrate Lacy's lands in England and Normandy for actions taken in Ireland; alternatively, Richard may have taken exception to Lacy's subsequently reaching an accommodation with John in respect of his Irish lands, and sought to maintain his overriding lordship there.[115]

In light of Richard's role in securing Walter's reconciliation with John in 1195, neither alternative is very likely. The only evidence that could support either interpretation comes from the fine roll of the first year of John's reign, in which he ordered the justiciar of Ireland, Meiler fitz Henry, to restore Henry Tyrell's lands and to inquire into his service, specifically establishing whether he had sided with John de Courcy and Walter de Lacy in destroying the king's land of Ireland.[116] This should not be seen as a link to Walter's actions in 1195, or evidence that John was simply 'biding his time to revenge himself on de Courcy and de Lacy' while under Richard's watchful eye.[117] The actual course of events shows that John and Walter were reconciled in the interim, while it was Walter's relationship with Richard that deteriorated. One of Count John's illegal alienations in Meath had been to his then sergeant Henry Tyrell in July 1192.[118] Consequently, the 1199 mandate may have sought to determine whether Henry had abandoned John and joined forces with Walter de Lacy and John de Courcy in 1195. This would have been an issue of personal allegiance, and would not imply any sustained or renewed enmity towards Walter, who was, after all, Richard's man in 1195.

Much of the blame for this confusion must be placed on the partitioning of history along modern national boundaries, which has placed artificial limitations on our understanding of the transnational aristocracy. For instance, the study of the Lacy family has been divided between English and Irish historiographies at the point of Hugh de Lacy's entry into Ireland in 1172. Joe Hillaby, a specialist in Jewish history and the western counties of England, restricted his article on Walter de Lacy to Ireland. This led him to see the 1199 mandate as proof of John's abiding enmity towards Walter, and to posit Irish matters as the reason for Richard's sequestration of Walter's lands (in which he includes Meath).[119] Even Brock Holden, who deals extensively with the Lacys in England and Wales seems at a loss and looks to Ireland for a convenient explanation. In his doctoral thesis, he follows the *Oxford Dictionary of National Biography* in attributing the sequestration to Walter's Irish activities of 1195. His published monograph has his revised opinion that it must have been 'for reasons having to do with the vagaries of Irish politics'.[120] If a concrete example is needed to justify a transnational approach to the study of transnational aristocrats, this episode certainly provides it.

Conclusion

The reign of King Richard is an exciting, but problematical period for the study of the Lacy family. To make matters worse, when Walter made an appearance on the historical scene, it was usually in the context of an event in which he played only a supporting role. His initial seisin of Meath had been attributed to 1194 for so long because this fits in nicely with the dynamic between King Richard and Count John as it was then understood, as well as the situation involving William Marshal. However, through careful investigation of the evidence surrounding the Lacy inheritance, a different picture emerges. Moreover, it is through this same study that a new insight into the actions of John while Richard was away on crusade may be gained, that is, his unchecked aggression towards seigniorial lordship in Ireland. John's decision to ignore Walter's rights in Meath and permanently to alienate portions of Walter's demesne was a legacy of Hugh de Lacy's conduct in 1185. However, Walter's divided allegiance may have played a part. Walter was John's man for his Irish holdings, and might have been expected to support John in 1192. For instance, in late 1191 William Marshal supported John against Chancellor Longchamp and accepted him as heir apparent in early 1192, before declaring in 1194 that, because he had sworn homage to John for Ireland, 'there is no man in this world who, if he sought to take Ireland, would not see me going with my forces to the side of him whose liegeman I am'. This, the Marshal pronounced in response to Chancellor Longchamp's suggestion that, in refusing to swear homage to Richard for his Irish lands, the Marshal was 'planting vines' with the lord of Ireland and heir to the English throne.[121] No evidence of Walter's political positioning exists for this period, but he was certainly a Ricardian by the king's return in 1194. The situation was soon to become much simpler, if not necessarily better, for Walter and his fellow Irish magnates upon Richard's death on 6 April 1199.[122] From that point the king of England and lord of Ireland were one and the same man. No longer was Ireland a refuge, or a place where Walter might easily forget where his ultimate loyalties must lie. Just as it had been before the council of Oxford in 1177, so it was again. The lord of Meath held all of his lands directly of the king of England: no more conflict of loyalties, no more ambiguity.

Notes

1 Howden, *Gesta*, i, p.350.
2 *Annales Cestrienses*, pp.34–5. Philip had been sent to Ireland in 1184 to pave the way for John's 1185 expedition. See Chapter 1.
3 Warren, *Henry II*, p.612.
4 'Roberti de Lacy filii mei et heredis mei', Balliol College Oxford MS 271, fo. 47v; *Monasticon Anglicanum*, iv, p.597.
5 *Pipe Roll 1 Richard I*, p.145.
6 Crouch, *William Marshal*, p.62; Warren, *Henry II*, chapter 16: 'The end of the reign'.
7 Howden, *Gesta*, ii, p.75.
8 *Hist. William Marshal*, lines 9367–8 (my italics).
9 *Ibid.*, lines 9373–408.
10 Painter, *William Marshal*, pp.83–5; Crouch, *William Marshal*, p.71.

11 Gillingham, *Richard I*, p. 101; John Gillingham, 'Henry II, Richard I and the Lord Rhys', *Peritia*, 10 (1996), pp. 225-36, at pp. 231-4.
12 BM Rouen Y201, fo. 61v; *Cal. Doc. France*, no. 618.
13 William was elected bishop of Ely on 15 September 1189 and consecrated 31 December 1189, Norgate, *Angevin Kings*, ii, pp. 277, 287.
14 *RBE*, i, p. 283; David Balfour, 'The origins of the Longchamp family', *Medieval Prosopography*, 18 (1997), pp. 84-5.
15 For instance, *Chart. St Mary's*, i, pp. 79-81; *Cart. Haughmond*, p. 149, no. 723.
16 *Pipe Roll 3 John*, p. 266.
17 Power, *Norman Frontier*, p. 146.
18 'Pro seruitio suo ... patri meo et fratri meo et mihi', BM Rouen Y201, fo. 61v; *Cal. Doc. France*, no. 618.
19 See the grant of Le Pin-au-Haras 'which had been Hugh de Lacy's' to William de Briouze in 1203, *Rotuli Normanniae in Turri Londinensi Asservati*, ed. T. D. Hardy (London, 1835), p. 74.
20 *Cartulaire Normand de Philippe-Auguste, Louis VIII, Saint-Louis et Philippe-le-Hardi*, ed. Léopold Delisle (Paris, 1882), no. 76.
21 *Ibid.*, no. 72.
22 Wightman, *Lacy*, pp. 239-40.
23 See Chapters 6 and 7.
24 BM Rouen Y201, fo. 61v; *Cal. Doc. France*, no. 618. Walter's father had granted his own charter to Durand in Dublin. See Chapter 1.
25 See Chapter 2.
26 Painter, *William Marshal*, pp. 79-80; Crouch, *William Marshal*, p. 70.
27 The charter granted Hugh the lands of Ratoath (Co. Meath), Treóit (parish Trevet, bar. Skreen, Co. Meath), Machaire Gaileang (bar. Morgallion, Co. Meath), the tuath of *Fithdwinterwod* (?), land of Cenél n-Enda (Kinalea, Co. Westmeath?), and the land of Cenél Láegaire (bar Upper and Lower Navan, Co. Meath?). *Gormanston Register*, pp. 143, 190. See Veach, 'A question of timing', pp. 176-80.
28 See Chapter 8.
29 Robin Frame, 'Aristocracies and the political configuration of the British Isles', in Frame (ed.), *Ireland and Britain, 1170-1450* (London and Rio Grande, 1998), pp. 151-70, at p. 156.
30 See Chapter 8.
31 In 1191, Ruaidrí sought (and was refused) support from the English of Meath to resume the kingship of Connacht, *AFM*, iii, p. 90 s.a. 1191.
32 *AFM*, iii, p. 78, s.a. 1187.
33 *ALC*, i, pp. 174-6, s.a. 1187; *AU*, ii, p. 210, s.a. 1187.
34 See: R. A. McDonald, *Manx Kingship in Its Irish Sea Setting: King Rǫgnvaldr and the Crovan Dynasty* (Dublin, 2007); McDonald, *The Kingdom of the Isles: Scotland's Western Seaboard, c.1100-c.1336* (East Linton, 1997).
35 *Irish Llanthony*, pp. 80-1, 213.
36 *Irish Llanthony*, pp. 78-9, 286. See Veach, 'A question of timing', p. 183.
37 *Reg. St Thomas*, pp. 224, 254, 270, 273.
38 *Reg. St Thomas*, pp. 7-9.

39 Hist. William Marshal, ii, lines 9581–618.
40 Painter, William Marshal, pp. 82–4; Crouch, William Marshal, pp. 66–7. The four were William Marshal, Geoffrey fitz Peter, Hugh Bardolf and William Brewer.
41 Painter, William Marshal, pp. 84–9; Crouch, William Marshal, p. 78; Norgate, Angevin Kings, ii, p. 297.
42 Howden, Gesta, ii, p. 236.
43 Gearóid Mac Niocaill, Notitiae as Leabhar Cheanannais, 1033–1161 (Dublin, 1961), pp. 38–9; Calendar of the Patent Rolls Preserved in the Public Record Office, Richard II, vol. iv, A.D. 1388–1392, (London, 1902), p. 300.
44 Calendar of the Patent Rolls Preserved in the Public Record Office, Edward III, vol. iii, 1334–1338 (London, 1895), pp. 415–16.
45 For the Pipards see Smith, Colonisation and Conquest.
46 Historic and Municipal Documents of Ireland, A.D. 1172–1320, ed. J. T. Gilbert (London, 1870), pp. 51–5; AI, p. 316, s.a. 1192; MCB, p. 72, s.a. 1192; Orpen, Normans, ii, pp. 145–6; Duffy, 'John and Ireland', pp. 235–6.
47 ALC, i, pp. 194–6, s.a. 1192.
48 AFM, iii, p. 92, s.a. 1192; ALC, i, p. 186, s.a. 1192. Ardnurcher (Cenél Fiachach) was held by Meiler fitz Henry of the Lacys, Song, lines 3138–41; Deeds, lines 3136–9.
49 ALC, i, p. 184, s.a. 1191.
50 BL MS Cotton Titus B XI, fo. 72r, and see below, p. 89.
51 Crouch, William Marshal, pp. 71–2, 76, 79, 85, 89–90, 116.
52 The Red Book of Ormond, ed. N. B. White (Dublin, 1932), p. 9. For place identifications see Flanagan, Irish Society, p. 132n.
53 Norgate, Angevin Kings, ii, p. 323.
54 Pipe Roll 6 Richard I, p. 5; Wightman, Lacy, pp. 236 (Frome), 203 (Stanton Lacy), 125 (Stanford), 122 (Marden).
55 Wightman, Lacy, p. 192. It reappears on the 1193 pipe roll accounting for two years, Pipe Roll 5 Richard I, pp. 86–7.
56 Pipe Roll 6 Richard I, pp. 136–7.
57 Gillingham, Richard I, pp. 248–51.
58 Crouch, William Marshal, pp. 81–2.
59 Hist. William Marshal, ii, lines 10295–340.
60 BL MS Hargrave 313; Gormanston Register, pp. 6, 177–8.
61 BL MS Harley 1240, fo. 27r, no. 26; Gormanston Register, p. 178.
62 Na Buirgéisí, i, pp. 172–3.
63 Bibliothèque Municipale de Troyes, MS 1316, fo. 39r.
64 Otway-Ruthven, Medieval Ireland, p. 73; Peter Crooks, '"Divide and rule": factionalism as royal policy in the Lordship of Ireland, 1171–1265', Peritia, 19 (2005), pp. 263–307, at p. 278.
65 See Chapter 1.
66 Perros [Walton], 'Shannon frontier', p. 126; W. L. Warren, 'King John and Ireland', in James Lydon (ed.), England and Ireland in the Later Middle Ages: Essays in Honour of Jocelyn Otway-Ruthven (Blackrock, 1981), pp. 26–42, at p. 30.
67 The cantreds were: Tri Tuatha (alias Tuatha Síl Muiredaig, Co. Roscommon),

Mag nAi (*alias* Machaire Connacht, Co. Roscommon), Mag Lurg-Tirerrill (bar. Boyle, Co. Roscommon), Corran (bar. Corran, Co. Sligo), Sliab Luga (bar. Costello, Co. Mayo and adjoining district in Co. Roscommon) and Leyny (bar. Leyny, Co. Sligo), *Rotuli Chartarum in Turri Londinensi Asservati*, ed. T. D. Hardy (London, 1837), pp. 139–40; Helen Walton, 'The English in Connacht 1171–1333', PhD (University of Dublin, 1980), pp. 22, 25.
68 Orpen, *Normans*, ii p. 147.
69 *Ibid.*, ii, p. 48.
70 For a narrative see F. X. Martin, 'John, Lord of Ireland, 1185–1216', in *NHI, ii*, pp. 127–55, at p. 129.
71 *AFM*, iii, p. 100, *s.a.* 1195; *ALC*, i, p. 190, *s.a.* 1195; *AI*, p. 320, *s.a.* 1195; *MCB*, p. 74, *s.a.* 1195.
72 *AI*, p. 320, *s.a.* 1195.
73 *AFM*, iii, p. 100, *s.a.* 1195; *ALC*, i, p. 190, *s.a.* 1195; *AU*, ii, p. 222, *s.a.* 1195.
74 Duffy, 'John and Ireland', p. 237.
75 Crooks, 'Divide and rule', p. 279.
76 *ALC*, i, p. 190, *s.a.* 1195.
77 Orpen, *Normans*, ii, p. 156.
78 *Grace's Annals*, p. 18, *s.a.* 1195; *Chart. St Mary's*, ii, p. 307, *s.a.* 1195; BL MS Additional 4792, fos 160-2, *s.a.* 1195.
79 Otway-Ruthven, *Medieval Ireland*, p. 72.
80 Orpen, *Normans*, ii, pp. 113, 162–3; Duffy, 'John and Ireland', p. 237.
81 'Iohannes dominus Hibernie comes Morton omnibus iusticiariis et baronibus et fidelibus suis Anglis et Hibernis salutem. Sciatis me ad instantiam domini Ricardi regis fratris mei remississe Waltero de Lacy et omnibus heredibus suis occasionem iram et malignationem quas versus eos consc[e]peram, et omnes excessos quas huc usque erga me fecerunt et predictum Walterum et omnes homines suos ad gratiam recepi et predicto Waltero omnia iura sua in Hibernia reddidi per MM. et D. markas argenti quas idem Walterus pro inde dedit. Quare precipio vobis quod eum et omnes suos sicut fideles meos habeatis et eos manutenetis, protegatis et defendetis, nec eius nec suis mollestiam aut grauamen faciatis vel fieri permittatis, et si quis ei vel suis in aliquo fecerit, id ei sine dilatione facietis. T(este) etc.' Bodleian Library MS Rawlinson B 498, fo. 63r, loose leaf.
82 *Pipe Roll 10 Richard I*, p. 213.
83 BL MS Harley 1240, fo. 27r, no. 26; *Gormanston Register*, p. 178 (excludes dating clause).
84 BL MS Cotton Titus B XI, fo. 72r.
85 'Conmaicne' in Edmund Hogan, *Onomasticon Goedelicum* (Dublin, 1910).
86 Painter, *William Marshal*, pp. 79–80; Crouch, *William Marshal*, p. 70.
87 *Gormanston Register*, pp. 143-4, 191-2. The cantreds were: *Tri Tuatha*, *Magh Lurg-Tirerrill*, Corran, *Sliabh Lugha*, Leyny, Carbury-Drumcliff, Tireragh, Erris and the two cantreds of Tirawley. Those in italics had been granted to Hugh by John in his earlier charter. See above, p. 86.
88 Kenneth Nicholls, 'A charter of William de Burgo', *Annalecta Hibernica*, 27 (1972), pp. 120–2, at p. 121.

89 Smith, *Colonisation and Conquest*, pp. 31-2
90 Mark Hagger, *The Fortunes of a Norman Family: The de Verduns in England Ireland and Wales, 1066-1316* (Dublin, 2001), pp. 34-59, 248.
91 TCD MS 1281, *s.a.* 1196; *AFM*, iii, p. 106n; Richard Butler, *Some Notices of the Castle and of the Ecclesiastical Buildings of Trim* (Trim, 1835), p. 10.
92 *Gormanston Register*, pp. 7, 179. For Limerick see Orpen, *Normans*, ii, pp. 156-8.
93 Orpen, *Normans*, ii, p. 157; Otway-Ruthven, *Medieval Ireland*, p. 73.
94 *Chancellor's Roll 8 Richard I*, p. 92.
95 'Vicecomes habet capere in manu Regis totam terram Walteri de Laci et respondere. Et Gaufridus Cambitor h.r. de exitu eiusdem terre de anno (preterito)', *Miscellaneous Records of the Norman Exchequer, 1199-1204*, ed. S. R. Packard (Northampton, 1927), p. 18.
96 Wightman, *Lacy*, p. 225.
97 Gillingham, *Richard I*, pp. 297-8.
98 J. T. Appleby, *England Without Richard, 1189-1199* (Ithaca, 1965), pp. 197-8; John Lloyd, *History of Wales*, 2 vols (London, 1939), ii, pp. 580-3.
99 Gillingham, *Richard I*, p. 280.
100 *Brut y Tywysogyon or the Chronicle of the Princes, Red Book of Hergest Version*, ed. Thomas Jones (Cardiff, 1955), p. 177, *s.a.* 1196.
101 *Chancellor's Roll 8 Richard I*, pp. xx-xxi.
102 Norgate, *Angevin Kings*, ii, pp. 349-50; Gillingham, *Richard I*, pp. 280-1. I misdate this to 1196 in Veach, 'King and magnate', p. 188.
103 Kate Norgate, *John Lackland* (London, 1902), p. 122.
104 The custodians of Hereford and Bridgenorth castles were also changed, Howden, *Chronica*, iv, p. 35.
105 *Pipe Roll 10 Richard I*, p. 212.
106 *Magni Rotuli Scaccarii Normanniae sub Regibus Angliae*, ed. Thomas Stapleton, 2 vols (London, 1840-44), ii, pp. lxx, 368-9.
107 Ibid., ii, p. 482.
108 TNA E 40/5924.
109 *Pipe Roll 10 Richard I*, p. 213.
110 *Gormanston Register*, pp. 142-3, 190-1.
111 *Pipe Roll 10 Richard I*, p. 213.
112 See for instance: Eyton, *Shropshire*, v, p. 257; Norgate, *John Lackland*, p. 143.
113 Wightman, *Lacy*, p. 224; *Mag. Rot. Normanniae*, pp. lxx, 368-9.
114 J. C. Holt, 'Review: The Lacy family in England and Normandy, 1066-1194. by W. E. Wightman', *The Economic History Review, New Series*, 20/2 (August 1967), pp. 385-86, at p. 385.
115 M. T. Flanagan, 'Lacy, Walter de (d. 1241)', *Oxford Dictionary of National Biography* (Oxford, 2004).
116 *Rotuli de Oblatis et Finibus in Turri Londinensi Asservati*, ed. T. D. Hardy (London, 1835), p. 74.
117 Otway-Ruthven, *Medieval Ireland*, p. 73.
118 See above, p. 84.
119 Hillaby, 'Colonisation, crisis-management and debt', pp. 8-9.

120 Brock Holden, 'The aristocracy of western Herefordshire and the middle march 1166–1246', DPhil (University of Oxford, 2000), pp. 224–5; Holden, *Lords*, p. 171.
121 *Hist. William Marshal*, ii, lines 10325–33.
122 Norgate, *Angevin Kings*, ii, p. 386.

4

Factionalism: 1199–1206

The accession of King John marks a turning point in the history of the Lacy family. In this period, Ireland was brought under the direct lordship of the king of England, and Normandy was lost. The balance of the king's administration and attention (if not his ambition) was shifted westwards, and he sought to exploit his insular realms for resources to retrieve his continental inheritance. John's brother and father had relied upon strong local magnates to drive the Irish royal administration in their absence, but, after fifteen years as lord of Ireland, John was used to enjoying greater personal oversight of his lordship there. His mechanism for control in the western British Isles left a lasting legacy and speaks to the general character of his rule. Magnates were played off against one another, and the predatory aspect of aristocratic lordship meant that such men all but queued up for a chance to do it. The loss of Normandy was felt by the aristocracy as much as the king, and cross-Channel magnates somehow had to make up for their Norman losses elsewhere. The commencement of the great series of royal enrolments allow for a detailed view of these processes, especially royal lordship. Consequently, the mechanics of the relationship between king and magnate are more visible than ever before, and no more so than with the Lacys.

Walter de Lacy began John's reign in a strong position. He had a decade of experience as John's vassal in Ireland to draw upon in his dealings with the new king, and enjoyed a recent history of amicable relations. Walter's marriage to Margery, daughter of the king's familiar William de Briouze, was a manifestation of this good will, and formed an indelible alliance between the two families of Lacy and Briouze. The two families thrived under John's patronage, thanks in large part to their shared ambitions. By the end of this period, the Lacys and Briouzes had ridden the tide of royal favour to attain the crest of power in Ireland and the central Welsh march. It remained to be seen whether they could trust the king whose factionalist policies had helped them there, or he them.

Walter in Normandy: 1199-1200

King Richard died on 6 April 1199, leaving two potential heirs: his nephew, Arthur of Brittany (who was still a minor), and his brother, Count John. This provided scope for dissension and intrigue and ushered in a period of uncertainty throughout the Angevin empire. Consequently, John was forced from the very beginning of his reign to secure Richard's inheritance in the face of an alternative heir and the omnipresent antagonist, King Philip Augustus of France. It is important to appreciate the significance of John's French preoccupations, as they constituted the driving force behind many of his – and his magnates' – actions which might otherwise seem unrelated. Despite Richard's supposed deathbed pronouncement in favour of John, Arthur was recognised as heir to Anjou, Maine and Touraine by their magnates, while John was accepted by the English and Normans. Aquitaine remained in the hands of John's mother, Eleanor, which effectively made it John's as well.[1] John quickly moved against Anjou, and on 14 April captured the castle and treasury at Chinon. He managed to avoid the forces of Arthur and King Philip and proceeded to Rouen, where he was invested as duke of Normandy on 25 April. After a brief retaliatory raid to punish the Angevins for their support of Arthur, John crossed to England, where he was crowned king on 27 May 1199. He wasted little time in calling out the feudal host and sailing for France on 20 June.[2]

Whether Walter de Lacy had been in Normandy or England when Richard died, he was with King John when war broke out that September. Some historians have argued that Walter's sojourn at court resulted from King John's specific suspicions of him.[3] Their recent relationship suggests otherwise, as does the charter evidence, which shows that Walter remained in Normandy while the king journeyed to Anjou and Aquitaine.[4] On 3 September 1199 they were together at Rouen.[5] Three days later, Walter was joined by his brother Hugh in the witness list of a royal grant to William, baron of Naas.[6] John was at this point issuing many new grants in Ireland, which James Lydon has calculated came to total some thirty-six knights' fees and thirty-one carucates of land in the space of about a week.[7]

The following month, King John made a truce with King Philip Augustus to last until the feast of St Hilary (13 January), which was eventually extended until midsummer 1200. John took advantage of this respite to journey to Aquitaine and England.[8] During this period, Walter de Lacy most likely remained in Normandy, concerning himself with his own interests in the duchy. He reappears at court only after John's return to Normandy. On 3 June 1200, Walter was at Caen where he witnessed a royal grant to William de Briouze.[9] The following day, 4 June, Walter witnessed two royal charters at Falaise.[10] It is difficult to ascertain the length of Walter's stay at court from this bare evidence, and it is not unlikely that he was in unattested attendance before 3 June. However, Walter seems not to have remained long after 4 June. King John rode to Argentan the next day, before leaving Normandy altogether.[11]

On 22 May 1200, King John accepted the Treaty of Le Goulet, in which he ceded the Norman Vexin, the Auvergne, the greater part of the county of Évreux, and the lordships of Issoudun, Graçay, and Bourges to the king of France in return for King Philip's recognition of him as heir to all of Richard's lands. John thereupon paraded his military might throughout Aquitaine as part of a larger effort to consolidate and govern the whole of his vast inheritance.[12] John also moved to reorganise the Welsh march and Ireland, which had a direct impact upon Walter. The first step had been taken that April, when King John made Henry de Bohun earl of Hereford, granting him £20 a year and the third penny of Herefordshire.[13] Historically, the Lacys' relationship with the earls of Hereford had been ambivalent at best, the latter having procured a grant of the Lacys' English honor and actively pursued the destruction of Walter's grandfather, Gilbert de Lacy, during the turbulent days of King Stephen's reign.[14] The resurrection of the comital title would have placed a block on Walter's influence in the English west midlands and the central march of Wales.

While Walter's influence was being curtailed, that of his fellow marcher baron William de Briouze was augmented. William was a beneficiary of the break-up of the earldom of Hereford, which had been parcelled out among heiresses when the male line failed in 1165. His mother was a daughter of Miles of Gloucester, earl of Hereford, and, when her brother William (her father's last surviving son) died without issue, she inherited a strong position in the southern march. She then passed the lordships of Radnor, Brecon and Abergavenny to her son William, who also held Bramber in Sussex and Barnstable and Totnes in Devon from his father's inheritance.[15] The charter that Walter witnessed on 3 June 1200 at Caen extended William's authority, granting him all the lands which he could acquire in Wales around his lordship of Radnor.[16] King John may have had good reason to favour William with such a licence to conquer, as, by the reckoning of some, William and his fellow familiars at Richard's deathbed had facilitated his succession. Roger of Howden claims that, as King Richard lay dying, he named John as his heir.[17] The somewhat obscure and rather late source, the annals of Margam, an abbey in the Welsh march, which some historians have argued were well placed to gather news of events relating to the barons of the southern march (and, according to Powicke's suggestion,[18] may have even had William de Briouze or his wife as a source) claim that those attending Richard – especially Briouze – effectively gave John the inheritance: '[John] was crowned despite the judgement against him [in Richard's court] at the fervent insistence of William de Briouze and his other supporters.'[19] This meant either that William and his associates convinced Richard to declare John his heir or that Richard made no such declaration and the group of men merely claimed that he had.[20] Either way, King John showed his gratitude by advancing those whom he regarded as having helped him to the throne.

Another baron of the Welsh march, William Marshal, was also integral to securing Richard's inheritance for John, and reaped very generous rewards in the early years of the new reign. When King Richard died, William and the archbishop of Canterbury, Hubert Walter, were in possession of the tower of Rouen, home of the ducal treasury. The Marshal's biography recounts a scene in which, upon hearing of Richard's death, William stood unequivocally on the side of John in a midnight debate with the archbishop of Canterbury over the succession.[21] For his efforts, John made the Marshal earl of Striguil.[22] The new earl also received the promise of the restoration of Pembroke, which came at some point between October 1200 and May 1201. The shrievalty of Gloucestershire was once again granted to him, along with custody of Gloucester and Bristol castles. The rewards kept coming so that by the end of 1201, in the opinion of one modern biographer, he was 'raised by his lord to be the most powerful magnate in the southern Marches of Wales'.[23] The position of William de Briouze leaves this statement open to debate, but the point remains that two influential barons of the Welsh march reportedly helped John to power, and were richly rewarded through to the summer of 1200.

On 24 September 1200, William de Briouze's son Giles de Briouze was consecrated as bishop of Hereford. This gained the Briouze family a block of fees along the Welsh border, including Bishop's Castle (Shropshire),[24] approximately 17 miles north-west of the Lacy castle of Ludlow. As a result of John's grants, Walter's English honor was hemmed in by powerful men, as the southern Briouze and Marshal lordships joined the resurrected earldom of Hereford and the earldom of Chester to form a protective shield against Welsh incursions. Walter was in danger of seeing his sphere of influence constricted, but he soon made the best of the situation. On 19 November 1200, King John confirmed Walter de Lacy's marriage to Margery, daughter of William de Briouze.[25] The marriage had much to recommend it in terms of the Welsh border. The Lacys' English honor shared a number of tenants with the Briouze lordship of Brecon, including the powerful knightly families of Baskerville, d'Évreux, Fourches, Muscegros and Pichard.[26] It is clear what William hoped to get from the marriage. In the marriage settlement, it was stipulated that Walter should not alienate any of his English or Norman lands without William's consent. Briouze went so far as to proffer 20 marks and a palfrey for King John's confirmation of Walter's charter to that effect.[27] Their alliance secure, Walter and his father-in-law remained at court for the time being, following John to Lincoln, where they witnessed King William of Scotland's homage to King John.[28] The pair likely remained with King John over Christmas, because after an extended period of negotiation, John granted William de Briouze the honor of Limerick in Ireland (i.e. that part of Thomond no longer in Irish hands) on 12 January 1201, excepting the service of William de Burgh, the city of Limerick, the gift of bishoprics and abbeys 'and anything that pertains to the Crown', the Ostmen's cantred, the Holy Island and 'the Irish and those that are with them'.[29] The grant was a renewal of Henry II's unrealised grant to William's uncle Philip de Briouze in 1177, but the timing of the grant suggests that it may have been predicated upon the Lacy/Briouze marriage alliance. Just as members of the ninth-century Carolingian *Reichsaristocratie* had relied upon extended family networks to maintain connections in far-flung (and sometimes politically fragmented) corners of the empire,[30] so these two Anglo-Norman aristocrats formed a marriage alliance that strengthened their positions in four realms of the Plantagenet empire. Once he had his Irish grant, William immediately crossed to Ireland to establish his personal lordship there.[31]

Balancing powers: Wales and Ireland: 1200–1

An under-appreciated chronicler of this period, the Anonymous of Béthune, author of the *Histoire des ducs de Normandie et des rois d'Angleterre*, had a close connection to the Briouzes. He was attached to the family of Béthune, with Baldwin de Béthune, count of Aumale, serving as a hero of the text.[32] Importantly, Baldwin was the nephew of William de Briouze's wife, Matilda de St Valery, to whom the *Histoire* pays specific attention. Before boasting of the strength of Matilda's lordship (which included her dominant personality and impressive dairy herds),[33] the *Histoire* describes King John's rule by saying: 'he always wanted his barons at odds with each other and was never happier than when he saw enmity among them'.[34] A more sympathetic commentator might characterise this as a propensity to 'counterbalance' his barons against one another, but it was a recurrent theme in King John's reign. The grant of Limerick should be viewed in this light. From late 1200 to early 1201, King John used the two families of Burgh and Briouze as blocks against each other in their respective strongholds, with Walter de Lacy the balancing point of the equation.

As mentioned above, from 1185 John had promoted William de Burgh to a position of great authority and influence in Thomond. Burgh had done much to consolidate that power through his diplomatic ties to the native Irish of the region, the Uí Briain kings of Thomond in particular. Similarly, William de Briouze was now being elevated in the march of Wales, and his own pragmatic diplomacy secured his position.[35] Although William de Burgh's territories were excepted from the grant of Limerick, the revival of Henry II's unrealised endowment intruded a royal favourite into the politics of Munster with the territorial prestige, if not the regional familiarity, to match Burgh. John explicitly stated that Briouze was to hold the honor of Limerick as freely as the other chief barons ('*capitales barones*') of Ireland.[36] Although John's reservation of the royal prerogatives in Limerick meant that the statement was not necessarily true, it was all the more important for its fallacy.[37] It clearly signalled John's desire to grant William de Briouze the social and political esteem enjoyed by the greatest magnates of Ireland, without reverting to the 'bad old days' of Henry II and Richard I, when security had made baronial dominance a necessary evil for the Crown to allow. The example of the elder Hugh de Lacy could not have been far from John's mind, considering how much he suffered from it. However, by inserting William de Briouze between himself and the barons of northern Munster, John forfeited his direct connection with many of his own grantees in the region. All those whose lands were subsumed by the honor of Limerick were no longer tenants-in-chief, being instead downgraded to Briouze's sub-tenants. At a stroke, King John had upset the socio-political nexus of the region that William de Burgh had manipulated to his advantage.

Meanwhile, William de Briouze's removal as sheriff of Herefordshire that autumn had seen him replaced by William de Burgh's younger brother, John's chamberlain, Hubert. Hubert de Burgh also received custody of the Three Castles of Grosmont (Monmouthshire), Skenfrith

(Monmouthshire) and Llantilio (Whitecastle, Monmouthshire), which divided the Briouze lordship of Abergavenny from the Lacy lordship of Ewyas Lacy.[38] The shrievalty of Herefordshire allowed Hubert to monitor the already constrained Lacy holdings in the county, as well as Giles de Briouze's see of Hereford. King John further limited Walter de Lacy's influence by confiscating Ludlow castle once more. The fact that Hubert de Burgh's appointment to William de Briouze's old office came just a month before John's confirmation of the Briouze/Lacy marriage contract suggests that there was more to the administrative reshuffle than a simple rotation of royal officials.

After the grant of Limerick, Walter de Lacy drops out of view for an extended period. Roger of Howden places him in Ireland in 1201, which perhaps means that he journeyed there with his father-in-law. In May 1201, King John mounted an expedition to France in order to quell the revolt of the Lusignans.[39] The absence of both William de Briouze and Walter de Lacy from the Welsh march required new arrangements for its defence in John's absence. According to Roger of Howden, Hubert de Burgh was made warden of the march and given one hundred knights to aid him.[40] What is more, Walter's brother-in-law, William fitz Alan,[41] was removed from his position as sheriff of Shropshire. William returned to royal service in the shire the following year,[42] but his removal, alongside Ludlow's confiscation and Hubert de Burgh's promotion, effected a further power shift in the march.

Sidney Painter ties Hubert's detachment of knights and William fitz Alan's removal to the activities of the famous rebel Fulk fitz Warin. The thirteenth-century romance 'Fouke le Fitz Waryn' claims that one hundred knights were sent after Fulk, which Painter argues is as plausible as Howden's explanation for them. Painter points out that a good proportion of Fulk fitz Warin's friends were tenants of William fitz Alan in Shropshire, making it possible that William's removal was connected with Fulk's rebellion.[43] However, the romance is hardly a reliable source for specific facts. For instance, it substitutes 'Walter' de Lacy for his grandfather Gilbert in the latter's dispute with Fulk's grandfather, Joce de Dinan (d. 1166) over Ludlow Castle.[44] Its author was plainly aware of some relevant detail, correctly describing Walter's coat of arms,[45] but none the less also succumbs to flights of fancy. For instance, it has 'Walter' de Lacy receiving aid from his Irish estates when fighting Joce de Dinan, a man who died three years before the English invasion of Ireland. Fulk fitz Warin's threat to the region should not be discounted, but neither should a colourful narrative overinflate his importance and be preferred to Howden's testimony. The march of Wales was a dangerous place populated by dangerous men. Its security had been, and would remain, of paramount importance to departing kings of England.

Ireland: 1199-1201

By the middle of 1201, Walter de Lacy had been absent from Ireland for at least two years. During that time, Connacht gradually emerged as the battleground between the resident elites for pre-eminence in Ireland, with a protracted succession dispute providing the backdrop. The first rumblings reached the borders of Meath in 1199. In that year, Cathal Crobderg Ua Conchobair burned Meiler fitz Henry's castle of Ardnurcher in Meath.[46] This was the first act of aggression to come from Connacht since the 1195 Athlone meeting, and occurred while both Walter and his brother Hugh were in France.[47] The following year (1200) Cathal Crobderg mounted another hosting (a native Irish military expedition) into western Meath, accompanied by the erstwhile Meath baron, Gilbert de Angulo, which met with mixed success.[48] He then turned on his rival for the kingship of Connacht, his nephew Cathal Carrach (with whom he had agreed a peace), but was initially defeated. At about this time, Cathal Carrach met with the Irish justiciar Meiler fitz Henry at Clonmacnoise.[49] Cathal Carrach then enlisted the help of William de Burgh, who brought forces from Dublin and Leinster (suggesting the justiciar's support) in addition to his own from Munster and helped to drive Cathal Crobderg from Connacht, giving Cathal Carrach the kingship.[50]

The fragmented political geography of Ireland provided tremendous scope for intrigue for the English king and his administrators, but also for the local elites, upon whom much of the real power in Ireland was devolved. Consequently, Irish succession disputes were political minefields, dangerous for all involved. The Lacys were pulled into (and sought to profit from) the Connacht dispute, alongside Walter's sometime ally John de Courcy, lord of Ulster. The intervention of the lords of Meath and Ulster ultimately led to a reversal of royal policy towards support for Cathal Crobderg.[51] Having been expelled from Connacht, Cathal Crobderg travelled to Ulster, where he eventually enlisted the support of John de Courcy and Walter's brother, Hugh de Lacy. Hugh gathered a force from Meath and with Cathal Crobderg and John de Courcy mounted an unsuccessful expedition to Connacht, where they were defeated by Cathal Carrach near Kilmacduah (Co. Galway).[52] Following an entry in the annals of Loch Cé, it has generally been held that 'as soon as the

Foreigners arrived in Mide they arrested Cathal Crobderg as a pledge for the payment of wages; and John was taken to Ath Cliath [Dublin] until he gave pledges from himself that he would obey the king of the Saxons'.[53] However, Orpen observes that the original passage in the annals of Loch Cé read that *Cathal Crobderg* was taken to Dublin until he gave pledges to obey the English king, the name of *Eoain* (John) having been interlined at a later date. Orpen takes the original statement to be the more likely as Cathal Crobderg was from this point the favoured candidate of the English Crown.[54] This interpretation is consonant with Roger of Howden's testimony. Howden is especially well informed about John de Courcy in this period, and may have had his information from sources close to Courcy himself.[55] Under 1201, Howden relates:

> In the same year, Walter de Lacy, a powerful man in Ireland, had a meeting with John de Courcy, lord of Ulster, and treacherously attempting to seize him, killed many of his people. Once John had fled, Hugh de Lacy, Walter's brother, said to him: 'My lord, come with me, and I will receive you in my castle, for which I am your man, until your troops have assembled, so that you may take vengeance on those who have always held you in hatred.' John therefore believed him, and entered his castle under safe conduct from Hugh. But when he wished to depart, Hugh would not let him depart; indeed, he had taken him for the purpose of delivering him up to the king of England, who had long wished to take him. However, John's men did not cease night and day to ravage with fire, sword, and famine the lands of Walter and Hugh de Lacy, until they had delivered their lord, John de Courcy, from Hugh de Lacy's custody.[56]

Howden died in 1201 or 1202, so this account cannot have been influenced by the later conflict between the Lacy brothers and John de Courcy, or by King John's treatment of Ulster (discussed below). The annals of Clonmacnoise, which have a particular concern for events in Meath, state that Cathal Crobderg was himself taken to Hugh's castle of Nobber.[57] Consequently, it appears that the Lacys captured both Cathal Crobderg and John de Courcy for transport to Dublin. John de Courcy's followers were able to save him for the time being, but, in the wake of defeat, Cathal Crobderg garnered no such support. The Lacys duly packed him off from Nobber to Dublin to be dealt with by the royal government.

The factional breakdown of English intrusion into the Connacht succession dispute – William de Burgh and the Irish justiciar supporting Cathal Carrach versus Hugh de Lacy and John de Courcy supporting

Cathal Crobderg – is especially interesting given King John's attempts to counterbalance the Burghs and the Briouzes/Lacys. In the wake of their defeat in Connacht, the Lacys' capture of John de Courcy and Cathal Crobderg shows their willingness to intrigue with King John, and their anticipation of royal favour in return. As it happened, once Cathal Crobderg was released from captivity, he immediately went to William de Burgh for aid against Cathal Carrach in Connacht.[58] William de Burgh was clearly an instrument of royal policy, as is clear from a letter sent by King John to the barons of Meath on 2 November 1201. It instructed them to have faith in what the Irish justiciar Meiler fitz Henry, William de Burgh and Geoffrey de Costentin should tell them.[59] The king had granted Geoffrey two cantreds in Connacht earlier that year, so Otway-Ruthven is likely correct that the letter had to do with Connacht 'for any attack on which Meath was of course a natural base'.[60]

It is interesting to note that King John bypassed Walter de Lacy by communicating directly with the barons of Meath. That same year, John intruded into Walter's judicial lordship when one Aubrey of Curtun claimed that he had been unjustly disseised of a knight's fee within Meath by Walter's father, Hugh. John accepted Aubrey's fine, and ordered the suit to be brought at the first county court of Dublin 'if the state of the land of Ireland allows this to be done without danger', and to put Aubrey in possession of the lands if it could be shown that Hugh had unjustly disseised him.[61] This was a new development in the English king's position regarding the lordship of Meath. When Hugh de Lacy was granted Meath in 1172, he was given absolute control of its judicial process. These powers were confirmed by King Richard in 1194, and John, as lord of Ireland, in 1195.[62] However, as will be seen over the course of the next two chapters, from the beginning of his reign in England, King John went to great lengths to erode the liberties enjoyed by the great Irish lordships. In 1204, three years after the royal court heard Aubrey of Curtun's case, Robert fitz Jordan brought another suit for land in Walter de Lacy's manor of Ardmulchan (bar. Skreen, Co. Meath).[63] In the event, Walter won this second suit, and Robert's widow, Christiana, raised the matter again in 1225 – just after the Crown pleas were decisively taken from the Lacys in Meath.[64] By the early thirteenth century, the settler community of Meath was coalescing into a coherent political force in its own right, and the king was keen to emphasise his direct connection to Walter's tenants as lord of Ireland.

While the Lacys aligned themselves against William de Burgh (and perhaps Meiler fitz Henry) in Connacht and captured John de Courcy in

Meath, the colonists fought against each other in Limerick. Under 1201, the Munster annals of Inisfallen record 'great warfare between Philip of Worcester and the son of William de Briouze (*Mac Uilliam Hebreus*) and other foreigners, the greater part of Mag Feimin being devastated'.[65] This is the same Philip of Worcester who had so often acted on the John's behalf in Ireland, and whose land formed part of the honor of Limerick.[66] Roger of Howden reports that, upon hearing of King John's grant of Limerick to William de Briouze, Philip escaped with difficulty from the king's court, made his way to Ireland via Scotland, and set about recovering his lands by force. This was small wonder. In addition to losing his privileged status as tenant in-chief, the loyal administrator had to proffer a fine and perform homage to William de Briouze to retain his lands.[67] For his part, the Irish justiciar, Meiler fitz Henry refused to help William combat Philip's attacks. Perhaps, being one of the first adventurers to Ireland and the hero of the original assault to take Limerick city in 1175,[68] Meiler also resented the introduction of a powerful newcomer to the area. On 22 December 1201, Meiler was warned that he would be recalled if he did not perform his duties touching William de Briouze in Ireland.[69] Four months later, in April 1202, King John had to send a series of mandates ordering the restoration of William's castles and rights in Limerick. These included one to Philip of Worcester, and another enjoining William's tenants to aid Meiler fitz Henry in carrying out the king's instructions regarding Limerick.[70] In a fragmented society with devolved power structures such as Ireland, local opposition could be difficult to overcome. This perhaps shows why the grant of Limerick was made only after William's alliance with Walter de Lacy. He may have been a terror in the Welsh marches, but William was a greenhorn in Ireland.

Division of Labour: 1202-4

The resumption of war in France soon saved William de Briouze. In July 1202, William joined the king in Normandy, where he was given the sensitive role of gaoler to the king's nephew and rival, Arthur of Brittany.[71] The signs of royal favour soon materialised. William was given custody of the land of William de Beauchamp, lord of Elmley castle in Worcestershire, worth over £300 a year, as well as the Welsh marcher lordships of Glamorgan and Gower.[72] He was also forgiven his outstanding debts to Kings Henry II and Richard.[73] More importantly for the present discussion, William was granted custody of Walter de Lacy's Norman lands, for which he was answerable to the king.[74] These would appear to have been the two fees in the honor of Pont Audemer, held in chief since the fall of Count Robert of Meulan in 1195.[75] Walter's brother Hugh held the honor of Le Pin-au-Haras (which was given to William the following year), and his brother Gilbert held the honor of Lassy (which was taken from him by King Philip Augustus in 1204).[76] Wightman presumed the grant of Walter's lands to be a sign of royal displeasure,[77] but this seems at odds with the relationship between Walter and King John to this point. An examination of the grant's context reveals it to be both part of King John's defensive organization of Normandy and a pragmatic arrangement for the administration of the transnational holdings of Lacy and Briouze.

In 1202, the situation in Normandy was dismal. Not only was the king of France on the offensive, but the Norman barons were grumbling about John's military regime.[78] Consequently, trust was in short supply. The presence of his trusted favourite, William de Briouze, would have been most welcome to the embattled king. Foreshadowing the situation in later medieval Ireland, cross-Channel landholding meant that many of the duchy's barons were absentee landlords who left their territories underguarded. Consequently, Walter de Lacy was absent from Normandy during this most desperate period. In his absence, King John sought to secure Walter's lands and to divert their proceeds to his war effort. In January 1203, Count Robert of Sées betrayed John, handing over Alençon (Orne) to Philip. King John promptly confiscated the lands of the count and his men, and enlisted William de Briouze's support in distributing them among his supporters.[79] Shortly thereafter, on 6 February 1203, John granted William custody of Hugh de Lacy's honor of Le Pin-au-Haras, which lay approximately 27 miles north of Alençon and only 6½ miles north of the Briouze lands at Lisieux (Calvados).[80] With the Lacys busy in Ireland, John hoped to secure the region under his trusted favourite.

This does not mean that the Lacys were forcibly disseised. William de Briouze's custody of the Lacys' lands was also part of a fascinating arrangement whereby the Lacy and Briouze families sought to exploit their far-flung possessions. This involved each acting as steward for the other while they were on opposite sides of the Irish Sea. This was by no means unprecedented in transnational history. For instance, David Crouch has pointed out how the twin brothers Waleran of Meulan and Robert of Leicester divided their interests at the English Channel during the troubled period 1139 to 1153, Robert supervising Waleran's interests in England, while Waleran attempted with less success to salvage his brother's position in Normandy.[81] Waleran even looked after the recently acquired English interests of his uncle, Ralph, count of Vermandois, who was much more at home in the northern French milieu.[82]

Since Briouze was a magnate of some importance in Normandy, while the Lacys were mere sub-tenants there, there were pragmatic reasons for the division of responsibility. Consequently, while William held the Lacys' Norman honors, Walter oversaw the Briouze honor of Limerick in Ireland. William was also employed to manage Walter's English (and perhaps Welsh) territories. The pipe roll for 1202/3 records that William de Briouze had custody of Walter's English territories.[83] It is not clear whether this was William or his son of the same name, to whom at least a portion of the Briouze inheritance may have been demised by this point.[84] What had heretofore been implicit in Walter de Lacy's pledge to refrain from alienating any of his English or Norman lands in 1200 was therefore made manifest by the Briouzes' personal oversight of those territories. His English and Norman lands looked after, Walter de Lacy defended William's honor of Limerick.

In 1203, the Irish annals report a hosting by William de Burgh 'accompanied by the Foreigners of Munster and Meath' into Connacht.[85] The expedition's aim was the removal of Cathal Crobderg Ua Conchobair and the realisation of William's claim to Connacht.[86] As discussed above, William de Burgh had only recently been employed to install Cathal Crobderg in Connacht, and his offensive prompted the Irish justiciar to complain to King John. On 7 July 1203, William de Burgh was called to answer the charges laid against him, and the following day his stronghold on the river Shannon, the city of Limerick, was granted to William de Briouze during pleasure.[87] Walter de Lacy joined the Irish justiciar, Meiler fitz Henry, in his march to receive William de Burgh's submission and possession of the city.[88] The annals of Clonmacnoise report that Meiler was also joined by Cathal Crobderg.[89] This would explain the testimony of the annals of Loch Cé that, when William de Burgh and his men ultimately deserted the city, its castle was razed by the Connachtmen.[90] The annals also report that Cathal Crobderg banished his nephew, Toirdelbach Ua Conchobair, into Meath. Toirdelbach was a son of the former high king Ruaidrí Ua Conchobair, and therefore an uncle of Walter's half-Irish brother, William 'Gorm' de Lacy. Consequently, William de Burgh's expulsion became the setting for a general regularisation of relations in the area. Walter and Meiler fitz Henry helped to negotiate a peace between Cathal Crobderg and Toirdelbach Ua Conchobair,[91] and Meiler received the submissions of Cathal Crobderg for Connacht, and Muirchertach Ua Briain for Thomond.[92] William de Burgh delivered hostages to Meiler and left Ireland for the royal court in Normandy, after which Meiler departed to assert English royal lordship in the north of Ireland.[93] Just as William de Briouze would have benefited from the English and Norman components of the Lacy inheritance, holding both Meath and Limerick gave Walter a territorial advantage with which he could better secure and promote his family's interests in Ireland. Walter had learned his lesson in the 1190s, when focusing on Ireland caused him to neglect his Norman obligations. With Normandy once again the focus of royal attention, Walter de Lacy and William de Briouze sought to overcome the difficulties of far-flung inheritances by sharing the burden of lordship. In times of strife, intensive lordship was best confined to as few realms as possible.

Royal agent: Munster and Connacht: 1204

Walter may or may not have had a role in the removal of William de Burgh from Limerick in 1203, but he was clearly an instrument of royal policy from February 1204. His first assignment was vital to the king's continental interests. At the beginning of 1204, the situation in Normandy was dire. King John had fled the duchy in December 1203, at which point Norman resistance to King Philip Augustus all but collapsed.[94] This was the beginning of Holt's 'ten furious years', which saw King John devote tremendous effort to recovering his continental inheritance.[95] Consequently, a commission comprising Walter de Lacy, Geoffrey Luterel, the archdeacon of Stafford (Henry le Blund) and William le Petit was charged with levying an aid on both the clergy and laity of Ireland in support of the war in Normandy.[96] The group was also to advise the Irish justiciar on imposing fines on escheats.[97] The imposition of financial burdens in aid of a distant war was never going to be a popular proposition, and it made sense to enlist the support of powerful local lords for its enactment. None was more prominent than the lord of Meath, especially since William de Burgh, William Marshal and William de Briouze were all absent, and John de Courcy was under assault (from Walter's brother) in Ulster. Walter's constable of Meath, William le Petit, was also a natural choice. Geoffrey Luterel was one of the king's men, who, being a stranger to Ireland, required royal funding for his maintenance.[98] Henry le Blund, archdeacon of Stafford, is better known to historians as Henry of London, the future archbishop of Dublin.[99]

From about the middle of March, John's intentions regarding Connacht become clearer. Having granted away Connacht to William de Burgh in the early years of his rule as lord of Ireland, King John now manoeuvred to secure the best part of the Irish kingdom for himself. First, Walter de Lacy was ordered to counsel the Irish justiciar and archdeacon of Stafford on their embassy to Cathal Crobderg, king of Connacht, where discussions over a partitioning of the kingdom must have taken place.[100] Then, on 26 March 1204, Walter and his fellow committee members were called upon to judge the dispute between the Irish justiciar and William de Burgh that had caused Burgh's removal from Limerick the previous year.[101] The only problem was that William de Burgh was needed for the king's proposed war in Normandy. King John granted him respite on 29 April 1204, and ordered all of his lands save Connacht and those given to William de Briouze to be returned to him. If an indignant Meiler fitz Henry refused to comply, then Walter and his associates were to enforce the king's will.[102] That Connacht was not included in the restoration, despite being the point of contention between Burgh and the Irish justiciar, is hardly surprising. The earlier mission to Cathal Crobderg had been a resounding success. The king of Connacht agreed to hold one-third of Connacht as King John's vassal at a yearly rent of 100 marks, and to surrender the remaining two-thirds into the hands of the English king. On 31 August 1204, Meiler was ordered to choose the best two-thirds of Connacht for the king and to set matters in order there.[103] Walter and his associates were reorganising the political map of Ireland in the king's name, and a repeat of the king's order to restore William de Burgh's lands on 16 September suggests that they were not in a hurry to implement his will if it did not match their own.[104]

The order of 16 September arose from William de Burgh's return to Ireland to answer the charges against him. Finally, the Irish justiciar's appeals were able to proceed, and the king's mandate makes it clear that a judgement incurring peril to life or limb was a real possibility. No record of the trial's outcome survives, but there are a few clues. In a charter issued between 16 September 1204 and 23 March 1205, William de Burgh granted William le Petit (one of the justices involved in deciding his case) lands in Connacht and Thomond, as well as those lands in Meath that Walter de Lacy had granted the Burgh brothers in the 1190s.[105] The witness list of the charter is also interesting. Among the lay magnates were Walter, Hugh and Robert de Lacy, John Marshal (William Marshal's nephew and steward of Leinster) and several other barons of Meath. It would have been odd for William le Petit to have accepted (or even been offered) the grant if judgement, which included the right to Connacht, had been made against William de Burgh. If, on the other hand, the case was still open, then this was a highly visible bribe of one of the judges, one witnessed by another. Indeed, as King John agreed in principle to terms that allowed Cathal Crobderg to retain a third of the province in August 1204, this seeming recognition of William de Burgh's right to Connacht by one of King John's representatives is puzzling. Perhaps then, judgement had been made in favour of William de Burgh (at least in the minds of the magnates involved).

Meanwhile, on 2 November 1204, the king stated that he had been informed that he could not rule or maintain peace in his lands of Connacht and Cork without the city of Limerick, custody of which he had committed to William de Briouze during pleasure. Meiler fitz Henry was no doubt the king's informant in this regard, and the order for Walter de Lacy to hand the city over to Meiler should be seen in light of the trial of William de Burgh.[106] Custody was re-granted to William de Briouze on 23 August 1205,[107] after William de Burgh's grants to William le Petit.

Lacy v. Courcy 1201-5

While Walter was busy in Munster, his brother Hugh once again attacked John de Courcy, lord of Ulster. As seen above, John de Courcy had perhaps fallen foul of King John as early as 1201, when the Lacy brothers attempted to deliver him to Dublin after their abortive Connacht expedition.[108] In July 1202, John de Courcy was given safe conduct to the king's court, which proves that he was not at peace with the king by this point.[109] If he made the trip, it was unsuccessful in securing peace for, in what seems to have been a sanctioned (if not royally sponsored) enterprise the following year (1203), Hugh de Lacy marched against Courcy and defeated him at his lordship's capital, Downpatrick (Co. Down).[110] King John issued another safe-conduct to and from his court to John de Courcy that September (the same month in which William de Burgh first joined the king in Normandy), which shows that John de Courcy was still outside the king's peace, and gives credence to the theory of King John's complicity in Hugh de Lacy's attacks.[111] The following year the king gave Walter a role in the destruction of John de Courcy. Taking advantage of the delay in proceedings against William de Burgh, King John entrusted his successful partnering from Munster, Walter de Lacy and Meiler fitz Henry, with the task of pursuing legal proceedings against John de Courcy. On 31 August 1204, the same day that he ordered Meiler to make preparations for accepting Cathal Crobderg's submission of Connacht, King John ordered Walter and Meiler to summon John de Courcy to the king's service. They were also to make conditions for his attendance (by the council of the barons of

Ireland), to cause judgement to be taken in the king's court should he fail to meet those conditions, and to effect his forfeiture if that were the judgement of the court. Perhaps influencing Walter's decision was the further stipulation that, in the event of John de Courcy's forfeiture, the eight cantreds of the lordship of Ulster closest to Meath should go to Walter and Hugh.[112] Normandy had been lost to the French king by this point, and this clause has the appearance of compensation for the Lacys' lost territories there. The very next day (1 September), King John further rewarded Hugh de Lacy with a fee in Ireland worth 60 marks a year.[113]

John de Courcy was by this point in dire straits. He had the previous year (1203) handed over hostages for his good behaviour, who would be risked if he did not co-operate. Included among the hostages were a number of his vassals and their sons, which gave a certain menace to King John's letter to the barons of Ulster, dispatched at the day after Walter's commission, 1 September, ordering them to cause their lord to come to the king's service, lest the king proceed against their hostages and their lands ('*ad obsides vestros et ad feoda vestra nos capiemus*').[114] Rumours alleging King John's involvement in the murder of his own nephew, Arthur of Brittany, around 3 April 1203 would have been firmly set in the minds of those whose children he had just threatened.[115] Nevertheless, John de Courcy remained defiant.

Hugh de Lacy once again marched against Ulster, and this time took Courcy prisoner.[116] The annals of Loch Cé claim that he was released after having taken vows to go to Jerusalem, but if this is true then he reneged on his promise and instead made his way to Tír Eógain, though the Manx chronicle claims that he fled to his brother-in-law on the Isle of Man.[117] Another safe-conduct was issued on 21 October 1204, to no avail.[118] The situation is confused, but John de Courcy seems thereafter to have made two unsuccessful attempts to recover his lordship by force, one coming from Tír Eógain, and the other from Man and the Isles. Their exact chronology is unclear, and the entries may in fact be records of a single co-ordinated assault seen from two different perspectives. In both instances John de Courcy's ambitions were thwarted by Walter de Lacy at the head of a force from Meath.[119] Katharine Simms has made a convincing argument that Áed Méith Ua Néill, king of Tír Eógain was a vassal of the lord of Ulster, which would certainly explain the fact that he was willing to support John de Courcy in 1204 and his successor, Hugh de Lacy, in later years.[120] However, it was the involvement of King Rǫgnvaldr of Man and the Isles that caused King John more concern. The Manx king held a highly strategic position within the Irish Sea, and his fleet was a valuable asset to his allies. The fleet that King Rǫgnvaldr brought to Courcy's aid in 1205 was said to have comprised one hundred ships, which may have contained four to five thousand warriors.[121] Although Walter de Lacy was able to overcome the force, the English king could not afford to leave such a dangerous weapon in the hands of his enemies.

King John first moved to break up another alliance that Rǫgnvaldr had been negotiating with one of his Irish Sea neighbours, Llywelyn ab Iorwerth, prince of Gwynedd. Llywelyn had, since the death of his uncle Rhodri ab Owain in 1199, been in negotiations with the pope over his proposed marriage to Rhodri's widow, Rǫgnvaldr's daughter. Before that marriage could take place, however, King John offered his own eldest child and illegitimate daughter, Joan, to Llywelyn – an offer that could not be refused.[122] The marriage proposal was made during the summer of 1204, that is, at the precise time that King John orchestrated John de Courcy's downfall.[123] Having prevented one seaborne alliance, the English king moved to break up another. On 8 February, King John took King Rǫgnvaldr under his protection.[124] This act detached the Manx king from John de Courcy, and ensured that the Lacy brothers would not further destabilise the region by mounting any retaliatory actions against Man and the Isles. Rǫgnvaldr was from this point courted by King John, and became a more or less loyal vassal of the king of England.[125]

Meanwhile, the final clause of King John's 21 August mandate was carried out on 13 November, when Walter and Hugh de Lacy were granted eight cantreds of John de Courcy's forfeited lordship of Ulster.[126] That same day, Hugh de Lacy was further rewarded with the grant of six cantreds of Connacht (a fifth of the province) as had been agreed when the king was count of Mortain.[127] On 5 May 1205, the situation was amended, with Hugh de Lacy receiving a grant of the entire lordship of Ulster,[128] and on 29 May he was belted as earl.[129] Hugh's elevation to comital status has caused confusion amongst historians of medieval Britain and Ireland, especially since it elevated Hugh above (and may have come as an affront to) the other great lords of Ireland, including the king's favourite, William de Briouze, and Hugh's elder brother, Walter de Lacy. Sidney Painter found the move so incomprehensible that he wrote: 'perhaps the king could not resist the temptation to annoy every one to some extent.'[130] While King John's capacity to antagonise his barons is legendary, David Crouch has offered a more pragmatic explanation of Hugh's promotion.[131] In an article on earls in Wales and Ireland, Crouch rebuts the notion that Hugh's earldom was a nod to Ulster's relative independence under John de Courcy, and places the earldom of Ulster in its broader context. Hugh was not the first English earl in Ireland. That honour belonged to Strongbow, lord of Leinster and earl of Striguil. After his death, the restoration of Pembroke to his inheritance meant that his heir, William Marshal, controlled the southern Irish Sea littoral. To be an earl was to hold a privileged social place among the aristocracy, and earls were obvious focal points of regional polities. Crouch suggests that it was John's desire to counterbalance the Lacys against William Marshal's potential dominance in the region that prompted Hugh's elevation as earl of Ulster.

There is much to recommend Crouch's argument. Hugh's belting on 25 May occurred as relations between William Marshal and King John were at their nadir. John had granted William leave to come to terms with King Philip Augustus in order to save the Marshal territories in Normandy. However, William swore 'liege homage on this side of the sea' to the French King, dividing his allegiance at the English Channel and denying John his continental service. William flatly refused to fight to reclaim John's lost continental inheritance just days after Hugh's belting.[132] What is more there is plenty of evidence that John's purpose of dividing and ruling was fulfilled in later events. The subsequent rebellions of Hugh de Lacy (1223-24) and Richard Marshal (1233-34) were to pit the Lacys against the Marshals, and, by harnessing baronial competition to put down the rebellions, showed how such royally supported factionalism might work for the king's benefit.[133] In the short run, however, no such competition was immediately apparent. It is true that the Irish barons looked to the Lacys rather than William Marshal for their leadership in the Irish crisis of 1207, but they fought for the same cause.[134]

If, as seems quite likely, King John elevated a Lacy to counterbalance William Marshal in Leinster, why was Hugh de Lacy chosen? Walter was the one who could mobilise the resources necessary to compete with Leinster, which resources were instrumental in securing John de Courcy's defeat. According to Howden, it had been Walter who had captured John de Courcy in 1201. Hugh was the victor at Downpatrick in 1203 and captured John de Courcy in 1204, but this was done with an army drawn from Meath. Once Courcy escaped, it was Walter who repulsed the armies from Tír Eógain and the Isle of Man as they attempted to retake Ulster. William Marshal's interests spanned the Irish Sea, providing further resources and a means of royal oversight. Hugh's did not, but Walter's did. This imbalance of power between the Lacy brothers is recognised in a grant by Hugh's own son-in-law, David, baron of Naas, about 1234. Walter comes second only to the Irish justiciar in the charter's witness list, preceding (among others) Earl Hugh and the powerful lord of Connacht, Richard de Burgh (Walter's son-in-law).[135] In this light, the choice of Hugh over Walter makes little sense.

Ireland in 1205

There are at least two problems with the scenario set out above. It is a scenario determined by hindsight, and displays a preoccupation with southern Irish politics. At the beginning of 1205, the political structure of Ireland hung in the balance. Of Ireland's five provinces, only Meath and Leinster remained relatively stable. In Connacht, a tenurial relationship between the English king and the ruling Ua Conchobair was being negotiated, while Hugh de Lacy held a royal charter for six cantreds, and William de Burgh's right to the entire province was being judged (and possibly confirmed). In Ulster, the expulsion of John de Courcy had heaped territorial rewards upon his enemies, the Lacy brothers. William de Burgh's trial also had implications for Munster, where his chief opponent, Meiler fitz Henry, sought to dominate the province from the royal stronghold at Limerick. However, by the end of 1205, William de Burgh was dead, Cathal Crobderg held Connacht on much more favourable terms than those he proposed in 1204,[136] Hugh de Lacy had lost his stake in Connacht, but held all of Ulster as its earl, and the city of Limerick was in the hands of William de Briouze's custodian, Walter de Lacy. Involving similar issues and personnel, the reorganisations of Connacht and Ulster were inextricably linked. When King John granted Hugh de Lacy six cantreds of Connacht in November 1204, it impacted upon Walter de Lacy's position as adviser in negotiations with Cathal Crobderg, and as judge in the trial of William de Burgh (who had already made Hugh a grant of ten Connacht cantreds in the 1190s).[137]

Had King John immediately accepted and enacted Cathal Crobderg's 1204 proposal that he hold one-third of Connacht by charter and surrender the remaining two-thirds to the king, then Hugh's six cantreds could have come out of the roughly twenty Cathal released to John. But John was not quick enough. By May 1205, William de Burgh was in a position to grant one of his judges land in Connacht, which may suggest that his right to the province had been confirmed. In this case, Hugh de Lacy would have expected to hold his ten cantreds in Connacht of William de Burgh. King John would have had to dip further into his own pockets to compensate Hugh for his Norman lands, and reward him for his role in John de Courcy's downfall. Instead of sharing eight cantreds of Ulster with his brother Walter, Hugh was granted the entire lordship. His belting as earl may well have been to counterpoise William Marshal in Leinster, but it may also have been to ensure his loyalty now that he held a third of Connacht of William de Burgh. This much is speculation based largely upon the interpretation of William de Burgh's grant to William le Petit, but, if accurate, then it paints a picture of an Ireland dominated by two earls: Hugh de Lacy in the north and west, and William Marshal in the south-east. This could explain why Walter de Lacy was not made earl instead of Hugh. Walter held a much better position in England, Ireland and Wales, but in May 1205 an ascendant Hugh was in a better position to assume and hold the first Irish earldom.

Here the second problem presents itself. So far the discussion has focused on southern Irish politics, which looked east to England and Wales. But Ulster faced Galloway, Strathclyde and the Western Isles.[138] William Marshal was not the closest earl by a long shot. The northern maritime nexus drew Hugh into a world populated by the earls of Atholl, Carrick, Caithness, Lennox, Orkney, Ross and Strathearn, not to mention the king of Man and the Isles and the quasi-regal lord of Galloway. John de Courcy's fall, coupled with the loss of Normandy, caused the English king to take ever greater interest in the politics of this northern region. As mentioned above, he prevented a marriage alliance between King Rǫgnvaldr of Man and Llywelyn ap Iorwerth of Gwynedd, before binding Rǫgnvaldr into a web of English royal patronage.[139] When King John later drove Hugh de Lacy from Ireland in 1210, Hugh used his connections to escape through Lennox to St Andrews, while King John bestowed large grants in Hugh's confiscated earldom upon the Galloway family, including the lord of Galloway and earls of Carrick and Atholl.[140] More examples of Ulster's northern maritime orientation could be marshalled, some of which will be discussed in due course below. For the moment, it is perhaps enough to say that, when he was made earl in 1205, it appeared as though Hugh de Lacy would dominate northern Irish politics, act with his brother as an effective counterpoise to William Marshal in Leinster and be King John's man in the earl-rich world of Britain's north-Atlantic archipelago.

However, William de Burgh's death that year ruined King John's position in Connacht.[141] With no viable alternative other than Burgh's underage son Richard, the English king was forced to treat with Cathal Crobderg or risk further destabilisation. Cathal proposed revised terms, which King John accepted on 20 December 1205. The Irish king was still to hold one-third of Connacht in fee, but, instead of surrendering the other two-thirds, he was merely to render tribute for them. Only two cantreds were reserved to the English king.[142] Consequently, no room was left for

Hugh de Lacy. When he eventually received and successfully subinfeudated five cantreds in Connacht long afterwards, in the 1230s, it was by grant of William's son, Richard de Burgh.[143] Until then, Hugh had to be content with his earldom of Ulster.

The trial and subsequent death of William de Burgh signalled an end to the temporary balance of power between the families of Burgh, Briouze and Lacy in Ireland and Wales that King John had initiated in 1200. This was not just about William in Connacht. In the spring of 1205, Hubert de Burgh was captured at Chinon by Philip Augustus.[144] The king then granted Hubert's shrievalty of Herefordshire to the royal seneschal, William de Cantelupe. The Three Castles, which had been granted to Hubert in October 1200 to provide a check on the Briouze/Lacy lands, were then granted in fee to William de Briouze.[145] Clearly, the Burghs were no longer an effective counterbalance. What is more, after being belted as earl of Ulster at the English court, Hugh de Lacy was sent back to Ireland on 30 June with letters instructing the justiciar to place undoubted reliance on Hugh's advice regarding the king's interests in Ireland, and to wage no war against those of the march unless by the advice of Walter and Hugh de Lacy, and others, whose fidelity and service were necessary to maintain the war.[146] On 23 August, custody of the city of Limerick was restored to William de Briouze, which in effect gave possession of it to Walter de Lacy.[147] Limerick, like Athlone further north, controlled the Shannon as it flowed through its hinterland. As lord of Meath and custodian of Limerick (both honor and city), Walter de Lacy now possessed the main southern and eastern approaches to Connacht, and, consequently, was well placed to intrigue in that province. Indeed, with significant stakes in Meath, Ulster and Munster, the Lacys were able to exert their will directly in three of the historic fifths of Ireland. Walter's position along the Shannon brought Connacht within range, and the continuing absenteeism of the Marshal lord of Leinster meant that the local settler community might have to look further north for a leader. By the autumn of 1205, the Lacy/Briouze coalition was in the ascendancy.

Conclusion

The first seven years of John's reign were a time of great advancement for the Lacy family. Walter's amiable relationship with the new king facilitated his marriage to Margery, daughter of John's familiar William de Briouze. Lacking the power to impose a strong centralised administration in Ireland, or to extend his direct authority into the Welsh march, King John used what power he had to pit his frontier barons against one another.

By devolving lesser power on these men, John was still able to direct the course of politics in Ireland, without facing the risks posed by an omnicompetent magnate justiciar. He had learned his lesson from the example of the elder Hugh de Lacy in 1185. Consequently, the Lacys and Briouzes were used to counterbalance the Burgh brothers in Ireland and Wales (and vice versa), illustrating the close ties between Wales and Ireland, and suggesting that, sharing similar personnel, the two realms were thought of as a political commonalty.

However transnational the holdings, early thirteenth-century lordship remained very personal, based in most cases on regular oversight by individual lords. Experience had shown that, while possessing lands in more than one realm added to a lord's prestige, the effective exploitation of any frontier components was complicated by distance and divided attention. Walter de Lacy and William de Briouze, therefore divided their attention at the Irish Sea. Walter made William custodian of his English and Norman honors, while Walter oversaw the Briouze honor of Limerick in Ireland. Such co-operation is reminiscent of the co-operation between the Beaumont twins in the mid-twelfth century, and indicates the possible strength of the marriage bond between families in the thirteenth century. This arrangement also allowed the scales of power to be tipped in favour of the Lacy/Briouze alliance, a process accelerated by the loss of Normandy in 1204. When William de Burgh overstepped his bounds and began to eye Connacht too greedily, Walter helped the Irish justiciar remove him from Limerick, and was on the royal commission to judge the charges against him. At the same time Walter and his brother Hugh were the chief agents in King John's destruction of the lord of Ulster, John de Courcy. The defeat and supplanting of John de Courcy is the first manifestation of a significant trend in the Lacy brothers' career. Time and again they acted in concert, with Hugh providing military endeavour and Walter official legitimacy. The addition of Ulster in 1204 more than made up for the loss of the family's Norman sub-tenancies, and made the Lacys the dominant force in Ireland. When King John belted Hugh earl of Ulster in 1205, he broadened his impact, placing Hugh on par with the neighbouring sea-borne earls of western Scotland and the Isles, and counterbalancing Earl William Marshal's control of the southern Irish Sea from Pembroke to Leinster.

Notes

1 Sidney Painter, *The Reign of King John* (Baltimore, 1949), pp. 1–16.
2 Norgate, *Lackland*, pp. 65–8; Painter, *King John*, pp. 15–16.

3   Hillaby, 'Colonisation, crisis-management and debt', p. 9.
4   See below, p. 103.
5   *Rot. Chart.*, pp. 23-4.
6   *Gormanston Register*, p. 163.
7   James Lydon, *The Lordship of Ireland in the Middle Ages* (2nd edn, Dublin, 2003), p. 62.
8   Norgate, *Lackland*, pp. 72-3.
9   *Rot. Chart.*, pp. 66-7.
10 BL MS Lansdowne 229, fo. 23r; *Rot. Chart.*, p. 69.
11 See itinerary in *Rotuli Litterarum Patentium in Turri Londinensi Asservati*, ed. T. D. Hardy (London, 1835).
12 Powicke, *Loss of Normandy*, pp. 134-40; W. L. Warren, *King John* (London, 1961), pp. 54-5.
13 *Rot. Chart.*, pp., 53, 61.
14 W. St C. Baddeley, *A Cotteswold Manor: Being the History of Painswick* (London, 1929), p. 53; Z. N. Brooke and C. N. L. Brooke, 'Hereford Cathedral dignitaries in the twelfth century – supplement', *Cambridge Historical Journal*, 8/3 (1946), pp. 179-85, at p. 185.
15 Norgate, *Lackland*, pp. 139-40; Painter, *King John*, p. 41.
16 *Rot. Chart.*, pp. 66-7.
17 Howden, *Chronica*, iv, p. 83.
18 Powicke, *Loss of Normandy*, appendix I. It should however be noted that the Margam account was written in the 1240s and shows the influence of Roger of Wendover or a similar source which subscribed to the anti-Johannite baronial propaganda of the reign.
19 'Contra hoc inquam judixium coronatur, Willelmo de Brause, cum fautoribus suis ad ejus coronationem vehementius instante.' 'Annala de Margan', in H. R. Luard (ed.), *Annales Monastici*, 5 vols (London, 1864-69), i, p. 24.
20 Painter, *King John*, p. 7.
21 *Hist. William Marshal*, ii, lines 11836-908.
22 Crouch, *William Marshal*, pp. 86-7. The justiciar, Geoffrey fitz Peter, was also rewarded, being made earl of Essex.
23 *Ibid.*, pp. 86-90 (quote at p. 90).
24 Painter, *King John*, p. 44.
25 *Rot. Chart.*, p. 80.
26 Compare the list of Brecon tenants in Holden, *Lords*, p. 70, to the list of Lacy tenants in Appendix 2.
27 *Rot. Obl. et Fin.*, p. 81; *Rot. Chart.*, p. 80; *Pipe Roll 3 John*, p. 87.
28 *Rot. Chart.*, pp. 79-80; Howden, *Chronica*, iv, p. 141.
29 'Et aliorum omnium ad coronam regiam pertinentium'; 'de omnibus hominibus exceptis Hiberniensibus et illis qui cum eis sunt', *Rot. Obl. et Fin.*, pp. 94, 99 (quotes p. 99); *Rot. Chart.*, p. 84; *Pipe Roll 3 John*, p. 8.
30 Marios Costambeys, Matthew Innes and Simon MacLean, *The Carolingian World* (Cambridge, 2011), p. 308.
31 *Rot. Chart.*, p. 100b.

FACTIONALISM: 1199-1206

32 John Gillingham, 'The Anonymous of Béthune, King John and Magna Carta', in J. S. Loengard (ed.), *Magna Carta and the England of King John* (Woodbridge, 2010), pp. 27-44.
33 *Histoire des ducs de Normandie et des rois d'Angleterre*, ed. Francisque Michel (Paris, 1840), pp. 111-12.
34 'Ses barons melloit ensamble quanques il pooit; moult estoit liés quant il veoit haine entre els.' *Histoire des ducs*, p. 105.
35 Painter, *King John*, p. 46.
36 *Rot. Chart.*, p. 84.
37 Warren, 'King John and Ireland', p. 34.
38 *Rotuli de Liberate ac de Misis et Praestitis, Regnante Johanne*, ed. T. D. Hardy (London, 1844), p. 19.
39 Norgate, *Lackland*, p. 79.
40 Howden, *Chronica*, iv, p. 163.
41 William married Walter's sister, *Rot. Hundred.*, ii, pp. 69, 76, 80.
42 *Pipe Roll 4 John*, pp. 45-6.
43 Painter, *King John*, pp. 48-50.
44 *Fouke Le Fitz Waryn*, eds E. J. Hathaway, et al. (Oxford, 1975).
45 'Or, a fess gules', *Matthaei Parisiensis, Monachi Sancti Albani, Chronica Majora*, ed. H. R. Luard, 7 vols (London, 1872-83), vi, p. 474.
46 *ALC*, i, p. 206, *s.a.* 1199. For identification, Perros [Walton], 'Shannon frontier', p. 128.
47 *Rot. Chart.* pp. 23-4; *Gormanston Register*, p. 163.
48 *ALC*, i, pp. 208-10, *s.a.* 1200; *MCB*, p. 80, *s.a.* 1200. In Ireland, a hosting traditionally involved the theft of an enemy's cattle, and could include the destruction of buildings and the taking of slaves.
49 *Ann. Clon.*, p. 216, *s.a.* 1200 [*recte* 1201]; *AFM*, iii, p. 124, *s.a.* 1200 [*recte* 1201]; Walton, 'The English in Connacht 1171-1333', pp. 32-3.
50 *ALC*, i, pp. 210-14, *s.a.* 1200; *AI*, p. 326, *s.a.* 1200; *MCB*, p. 80, *s.a.* 1200; *AU*, ii, p. 234, *s.a.* 1201 [*recte* 1200]; *Ann. Clon.*, pp. 213-14, *s.a.* 1199 [*recte* 1200]; *AFM*, iii, p. 118, *s.a.* 1199 [*recte* 1200]; Freeman, 'Cottonian Annals', *s.a.* 1200.
51 Orpen, *Normans*, ii, pp. 189-90.
52 *ALC*, i, pp. 218-22, *s.a.* 1201; *AU*, ii, pp. 234-6, *s.a.* 1201; Freeman, 'Cottonian Annals', *s.a.* 1201; *Ann. Clon.*, pp. 216-17, *s.a.* 1200, *AFM*, iii, p. 120, *s.a.* 1199.
53 *ALC*, i, p. 222, *s.a.* 1201. See also: *Ann. Clon.*, p. 207, *s.a.* 1200 (Cathal taken to castle of Nobber), *MCB*, p. 82, *s.a.* 1201 (Lacys took Courcy prisoner).
54 Orpen, *Normans*, ii, p. 188n.
55 Gillingham, 'Travels of Roger of Howden', p. 164.
56 'Eodem anno Valterus de Lasci, vir potens in Hibernia, cepit colloquium cum Johanne de Curci, domino de Ulvestire, et volens eum proditiose capere, multos de suis interfecit. Cum autem praedictus Johannes verteretur in fugam, dixit ei Hugo de Lasci, frater praedicti Valteri, "Domine, veni mecum, et receptabo te in castello meo, de quo homo vester sum, donec exercitus vester congregetur, ut possitis vindicare vos de iis qui te oderunt semper." Credidit ergo illi praedictus Johannes, et intravit castellum tutus de praefato Hugone.

Sed cum inde exire vellet, non permisit eum Hugo exire: immo cepit, traditurus eum regi Angliae, qui a multo tempore desiderabat eum tenere. At homines praedicti Johannis die ac nocte non cessabant devastare ferro, flamma, fame, terras praedictorum Valteri et Hugonis de Lasci, donec liberaverunt dominum suum Johannem de Curci de captione praefati Hugonis de Lasci.' Howden, *Chronica*, iv, p. 176. Walter Bower also claims that John de Courcy was Hugh de Lacy's lord, though no definite evidence exists, Walter Bower, *Scotichronicon: in Latin and English, Vol. iv: Books vii and viii*, eds David J. Corner et al. (Aberdeen, 1994), p. 461.

57 *Ann. Clon.*, p. 217, s.a. 1200.
58 *ALC*, i, p. 222, s.a. 1202, *Ann. Clon.*, p. 217, s.a. 1200.
59 *Rot. Litt. Pat.*, p. 2.
60 *Rot. Chart.*, p. 103b; Otway-Ruthven, *Medieval Ireland*, p. 76.
61 *Rot. Obl. et Fin.*, pp. 180–1.
62 *Gormanston Register*, pp. 177–8.
63 *Rot. Obl. et Fin.*, p. 222.
64 *Rotuli Litterarum Clausarum in Turri Londinensi Asservati*, ed. T. D. Hardy, 2 vols (London, 1833–44), ii, 64, and see Chapter 7.
65 *AI*, p. 328, s.a. 1201. Mag Feimin is a plain extending from Cashel to Clonmel in modern Co. Tipperary. It was then in the honor of Limerick.
66 See above, Chapters 2 and 3.
67 Theobald Walter paid Briouze a 500 mark fine for his territories, Howden, *Chronica*, iv, p. 153.
68 *Song*, lines 3412–55; *Deeds*, lines 3410–53; *Expugnatio Hibernica*, p. 150.
69 *Rot. Litt. Pat.*, p. 4.
70 *Ibid.*, p. 16b.
71 Painter, *King John*, p. 28.
72 *Pipe Roll 4 John*, p. 20; *Rot. Litt. Pat.*, p. 19.
73 *Rot. Litt. Pat.*, p. 18.
74 *Rot. Norm.*, p. 59.
75 Powicke, *Loss of Normandy*, p. 71.
76 *Rot. Norm*, p. 74; *Catalogue des actes de Philippe-Auguste*, ed. Léopold Delisle (Paris, 1856), p. 185; *Cartulaire Normand*, nos 72, 76.
77 Wightman, *Lacy*, pp. 223–4.
78 Powicke, *Loss of Normandy*, pp. 145–7.
79 Daniel Power, 'The end of Angevin Normandy: the revolt at Alençon', *Historical Research*, 74/186 (Nov. 2001), pp. 444–64. *Rot. Norm.*, pp. 70ff.
80 *Rot. Norm.*, p. 74.
81 Crouch, *Beaumont Twins*, pp. 51ff.
82 Ralph's main interests were in Picardy and Artois. David Crouch, 'Between three realms: the acts of Waleran II, Count of Meulan and Worcester', in Nicholas Vincent (ed.), *Records, Administration and Aristocratic Society in the Anglo-Norman Realm* (Woodbridge, 2009), pp. 75–90, at p. 86.
83 *Pipe Roll 5 John*, pp. 63, 70.
84 Ifor W. Rowlands, 'William de Braoze and the lordship of Brecon', *Bulletin of*

the Board of Celtic Studies, 30 (1982), pp.123-33; Brock Holden, 'King John, the Braozes, and the Celtic fringe, 1207-1216', Albion, 33/1 (2001), pp.1-23, at pp.11-13.
85 ALC, i, p.228, s.a. 1203; AI, pp.330-2, s.a. 1203.
86 Orpen, Normans, ii, pp.191-2.
87 Rot. Litt. Pat., i, pp.31-2.
88 ALC, i, pp.228-30, s.a. 1203; Ann. Clon., p.219, s.a. 1202 [recte 1203]; AI, p.332, s.a. 1203.
89 Ann. Clon., p.219, s.a. 1202.
90 ALC, i, p.230, s.a. 1203.
91 ALC, i, p.230, s.a. 1203; AU, ii, p.240, s.a. 1203.
92 AI, p.332, s.a. 1203.
93 Rot. Liberate, p.70; ALC, i, p.230, s.a. 1203.
94 Norgate, Lackland, p.99.
95 J. C. Holt, The Northerners: A Study in the Reign of King John (Oxford, 1992), p.144.
96 Rot. Chart., pp.133-4; Rot. Litt. Pat., p.39; Rot. Liberate, p.106.
97 Rot. Chart., p.133.
98 Rot. Liberate, p.83.
99 For the Blunds see E. St J. Brooks, 'Archbishop Henry of London and his Irish connections', Journal of the Royal Society of Antiquaries of Ireland, 4th ser., 60 (1930), pp.1-22. Although 'le Blund' (or Blundus, White, etc.) is a very common name, it is interesting to note that the elder Hugh de Lacy's widow (the daughter of Ruaidrí Ua Conchobair) remarried to a Blund at some point after 1186. Royal Letters, i, p.502; and see Chapter 7.
100 Rot. Liberate, p.83.
101 Rot. Litt. Pat., p.39.
102 Ibid., pp.39-41; Rot. Liberate, p.67.
103 Foedera, I, i, p.91; Rot. Litt. Claus., i, p.6.
104 Rot. Litt. Pat., p.46.
105 Kenneth Nicholls, 'A charter of William de Burgo', Annalecta Hibernica, 27 (1972), pp.120-2.
106 Rot. Litt. Pat., p.47.
107 Rot. Litt. Claus., i, p.47.
108 See above, p.109.
109 Rot. Litt. Pat., p.15.
110 AFM, iii, p.136, s.a. 1203; ALC, i, p.232, s.a. 1203; Ann. Clon., p.220, s.a. 1203; MCB, p.82, s.a. 1203; AU, ii, p.240, s.a. 1204 [recte 1203].
111 Rot. Litt. Pat., p.34.
112 Ibid., p.45.
113 Ibid., p.45b.
114 Ibid., p.45b.
115 Painter, King John, p.27.
116 ALC, i, pp.232-4, s.a. 1204; AFM, iii, pp.138-40, s.a. 1204; AU, ii, p.240, s.a. 1204; MCB, p.82, s.a. 1203; Ann. Clon., p.220, s.a. 1204; Grace's Annals, pp.21-3, s.a.

1204; *Clyn's Annals*, p. 139, *s.a.* 1204; *Chart. St Mary's*, ii, pp. 308–10, s.a 1204; *Chronica de Mailros*, ed. Joseph Stevenson (Edinburgh, 1835), p. 105, *s.a.* 1204.

117 *ALC*, i, pp. 232–4, *s.a.* 1204; *Cronica Regum Mannie & Insularum*, ed. George Broderick (Belfast, 1979), fo. 41v.

118 *Rot. Litt. Pat.*, p. 47. Extended 8 February, ibid., p. 50.

119 From Tír Eógain: *MCB*, p. 84, *s.a.* 1204. From the Isles: *ALC*, i, p. 234, *s.a.* 1205; *Cronica Mannie*, fo. 41v.

120 Katharine Simms, 'The O'Hanlons, the O'Neills, and the Anglo-Normans in thirteenth-century Armagh', *Seanchas Ardmhacha: Journal of the Armagh Diocesan Historical Society*, 9/1 (1978), pp. 70–94, at p. 77.

121 McDonald, *Manx Kingship*, p. 121. For Manx sea power see Seán Duffy, 'The prehistory of the galloglass', in Duffy (ed.), *The World of the Galloglass: King, Warlords and Warriors in Ireland and Scotland, 1200–1600* (Dublin, 2007), pp. 1–23. R. Andrew McDonald, 'Dealing death from Man: Manx sea power in and around the Irish Sea, 1079–1265', in Seán Duffy (ed.), *The World of the Galloglass: Kings, Warlords and Warriors in Ireland and Scotland, 1200–1600* (Dublin, 2007), pp. 45–76, esp p. 53.

122 Lloyd, *Wales*, ii, p. 617; McDonald, *Manx Kingship*, p. 103.

123 Lloyd, *Wales*, ii, p. 616. The offer had been made by 15 October 1204, *Rot. Litt. Claus.*, i, p. 12.

124 *Foedera*, I, i, p. 44.

125 McDonald, *Manx Kingship*, p. 131.

126 *Rot. Chart.*, p. 139. The price of the grant is listed as 550 marks in 200 mark instalments, *Rot. Obl. et Fin.*, p. 227.

127 *Rot. Chart.*, pp. 139–40. The cantreds were those closest to Meath, namely: Tri Tuatha, Mag nAi, Mag Lurg-Tirerrill, Corran, Sliab Luga and Leyny, see Chapter 3.

128 *Rot. Litt. Pat.*, p. 54.

129 *Gormanston Register*, p. 142; *Rot. Chart.*, p. 151.

130 Painter, *King John*, p. 47.

131 David Crouch, 'Earls in Wales and Ireland' in Crouch (ed.), *The Earl in Medieval Britain* (forthcoming).

132 Warren, *King John*, pp. 113–15.

133 See Chapter 7.

134 See Chapter 5.

135 *Gormanston Register*, pp. 145–6, 195.

136 *Rot. Litt. Claus.*, i, p. 62.

137 See Chapter 3.

138 For the Galloway and Strathclyde nexus see K. J. Stringer, *The Reformed Church in Medieval Galloway and Cumbria: Contrasts, Connections and Continuities*, Eleventh Whithorn Lecture (Whithorn, 2003).

139 See above, p. 118.

140 Seán Duffy, 'The lords of Galloway, earls of Carrick, and the Bissetts of the Glens: Scottish settlement in thirteenth century Ulster', in David Edwards (ed.), *Regions and Rulers in Ireland, 1100–1650: Essays for Kenneth Nicholls* (Dublin, 2004), pp. 37–50. And see Chapter 5.

141 *ALC*, i, p.234, *s.a.* 1205; *Ann. Clon.*, p.220, *s.a.* 1204 [*recte* 1205].
142 *Rot. Litt. Claus.*, i, p.62.
143 *Rot. Chart.*, pp.218-19, and see Chapter 6.
144 Painter, *King John*, p.45.
145 *Rot. Litt. Pat.*, p.57; *Rot. Chart.*, p.160b.
146 *Rot. Litt. Claus.*, i, p.40.
147 *Ibid.*, i, p.47.

5

Royal v. aristocratic lordship: 1206–16

King John's policy for Ireland in the opening years of his reign was one based on political pragmatism and expediency. His administration lacked the resources to compete with the great provincial lordships, so he was forced to work with them to achieve his ends. John's promotion of the Lacys and William de Briouze during the factionalist disputes of the previous years meant that, by 1206, the resident Lacy brothers were without rival in Ireland. Although it was a situation of his own making, this prominence of aristocratic lordship in Ireland was far from ideal for John. Lacy supremacy in Ireland harked back to the days of the elder Hugh, and John's embarrassment in 1185. For John, the limitation of magnate power was essential. The ensuing period in Ireland was one of conflict between royal and aristocratic lordship, soon to be replicated throughout the Angevin empire. Indeed, it is intriguing to speculate what might have happened had the baronial revolts in Ireland (1207–8) and England and Wales (1215–17) not been separated by seven years. In the event, the respite allowed King John time to regroup his forces. His 1210 expedition to Ireland was a delayed, but necessary, response to the flouting of his authority since 1207. The manifestation of unrepentant aristocratic power in Ireland, the Lacy/Briouze alliance, was sacrificed so that the strength of John's personal lordship would be embedded in the colony. By the time that civil war broke out in England and Wales in 1215, several of John's enemies from 1207 were his firmest supporters. In particular, Walter de Lacy's return from exile demonstrates the essential strength of the symbiotic relationship between royal and aristocratic lordship, even at a time of conflict.

The Irish crisis of 1207

On 3 April 1206, King John sent two mandates which were meant to redress the imbalance of power in Ireland. One ordered the Irish justiciar, Meiler fitz Henry, to take the former lands of the recently deceased William de Burgh and Theobald Walter into the king's hand.[1] William's lands provided the Crown with a significant stake in Thomond, but Theobald's were more widespread sub-tenancies held of the lords of Limerick, Meath and Leinster. Prerogative wardship meant that they all reverted to the Crown and punched holes in three of the colony's four provincial lordships. John's second mandate commanded the justiciar to establish the boundary between Limerick and Cork (colonial Thomond and Desmond), as a preliminary to the shiring of the region.[2] Meiler's commission in 1206 was thus clearly aimed at limiting Briouze's lordship in Limerick. At the same time, William de Briouze had his Welsh lordship of Brecon threatened through English litigation.[3] John's April initiatives put royal and aristocratic enterprise on a collision course in western Ireland, and, as custodian of Limerick, Walter de Lacy was at the centre of the storm.

The real trouble began in the winter of 1206-7. On 13 January 1207, Walter, Hugh, Robert and William de Lacy gathered at Rathbeggan (bar. Ratoath, Co. Meath) with the greater barons of Meath.[4] At about the same time, roughly 130 miles away, Meiler fitz Henry's son Meiler took the honor of Limerick by force. Winter campaigns were risky, especially as the weather and terrain in western Ireland could be daunting. Consequently, Meiler's attack seems to have taken everyone by surprise. King John was quick to distance himself from such an overt act of aggression, rebuking the Irish justiciar in a mandate dated 12 February 1207.[5] Although his letter stressed the fidelity of William de Briouze, and the esteem in which William was held, it also ordered Meiler to retain the royal city of Limerick if it had been taken. However, that was easier said than done. Meiler's assault had challenged Walter de Lacy's reputation (as custodian of Limerick), and contemporary conceptions of honour dictated that Walter respond 'manfully' to the insult. Consequently, Walter attacked Meiler as the latter attempted to retain the city of Limerick. In a letter to the barons of Meath and Leinster dated 21 February 1207, the king thanked them for their fidelity when dissension arose between their lord and the Irish justiciar over the city of Limerick, and because they had tried their hardest to avert evil from Walter. Walter also seems to have attempted to chastise the young Meiler for his role in the assault, which, because the elder Meiler held Ardnurcher of Walter in the lordship of Meath, may have had the character of a lord disciplining a disobedient tenant. However, King John then quickly moved to protect his Irish justiciar's son from baronial justice. On the same day as his letter to the barons of Meath, the king ordered that the young Meiler not answer for Limerick's taking except before the king, and reiterated his desire that the city be retained.[6] The ill-disguised deviousness on display here accounts for much of what happened next. It was impossible to trust the professions and motives of such a man as John.

Meanwhile, John had accelerated his plans to reinforce royal lordship in Ireland. On 14 February, two days after his letter stressing royal support for William de Briouze in Limerick, the king ordered the constable of Bristol to find a ship to transport fifteen royal crossbowmen to Ireland.[7] Their likely destination was Dublin, which the barons and knights (*barones et milites*) of Meath and Leinster were ordered to help Meiler fitz Henry fortify while retaining their fidelity to the Crown. Since John held hostages from these colonists, the seriousness of his injunction was clear.[8] By communicating directly with Walter de Lacy's military tenants, John hoped to rob their lord of the support he needed against Meiler fitz Henry. This piece of duplicity did not work. It merely confirmed suspicions. On 2 March, Walter, his brothers, and the leading barons and knights of Meath gathered together in a show of support at Galtrim (Co. Meath).[9] Two days later, King John gave Philip d'Aubigné custody of Ludlow castle, only recently restored to Walter for a large fine.[10] Finally, on 14 April, Walter was called to judgement in England.[11]

In the meantime, Walter and his brother Hugh had marched on Meiler's castle of Ardnurcher, expelling him from it and from Walter's neighbouring territory of Fir Cell (bars Ballycowan, Ballyboy and Eglish, Co. Offaly), which Meiler seems to have occupied unlawfully.[12] It was only after Walter and Meiler had come to blows in Munster, and around the time of their conflict in western Meath, that William Marshal arrived on the scene. The lord of Leinster nevertheless played a leading role in the subsequent conflict. Meiler had seized the Marshal's territory of Uí Failge in northern Leinster, which bordered Walter's land of Fir Cell and four of Theobald Walter's former Limerick tenancies, Éile Uí Cearbaill (Co. Offaly), Éile Uí Fogartaig (Co. Tipperary), Urmuman (Co. Tipperary) and Ara (Co. Tipperary). The problems in Limerick, Fir Cell and Uí Failge were quite similar, and, when taken together, involved a substantial portion of the Irish midlands. The lord of Uí Failge, Gerald fitz Maurice, had died before 15 January 1204, when King John ordered that William

Marshal have custody of his land and heir.[13] However, as with Theobald Walter, prerogative wardship meant that the Crown had the ultimate right to custody of Gerald's lands. With this justification, and despite John's initial orders to the contrary, Meiler fitz Henry seized Uí Failge. Whether or not John was complicit in Meiler's actions, he again threw his support behind the Irish justiciar.

William Marshal prepared to journey to Ireland at the end of February or early March. Another magnate harbouring a grudge against the Irish justiciar was the last thing that the king needed in Ireland, and John belatedly (though unsuccessfully) attempted to prevent William's crossing.[14] A significant number of colonial barons sided with the lords of Limerick, Meath and Leinster against the Irish justiciar, and together wrote to the king. On 23 May 1207, John replied. His list of addressees show the authors of the barons' letter: Walter, Hugh and Robert de Lacy, William le Petit, Richard de Tuit, Adam of Hereford, Philip de Prendergast, William baron of Naas, John de Clahull, Maurice of London, Thomas of Hereford and other barons (though, interestingly, not knights) of Leinster and Meath.[15] In his letter John 'marvelled' that they seemed prepared to create a 'new assize' (*nova assisa*) in Ireland without him. He reprimanded them for their attempts to get Meiler to restore Uí Failge without the king's consent, when (he insisted) Meiler had taken it by his order. There was clearly more behind the barons' letter than one isolated court action, but historians have tended to confine their examinations to William Marshal and the lordship of Leinster (because, no doubt, of the specific mention of Uí Failge and the prominence of the Marshal's biography in the historical record). As H. G. Richardson observes, 'it looks indeed as though the protest were not in the interest of the Marshal but, in circumstances we do not understand, in the interest of Walter de Lacy; and while some of the Marshal's tenants, including the disloyal Philip de Prendergast, joined in the protest, the lead was clearly taken by the barons of Meath'.[16] Marie Therese Flanagan has shed further light on the complex situation in Leinster, and concludes that 'Meiler's action in taking Uí Failge into his own hand in the name of the king had provoked a collaborative response from the barons of Leinster and Meath'.[17] By limiting themselves to Leinster, such analysis gives the impression that hostilities were mostly Leinster-based, when actually they were not. Instead, the conflicts of 1207 turned on the expansion of royal lordship throughout the colony, with protests against the abuse of prerogative wardship eliciting a direct response from the king over Uí Failge.

Walter de Lacy's appearance in King John's letter suggests that he was still in Ireland at the time, as does a second letter sent that same day which authorised Meiler to distrain Richard Tyrell to send the agreed hostage for Walter's good behaviour.[18] This second letter also hints at the extent of the conflict. It ordered Meiler to arrest several Briouze and Lacy tenants for their 'robberies' and for breaking the king's peace. Furthermore, John ordered that Meiler hold in the king's hand the cities of Limerick and Cork, and expel those who had gone there against the Crown. John also decreed that Meiler's recent land grants in Desmond should stand. This is convincing evidence that the Irish justiciar had been acting on his own in the name of the king by alienating land in Desmond (perhaps as a result of the 1206 border inquest). John also made specific mention of a man named Norman Clatere who had left Dublin, of which he was a citizen, and gone to live in Walter de Lacy's lands. Norman's lands, chattels and body (if he could be found) were to be retained at the king's pleasure. Placed alongside John's angry letter to the barons of Meath and Leinster, this shows that the colonial communities of Meath, Munster and Leinster were all at odds with the Irish justiciar, with colonial forces in Munster occupying the royal cities of Limerick and Cork against the king, and the lordship of Meath used as a safe refuge from the Crown.

Compromise: 1207–8

The nature of lordship in this period was such that armed resistance against one's lord was not unforgivable, as long as the validity of that lordship was eventually acknowledged. The rapprochement between John and Walter de Lacy in 1195 is one example.[19] Another came in 1207. From midsummer, warfare still raged in Ireland, but Walter de Lacy and William Marshal submitted to King John, admitting the legitimacy of his authority over them. William de Briouze's failure to do likewise, if not the initial cause of disaffection between king and magnate, posed a direct challenge to John's rule and hardened the king's resolve to bring him down.[20]

Over the summer of 1207, the Irish annals report that 'a great war broke out among the English of Leinster; i.e. between Meiler, Geoffrey de Marisco, and William Marshal. Leinster and Munster suffered severely from them.'[21] This led John to try to gain support from Meath. On 13 July, King John ordered the custody of Ludlow castle and town, only recently taken from Walter, to be given to his 'dear and faithful William de Briouze', thus restoring it to Walter's custodian (and showing that William was still ostensibly in favour in mid-July 1207).[22] Three days later, Walter was with the king at Winchester, where he witnessed John's grant of a fair at

Mullingar to Walter's constable, William le Petit.[23] Walter then kept in regular contact with John, witnessing the king's charters at Worcester on 23 August, Bristol on 17 September, Windsor on 25 October and Malmesbury on 23 November 1207.[24] On 4 December one of Walter's hostages, Richard de Capella, was released.[25]

Late in the year, the main combatants of the summer conflict met with King John at Woodstock to settle matters.[26] At the council, on 9 November, John decreed that the pleas of the Crown and those touching free tenements were to be reserved to the Crown in Ireland, and asserted his monopoly over the circulation of coin in Ireland.[27] This was the culmination of John's efforts since his coronation in England to install the English model of royal lordship in Ireland, efforts which had involved intruding into the judicial process in Meath and Leinster, and instituting a clause reserving Crown pleas in new Irish grants.[28] In 1207, John's decree severely limited the liberties of Meath and Leinster: a powerful blow to aristocratic autonomy in Ireland. We see this in the terms written into the revised charters for their lordships that Walter and William Marshal obtained from John the following year.[29] John also granted (or confirmed) lands in Ireland to some of those present, with the barons and knights of Leinster gaining the most.[30] Importantly, William de Briouze and his new custodian of Limerick, Geoffrey de Marisco, were both absent from the meeting. The well-placed annals of Worcester report under 1208 that King John suspected Briouze of ordering Geoffrey to seize the city of Limerick and other castles in Ireland, and that John called him to his court in order to answer these charges. The annals then claim that William de Briouze refused the summons and instead fortified his Welsh castles, which led directly to his persecution, flight and ruin.[31] This scenario is quite plausible. In addition to the warfare involving Geoffrey de Marisco in Leinster and Munster in the summer 1207, the annals of Loch Cé report under 1208 a 'great war ... between the sons of Hugh de Lacy [the elder], and Meiler, and Geoffrey de Marisco',[32] and one set of Dublin-based Latin annals records 'a great massacre at Thurles in Munster upon the men of the Irish justiciar by Sir Geoffrey de Marisco'.[33] As seen above, in 1204, King John's confiscation of the lordship of Ulster seems to have been justified by John de Courcy's failure to appear before the king's judicial committee (which included Walter de Lacy) in Ireland. It was a convenient pretext for a draconian act, and indeed the same that King Philip Augustus had used against John himself in 1203 when he confiscated Normandy.[34] It is no surprise that the annals of Worcester mention a similar default on the part of William de Briouze in 1208.

A month after the council of Woodstock, on 5 December, King John granted his 'faithful and beloved' Walter de Lacy the cantred of Ardmayle (Co. Tipperary) during pleasure, for which he was to answer to the king.[35] Ardmayle was part of the Briouze honor of Limerick,[36] and the terms of its granting can only have signalled the break-up of the Briouze honor. Meanwhile, as John made strides in reorganising colonial Ireland, his justiciar had yet to win a decisive victory on the ground. The war had been carried out by proxy throughout the autumn, with Meiler rejoining it after the council that November.[37] Hard pressed by Meiler's forces in Leinster, William Marshal's deputies called upon Ulster for aid. Hugh de Lacy had not been summoned to England for the council of Woodstock, and he rode to the rescue with a substantial force, devastating Meiler's lands.[38] Thus, while in England Walter regained the trust of the king, Hugh helped to defeat the Irish justiciar across the sea. Such were the surprising possibilities of transnational lordship.

Hugh's victory went unheralded in England for the time being, however. Severe weather halted communications via the Irish Sea, a reminder that the sea had the power to divide as well as unite.[39] The lack of news was especially frustrating for King John, who, with the great men of the Irish colony attending him in England, stood on the brink of assuming unprecedented control over Irish affairs. Finally, after months of silence, John lost his patience. On 20 February 1208, he forbade the mariners of the Welsh coast to cross to Ireland for anyone, ordered them to be ready for a royal expedition to Ireland on 16 March and threatened to hang all who refused to comply.[40] This indicates the importance which the successful assertion of royal lordship in Ireland held for John, and shows that his Irish expedition was supposed to have been mounted in 1208 (not 1210) as a direct response to the Irish barons' recalcitrance. Before the expedition could get under way, however, news from Ireland finally came. Meiler had been captured, made peace and delivered his son as a hostage.[41] The barons were victorious. As quickly as he had moved to back Meiler against the magnates when that course looked advantageous in early 1207, John reversed course once the Irish justiciar had been defeated. Meiler was soon replaced, and John fell back on the older policy of appeasement with the powerful lords of Meath and Leinster his father had used.[42] To have been forced to swallow his pride and bow to the superiority of the magnates' forces could not have sat well with the king, whatever his public declarations. The seeds of conflict that were to burst forth in 1210 were already sown, but they needed time to germinate.

The storm gathers: 1208–9

For the time being, John's change of heart convinced the barons. However, while the king was unable to humble the Lacys or William Marshal in Ireland, William de Briouze was a different matter. On the same day that Walter made peace with King John, 19 March 1208, he was ordered to hold William de Briouze the younger as a royal hostage for the elder William's good behaviour.[43] Two days later, on 21 March, Philip of Worcester, Roland Bloet and Master Robert of Cirencester were sent to Ireland with a commission to be present at the justiciar's councils, to enact the king's will (if so required) and to review the state of Ireland.[44] As mentioned above, Philip of Worcester had fought against Briouze's overlordship in Limerick in 1201.[45] Just as importantly, Philip's former lands formed the bulk of the territories that the Irish justiciar was supposed to inspect (and possibly take into royal demesne) in 1206, lands to which Philip was ultimately restored as tenant-in-chief in 1215.[46] Given the turmoil sparked by the royal commissions of 1206, it is little wonder that King John was anxious to ensure that William de Briouze accepted Philip's findings.

Meanwhile Walter and William Marshal rode high in royal favour. On the same day that the commissioners were sent to Ireland, Meiler fitz Henry was ordered to deliver seisin of Uí Failge to the Marshal. Two days later, on 23 March, Walter, the Marshal and other Irish barons counselled the king at Southampton, where John ordered that Irish brigands (*latrones*) be expelled from Ireland and brought to judgement according to English law.[47] On 28 March, William Marshal was granted a new charter for Leinster. However, a similar confirmation of his lordship did not immediately follow for Walter de Lacy. Instead, on 9 April, the king directed Robert de Vieuxpont to take Hugh de Lacy, probably Walter's nephew of that name, hostage for Walter's good behaviour.[48] This ensured that Walter did not interfere with the Crown's distraint of Briouze's Welsh marcher lands about this time.[49] Once John's men had completed their task against Walter's father-in-law, Walter received his new charter for Meath. The charter was issued on 24 April at Hereford, at the same time and place that William de Briouze negotiated his own settlement with the king.[50] Perhaps unsurprisingly, Walter de Lacy and William de Briouze were being treated as close allies. The limited terms on which Meath was from now on to be held reserved to the king pleas of the Crown and episcopal investitures, and stated that the king's writ was to run throughout Walter's lands. Walter therefore agreed to surrender the autonomy of his liberty in Meath. In return, John renounced his right of prerogative wardship of the tenants of Meath who held lands elsewhere of the king. Walter wasted little time and crossed to Ireland in May or early June 1208.[51]

From the summer of 1208, the near-absence of chancery enrolments makes events very difficult to read. What can be fathomed for the second half of 1208 is already fairly well known.[52] Dissatisfied with the conditions of his settlement with the king, William de Briouze rebelled, but failed to garner any support among his tenants. This highlights the crisis of aristocratic lordship that underlay his destruction. Instead, he and his family were forced to flee to Walter de Lacy in Ireland. It was at this point that John confiscated all of William's territory, completing his financial and political ruin. William de Briouze and his family were now fugitives, and should have been apprehended by any of John's loyal subjects. However, while royal will had just been enforced in the Welsh march, detaching William's power base at the moment of his rebellion, the events of 1207 had all but proved that Ireland was beyond John's grasp militarily. Instead of turning the Briouzes over to John's officials, the Irish magnates closed ranks against the king. Rough seas forced the fugitives to land in Wicklow, where they were harboured by William Marshal. The new Irish justiciar, Bishop John de Gray, ordered that they be delivered to him, which order the Marshal defied on the grounds that he could not betray his lord, William de Briouze. Whatever the difficulty in proving a tenurial link between the two magnates, the Marshal's actions show the potential strength of seigniorial lordship against a royal challenge. The Lacys then sheltered the Briouzes and proceeded to negotiate with King John on their behalf.

In 1210, King John produced his *Querimonia*, a solemn document sealed in council, in which he explained and justified to the community of his kingdom his destruction of William de Briouze.[53] According to John's testimony, an agreement was reached whereby William was to remain with the Lacys as he undertook to come to the king and make satisfaction for his crimes. If he failed to do so within an allotted time, Walter and Hugh agreed neither to harbour him nor permit him to remain in Ireland.[54] It had only been a matter of months since Walter received a renewed charter for Meath and other concessions from the king, yet this episode exposes the hollowness of these acts of patronage. They merely papered over the cracks in the relationship between king and magnates. King John's anger at the Lacys is palpable in his *Querimonia*, and by 1209 or early 1210 there is evidence that Walter and Hugh were intriguing against King John with King Philip of France.

Knowledge of their apparent treason comes from a letter of King Philip Augustus:

Philip by the grace of God king of France to his dear friend J. de Lacy (*J. de Latiaco*), greeting and affection. We inform you that we shall hold to such a plan concerning your predecessors' lands in England that we shall not be swayed on the subject, if you honour with us the agreement about which our beloved and faithful Roger des Essarts has informed us on your behalf, that is, making war upon King John in England with the friends and allies which Roger says you have, and likewise in Ireland, through your friends and the fortifying of castles, as soon as we know as surely as can be known that this has been done. Paris 1209.[55]

This letter survives only in the Capetian chancery archive, and can therefore be assumed to be a genuine piece of Capetian diplomatic correspondence. At first glance, 'J. de Latiaco' would seem to indicate J(ohn) de Lacy, and, in his study of the reign of King John, Sidney Painter struggled to reconcile the letter's contents with the actions of John de Lacy, the seventeen-year-old son of Roger de Lacy, constable of Chester.[56] However, the addressee of the letter can only have been either Walter or Hugh de Lacy. At the time the letter was composed, John de Lacy was a landless minor, whose father, friends and relatives were all still loyal to the English king. The holdings of the Pontefract Lacys' lands had not been diminished in England (as the implied promise of restoration would argue) and they had no possessions in Ireland.[57] The contents fit the circumstances of Hugh and Walter. For, in addition to holding lands on either side of the Irish Sea, Walter and Hugh de Lacy had recently made war against the king's justiciar in Ireland and were in 1209 sheltering the fugitive Briouze family.

The addressee's intermediary with the French king, Roger des Essarts, was soon to be Hugh de Lacy's companion on the Albigensian Crusade.[58] This link is all the more striking in light of the Dunstable annalist's record, under 1210, of a rumoured plot to drive John from his throne and set up the leader of that crusade, Simon de Montfort (d. 1218), in his stead.[59] Hugh eventually entered a tenurial relationship with Simon, being granted the lordships of Laurac (Aude, cant. Fanjeaux) and Castelnaudary (Aude), near Carcassonne.[60] As explored in Chapter 1, the Lacy brothers' grandfather, Gilbert de Lacy, had been a tenant of the Montfort counts of Évreux, and Gilbert's sons Hugh the elder and Amaury witnessed charters of Simon III de Montfort, count of Évreux (d. 1181). Although the Lacys' Évreux sub-tenancy had passed to a cadet branch under Amaury, both Hugh the elder and Walter de Lacy maintained connections to the region through, for instance, their patronage of the monastery of Saint-Taurin d'Évreux.[61] Hugh granted the monks the churches and tithes of Fore (Co. Westmeath), as well as the neighbouring wood and mill of St Fechin.[62] Walter made further Irish grants to the monastery,[63] and may have counted the then abbot's nephew, John fitz Alured, among his lay tenants in Meath.[64] Saint-Taurin d'Évreux had a long connection with the Montforts, and it was where that Walter and Hugh the younger fled when they were expelled from Ireland in 1210. Hugh's escape was aided by a French connection, the bishop of St Andrews, William Mauvoisin. William appeared alongside the elder Hugh de Lacy in several Norman charters, including one issued by Henry II *c*.1174 granting the liberties of Breteuil to the men of Condé-sur-Iton (Eure, cant. Breteuil) under the bishop of Évreux.[65] Simon de Montfort's son, the more famous baronial reformer Simon de Montfort (d. 1265), witnessed Hugh de Lacy's grant to the church of St Andrews in 1237, less than a year before Bishop William's death.[66] Thus it seems that, only months after Walter's reconciliation with King John for his war against the Irish justiciar, the Lacy brothers were harbouring a known fugitive and were negotiating rebellion with the king of France.

John's treatment of William de Briouze had all too obvious implications for Walter's own standing and security, which may have been too much for Walter to countenance. Rumours of conspiracy, both foreign and domestic, were rife in the wake of the interdict and in anticipation of King John's excommunication, which may have been reason enough for Walter's conspiracy. Evidence of John's insecurity, and the extent of the French king's intrigues, came in the spring of 1209, when negotiations over a marriage alliance between Scotland and France were probably betrayed.[67] When confronted with an English army brought north that summer to ensure his loyalty, King William treated for peace. Roger of Wendover records that King John admonished William for having harboured John's fugitive subjects and open enemies.[68] A wave of episcopal refugees had fled England after the interdict and found refuge in Scotland,[69] and the parallel with the Lacys' harbouring of the Briouze family is obvious. John appears to have decided on decisive action against all rumours of French conspiracy, and, when a Franco-Welsh treaty of alliance was discovered in 1212, John's grand Welsh expedition was halted only as a result of threats from the English baronage.[70]

Although he had not pronounced the interdict in 1208, Walter's brother-in-law, Giles de Briouze, bishop of Hereford was connected with its imposition and had fled to France with those responsible.[71] So while one fugitive Briouze was in exile in France and the others safely tucked away in Meath, letters of conspiracy passed between King Philip and a member of the Lacy family. After King John had forcefully dealt with Scotland, he turned to Wales. The outlawry of William de Briouze in 1208 meant that his vast territories had reverted to the Crown. This gave King John a substantial foothold in the southern and central marches of Wales, and the ability to deal more forcefully with the Welsh princes. On 18 or 19 October 1209, this expansion of royal lordship was made manifest in the homage that the princes of north and south Wales did to John at Woodstock.[72] Once Scotland and Wales were secured, King John could turn to his unfinished business in Ireland.

King John's Irish expedition: 1210

A royal voyage to Ireland was a significant enterprise. Only one other reigning king of England, Richard II, visited the colony between 1172 and 1689.[73] The scale of, and planning involved in, the campaign have been dealt with elsewhere.[74] Suffice to say that it was a major undertaking. In 1210, it was also well timed. While the rest of John's reign could be characterised by a scarcity of financial resources, the period of the interdict, from 1208 to 1213, brought a windfall. John confiscated the property of those clerics who, in accordance with the interdict, refused to perform their spiritual tasks.[75] What is more, at the beginning of 1210 the king compelled the Jews of England to part with much of their wealth, which according to the Waverley annalist amounted to 66,000 marks.[76] With his borders secure and with unprecedented levels of income, King John was ideally placed to mount an expedition to Ireland.

William Marshal and William de Briouze saw the writing on the wall, and hastened to court before the expedition set sail. The Marshal submitted to the king and proved his loyalty by joining the embarking army.[77] Briouze, however, either distrusting John or refusing to proceed with the king against his family, remained behind.[78] That William de Briouze was suffered to remain in Wales while King John and his army crossed the Irish Sea indicates the extent of his political marginalisation, a view only reinforced by the failure of the several incursions he orchestrated with the Welsh (and possibly Hugh de Lacy) in the king's absence.[79] If these were the co-ordinated attacks 'by friends and allies' mentioned in King Philip's letter the previous year, they proved dismally anticlimactic.

King John landed in Ireland on 20 June 1210. The progress of the royal army shows that his expedition was concerned with reasserting royal lordship in Ireland while bringing its magnates, the Lacy brothers in particular, to heel. Had the honor of Limerick been the issue central to John's Irish expedition, as he claimed in his *Querimonia*, he might have been expected to express his personal lordship over it by touring the territory (as he was to do in Meath). Instead, after making land at Crooke (Co. Waterford), John lingered in Waterford, where he received the submission of Donnchad Cairprech Ua Briain, king of Thomond. According to Mac Carthaigh's Book, John established a tenurial relationship with the Irish king through a grant of the lordship (*tigernas*) of Carrac Ui gCoinneall (Carrigogunnell, bar. Pubblebrien, Co. Limerick) on the Shannon, and even made Donnchad a knight (*ridire*).[80] It is significant that Ua Briain was obliged to journey to Waterford, not Limerick (the obvious setting for his submission). Instead of going west, John now made for his true targets: the unrepentant Lacy brothers. After parading his royal authority through the Marshal's lordship of Leinster, King John halted in Dublin.[81]

The 1209 French letter mentioned the readying of castles in Ireland, but Walter lost his nerve. Only his brother Hugh put up any resistance to the royal army. The difference between the two brothers was that Ireland was Hugh's only real concern, while Walter had his English and Welsh lands to consider. What is more, Hugh had personally enfeoffed many of his tenants in Ulster, who proved themselves loyal to him in the face of the king on this and other occasions. By contrast, King John had intrigued in Meath since 1186. He also had bestowed patronage upon the senior members of Meath's colonial community since they last stood with Walter against the Crown in 1207. If Walter wanted to oppose John in 1210, the capitulation of William Marshal in Leinster and the uncertain loyalty of his own knights may have shaken his resolve. However, Walter waited too long to decide. In failing to emulate William Marshal and William de Briouze by submitting himself to John before the royal army set out from Wales, Walter left himself open to attack.

The manoeuvre that Walter then performed was adroit, if not immediately successful. On 28 June, his messengers approached the king at Dublin, offering his total submission and his brother Hugh de Lacy as a scapegoat.[82] Through this, Walter hoped that John would see him as the (blameless) law-abiding brother and Hugh as the reckless adventurer: the roles they had played so well since 1203. Nevertheless, King John immediately banished Walter, and seized his inheritance.[83] With Hugh still defiantly harbouring the Briouze family in Ulster, King John sent his fleet north to wait for him at Carlingford (Co. Louth). John then did in Meath what he did not bother doing in Limerick: he made a progress through his confiscated lordship with its most powerful tenants in attendance.[84] The psychological effect of this triumphal tour should not be underestimated. On 30 June, King John granted Hugh de Lacy's Meath sub-tenancy at Ratoath to Philip of Worcester. Ratoath had been alienated by John after 1186, and its bestowal upon the Lacys' old administrative rival (and Briouze's enemy) was steeped in symbolism.[85] The grant was witnessed by many of Walter de Lacy's tenants, including three of his messengers to the king at Dublin: William le Petit, Richard de Tuit and Richard de Feipo.[86]

Progressing to the *caput* of Walter's lordship, John took the castle of Trim and held court outside its walls from 2 to 4 July. The royal army then moved on to Kells, where it camped from 4 to 5 July.[87] On the way from Trim to Kells, its ranks were swelled by the arrival of the forces of the king of Connacht, Cathal Crobderg, who submitted to John at Ardbraccan (bar. Lower Navan, Co. Meath).[88] From Kells, the king dispatched a force under John Marshal, probably to secure the other Lacy castles in Meath.[89] It was only then that the bulk of the royal army turned north. John's circuit of Meath allowed Hugh de Lacy and the Briouzes time to escape from Ireland at his approach. By the time of the fall of Hugh's stronghold at Carrickfergus (Co. Antrim), the fugitives had crossed to Scotland.[90]

John made another circuit of Meath upon his return from Ulster, before turning to the matter of William Marshal at Dublin. William had flouted John's authority in 1207, and sheltered the fugitive Briouze family in 1208. The latter was a treasonable offence, yet the Marshal's biography (ever anxious to talk up William's prowess) claims that he was saved because no one dared face him in a trial of combat to prove his transgressions.[91] Perhaps William's timely submission to John's authority before the expedition also counted. By contrast, the Lacys remained defiant until John was at their door (and Hugh remained so thereafter, even when driven to Scotland). They had left the question of their loyalty open for too long for John to tolerate while he had the power to do otherwise. An example had to be made, and it was only their timely escape that prevented the Lacy brothers from feeling the full force of the famous Angevin temper.

Nothing is known of Walter's route from Ireland, but the anonymous of Béthune records that Hugh de Lacy, Matilda de St Valery (Briouze's wife) and William de Briouze the younger fled to the Isle of Man, where they rested for four days, before continuing to Scotland.[92] This is intriguing. The king of Man was Rǫgnvaldr Guðrøðarson, brother-in-law of the former lord of Ulster, John de Courcy, and a man unlikely to show Hugh de Lacy hospitality. What is more, Man served as a supply depot for King John's Irish expedition.[93] However, according to the Bagler sagas

(*Böglunga sögur*), King Inge of Norway attacked the island that summer and forced King Rǫgnvaldr to submit to him.[94] This would have allowed the fugitives safe passage. The sagas assert that King Rǫgnvaldr was absent from Man (possibly with King Inge in Norway) when an English fleet ravaged it in the wake of the fugitives' escape.[95] King John had taken Rǫgnvaldr under his protection as early as February 1205, and was shortly to establish a tenurial bond with the Manx king, in 1212.[96] John's assault on Man was aimed at reasserting English hegemony over the island by attacking those who had profited from the Norse invasion and allowed the fugitives to escape.

Meanwhile, Hugh de Lacy and the Briouzes crossed to Galloway, where Matilda, her son William and others of their party were taken captive by Duncan, earl of Carrick.[97] Hugh de Lacy and Reginald de Briouze (the Briouzes' second son) escaped and fled to Lennox (Dumbartonshire and part of Stirlingshire). Hugh left his own sons with the lord of the area, probably Alwin, earl of Lennox (d. *c*.1217), and journeyed with a handful of men to St Andrews (Fife).[98] Here they were received by the bishop, William Mauvoisin, whose connection to the Lacys has been mentioned above.[99] Walter Bower claims that spies in search of Hugh de Lacy reached St Andrews only shortly after Hugh's departure by ship for France. Not finding him, the agents left cheated of their hopes.[100]

Walter and Hugh de Lacy were reunited in France. Several later Anglo-Irish annals relate that, after escaping the king in Ireland, the Lacy brothers secretly fled to the abbey of Saint-Taurin d'Évreux in Normandy, serving in various menial employments. Being at last discovered by the abbot, the brothers were reconciled with the king through his entreaties.[101] Not all aspects of this tale are altogether implausible considering the Lacys' ties to the monastery, and the prospect that Walter and Hugh came together in exile is enticing. In the face of the royal army, Walter had disavowed all connection to his brother, relinquishing Hugh's subtenancies in Meath to the king and complaining of losses suffered at his hands. Their reunion in exile would suggest that the brothers were in fact working together, a strategy used by other Anglo-Norman families, such as the Marshal brothers in the period of King Richard's absence and captivity, 1190–94.[102]

Ireland without the Lacys

The immediate and total withdrawal of the colony's leading family naturally had drastic implications for the political landscape of Ireland. The Lacys' removal created a power vacuum in Ireland, and removed the main barriers to the expansion of royal lordship there. Consequently, the early days of post-Lacy Ireland display definite signs both of the emergence of a strong central authority and of the clear absence of a stabilising force as King John sought to capitalise on his victory. Holding Limerick and Meath as Walter de Lacy had in 1206, King John now controlled the main approaches to Connacht. Unsurprisingly, he was quick to improve his position, authorising the construction of a bridge over the Shannon and a stone castle at Athlone.[103] The king then set about supplanting the old lord of Meath by bestowing patronage upon a number of his tenants. When John de Gray was called away to attend the king's Welsh expedition the following year, King John replaced him as Irish justiciar with Walter's former captain, Richard de Tuit.[104] However, Richard was not long in his office before he was killed by a collapsing tower while overseeing the construction of Athlone Castle.[105] John then handed the reins of the royal administration to Walter de Lacy's former constable, and recently appointed royal steward of Meath, William le Petit.[106]

William's term in office is known from the Irish Pipe Roll 14 John, which is an invaluable source for historians of early thirteenth-century Ireland. Of vital importance to the assertion of royal lordship in the aftermath of John's victory is its record of expenditure on the repair and fortification of the colony's defences. Within the former Lacy hegemony, the castles of Trim, Nobber and Athboy (Co. Meath), Athlone and Kilbixy (Co. Westmeath), Incheleffer (Co. Longford), Kilmore and Belturbet (Co. Cavan), were fortified, while over £44 was spent for the ward and garrisoning of the castles of Galtrim, Kells, Nobber, Duleek and Drogheda (Co. Meath), Lough Sewdy and Fore (Co. Westmeath) and Incheleffer.[107] These improvements were physical manifestations of John's immediate lordship in Meath. Anyone who looked upon these castles would know that they were now royal castles. King John was clearly in charge.

John's defensive improvements were also desperately needed thanks to his domineering approach in 1210. John had cowed William Marshal and defeated the Lacys, but he also had alienated the powerful Irish kings Cathal Crobderg Ua Conchobair and Áed Méith Ua Néill. With the lords of Meath and Ulster gone, the main blocks against Connacht and Tír Eógain were removed.[108] Only months after John's departure from Ireland, Gofraid, son of Domnall mac William, a claimant to the Scottish throne, led an invasion of Scotland from the north of Ireland. In this he likely had the active support of the king of Tír Eógain.[109] To block Ua Néill's growing independence, in May 1212 John installed in Ulster the family of the great sea-captain Alan of Galloway. Alan was granted 140 knights' fees, comprising almost all of the northern counties Antrim and Londonderry (including lands belonging to Ua Néill). Others, including Alan's younger brother, Earl Thomas of Atholl, his cousin, Earl Duncan of Carrick, and kinsman by marriage, King Rǫgnvaldr of Man, also received grants in Hugh de Lacy's former earldom.[110] The impact of these grants was immediate. In 1212, Earl Thomas joined with the sons of Rǫgnvaldr Somerliðisson (Ragnall mac Somairle) of the Isles (to whom the Gallowegians were also connected by marriage) in a punitive expedition against Derry (Co. Londonderry) for Ua Néill's support of the Mac Williams.[111] This episode shows the extent of the English king's hegemony over the region, but it also displays the relative impotence of the royal steward of Ulster, who could not constrain the Uí Néill. The English king once again had to rely upon his magnates, including the Gallowegians, to enact his will in the region.

As in Ulster, Meath also felt the loss of its lord. In 1172, the Lacy lordship of Meath had been created to replace the Uí Máel Sechlainn kingdom of Mide. Although the Lacys met with a great deal of success in the conquest of Meath, its traditional ruling dynasty had never gone away. The transfer of lordship from Walter de Lacy to the distant English king provided an opportunity for the native dynasty to reassert itself. In 1212, Cormac mac Art Ua Máel Sechlainn wrested control of Delbna Ethra (bar. Garrycastle, Co. Offaly) from the settlers, with his son, Máel Sechlainn, defeating the local English defensive force and killing its constable, Robert of Duncomar.[112] Evidence of this war, referred to as 'MacArt's war' (*gwerram de Machart*), is also found in the Irish Pipe Roll 14 John.[113] The Irish justiciar, John de Gray, joined with a force from Munster under Donnchad Cairprech Ua Briain and attacked Cormac at Kilnagrann in Fir Cell. The royal forces were beaten, however, and it was not until Cormac was faced by an assembly of Irish forces that he was at last brought to obedience.[114] A series of dynastic battles then consumed the Uí Máel Sechlainn, drawing in a number of colonists and adding further instability to the Irish midlands.[115]

Thus, while King John's victory over the Lacys had been total, it was not accompanied by the proportional extension of royal lordship in Ireland he had hoped for. The reasons for this are many, but in the former Lacy lordships of Meath and (to a lesser extent) Ulster much of the blame must be placed on John's decision to retain most of his new territories as royal demesne. He had several reasons to do so. F. X. Martin highlights the financial benefits: 'taking over the lordships of Meath and Ulster was to be part recompense for the financial outlay of the expedition to Ireland', though Martin underestimated the king's resources for the expedition.[116] More importantly, the disturbances of 1207 had reminded John of the dangers of powerful provincial lordships. However, it is also worth noting the personal relationship between magnate and king. For all of his seeming treachery, Walter de Lacy remained a powerful and well-connected baron. The speed with which he was eventually reconciled with John hints that reconciliation was always at the back of the king's mind. This could explain why John kept the lordship of Meath intact, only granting away non-demesne manors, such as Hugh de Lacy's Ratoath. For the time being, John's policy brought him more authority, but his colony less security, within Ireland.

From exile to reconciliation: 1210-13

While their lands were laid open to royal administrators and Irish assaults, the Lacys remained in France. As mentioned above, the story of their stay at Saint-Taurin d'Évreux states that its abbot secured their reconciliation with King John.[117] While their long-standing connection with the abbey makes a three-year covert existence there unlikely, the circumstances of 1213 suggest that King John would have listened to an ecclesiastical intercessor. John's protracted political duel with the Church over the disputed Canterbury succession was ever in the background as the king faced a Welsh uprising, mounting baronial discontent and threats from King Philip. On 13 May 1213, John finally relented. He made peace with the pope, formally surrendering 'the entire realm of England and the entire realm of Ireland', and receiving them back as papal fiefs.[118] As well as removing a name from his long list of enemies, this also secured John ecclesiastical protection. Rather than fighting *for* the Church against an excommunicate king, any aggressor would hereafter be attacking the pope's vassal. The papal legate Pandulf immediately crossed to France, forbidding King Philip to follow through with his planned invasion of England. The French king was indignant, but ultimately acquiesced.[119]

Walter de Lacy's fortunes changed soon thereafter. At the beginning of June 1213, two weeks after his rapprochement with the pope, King John issued letters recalling Walter from exile.[120] Walter's decision to seek reconciliation is noteworthy. While Walter had been able to flee to a Norman monastery in 1210, his wife's family was not so lucky. After their capture in Scotland, her mother and brother (Matilda de St Valery and William the younger) had starved to death in John's prison at Windsor.[121] To lose sight of that fact would be to underestimate Walter's decision to re-enter

John's service in 1213. Loath though he might have been to admit it, Walter de Lacy needed King John. King Philip had been willing to make vague promises to a strategically placed aristocrat in 1209 or early 1210, but there is no evidence that he actually assisted Walter in exile. The only way to prevent the Lacy family from fading away into obscurity was to return to England. No royal record of a fine survives, though one Dublin-based set of annals mention that Walter paid the king 2,500 marks.[122] Whether this was born of a spirit of reconciliation or strict pragmatism, by the summer of 1213 Walter de Lacy was once again King John's loyal magnate.

The specifics are impossible to determine, but, if the abbot of Saint-Taurin d'Évreux pleaded on Walter's behalf, his cause may have been tied to the pope's. John's settlement with Pope Innocent stipulated that the king was to restore and receive back into favour those clerics and laymen connected with their dispute. Elsewhere, the rebel barons Eustace de Vesci and Robert fitz Walter convinced papal representatives that they ought to be named specifically in the agreement, so it is possible that Walter's restoration was in some way linked to this order.[123] However, Joe Hillaby contends that Walter's return had 'almost certainly' been negotiated by the Irish barons around the time of their famous profession of loyalty in 1212.[124] The problem with this interpretation is that, when Walter re-entered John's service in 1213, only his English lands were restored.[125] Negotiations over Meath probably began as well, and terms may well have been agreed, but its restoration was not ordered until 1215 and not fully achieved until Walter visited Ireland in 1220.[126] Hillaby also speculates that Walter was re-established in the Welsh march to curb the growing power of his brothers-in-law, Reginald and Giles de Briouze. Brock Holden agrees, asserting that the troubled state of the Welsh march prompted John to welcome Walter back.[127] This scenario is more plausible, because the restoration of Walter's English lands, minus Ludlow, was ordered on 29 July 1213, just after Giles's return from exile, and three days before a truce with the Welsh was scheduled to end.[128] However, although this timing is unlikely to be a coincidence, there is reason to believe that the security of the Welsh march was not the primary factor in Walter's return.

The Welsh march was always important to the English king, but the situation was far more pressing elsewhere. John's surrender of England and Ireland to Innocent III had removed any threat that a Welsh uprising might be characterised as a war in support of the pope. With King John his loyal vassal, the pope ordered his legate Pandulf to negotiate a truce between John and the Welsh.[129] Walter's return from exile on June 2 came a day before the truce was agreed on 3 June.[130] Although the truce expired on 1 August, the papal position made it unlikely that hostilities would recommence. Indeed, on 25 August, King John authorised the wardens of the Welsh march to prolong the truce to 1 November.[131] The truce then seems to have remained in effect for the rest of 1213 and throughout 1214.[132] The state of affairs along the Welsh march had been much worse for John during the Welsh offensive the previous year when a Franco-Welsh treaty of alliance was negotiated and 'the king had nearly as many enemies as he had magnates'.[133] Circumstances would eventually grow desperate enough to require Walter de Lacy's presence during the civil war, but in the summer of 1213 King John's surrender to the pope meant that his position in the region was markedly better than it had been for years.

Walter was not merely an Irish baron, or Welsh marcher. He was an international aristocrat and seasoned veteran. As such, his role in John's Poitevin expedition deserves consideration as a cause of his restoration.[134] As Rees Davies points out, 'there was no quicker route to re-establish an aristocratic family's fortune or to win the trust of the king' than proven military prowess.[135] Walter's recall was immediately preceded by a muster of forces for the defence of England against French invasion that spring, and a crushingly successful seaborne assault against King Philip's fleet at Damme (West-Vlaanderen) on 30 May 1213.[136] With the French navy more than decimated, King John moved to press home his advantage. Shortly after Lacy's recall, John dispatched William, earl of Salisbury, with money and reinforcements to support the count of Flanders against King Philip's army in the north, and reassembled his forces in order to mount an expedition to Poitou.[137] In this light, Walter de Lacy was a valuable soldier in his ongoing war against King Philip.

The Poitevin expedition of 1213 never materialised, because the assembled aristocracy refused to accompany John overseas. Although King John is famous for his use of mercenary armies, the aborted Poitevin expedition is a reminder that, for the major campaigns at least, royal armies depended on troops provided by the barons. These large armies were therefore as much manifestations of aristocratic dependence as royal. In this instance, the barons took issue with the terms of service John demanded of them, some airing the old claim that their military obligation pertained only to England. According to Roger of Wendover, the barons also refused to follow John while the sentence of excommunication still hung over him.[138] Norgate takes a rather more cynical view of the barons' reticence, pointing out that the same men had for years fought and dined with the excommunicate king.[139] While it would be naive to ignore the larger context of mounting baronial dissatisfaction with John's rule, there may be more to Wendover's claim than Norgate allowed. The host assembled in July 1213 was to be used to support a suspected heretic, John's ally Count Raymond of Toulouse. To make matters worse, the barons would be combating not only the forces of Philip Augustus but potentially the crusaders who had been fighting to rid Languedoc of the Albigensian heretics since 1209. The Albigensians had long been demonised in the lands of Plantagenet and Capetian kings, and as far back as the 1170s the call to put down their heresy had been used by Henry II and Louis VII to justify armed intervention *against* the counts of Toulouse.[140] Roger of Wendover at least saw a link between John's expedition and the crusade. Immediately after his account of the barons' refusal to follow John to Poitou, Wendover reminds his audience of the Albigensian heresy, and provides a rather sympathetic history of the crusade to that point.[141] Popular opinion in England was on the side of the crusaders, with whom many nobles identified. Given the pope's continued support of the crusade, the English barons' desire not to be led against a crusade by an excommunicate king is understandable.

The rewards of military service: 1214-15

Interestingly, while Walter de Lacy may have been recalled in order to fight for King John in Wales or Poitou, his brother Hugh de Lacy was already in Languedoc as a crusader. After being reunited with Walter in the abbey of Saint-Taurin, Hugh set off south. In Languedoc Hugh fought alongside the Lacys' intermediary with the king of France, Roger des Essarts, and the rumoured figurehead of rebellion in 1210, Simon de Montfort.[142] The crusade offered a martial outlet for some Norman lords who found themselves constrained by the Capetian conquest of Normandy in 1204, and Montfort granted a number of them confiscated lands for following him long after their crusading vows had been fulfilled.[143] Expelled from Ulster, Hugh de Lacy likewise relished the prospect of campaigning in Languedoc. For his service, Simon de Montfort granted Hugh the conquered lordships of Laurac (Aude, cant. Fanjeaux) and Castelnaudary (Aude), near Carcassonne.[144] Hugh was consequently able to shun until 1221 all overtures of reconciliation from the Plantagenet royal government that his brother Walter negotiated for him.[145] By attacking the Albigensians and their patron, Raymond of Toulouse, Hugh and his comrades were by extension attacking Raymond's ally, King John. The pope suspected King Philip's son Louis of playing a similar game when he eventually took over the leadership of the crusade in 1219.[146] It may not be a coincidence that

Simon de Montfort was rumoured to have coveted the crown of England for himself in 1210 (with several of his fellow crusaders being implicated in a treasonous conspiracy), while Prince Louis actually had himself elected king of England in 1216. The failure of both attempts in England brought fresh impetus to the Albigensian Crusade.

By the end of 1213, Count Raymond's position in Languedoc was dire, and King John could wait no longer. He first ensured that the war against King Philip would proceed in the north without him, and then heeded Raymond's calls for aid in February 1214.[147] Walter de Lacy meanwhile mobilised his resources and landed at La Rochelle (Charente-Maritime) about 14 March.[148] Walter's movements are difficult to chart, but he had joined the king by the beginning of April, when the pair visited the Grandmontine priory in La Marche (Haute-Vienne, cant. Ambazac).[149] He then accompanied the king as far as La Réole (Gironde), where, on 13 April, he was issued with a curious task. Walter was sent south, ostensibly to purchase horses in Narbonne (Aude).[150] The men of Narbonne were given the king's bond for 100 marks to assist the purchase, which, combined with whatever other money Walter had available to him for the purchase, might have bought more than one hundred mounts. It is unfortunate that nothing more is known of this mission, for the possibilities surrounding it are intriguing. Situated on the Mediterranean coast, Narbonne is approximately 210 miles south-east of La Réole, where Walter was assigned his task. To reach the city, Lacy had to negotiate the rugged territory occupied by the Albigensian crusaders, passing both Toulouse and Carcassonne on the way. There is no previous evidence of Walter ever being south of Normandy, let alone to the Mediterranean, so John was sending Walter into unknown country. It may be that the mission was only partly to do with its professed purpose. The only tie that Walter had to Languedoc was through his brother Hugh, and the only reason to send Walter, instead of a knight or local lord, would have revolved around this detail. In the following year, 1215, King John reminded Hugh de Lacy that Walter had long since made a fine with him for the restoration of Hugh's territory of Ulster, and that John had tarried in Hugh's neighbourhood for longer than he had liked without Hugh paying that fine.[151] This can have referred only to the 1214 Poitevin expedition, when John and Hugh were both in southern France. Consequently, Walter's mission likely turned on John's attempts to return Hugh to his allegiance. Unfortunately, nothing further is heard of the matter, or of Walter de Lacy, until the fateful end of John's Poitevin expedition that autumn.

After a period of initial success, the war did not go well for John.[152]

On 9 July 1214, he wrote to England asking all who were not engaged in the governance of the kingdom to hasten to him in Poitou. Like Walter de Lacy, their service was to be rewarded with the relaxation of any ire which John might have conceived towards them.[153] The king's dispatch was all but ignored. On 27 July, John's imperial allies, aided by the earl of Salisbury, suffered a catastrophic defeat by King Philip's army at Bouvines (Nord, cant. Cysoing). Whether or not one agrees with Holt's famous pronouncement that 'the road from Bouvines to Runnymede was direct, short and unavoidable',[154] John feared the worst. Baronial discontent had been mounting in England throughout the Poitevin campaign, and, upon hearing the news from Bouvines, John sent orders relating to the defence of his castles and person.[155] He was nevertheless determined to continue his campaign and face the forces of France alone, but was ultimately persuaded by the pope to negotiate a cessation of hostilities. In September 1214, King John concluded a truce with Philip Augustus to last for five years from Easter. He took ship for England the following month.[156]

Upon reaching England, Walter de Lacy reaped his reward for faithful service. Before 7 May 1214, terms for the restoration of the manor of Ludlow (which had not been restored with the rest of Walter's English lands) were set at a £40 render towards the custody of its castle.[157] By the end of Walter's term on the continent, this had changed. On 23 October, the sheriff of Herefordshire was ordered to restore the manor of Ludlow to Walter, without any mention of a fine.[158] Indeed, it seems as though Walter had been able to renegotiate so that the king paid *him* for the retention of Ludlow castle. An order to the same sheriff several days later makes the situation clear. On 2 November John wrote that, while it might have been more sensible to restore Ludlow castle to Walter than to pay 40 marks a year for its custody, he wished the sheriff of Herefordshire to retain the castle and allow Walter the manor as per the agreement between them, because he did not wish to renege on that agreement.[159] Finally, on 26 December 1214, John restored to Walter 'all of the liberties (*libertates*) which his father Hugh de Lacy rightfully had in the time of Henry II'.[160] Although Ludlow castle remained in the hands of the Crown, Walter's lordship was reinstated fully in England and the Welsh march a year and a half after his recall from exile.

As the situation in England grew ever more desperate for John, Walter turned his attention to the recovery of Meath. The fact that the components of the Lacy inheritance either side of the Irish Sea were dealt with separately is instructive. King Richard had sequestrated Walter de Lacy's Norman lands in 1196, and had taken his English (and probably Welsh) territories for failing to pay the resultant 1,000 mark fine. In 1198, all were restored for the same fine.[161] The fact that John was unwilling to do the same for Walter's English, Welsh and Irish lands suggests that he was eager to emphasise Ireland's separate status. On 10 February, a vital step towards Walter's restoration in Ireland was taken with the release of his half-brother, William de Lacy, who was to serve as Walter's seneschal in Meath.[162] Just over a month later, on 15 March 1215, Walter made a fine of 4,000 marks with the king for the restoration of his Irish lands.[163] When compared with the 2,500 mark fine that Walter had agreed with John for Meath in 1195, the 1,000 mark fine King Richard demanded for his Norman lands in 1196 and the 3,100 mark fine that Walter ultimately agreed for the restoration of his English (possibly Welsh) and Norman fees in 1198,[164] the new fine highlights the rising cost of reinstatement. Furthermore, King John expected to be paid promptly. The following day, he wrote that he had deposited the charters for Walter's English and Irish possessions in the New Temple, London, to be returned to Walter once he had satisfied his fine.[165] In an age when the possession of a written title to land was increasingly important, the implications were clear. One month later, on 22 April, John wrote to Hugh de Lacy expressing his displeasure at Hugh's failure to pay the negotiated fine for Ulster, and declaring that he had no choice but to convert Ulster to profit as his own.[166] Whatever Walter's string of restorations might suggest, in the period of heightened anxiety on the eve of civil war, the king was taking no chances.

Civil war: 1215-16

The actual order for Walter's seisin of Meath did not come for another four months, in which time England descended into civil war. The steady march towards war lay in the background to all of the king's dealings with Walter in this period. For instance, the reason for John's initial retention of Ludlow castle was almost certainly the security of the Welsh march against the rising tide of baronial discontent. The Crown's resources were stretched, however, and on 12 April 1215 John found that he had no choice but to entrust the castle to Walter and rid himself of its upkeep, garrisoning and rent.[167] For the past few months, King John had sought to nullify the threat from Wales both by ameliorating his relations with the Welsh themselves and by securing the fidelity of his marcher barons. However, his mismanagement meant that a united Welsh opposition allied itself with a league of disaffected English barons to present John with a significant challenge to his kingship that spring.[168] What is more, there was even dissension within the march. Walter's brothers-in-law, Reginald and Giles de Briouze, whose family interests had only just been restored, aligned themselves against the king,[169] as did Henry de Bohun, earl of Hereford, Fulk fitz Warin and several others.[170] The king wrote to the border sheriffs in the spring of 1215 to determine who in their shires had rebelled, and who remained loyal. For the central border with Wales, the sheriff of Shropshire wrote that several barons of note and their knights were rebelling in Shropshire, while Earl Ranulf of Chester and William Marshal had come to Shrewsbury (Shropshire) in royal service and Walter de Lacy, Walter of Clifford and John le Strange had taken up arms in the king's defence.[171] The sheriff of Herefordshire (Walter of Clifford) sent the king the disturbing news that 'the whole county of Hereford, besides the barons and their men, was with the bishop of Hereford [Giles de Briouze] against the king, and bore arms against the king or sent armed men'.[172]

The royalist barons of the march mustered under Walter de Lacy, John of Monmouth, Hugh de Mortimer and Walter of Clifford at Gloucester by the end of April 1215.[173] On 27 April, the rebels handed the king's representatives their demands, which, upon reading, John roundly rejected. The rebel barons sent John a formal renunciation of their homage and fealty on 3 May, advanced to Northampton, occupied the town and laid siege to the castle.[174] John had by then pulled Walter de Lacy and his comrades away from the march, ordering them, on 30 April, to proceed south-east to Cirencester (Gloucestershire) by the following Monday (3 May) well furnished with horses and arms and all the men they could get.[175] While the order told them to await the king's further commands at Cirencester, a separate dispatch shows that the marchers were to act as they saw fit until those commands came.[176] This gave them licence to pursue private warfare in the king's name, for which they were granted horses on 17 May.[177]

The general progress of the civil war need not be rehearsed here, but matters grew steadily worse for King John.[178] On the same day that the marchers were granted chargers, the rebels took London. The capture of London not only proved the rebellion viable but swelled its ranks. Just as alarmingly for Walter and his fellow marchers, the town of Shrewsbury surrendered to Llywelyn without a fight shortly thereafter.[179] The Briouze brothers then retook a number of their father's castles and territories from royal custodians, establishing a rebel bridgehead in the central march.[180] Further advances were made by the Welsh against the Marshal interests in the southern march, and a fresh outbreak of rebellion flared up in Devon.[181] The royalists needed to regroup and gather their strength.

The agreement witnessed by Magna Carta on 15 June 1215 bought the royalists time, but little else. For Walter, this meant a chance to focus on Ireland. On 5 July, the earlier agreement for Meath's restoration was finally enacted.[182] Drogheda was retained in the king's hand for three years, during which time the king allowed a rent of 30 marks against Walter's fine. As security, Walter's son and heir Gilbert was handed over as a hostage.[183] The next day, 6 July, John ordered the Irish justiciar to restore Walter's Irish castles once sureties for his fine had been obtained. However, all did not go smoothly. The king was, after all, preoccupied with English affairs. It took until 27 July for him to order Walter's knights and tenants in Meath to be attentive to him. Just five days later, on 1 August, this order was amended to stipulate that Walter's knights and tenants were to be attentive to him only *after* sureties for his fine had been found.[184] Walter was apparently having a difficult time finding anyone to guarantee his fine in that troubled period. John then ordered the Irish justiciar to restore Walter to his lands and tenements even if he was only able to find surety for 1,000 marks, a quarter of the fine.[185] Whatever Walter's difficulties, on the following day, 2 August, the Irish justiciar was ordered to restore Walter's ships.[186] Walter then sent William de Lacy to Ireland to look after the family's interests.[187] The months from May to July were especially busy ones for messengers conveying the king's mandates to Ireland. They included grants to towns, individual barons and religious foundations, as well as matters of defence and local administration.[188]

The Irish activity was such that it led Norgate to conclude that John 'was specially endeavouring to win for himself the support of the nobles, clergy and people of the Irish March as a counterpoise to the hostility and disaffection which surrounded him in his English realm'.[189] The situation was likely more complicated than that, for the native Irish were not idle while the king of England foundered.[190] What is more, there is evidence that John viewed Ireland as a possible last redoubt in the event that the rebels defeated him in England.[191] The Anonymous of Béthune reports that John sent his wife, Isabella, and eldest son, Henry, to Corfe castle (Dorset) at the beginning of the rebellion, where they were protected by Savaric de Mauléon. The Anonymous mentions young Henry being there in June 1216, but the Dunstable annalist places him at Bristol (which Savaric was then holding) in October 1216.[192] A movement from Corfe to Bristol makes sense, because, by summer 1216, Corfe was too close to Louis's troops in Hampshire. Whether to preserve an escape route, or simply to prevent the rebellion from spreading to another of his realms (which, as will be seen, was quite possible), John sought to secure Ireland in 1215.

In addition to fortifying Ireland, John used the break in hostilities to gather his forces in England, and redouble his efforts to secure papal support against the rebels. Those efforts bore fruit for the Welsh march that October, when, under pressure from the pope, Giles de Briouze agreed to terms.[193] Giles's defection largely stabilised the region, even more so when, upon his death less than a month later (17 November 1215), custody of his lands and castles was given to the steadfast royalists William Marshal (the elder) and Walter of Clifford.[194] Llywelyn captured a number of castles in southern Wales that December,[195] but the central march remained largely untouched by his aggression. That said, on 26 December 1215, the sheriff of Herefordshire, Engelard de Cigogné, was once again ordered to allow Walter de Lacy his liberties and to prevent any acts against Walter or his men,[196] which implies some threat (military or bureaucratic) to Walter's lordship in the region. Walter may have been away from the march with one of the two main branches of John's army, marching north or to London.[197] By 4 April he and his men were along the southern coast of England, guarding it against another expected French invasion.[198]

King John patrolled the Kent coastline before the end of the month, but was unable to prevent King Philip's son Louis from landing in England on 21 May 1216.[199] Now more than ever, John needed to recoup support from the barons. On 24 May, Walter and a few fellow marchers aided the king's negotiations with Reginald de Briouze. The talks did not go well, with John writing to Reginald on 28 May to negotiate 'in the spirit of saner council'.[200] These fruitless negotiations, coupled with the belief that Louis might soon strike at the region, brought King John to the Welsh border. There, while Louis sat in London, John unsuccessfully sought to gain the submissions of Reginald de Briouze and a number of native Welsh lords. John managed to burn the rebel castles of Hay, Radnor and Oswestry (Shropshire), but dared not hazard a direct confrontation with Llywelyn.[201] Reconciliation with Reginald de Briouze had still not been achieved by 7 August,[202] whereupon John decided to consolidate his position in the region by promoting Walter de Lacy. John knew that a powerful local magnate could become intractable if granted too much authority, but there was no more cost-effective solution to a region's security than the devolution of royal authority upon one better able to mobilise forces for its defence. As noted above, the earl of Hereford, Henry de Bohun, had been in rebellion since the spring of 1215, so Walter was raised as an alternative to him in Herefordshire. On 8 August 1216, Walter and his comrades were granted the custody of Elmley Castle, Worcestershire.[203] Ten days later, on 18 August, Walter was granted the shrievalty and royal castle of Hereford.[204] When, on 30 August, Walter was given custody of the temporalities of the vacant see of Hereford, his position in the region was practically unassailable.[205]

In Walter's commission as custodian of Hereford Castle, it was allowed that, if Louis besieged Hereford Castle so that the siege could not be raised without the intervention of an army, then Walter de Lacy did not have to risk himself in the castle. Instead, he had only to ensure that it was garrisoned by those who could be trusted to defend it without loss to the king's honour and advantage.[206] Walter immediately had to find such a force. By this point John had received better intelligence regarding Louis's activities and, gathering a large host from the garrisons of the region, including Walter de Lacy, left the march to harass the rebel army that was besieging Windsor Castle (Berkshire), before striking the rebels in the east of England.[207] From 21 September to 8 October King John cut an impressive path of destruction through rebel territory, relieving Lincoln castle in the process through the sheer terror of his progress.[208] Things were also looking up for the king elsewhere. Louis was losing ground in England, with several of his adherents, including William de Fors, count of Aumale, rejoining John. However, on 9 October the royal army entered the town of Lynn (Norfolk), where an attack of dysentery forced him to consider his mortality.[209] The following day, while in considerable discomfort, John granted three carucates of land in the forest of Aconbury (Herefordshire) to Walter's wife, Margery de Briouze, to found a house of nuns for the souls of her father, mother and brother.[210] Unlikely to elicit any political advantage for the dying king, this seems to have been restitution for his destruction of William de Briouze and cruel starving of Margaret and William the younger in 1210. King John died nine days later at Newark.[211] The Welsh marcher barons who had followed John east were well represented at his deathbed, with Walter de Lacy and John of Monmouth being named among the executors of his will.[212]

Conclusion

In the early days of the English invasion of Ireland, King Henry II had sought to control his new volatile territory by more or less emulating the practice of the early Norman kings regarding Wales. Lacking the resources to mount a thorough conquest of Ireland, Henry had allowed new imports from the Welsh march (such as Strongbow and Hugh de Lacy) something approaching marcher liberties in Ireland. In Ireland, as in Wales, these lords had been granted a great deal of control over their frontier territories in order to support their lordship in a hostile and ethnically mixed realm. However, John, as lord of Ireland, sought to revoke the independent character of colonial lordship in Ireland. Some of John's first grants as lord of Ireland in 1185 reserved the Crown pleas and ecclesiastical investiture, with a standard clause inserted into grants from about 1199. This was the year of John's coronation in England, which (as seen in Chapter 4) rendered Ireland peripheral to John's plans for some time. However, despite being forced to work with the Lacys and Briouzes to achieve his ends in Ireland and Wales, John nevertheless tried to undermine their lordship in Ireland by allowing at least two pleas relating to Meath to be heard in the royal court at Dublin.

The loss of Normandy in 1204 had a profound effect on the Plantagenet empire, as 'ten furious years' saw John use every means at his disposal to extract more and more money from his English subjects to fund the reconquest of his continental inheritance. It was this abuse of royal lordship (of which the English already had wearisome experience in the reigns of Henry II and Richard) that ultimately led to the English barons' rebellion and Magna Carta in 1215. In England, therefore, it was the abuse of royal lordship not its prevalence which was at issue; the baronial reformers (who, as will be seen in Chapter 6, eventually included Walter de Lacy and his fellow royalists, who together reissued Magna Carta in Henry III's name) merely sought to standardise its application. A well-regulated royal administration, including swift recourse to the royal courts when needed, was a welcome addition to the relatively peaceful, and increasingly litigious, society in England. Ireland was a different matter. Although the entire island theoretically constituted a *regnum*, over all of which John claimed lordship, Ireland was socially and politically fragmented. John's attempts to replicate English royal lordship in Ireland ignored the realities of frontier life, and set his Irish justiciar against the colony's most powerful lords.

The collision between royal and aristocratic lordship, first felt in Munster in the winter of 1206-7, sent shockwaves through Ireland. John's initiatives disturbed and galvanised the settler community, and in 1207 there was a violent reaction against Meiler fitz Henry's justiciarship. The new intrusiveness of royal lordship lay at the root of matters, with prerogative lordship intruding Crown administrators into Meath and Leinster, and threatening the very existence of the honor of Limerick. It was explicitly excluded from Meath and Leinster in the aftermath of the conflict, but this concession was more than offset by the removal of the Crown pleas from these same lordships. Victory over the king in Ireland could not be total for those holding lands of him elsewhere. Two years later, King John's 1210 Irish expedition was the delayed culmination of the issues of 1207-8. It was launched to suppress the style of aristocratic lordship that John had nurtured in the years before 1206, but which had become out of control and which defeated his Irish justiciar in 1208. In 1210, its only survivors were William Marshal, who wisely submitted to the king before John's expedition, and the treasonous Lacy brothers, who were cut down and expelled from the Angevin empire.

Walter de Lacy's restoration was eventually achieved in 1213 because, for all their conflicts, king and magnate needed each other. King John faced baronial opposition in England, and was in desperate need of able commanders for his expedition to Poitou, while Walter was landless in exile. Understanding that his lordship was dependent ultimately upon his king's survival, Walter remained loyal throughout the Magna Carta civil war. Indeed, Walter de Lacy's decision to rejoin King John, the man against whom he had so recently plotted and who had reputedly starved Walter's mother-in-law and brother-in-law to death in the wake of his 1210 expedition, speaks to the strength of the bond between king and magnate in the early thirteenth century.

Notes

1 *Rot. Litt. Pat.*, p. 60b.
2 *Ibid.*, p. 60b; C. A. Empey, 'The settlement of the kingdom of Limerick', in J. Lydon (ed.), *England and Ireland in the Later Middle Ages: Essays in Honour of Jocelyn Otway-Ruthven* (Blackrock, 1981), pp. 1-25, at p. 16.
3 Brock Holden, 'King John, the Braozes, and the Celtic fringe, 1207-1216', *Albion*, 33/1 (2001), pp. 1-23, at p. 10.
4 *Calendar of Ormond Deeds*, ed. Edmund Curtis, 2 vols (Dublin, 1932 and 1934), pp. 364-6.
5 *Rot. Litt. Claus.*, i, p. 77; *AFM*, iii, pp. 146-8, *s.a.* 1205; *Ann. Clon.*, p. 221, *s.a.* 1205.
6 *Rot. Litt. Pat.*, p. 69.
7 *Rot. Litt. Claus.*, i, p. 77b.
8 *Rot. Litt. Pat.*, pp. 69, 72.
9 BL MS Additional 4797, fo. 43r.
10 *Rot. Litt. Pat.*, pp. 69b-70; *Rot. Litt. Claus.*, i, pp. 79-80.
11 *Rot. Litt. Pat.*, p. 70; *Rot. Litt. Claus.*, i, p. 81.
12 *ALC*, i, 236, *s.a.* 1207; *AFM*, iii, 156, *s.a.* 1207; *Ann. Clon.*, pp. 221-2, *s.a.* 1207.
13 For a detailed examination of the situation in Uí Failge (which was more complex

than its presentation here suggests) see M. T. Flanagan, 'Defining lordships in Angevin Ireland: William Marshal and the king's justiciar', in Martin Aurell and Frédéric Boutoulle (eds), *Les seigneuries dans l'espace Plantagenêt (c.1150–c.1250)* (Bordeaux, 2009), pp. 41–59.
14 *Hist. William Marshal*, ii, lines 13311–422.
15 *Rot. Litt. Pat.*, p. 72.
16 H. G. Richardson, 'Norman Ireland in 1212', *Irish Historical Studies*, 3/10 (1942), pp. 144–58, at pp. 152–3.
17 Flanagan, 'Defining lordships', p. 50.
18 *Rot. Litt. Pat.*, pp. 71b–2.
19 See Chapter 4.
20 See Colin Veach, 'King John and Royal Control in Ireland: Why William de Briouze had to be destroyed', *English Historical Review* (forthcoming).
21 *AFM*, iii, p. 154, s.a. 1207. See also *Ann. Clon.*, p. 221, s.a. 1207.
22 *Rot. Litt. Pat.*, p. 74.
23 *Rot. Chart.*, p. 167.
24 BL Additional Charter 33658; *Rot. Chart.*, pp. 169–71, 173.
25 *Rot. Litt. Pat.*, p. 77b.
26 Otway-Ruthven, *Medieval Ireland*, p. 76–8.
27 *Rot. Litt. Pat.*, p. 76.
28 For Leinster see Flanagan, 'Defining lordships'.
29 See below, pp. 137–8.
30 *Rot. Chart.*, pp. 171–4.
31 'Annales prioratus de Wigornia', in H. R. Luard (ed.), *Annales Monastici*, 5 vols (London, 1864–69), iv, pp. 355–564, at p. 396, s.a. 1208.
32 *ALC*, i, p. 238, s.a. 1208.
33 *Chart. St Mary's*, ii, p. 311, s.a. 1208. Thurles was in Theobald Walter's former cantred of Éile Uí Fogartaig, one of the disputed territories.
34 Powicke, *Loss of Normandy*, pp. 145–69.
35 *Rot. Litt. Claus.*, i, p. 98.
36 The sheriff of Munster accounts for Ardmayle in 1211/12, making it part of Limerick. Irish Pipe Roll 14 John, pp. 68–70.
37 *Hist. William Marshal*, ii, lines 13551–670.
38 *Ibid.*, lines 13680–786; *Rot. Litt. Claus.*, i, p. 103; *AFM*, iii, p. 154, s.a. 1207; *Ann. Clon.*, p. 221, s.a. 1207.
39 *Hist. William Marshal*, ii, lines 13672–5.
40 *Rot. Litt. Pat.*, p. 79.
41 *Hist. William Marshal*, ii, lines 13787–888.
42 He did much the same in England in 1212, David Crouch, 'Baronial paranoia in King John's reign', in J. S. Loengard (ed.), *Magna Carta and the England of King John* (Woodbridge, 2010), pp. 45–62, at pp. 59–60.
43 *Rot. Litt. Claus.*, i, p. 106.
44 *Ibid.*, i, p. 107.
45 See Chapter 4.
46 Empey, 'Settlement of Limerick', pp. 8–10.

47 *Rot. Litt. Pat.*, p. 80.
48 *Rot. Litt. Claus.*, i, p. 110. This was likely the son of Walter's younger brother, Robert, who is mentioned as a hostage in 1207, *Rot. Litt. Pat.*, p. 72.
49 *Rot. Litt. Pat.*, p. 81; *Rot. Litt. Claus.*, i, pp. 112-13.
50 *Rot. Chart.*, p. 178. The charter also confirmed Walter's possession of seven knights' fees in Fingal, perhaps acquired during the elder Hugh's days as *custos* of Dublin.
51 *Rot. Litt. Pat.*, p. 84. He witnessed a concord between the Tyrell brothers at Westminster on 18 May 1208. TNA CP/1 Bundle 80/2, no 42.
52 The most recent treatments are in Crouch, 'Baronial paranoia'; Holden, 'King John, the Braozes'.
53 *Foedera*, I, i, p. 107; David Crouch, 'The complaint of King John against William de Briouze', in J. S. Loengard (ed.), *Magna Carta and the England of King John* (Woodbridge, 2010), pp. 168-79. Rymer and Crouch use different manuscript exemplars in their editions. Although that used by Rymer (Liber A of the Treasury of Receipt, TNA E 36/274) is a later copy, it seems to be superior to that used by Crouch (Little Black Book of the Exchequer, TNA E 164/12). Crouch's edition remains the only modern one, and the only English translation of the text. My thanks to Professor David Crouch for his help judging these sources, and tracking down Rymer's exemplar.
54 *Foedera*, I, i, p. 107; Crouch, 'Complaint of King John', pp. 170, 176.
55 'Philippus Dei gratia Francorum rex dilecto suo J. de Latiaco salutem et dilectionem. Mandamus vobis quod si conventiones nobis fueritis prosecutus quas Rogerus de Essartis dilectus et fidelis noster nobis ex parte vestra dixit, videlicet de guerra facienda in Anglia cum Johanne rege Anglie per amicos et imprisios quos ibidem vos dicit habere, et in Hibernia similiter per amicos et deffensionem castellorum, ita quod nos istud pro certo sciamus sicut melius poterit sciri, nos tale consilium habebimus de terra quam predecessores vestri habuerunt in Anglia quod de re redargui [*sic*, redargueri?] non poterimus. Actum Parisius, anno Domini Mo CCo nono.' *Recueil Philippe Auguste*, iii, no. 1079. In the French chancery the *mos gallicanus* (which reckoned the year from Easter) meant that 1209 went from Easter (29 March) 1209 to Easter (18 April) 1210.
56 Painter, *King John*, pp. 253-5.
57 For these arguments see Holt, *Northerners*, pp. 207-8; A. A. M. Duncan, 'John King of England and the Kings of Scots', in S. D. Church (ed.), *King John: New Interpretations* (Woodbridge, 1999), pp. 247-71, pp. 258-9.
58 *Recueil Philippe Auguste*, iii, no. 1079; William of Tudela and Anonymous, *The Song of the Cathar Wars: The History of the Albigensian Crusade*, ed. and trans. Janet Shirley (Aldershot, 1996), p. 28. Les Essarts (Eure, cant. Damville) was part of Simon de Montfort's demesne, *Recueil historiens*, xxiii, p. 714 e, f; *Cartulaire de l'Abbaye de Notre-Dame des Vaux de Cernay de l'Ordre de Citeaux au diocèse de Paris, Tome Premier, 1118-1250*, eds Lucien Merlet and Auguste Moutié (Paris, 1857), p. 188. The name Essarts is a very common one, but, in 1190, the sheriff of Shropshire paid Gilbert des Essarts 100s for the custody of Ludlow castle, *Pipe Roll 2 Richard I*, p. 124.

59 'Annales Prioratus de Dunstaplia', in H. R. Luard (ed.), *Annales Monastici*, 5 vols (London, 1864-69), iii, pp. 3-420, at pp. 33-4, *s.a.* 1210.
60 *Recueil historiens*, xix, pp. 170, 181.
61 An unidentified Robert de Lacy received 13 *livres* from the farm of the honor in 1198, *Mag. Rot. Normanniae*, ii, p. 462.
62 *Cal. Doc. France*, nos 302, 314-15.
63 AD Eure H 793 fos 70r-71r; *Cal. Doc. France*, nos 314-15.
64 *Reg. St Thomas*, p. 42. A Thomas fitz Alured witnessed the elder Hugh de Lacy's grant to William le Petit. *Song*, pp. 309-10.
65 *The Cartae Antiquae, Rolls 11-20*, ed. J. C. Davies (London, 1960), p. 91; *Recueil Henri II*, ii, pp. 84-5, 90, 92-5; *Cal. Doc. France*, no. 301.
66 *Calendar of Documents Relating to Ireland Preserved in Her Majesty's Public Record Office, London, 1171-1251*, ed. H. S. Sweetman (London, 1875), no. 2408; the entry in *Cal. Chart., 1226-57*, p. 232, omits the witness list.
67 Duncan, 'John and kings of Scots', pp. 260-1.
68 *Flores Historiarum*, ii, p. 50.
69 Norgate, *Lackland*, pp. 133-4.
70 See Rowlands, 'King John and Wales', pp. 283-4.
71 'Annales de Margan ', p. 29, *s.a.* 1208; *Mathaei Parisiensis Chronica Majora*, ii, 522. In 1212 King Philip granted Giles the French lands that his father had held at the time of his death, *Histoire des ducs*, p. 115.
72 *Flores Historiarum*, ii, pp. 50-1; *Matthaei Parisiensis, monachi sancti Albani, historia Anglorum*, ed. Frederic Madden, 3 vols. (London, 1866-69), ii, p. 119.
73 Duffy, *Medieval Ireland*, p. 158.
74 S. D. Church, 'The 1210 campaign in Ireland: evidence for a military revolution?', in Christopher Harper-Bill (ed.), *Anglo-Norman Studies XX* (Woodbridge, 1997), pp. 45-57.
75 Christopher Harper-Bill, 'John and the Church of Rome', in S. D. Church (ed.), *King John: New Interpretations* (Woodbridge, 2007) pp. 289-315, at pp. 304-7.
76 'Annales Monasterii de Waverleia', in H. R. Luard (ed.), *Annales Monastici*, 5 vols (London, 1864-9), pp. 129-411, at p. 264, *s.a.* 1210; *Flores Historiarum*, ii, pp. 54-5.
77 *Hist. William Marshal*, ii, lines 14240-6.
78 *Foedera*, I, i, p. 107.
79 *Ibid.*, I, i, p. 107; *Memoriale Fratris Walteri de Coventria*, ed. William Stubbs, 2 vols (London, 1872-73), ii, p. 202.
80 *MCB*, p. 86, *s.a.* 1210. For its significance, Verstraten [Veach], 'The anglicisation of the Irish nobility', chapter 2.
81 *Hist. William Marshal*, ii, lines 14259-66; *Rot. Liberate*, pp. 177-228.
82 *Cal. Doc. Ireland, 1171-1251*, no. 402.
83 *MCB*, p. 86, *s.a.* 1210.
84 *Ibid.*, p. 86, *s.a.* 1210; *Handbook and Select Calendar of Sources for Medieval Ireland in the National Archives of the United Kingdom*, eds Paul Dryburgh and Brendan Smith (Dublin, 2005), pp. 269-71.

85 See Chapter 3.
86 The others were Richard Tyrell, Peter de Meset, Martin de Mandeville and Adam Dullard, *Gormanston Register*, pp. 179–80.
87 For John's progress see *Rot. Liberate*, pp. 178–228.
88 *Ann. Clon.*, p. 223, s.a. 1208–9.
89 Orpen, *Normans*, ii, p. 250.
90 Duffy, 'King John's expedition'.
91 *Hist. William Marshal*, ii, lines 14283–318.
92 *Histoire des ducs*, p. 113.
93 *Rot. Liberate*, p. 209.
94 *Early Sources of Scottish History A.D. 500 to 1286*, ed. A. O. Anderson, 2 vols (Edinburgh, 1922), ii, pp. 378–81.
95 *Cronica Mannie*, fo. 41v; *ALC*, i, p. 242, s.a. 1210; *Early Sources*, ii, p. 381; McDonald, *Manx Kingship*, p. 136.
96 *Rot. Chart.*, p. 191. McDonald, *The Kingdom of the Isles*, p. 87.
97 *Foedera*, I, i, p. 107.
98 Bower, *Scotichronicon, iv*, pp. 461, 629. This section seems to be based upon a near-contemporary source from eastern Scotland, perhaps even the bishop of St Andrews. *Ibid.*, p. xxiv.
99 See p. 140.
100 Bower, *Scotichronicon, iv*, p. 463.
101 BL MS Additional 4792, fos 16or-2r, s.a. 1210; *Grace's Annals*, p. 24, s.a. 1210; 'The Book of Howth', in J. S. Brewer and William Bullen (eds), *Calendar of Carew Manuscripts Preserved in the Archiepiscopal Library at Lambeth*, vol v (London, 1871), pp. 1–260, at p. 121; *Chart. St Mary's*, ii, p. 311, s.a. 1210.
102 Crouch, *William Marshal*, pp. 73–80.
103 *ALC*, i, p. 244, s.a. 1210; *Ann. Clon.*, p. 224, s.a. 1210; *MCB*, p. 88, s.a. 1210; Irish Pipe Roll 14 John, pp. 24–5.
104 *AFM*, iii, p. 166, s.a. 1210 [recte 1211]; *Ann. Clon.*, p. 224, s.a. 1210. For Richard see Chapter 8.
105 *ALC*, i, 244–6, s.a. 1211; *Chart. St Mary's*, ii, pp. 279, 312, s.a. 1211; *AFM*, iii, p. 168, s.a. 1210 [recte 1211]; *Ann. Clon.*, p. 224, s.a. 1210 [recte 1211]; *Grace's Annals*, p. 24, s.a. 1211.
106 Irish Pipe Roll 14 John, p. 66; Richardson, 'Norman Ireland in 1212', p. 146.
107 Irish Pipe Roll 14 John, pp. 22–5, 30–1, 38–9, 44–5.
108 Duffy, 'King John's expedition'.
109 Bower, *Scotichronicon, iv*, p. 467; *John of Fordun's Chronicle of the Scottish Nation*, ed. William F. Skene (Edinburgh, 1872), p. 274; *Mem. Walteri Coventria*, ii, p. 206. See also Pollock, 'Rebels of the West', p. 23.
110 *Rot. Chart.*, pp. 186b, 194; *Rot. Litt. Pat.*, p. 98; *Rot. Litt. Claus.*, i, p. 587, 615. Alan of Galloway, Earl Thomas of Atholl and Earl Duncan of Carrick were related to King Rǫgnvaldr of Man and the sons of Rǫgnvaldr Somerliðisson through the marriage of Affrica of Galloway (daughter of Fergus of Galloway) to King Óláfr Guðrøðarson of Man. McDonald, *Manx Kingship*, pp. 27, 66, 75, 154.
111 *ALC*, i, p. 246, s.a. 1211 [recte 1212].

163

112 *ALC*, i, p. 246, *s.a.* 1212; *Ann. Clon.*, p. 225, *s.a.* 1211 [*recte* 1212]; *AFM*, iii, p. 172, *s.a.* 1211 [*recte* 1212].
113 Irish Pipe Roll 14 John, pp. 24–5, 52–3.
114 *ALC*, i, pp. 248–50, *s.a.* 1214; *Ann. Clon.*, pp. 225–6, *s.a.* 1212; *AFM*, iii, pp. 172–4, *s.a.* 1212.
115 *ALC*, i, p. 250, *s.a.* 1214, *Ann. Clon.*, pp. 226–8, *s. aa.* 1213–14; *AFM*, iii, pp. 174–6, 181–185, *s.a.* 1213–14.
116 Martin, 'John, Lord of Ireland', pp. 127–55, at pp. 140–1 (quote p. 141).
117 See above, p. 144.
118 'Totum regnum Angliae et totum regnum Hiberniae', *Foedera*, I, i, pp. 111–12.
119 Norgate, *Lackland*, pp. 184–5.
120 *Rot. Litt. Claus.*, i, p. 134b; *Rot. Litt. Pat.*, p. 99b.
121 Painter, *King John*, pp. 242–50.
122 *Chart. St Mary's*, ii, p. 311, *s.a.* 1210. This is hardly conclusive evidence, and may refer to the 4,000 mark fine Walter eventually proffered for Meath. See below, p. x.
123 *Flores Historiarum*, ii, pp. 80–1; *Mem. Walteri Coventria*, ii, p. 212.
124 Hillaby, 'Colonisation, crisis-management and debt', p. 15.
125 *Rot. Litt. Claus.*, i, p. 147.
126 See below, p. 153.
127 Hillaby, 'Hereford gold, part 2', p. 208; Holden, *Lords*, p. 185.
128 *Rot. Litt. Claus.*, i, p. 147 (restoration); Norgate, *Lackland*, pp. 186–7 (Giles); *Rot. Litt. Pat.*, p. 100 (truce).
129 Lloyd, *Wales*, ii, p. 641.
130 *Rot. Litt. Pat.*, p. 100.
131 *Ibid.*, p. 103b.
132 Lloyd, *Wales*, ii, 641.
133 'Rex tot fere habere hostes, quot habuit magnates.' *Flores Historiarum*, ii, p. 259 (quote); Rowlands, 'King John and Wales', pp. 283–4; R. F. Treharne, 'The Franco-Welsh treaty of alliance in 1212', *Bulletin of the Board of Celtic Studies*, 18/1 (1958), pp. 60–75.
134 See below, p. 151.
135 Davies, *Lords and Lordship*, p. 118.
136 Warren, *King John*, pp. 204.
137 Norgate, *Lackland*, p. 186.
138 *Flores Historiarum*, ii, p. 80; *Mem. Walteri Coventria*, ii, pp. 212, 217.
139 Norgate, *Lackland*, p. 186.
140 Nicholas Vincent, 'England and the Albigensian Crusade', in Björn Weiler and I. W. Rowlands (eds), *England and Europe in the Reign of Henry III (1216–1272)* (Aldershot and Burlington, 2002), pp. 67–97, at pp. 68–9, 75.
141 *Flores Historiarum*, ii, pp. 87–93.
142 Tudela and Anonymous, *Song of the Cathar Wars*, pp. 28, 50, 89, 101–2, 106, 133, 145, 147–8, 164, 168, 183; *Recueil historiens*, xix, pp. 145, 170, 181.
143 Vincent, 'England and Albigensian Crusade', p. 73; Power, *Norman Frontier*, p. 178; *A History of the Crusades, Volume ii: The Later Crusades, 1189–1311*, eds R. L. Wolff and H. W. Hazard (Madison, 1969), p. 294.

144 *Recueil historiens*, xix, pp. 170, 181.
145 *PR, 1216-25* (London, 1901), p. 301.
146 *Calendar of Entries in the Papal Registers Relating to Great Britain and Ireland. Papal Letters, vol. i, A.D. 1198-1304*, ed. W. H. Bliss (London, 1893), p. 67; *Diplomatic Documents Preserved in the Public Record Office, vol. 1, 1101-1272*, ed. Pierre Chaplais (London, 1964), no. 34.
147 Norgate, *Lackland*, p. 196
148 *Rot. Litt. Pat.*, p. 112.
149 Walter later founded a Grandmontine priory at Craswall, Herefordshire. *Monasticon Anglicanum*, vi, p. 1035.
150 *Rot. Litt. Pat.*, p. 113b.
151 *Ibid.*, p. 134. Many thanks to Professor David Carpenter for his thoughts on this possibility.
152 Norgate, *Lackland*, pp. 196-206; Warren, *King John*, pp. 217-24.
153 *Rot. Litt. Pat.*, p. 118b.
154 Holt, *Northerners*, p. 100.
155 *Rot. Litt. Claus.*, i, 202; Painter, *King John*, pp. 280-4; Holt, *Northerners*, pp. 100-1.
156 *Foedera*, I, i, p. 125; *Flores Historiarum*, ii, pp. 110-11.
157 *Rot. Obl. et Fin.*, pp. 480, 487.
158 *Rot. Litt. Claus.*, i, p. 175.
159 *Ibid.*, i, p. 173b.
160 *Ibid.*, i, p. 182.
161 See Chapter 4.
162 *Rot. Litt. Pat.*, p. 128; and see Chapter 7, p. x.
163 *Rot. Litt. Pat.*, pp. 131, 181; *Rot. Obl. et Fin.*, pp. 562-4, 601-3.
164 See Chapter 4.
165 *Rot. Litt. Pat.*, p. 131.
166 *Ibid.*, p. 134.
167 *Ibid.*, p. 132b.
168 Rowlands, 'King John and Wales', pp. 284-5.
169 Holden, *Lords*, pp. 178-9, 193.
170 Painter, *King John*, p. 289.
171 Eyton, *Shropshire*, x, pp. 326-7 (transcribed in full).
172 *Cal. Ancient Correspondence Wales*, p. 1.
173 *Rot. Litt. Pat.*, p. 134b.
174 Norgate, *Lackland*, p. 228; Warren, *King John*, pp. 233-4.
175 *Rot. Litt. Pat.*, p. 134b.
176 *Rot. Litt. Claus.*, i, p. 197b.
177 *Rot. Litt. Pat.*, p. 137.
178 See Norgate, *Lackland*, pp. 229-86; Warren, *King John*, 224-56; Painter, *King John*, pp. 308-77; Holt, *Northerners*, pp. 109-42; David Carpenter, *The Minority of Henry III* (London, 1990), pp. 5-44.
179 *Brut (RBH)*, p. 203, *s.a.* 1215; Lloyd, *Wales*, ii, p. 643.
180 Lloyd, *Wales*, ii, 644.

181 *Ibid.*, ii, p. 645.
182 See above, p. 153.
183 *Rot. Obl. et Fin.*, pp. 562-4, 601-3; *Rot. Litt. Pat.*, p. 181. Gilbert arrived at court on 9 July, *Rot. Litt. Pat.*, p. 149.
184 *Rot. Litt. Pat.*, pp. 148b, 151-151b.
185 *Rot. Litt. Claus.*, i, pp. 224, 228b.
186 *Ibid.*, i, p. 224.
187 Otway-Ruthven, *Medieval Ireland*, p. 89.
188 *Rot. Litt. Claus.*, i, pp. 218-19b; *Rot. Chart.*, pp. 210-13.
189 Norgate, *Lackland*, p. 240.
190 Duffy, 'John and Ireland', pp. 243-5.
191 William Marshal approved of a similar plan for the young Henry III after King John's death. *Hist. William Marshal*, ii, lines 15655-96.
192 *Histoire des ducs*, pp. 152, 172; 'Annales de Dunstaplia', p. 48, *s.a.* 1215 [*recte* 1216].
193 *Rot. Litt. Pat.*, p. 157b; *Cal. Pap. Let.*, pp. 40-1; *Brut (RBH)*, p. 205, *s.a.* 1215.
194 *Rot. Litt. Pat.*, p. 159-159b. Lacy was also granted land in Gloucestershire, *ibid.*, p. 157; *Rot. Litt. Claus.*, i, p. 241b.
195 Lloyd, *Wales*, ii, p. 648.
196 *Rot. Litt. Claus.*, i, p. 182.
197 Norgate, *Lackland*, pp. 255-61.
198 *Rot. Litt. Pat.*, p. 174.
199 Norgate, *Lackland*, pp. 255-69.
200 'Spiritum consilii sanioris' *Rot. Litt. Pat.*, p. 184-184b.
201 Lloyd, *Wales*, ii, 650n.
202 *Rot. Litt. Pat.*, p. 192.
203 *Ibid.*, p. 192b.
204 *Ibid.*, pp. 193-4; *Rot. Litt. Claus.*, i, p. 283.
205 *Rot. Litt. Claus.*, i, p. 285.
206 *Rot. Litt. Pat.*, p. 194.
207 Warren, *King John*, pp. 252-3.
208 Norgate, *Lackland*, pp. 278-9,
209 *Ibid.*, p. 279-81.
210 *Rot. Litt. Pat.*, p. 199b.
211 Warren, *King John*, p. 254.
212 *Foedera*, I, i, p. 144.

6

Sheriff of Herefordshire: 1216-22

Susan Reynolds writes that in most medieval instances 'protests and rebellions were fairly clearly against individual acts of oppression or individual rulers, rather than the structure they represented'.[1] In 1215, this was not the case. For all of King John's immoderation, the complaints against him were greater than the sum of his misdeeds.[2] Consequently, his death, instead of restoring the English Crown to the position it held under his predecessor Richard I, was a hammer-blow to the brand of kingship that had held England in its grip for the past sixty-two years. England's experienced and obdurate monarch, a man whose strength of will had driven a significant section of his baronage into revolt, was succeeded by a nine-year-old boy-king Henry III. The circumstances of the civil war also undermined the stability of the English Crown, leaving it penniless and largely impotent in broad sections of the kingdom. The most decisive factor in the transformation of the character and nature of English kingship in this period, however, was that, at precisely the same time that the rebel barons were championing the cause of baronial rights and the limitation of kingship, the keeping of the kingdom was delivered into the hands of the aristocracy. The regency government set up to rule in the young Henry III's name was one largely composed of the late king's most loyal magnates, who, like Walter de Lacy, would not have been strangers to the excesses of John and his immediate predecessors. The royalist barons' loyalty was not entirely disinterested, and they soon set about limiting English kingship through the several reissues of Magna Carta that followed.

After the war, the seismic shift in the balance of power was immediately apparent. There was a real danger that the kingdom would remain divided between areas where royal officials ruled their bailiwicks

167

semi-independently, and areas where aristocratic lordship was all-powerful.³ The regency government's ineffectualness was also displayed further afield in its failure to control its representatives in Poitou or, more pertinent for the current study, Ireland.⁴ The state of the kingdom of England and its associated territories largely convinced the political community that the recovery of royal authority was necessary for the fair and effective administration of the realm, especially since that authority was to be clearly circumscribed by the precepts of Magna Carta.⁵ Consequently, leading up to, and largely during, the great crises of the 1220s and 1230s, the Crown was able to claw back a great deal of power, albeit a power wielded in concert with the greatest men of the realm.

Magna Carta, 1216

King John's death left the royalist barons the task of winning the civil war. As an executor of John's will, Walter de Lacy's standing was temporarily enhanced, and he attended most, if not all, of the royalist barons' early councils. Their first tasks were to choose a new king and lure support away from Louis of France. The two duties were bound together in letters sent to Llywelyn and King Alexander of Scotland immediately after John's death, inviting them to take part in the 'election' of a new king of England.⁶ These overtures were quickly superseded, however, by the royalists' decision to crown John's young son Henry at Gloucester on 28 October.⁷ By that point, Walter had returned to Herefordshire as warden of the central march, where his presence was clearly needed.⁸ On the same day as the coronation, William Marshal's south Herefordshire castle of Goodrich was attacked either by Reginald de Briouze or by Llywelyn.⁹ William Marshal accepted the role of regent the following day, and was the head, if not the absolute head, of the regency government thereafter until his death in 1219.¹⁰

The newly formed royal council comprising the full strength of the royalist leadership (including Walter de Lacy) held its first meeting on 11 November at Bristol castle. The regional nature of the civil war was highlighted by the fact that eleven of the twenty-four barons present were from the Welsh march.¹¹ Their interests were served when, after causing every man present to swear fealty to King Henry III, the legate Guala laid an interdict upon Wales for its support of the rebel cause. He then repeated his excommunication of Louis, the rebels and their allies.¹² In less than a month the royalists had gone from inviting Llywelyn to participate in the election of the new king, to placing Wales under the interdict for its continued contumacy. This new ecclesiastical censure was a boon to those, like Walter de Lacy, who were charged with the security of the march.

If the new regency government was willing to use the stick to punish its enemies, it was also ready to use the carrot to entice them to its allegiance. On the second day of the conference at Bristol, 12 November 1216, the government issued its own version of Magna Carta.[13] This Charter, with some of the more contentious clauses from 1215 either removed or reserved for further deliberation, was an offer to negotiate with the rebels.[14] King John's death made the prospect of negotiations more appealing to the less ardent rebels, who now found themselves in open revolt against the young and blameless Henry III. As Carpenter puts it, 'Henry shrugged and the weight of John's crimes fell from his shoulders'.[15] The Minority government gave voice to the new conciliatory spirit in a letter to the Irish justiciar. It declared that the young Henry wished to remove the dissention that had arisen between his father and the nobles of Ireland because, whether justified or not, it had nothing to do with him. The Irish magnates were promised a restoration of their liberties 'to restore the good days of their noble ancestors'.[16] The main beneficiaries of this mandate were members of the council, such as William Marshal and Walter de Lacy, who had fought John over their liberties in 1207. Clearly, the royalists were determined to benefit from John's death.

The council next turned to the grievances of individual rebel barons. Walter joined with William Marshal, William de Cantelupe and Falkes de Bréauté in addressing a letter to the rebels, William Longespée, earl of Salisbury and William Marshal the younger, offering to negotiate their return to the royal allegiance. On 18 November, the regency council, through the advice of earls Ranulf of Chester and William Ferrers (of Derby), even offered restoration to Hugh de Lacy if he would return to fealty.[17] In the short term, however, the regency's overtures came to nothing, and the first defections of any consequence did not begin until Louis left England to gather reinforcements in February 1217, four months after the revised version of Magna Carta.[18]

The significance of the reissue went far beyond the immediate context of the civil war. In 1189, both William Marshal and Walter de Lacy had been victims of John's willingness to alienate permanently lands held in wardship. Accordingly, they retained the clauses in Magna Carta protecting lands held in wardship.[19] With the reissue of Magna Carta, Walter and his fellow royalist barons changed the nature of English kingship. Henceforth, the king of England was to have his authority fundamentally circumscribed. This may not have broken any new ground within the wider context of western European political thought or action, but it was a watershed in English politics.[20] The young King Henry III had been commended into the safekeeping of his father's most trusted magnates and the legate, and they had immediately taken steps to limit his rule and deprive him of the form of kingship that his grandfather, uncle and father had achieved.

Winning the war: 1216–17

The royalist barons of the regency council may have wielded considerable power in their redefinition of English kingship that autumn, but in a practical sense they were an all but spent force. Fear of Llywelyn and Reginald de Briouze kept the royal army close to the Welsh march, and forced the government into a truce with the rebels and Louis.[21] This was later extended when Reginald de Briouze rejected the Minority government's offer of restoration for his return to royal service.[22] Neither truce was honoured by either side, however, and the war persisted. On 14 January, the government sent a letter to the defenders of Bedford castle, urging them to stand firm against Louis's forces and assuring them that William Marshal, the earls of Chester and Derby, William Brewer, Hugh de Mortimer, Walter de Lacy, Walter of Clifford and others had sworn to be responsible for the ransoms of those who might be captured in the defence of royal castles.[23] Walter was now among those bankrolling the English Crown. Three days later, Pope Honorius authorised the legate Guala to suspend the crusading vows of those who fought for the royalists. Guala extended this commission, remitting the sins of those who joined the cause, signing them with the cross as if the fight against the rebels were a crusade.[24]

One month later, Walter helped to relieve the town of Rye (Sussex). On 28 February, William Marshal sent a letter to the men of Rye, which had only just fallen to Louis's forces, to take courage and give no hostages and negotiate no terms for surrender, because they would soon be saved. A powerful relief force was mobilised under the Marshal, and included a significant marcher contingent, including Walter de Lacy, Hugh and Roger de Mortimer, Walter and Roger of Clifford, William de Beauchamp and John of Monmouth.[25] It is unclear when the relief of Rye was achieved, but from this point the royalists steadily gained strength. Louis had sailed for France to collect reinforcements shortly after taking Rye, and, in his absence, two prominent rebels, William Marshal the younger and William Longespée, earl of Salisbury, defected to the Crown. The *History of William Marshal* contains a detailed account of how the two men who 'loved each other as if they were brothers' helped capture the castles of Knepp (Sussex), Wolvesey (Winchester, Hampshire) and Marlborough (Wiltshire) for the king.[26]

The following month, Walter de Lacy, Hugh de Mortimer, John of Monmouth and Walter of Clifford issued a charter granting in the name of the king the castle and shrievalty of Worcester to Walter de Beauchamp.[27] Walter de Lacy's actions from then until the end of the civil war are difficult to determine. The civil war's decisive battle took place on 20 May 1217 at Lincoln.[28] The Marshal, as regent, had marched north to reinforce the royalist siege of Mountsorrel (Leicestershire). However, once the rebels moved from Mountsorrel to blockade Lincoln, the Marshal pursued with the entire royalist army.[29] Walter may have been left along the Welsh border, where negotiations with Reginald de Briouze persisted,[30] but if he could have been risked for the relief of Rye, then he may have marched to Mountsorrel and Lincoln as well.

The royal army's victory at Lincoln was followed by a steady flow of defections to the Crown while the two sides negotiated unsuccessfully for a lasting peace.[31] Reginald de Briouze finally submitted at the end of June 1217. On 23 June, the Briouze inheritance in England was granted to Reginald,[32] followed the next day by the Irish component.[33] As sheriff of Herefordshire, a powerful marcher, and his brother-in-law, Walter de Lacy played a leading role in Reginald's restoration. Briouze's defection angered his father-in-law, and erstwhile ally, Llywelyn ab Iorwerth, who launched a retaliatory offensive within Wales.[34] This and his other shrieval duties tethered Walter to the march for the rest of 1217. He and his fellow marcher lords remained loyal instruments of royal authority in the region, helping to restore a number of former rebels and adjudicating the inevitable disputes.[35]

The civil war officially ended with the treaty of Kingston/Lambeth in mid-September 1217,[36] but it raged on in Wales. Llywelyn had done quite well for himself while his allies in the east foundered, and he had no desire to participate in a peace that required him to relinquish his conquests. It took a separate treaty, agreed at Worcester in March 1218, to bring the war in Wales to an end.[37] Rees Davies emphasises that the concessions that Llywelyn was able to gain, specifically the confirmation of his conquests, custody of the royal castles of Cardigan and Carmarthen, and custody of the lands of his rival Gwenwynwyn while the heir remained in wardship, were mitigated by the fact that he and his fellow Welsh princes were compelled to do homage to Henry III and thereby acknowledge their subservience to the English Crown.[38] The symbolic importance of the Welsh princes' homage was most welcome to the regency government, but the terms of their submission meant that the extension of royal authority was bought with the loss of real power in Wales. However, the war was over and peace the primary objective. What remained was for everyone to make the best of the situation. For Walter de Lacy, that meant exploiting his position as sheriff of Herefordshire to expand his lordship in England and Wales.

Walter's success in this endeavour was due more to the weakness of the Minority government than to his own capacities. For the next few years, almost every step forward was at the expense of the Crown. Walter was not alone. All over England, men who had been installed in the shires as military governors during the civil war remained in their posts. Supported by the belief that the Minority government could not overturn King John's appointments, Walter and his fellow royalist sheriffs continued the wartime practice of spending the fixed dues, proceeds of the county and hundred courts, and issues of the royal demesne manors within their shires as they saw fit, without first accounting for them at the Exchequer.[39] This was a crippling practice for the royal government, which thereby was denied a regular revenue from the localities. The situation was such that, by 1220, Pope Honorius III wrote that the great men of England were 'revelling in the royal goods while the king begs'.[40] From the end of the civil war in 1217 to the pope's letter in 1220, very little change is discernible in the relationship between Walter and the Crown. A weak royal government was a double edged sword, however, for, while it allowed Walter greater freedom of action in Herefordshire and the central march, it also denied him protection from over-mighty administrators in Ireland. This made his ascendancy a very local phenomenon, and frustrated Walter's attempts to secure peaceful seisin of his Irish interests.

The hazard of a weak royal government: Ireland, 1215-20

Walter de Lacy's position in England was markedly different from that in Ireland. The problem in Ireland began in 1215, with the question of the timing of Walter's lawful entry into Meath. King John had done his Irish justiciar no favours by issuing contradictory mandates to Walter's knights and free tenants in Meath, only days apart, first notifying them of the full restoration of their lord and commanding them to be attentive to him, and then demanding that they should be attentive only once the Irish justiciar had secured sureties for Walter's fine.[41] The Irish justiciar, Geoffrey de Marisco, received only orders along the lines of the second mandate, and this may have led to conflict. The Irish annals of Clonmacnoise report under 1215 a war between Walter's half-brother, William, and the Irish justiciar:

> William sonne of Hugh Delacye came from England and tooke upon him the kingdome of Meath and government thereof. Whereupon there arose great contention and warrs between the English of the south of Ireland in generall and him, whereby many Damages and losses of preys and spoyles were sustained by either party.[42]

Although this testimony is unique, it should not immediately be discounted. Being especially concerned with events within the Irish midlands,[43] the Clonmacnoise annalist was more likely to notice such a feud than his fellow Irish annalists. William de Lacy's struggle with the Irish justiciar could easily have blended in with MacArt's war (mentioned above),[44] masking Lacy's war to Irish annalists not particularly concerned with the politics of colonial Meath.

The timing of this dispute is difficult to determine, because the Clonmacnoise annals have a notoriously loose chronology. Walter paid the initial 1,000 marks of his fine by 12 April 1216, which entitled him to seisin under his renegotiated terms.[45] The first sign that Geoffrey de Marisco continued to withhold seisin came on 24 June 1216, when King John sent him a mandate ordering that he observe the agreements made between Walter de Lacy and the king touching Walter's land in Ireland.[46] Walter de Lacy joined the king only shortly thereafter, where he remained until John's death that October. If William de Lacy had already taken up arms against the Irish justiciar, John gave no indication of this in his dispatches concerning Meath on 18 August 1216 (the same day Walter was made sheriff of Herefordshire).[47]

The first hint that English sources give of William de Lacy's activities in Ireland is in a mandate sent around January 1217, wherein the king commanded William to restore to the Irish justiciar the castles of Dundrum (Co. Down) and Carlingford (Co. Louth), which William had taken. William was also ordered to satisfy the justiciar for the damage he had done to the king and his land by taking the castles.[48] The mandate appears on the patent roll between two directives to Geoffrey de Marisco concerning Walter de Lacy's interests. The first, on 20 January 1217, was for the restoration of the castle of Drogheda and the cantred of Ardmayle,[49] and the second, on 23 January, demanded that the lands and castles of Richard de Tuit be delivered to Walter once a debt of 200 marks had been paid.[50] Clearly, William de Lacy's dispute with the Irish justiciar did not impact negatively on Walter's position at court.

Less than a month later, on 14 February, Walter was given respite and quitclaim touching the arrears of the farm of Herefordshire from the previous Easter (10 April 1216). This effectively granted Walter the proceeds of the shire that he had amassed or spent during the civil war. That July, Ireland was once again discussed as the royalist magnates gathered in council at Gloucester. The Irish lands of two former rebels, Reginald de Briouze and Nicholas de Verdun, had just been restored,[51] yet Geoffrey de Marisco still refused Walter seisin of several territories. Geoffrey blamed William de Lacy's offensive for his failure to carry out the January mandates, but the council plainly thought that his motives ran deeper. On 2 July 1217, they sent a letter firmly warning Geoffrey that he ought to effect the restoration of the lands and castles in question without delay or other pretext. They also 'marvelled' at the great number of commands that he hindered, making it clear that William de Lacy's aggression was no reason to withhold Walter's lands along with his castles. The letter stated that Walter had given security that he would make amends for William's excesses towards the king, and ordered that Walter, and his men, lands and possessions, be protected and left in peace. It finished by denying the Irish justiciar the right to implead Walter or his men while Walter was on the king's service in England, except by special order of the king, and granted Walter de Lacy respite of his debt to the Crown.[52]

Given that Geoffrey used William de Lacy's aggression as an excuse, and that the council accepted this as good cause to withhold Walter's castles (if not his lands), there seems to have been more at issue than William's occupation of his brother Hugh's former castles of Carlingford and Dundrum. What is more, Geoffrey's conduct in this and future matters (discussed below) makes it all the more likely that he sought to delay or deny William custody of Meath as Walter's seneschal from 1215. Indeed, it appears that the Irish justiciar used his office to retain Walter's lands and castles for his own use. The council thought as much, and sent a letter to Archbishop Henry of Dublin and the barons of Ireland ordering them to aid Geoffrey in carrying out Walter's restoration.[53] As with other mandates of this type, their euphemistic 'aid' was to ensure that Geoffrey did as he was told.

The character of Geoffrey de Marisco's justiciarship, or at least the Minority government's view of it, was summed up at his supersession in 1221. In a letter to the natives and colonists of Ireland, on 17 July 1221 the council declared that it had received nothing whatever from the demesne lands, rents or escheats of Ireland since King John's death, and stated that, contrary to the council's explicit mandates, Geoffrey had caused the revenues of Ireland to be paid into his own chamber.⁵⁴ As early as April 1217, the Minority government already suspected Geoffrey of using Crown revenue for himself, when it ordered that the rents and fines of Ireland ought to be received only at the Exchequer, and kept by the treasurer until the king otherwise directed.⁵⁵ On that occasion, the government also sent Archbishop Henry, known as a loyal Angevin administrator and justice of many years' experience, to oversee the justiciar's activities and 'expedite the king's business'. Geoffrey was allowed to do nothing in Ireland without the archbishop's assent.⁵⁶

Given the Minority council's statement in 1221, Archbishop Henry was plainly unable or unwilling to curtail Geoffrey's embezzlement. There is even evidence that Archbishop Henry might have been complicit in the Irish justiciar's abuse of office, or was at least as guilty as he. For instance, on 20 June 1220 Geoffrey was ordered to restore Blathach Castle, near Limerick ('*Blathac juxta Limeric*'), to Walter de Lacy.⁵⁷ The problem was that the Irish justiciar at some point granted Blathach to the archbishop. Archbishop Henry, 'one of the greatest pluralists in medieval England',⁵⁸ served as justiciar of Ireland from 1213 to 1215, making it possible that he had alienated the castle himself. He was certainly not above such actions. For example, in 1217, as papal legate for Ireland, he had been granted custody of the vacant primatial see of Armagh, including its temporalities and those of all vacant sees within its province. However, from 1219, he failed to comply with several orders to deliver seisin to the new archbishop of Armagh, Luke de Netterville, so that by 1227 King Henry III was still complaining that full seisin had not yet been given.⁵⁹ The case of Blathach castle seems to point to co-operation between the archbishop and Geoffrey. Once Archbishop Henry had possession of Blathach, he conferred it upon his niece, Matilda, before her marriage to Geoffrey's son and heir, William de Marisco.⁶⁰ With the illegally alienated castle serving as the marriage portion in an alliance between the Irish justiciar and the man sent to Ireland to oversee his administration, it is little wonder that Walter had a difficult time recovering full seisin of his Irish territories.

Little effective supervision meant that Geoffrey de Marisco was able to retain, and profit from, Walter's possessions for several years. The order for the restoration of Drogheda Castle was repeated three more times in 1217, on 31 October, about 3 November and 10 November, with the archbishop of Dublin also being addressed in the third of these mandates.⁶¹ Another mandate followed that summer, on 20 June 1218, for the return of Drogheda Castle and Ardmayle, with the castle of Blathach now included.⁶² A rather opaque mandate followed two months later, on 27

August, in which the Minority government wrote that it had heard that Archbishop Henry wanted to be rid of the burden of Drogheda Castle, but ordered that it remain in his custody and that he be compensated for its upkeep.[63] If this meant that the government had decided to retain Drogheda Castle, then Geoffrey de Marisco's recalcitrance had cost Walter de Lacy dearly.

Walter was not the only magnate to be so treated. On 18 December 1217, the Irish justiciar was reprimanded for failing to restore to Reginald de Briouze the honor of Limerick, with the castle and city, as ordered six months earlier.[64] Similarly, King John's imports from western Scotland, Thomas of Galloway, Earl Duncan of Carrick and John fitz Alexander, complained of their maltreatment in Ulster.[65] What is more, Llywelyn ab Iorwerth had difficulty gaining seisin of his family's possessions in Dublin at this time.[66] There can be no question of Geoffrey targeting one particular faction, because the men involved had recently been enemies. Walter's commission during the civil war as a warden of the march had been due to the abiding hostility of Llywelyn and Reginald de Briouze in the region, while the men from Scotland's western seaboard had all played a part in the Lacys' downfall in 1210.[67] The only thing that the magnates of Meath, Limerick and Ulster, as well as Llywelyn, had in common was that they were all absentee lords whose rights could be infringed without fear of immediate reprisals. There must have been a very good reason for Walter to have remained in England until 1220, by which point a decade would have passed without a resident lord of Meath.

The benefits of a weak royal government: Herefordshire, 1216-20

Walter could afford to rely upon toothless royal mandates to battle Geoffrey de Marisco's encroachments in Ireland, because he was happily exploiting his own official position in Herefordshire. Like Geoffrey de Marisco in Ireland, Walter controlled disposal of justice within his bailiwick, which, when combined with his status as the most powerful baron in the vicinity, made him virtually unassailable locally. He was also, like Geoffrey, responsible for Crown revenues, including royal demesne and escheats. Walter's accounts show that he provided no more than a token render for Herefordshire at the Exchequer each year. The traditional farm for Herefordshire was £164 16s 5d, which was far below the actual revenue the sheriff was likely to receive. In 1218, Walter's deputy, Thomas de Anesy, paid in only 18s 8d,[68] which amounted to only 0.5% of the farm. The following year's returns increased to £16 13s 9d.[69] But a downward trend began thereafter and continued for the remainder of Walter's term as sheriff, with the account for 1222 being the only one to show an increased render compared with the previous year.[70] Every piece of expenditure had to be accounted for, yet, in the absence of a strong central figure in the minority of the king, Walter and his fellow sheriffs were left with little oversight in the revenue's distribution. Because it was widely held that King John's appointees could not be deposed until the new king came of age, there was little that the Minority government could do to rein the sheriffs' power.

Along the Welsh march, much royal revenue was diverted to local defence. With relative independence came vulnerability, as the Crown's weakness meant that the marchers could no longer rely upon the king to protect them from Llywelyn, whose 'superiority within native Wales from 1218 to 1240 was more fully articulated than that enjoyed by any other Welsh prince since the coming of the Normans'.[71] Even if it had been stronger, the Minority government's generous treatment of the Welsh from the Treaty of Worcester signalled that no royal backing would be given to baronial incursions into Wales. Lacking sufficient strength for offensive action, the marcher barons decided to buttress the march. A period of rigorous fortification followed, one to which the introduction of a great number of masonry castles likely belongs.[72] Hereford castle was strengthened under Walter's supervision,[73] and it is probable that some royal revenue wound up subsidising the fortification of Lacy's own castles.

The encastellation of an entire region required considerable amounts of money, and this may have figured in the Minority government's decision to authorise the foundation of a Jewish community at Hereford.[74] Jewish money-lenders were a ready source of income for knights and barons, but their security was the special preserve of the Crown. A great number of Jews had fled England during the tumultuous civil war, but the cash-strapped Minority government was eager to see this source of revenue back in business. With the cessation of hostilities, the Crown sought to mollify those Jews who had remained in England, and to entice others to return.[75] In May 1218, a great council at Westminster took great care to safeguard the Jews' interests as a lucrative aspect of the royal demesne.[76] On 29 June 1218, Walter, as sheriff of Herefordshire, was ordered to allow the Jews of Hereford to establish their own community in the town, and to protect them from harm. He was also to ensure that the bishop of Hereford was unable to implead them for debt in his ecclesiastical courts, jurisdiction over the Jews belonging to the Crown.[77] Walter's extensive borrowing from the Jewish community of Hereford was to haunt him later in life,[78] but for the time being he and his fellow marchers formed a symbiotic relationship with the Hereford community.

Buoyed by his commission as sheriff of Herefordshire, and by his consolidation of power within the region, Walter de Lacy was able to negotiate with the Minority government from a position of strength. The latter was still in the unenviable position of having to bestow patronage on its loyal followers, while dealing with virtually untouchable administrators and an inalienable royal demesne. A period of extensive negotiation and compromise ensued. Consequently, when Hubert de Burgh sought to exploit his own position as English justiciar to secure a grant of the Three Castles – Grosmont, Skenfrith and Llantilio – he was forced to negotiate with Walter de Lacy.[79] As discussed above, King John had granted Hubert custody of the Three Castles in 1200, when they served as a wedge between the lands of Walter de Lacy and William de Briouze. He later reversed his decision, taking them from Hubert and granting them in fee to William de Briouze in 1205, as part of the latter's aggrandisement.[80] They had been restored to Reginald de Briouze with the rest of his father's inheritance in 1217, but Hubert decided to press his tenuous claim. He brought a plaint before the justices in Herefordshire that same year, claiming that King John had disseised him without judgement and of his own volition.[81] Reginald ignored the court action, and, at a special session of the king's council, was adjudged to have lost the suit by default. Consequently, on 8 December 1218, Walter de Lacy was notified of the court's decision and ordered to deliver seisin of the Three Castles to Hubert.[82] This was apparently easier said than done, for a month and a half later, on 26 January 1219, armed intervention was deemed necessary. Walter was reinforced by Hugh and Robert de Mortimer, Walter III and Roger of Clifford, John of Monmouth, and others of the county, and once again ordered to deliver seisin to Hubert.[83] However, Walter was either reluctant to proceed militarily against his brother-in-law, unwilling to facilitate Hubert's re-entry into the region, or determined to profit from the transaction, for he once again failed to deliver seisin.

Hubert hoped that the latter was the case, and procured two concessions for Walter that summer. The first, a gift of one hundred oaks to Walter's wife, Margery, for her foundation at Aconbury, was granted on 4 July 1219, immediately after a meeting of the king's council at Hereford.[84] David Carpenter characterises this as an act of conciliation, which it may well have been.[85] If this specific favour to Margery de Lacy can also be seen as an inducement to assist Hubert in realising his claim to the Three Castles, it might indicate that she played a part in Walter's failure to wrest them from her brother earlier that year. The matter did not end there, however. That same day, Hubert and Peter des Roches, bishop of Winchester appointed local knights and barons as commissioners in each county to inquire into unauthorised assarts made since Henry III's coronation in all woods, royal or otherwise. All such assarts (and their proceeds) were to be taken into the king's hand, and those responsible were to appear before justiciar and council on 16 August to show by what right they had made them.[86]

In due course, Hubert received a letter from one of the Hereford commissioners, Michael the Welshman, who was having trouble carrying out his orders in the face of opposition from the Lacys. Michael reported that he had carried out Hubert's orders concerning Margery de Lacy's assarts and the woods of the monks of Dore (Herefordshire). However, the Lacys said that they wished to have the crops of the assart, and the monks wanted to make a profit from their wood. Margery had also sold the hundred oaks which Hubert had given to her for Aconbury, and claimed a further thirty three oaks in Aconbury, forbidding anyone else to buy them. Even more alarmingly, Walter de Lacy had set a force of footmen and horsemen to oppose Michael's royal commission.[87] Hubert responded on 14 August, decreeing that Margery ought to have peace touching the assarts of three carucates of land which had previously been agreed by royal order, but that anything outside those three carucates ought to be seized and held until further orders.[88] Nothing more is heard of the matter of Walter's armed intervention or of Margery's misconduct over the oaks, but the fact that the Lacys were willing to proceed thus in Walter's bailiwick shows the degree of Walter's independence.[89]

The second concession that Walter secured from Hubert de Burgh concerned his shrieval account, and was ongoing while these events were unfolding. Walter wrote to the justiciar at some point in July, stating that, as he had explained to him at Hereford (where the two were at the beginning of July), he was unable to render his account at the Exchequer before Michaelmas.[90] On 21 July 1219, Hubert issued the desired order to respite Walter's account,[91] which was followed on 20 September with another letter to the same effect.[92] Walter duly thanked the justiciar for his kindness, notified him that he was sending a clerk to account at the Exchequer, and asked for respite on several other royal debts that he owed.[93]

Despite the justiciar's actions on his behalf, Walter remained unable (or unwilling) to prise the Three Castles from Reginald de Briouze's grasp. In the same letter in which he had complained of Walter and Margery de Lacy, Michael the Welshman wrote that 'Reginald de Briouze is selling and destroying the wood of Skenfrith and Grosmont'.[94] The fact that Reginald was intensively exploiting two of the Three Castles despite a standing order for their transference to the English justiciar, while Walter de Lacy, the man charged with that transference, set an armed force against royal officials rather than against Reginald shows just how little authority the Minority government had in Herefordshire. The order for seisin of the Three Castles was repeated four months later on 8 December, and once again ignored.[95] Exasperated, Hubert decided to negotiate directly with Reginald de Briouze, and a compromise was reached whereby Hubert was to hold the castles from Reginald.[96]

Walter gained even more influence in the region thanks to the failure of the forest inquiries. On 28 October, the date assigned for those with illegal assarts to answer for their crimes before the king's council, a large group of angry men instead laid complaints before Hubert and the council about the whole forest administration. Faced with concerted resistance, Hubert went from chastising the barons as those in breach of forest law, to championing their cause against the very men whom he had sent after them in the first place.[97] On 8 November 1219, Hubert wrote to the forest officials ordering them to behave amicably towards those within the forest so that 'they no longer, through the oppressions of you and yours, have grounds for complaint'.[98] As a result, Walter de Lacy went from being a supposed disturber of the peace to a victim of the unjust forest administration. Hubert then appointed Walter de Lacy to the forest administration of Gloucestershire. The order came on 13 December, five days after the final unsuccessful order for the delivery of the Three Castles.[99]

Return to Ireland: 1220-1

In August 1220, Walter attended a royal council at Oxford, which was the scene for an airing of grievances against Geoffrey de Marisco's predatory administration as Irish justiciar. As a result, the Irish justiciar received a firm rebuke and had strict limitations imposed on his authority,[100] but, as a King John appointee, he could not so easily be removed from office. Although King Henry III had just undergone a second coronation on 17 May 1220, he was, at twelve, still seventeen months from his fourteenth birthday and any hope of securing widespread recognition of his majority.[101] The weakness of the Minority government in this regard, or its unwillingness to cede control to Henry, is clear from its decision not to publish two contemporaneous mandates from the pope aimed at the resumption of royal authority in the localities.[102] This decision may finally have prompted Walter to secure his Irish interests in person, giving him the security to leave England with Herefordshire firmly under his control. Walter's departure was delayed by rumblings within native Wales. On 21 August 1220, Hubert de Burgh wrote to the sheriffs of Herefordshire, Gloucestershire and Worcestershire, telling them that he had received intelligence that Llywelyn was mustering an army. Walter and his fellow sheriffs were ordered to ascertain whether the force was being gathered against Reginald de Briouze, or others of the king's barons, and to aid Reginald in defending his lands.[103] In the event, Llywelyn launched his offensive against the younger William Marshal in Pembrokeshire, which, though successful, was not enough to keep Walter in England.[104]

Walter's son and heir, Gilbert, also had come into his own by this point, giving Walter the option of placing a Lacy at the head of his English and Welsh administration (as he had with William de Lacy in Ireland). Gilbert had been granted the extensive Lacy demesne estate of Britford (Wiltshire), where, on 23 November 1219, he was granted a weekly market and yearly fair for a fine of 100s.[105] That said, there seems no reason to follow Brock Holden's line of reasoning (which he made regarding a grant of oaks to Gilbert for the construction of a chapel at his *curia* of Britford in 1222)[106] that such an expression of lordship implied that Walter had demised the English and Welsh components of the Lacy inheritance to Gilbert in their entirety.[107] In 1219, Walter was still too heavily involved in the politics of the region to have handed over the inheritance to his teenage son Gilbert. What is more, there is no evidence of Gilbert being associated with the lordship of the core Lacy lands at this point. It is possible that Walter may have introduced Gilbert to the complexities of honorial administration while he was away, but only as his deputy. There are several instances of this in the history of transnational lordship. Earl Robert II of Leicester deputed his son Robert de Breteuil to manage his extensive Norman estates while Earl Robert administered England as justiciar between 1155 and 1168. Likewise, Earl Robert's twin, Waleran, deputed his son Robert to manage his French county of Meulan while Waleran resided in Normandy.[108]

By the autumn of 1220, Meath had suffered a decade of absentee rule, half of this time in the custody of King John. An important aspect of Walter's return included the reordering of his administration and the settlement of disputes that arose from his protracted absence. To help, Walter brought with him his bailiff for the shrievalty of Hereford, Thomas de Anesy, who was replaced in Herefordshire by Warin of Grendon for the duration of Walter's stay in Ireland.[109] The 'Dublin annals of Inisfallen' ascribe the construction of the castle of Trim to this year, 1220, which historians traditionally have taken to signal some new building phase on the site.[110] However, because the annals' information seems to have come from a misdated and mistranslated entry in the book of Howth (which actually referred to the siege of Trim in 1224), there is little reason to suppose any great new building programme at Trim.[111]

From October to November 1221, Geoffrey de Marisco slowly relinquished control of the Irish administration,[112] and on 10 November the order for Walter de Lacy to receive seisin of his lands was repeated to the new justiciar, Archbishop Henry of Dublin.[113] The following summer, the situation regarding Walter's lands becomes clearer. On 26 June 1222, Archbishop Henry was ordered to give aid and council to Walter de Lacy in recovering seisin of his lands of Ardmayle, Ardnurcher and *Minaluwy* (?), which King John had taken from him, but which were no longer in the crown's possession.[114] Two weeks later, Archbishop Henry was ordered to remove any force he might find defending Ardmayle or Ardnurcher.[115] These two mandates may have been designed to buy Walter's compliance with an order of 24 June, to take the Herefordshire manors of Marden and Lugwardine, the mill of Marden and part of the wood of Marden into the king's hand.[116] Walter was custodian of these two manors (with Marden being a former Lacy subinfeudation),[117] and may have baulked at handing them over while his own lands remained alienated in Ireland. If so, than this was another instance of compromise necessitated by a weak royal government.

That same year (1222) Walter attempted to expand his direct lordship beyond Meath in Ireland, which also unleashed his half-brother William de Lacy upon the Irish of Bréifne. Walter's first step was to build a castle on the west bank of the Shannon at Athleague (now Ballyleague, Co. Roscommon).[118] Athleague, as well as being the site of a crossing over the Shannon and the northern entry point to Lough Ree, was extremely fertile owing to the silt deposits left by the annual flooding of the river.[119] The later manor of Athleague sat astride the Shannon, which allowed it to take full advantage of the rich soil and command maritime traffic in the vicinity. The successful fortification of that site would have greatly enhanced Walter's influence on the western extremity of his lordship, and provided a potential outlet for expansion into Connacht. The Irish annals report that most of a castle had been completed when the king of Connacht, Cathal Crobderg Ua Conchobair, approached at the head of his army. Walter's men fled, allowing the Connachtmen to pull down the unfinished fortifications.[120] The castle was later reconstructed by William de Lacy in 1227,[121] which indicates its importance for his own ventures beyond Meath.

Bréifne - 1220-33

It is not immediately clear what sparked Walter's desire to stab westward, but the Crown's decision on 13 August 1220 to retain his castle and vill of Drogheda for a yearly rent of £20, may have played a part.[122] Drogheda was Meath's link to the outside world, and, by controlling it, the government could regulate commerce along the rivers Boyne and Blackwater (the lifelines of Walter's Irish lordship), and disrupt Walter's participation in the politics of the Irish Sea. With the earldom of Ulster (and its own maritime network) still in the Crown's hands, the disputed territory of Bréifne offered the best opportunity for expansion.

Walter's activities in Bréifne were also designed to provide for his family. During King John's reign, Walter had helped to secure Ulster for his brother Hugh and had sought to consolidate the position of his father-in-law, William de Briouze, in Limerick. In 1220, he set out to establish an independent lordship for his half-brother, William de Lacy, in Conmaicne and the territory of the Uí Ragallaig in east Bréifne.[123] The laconic annals of Bréifne, fragmentary for this period, record that, in 1220, Walter de Lacy brought a strong force to Ireland on behalf of the English king, and took hostages from the Uí Ragallaig.[124] The annals of Loch Cé further situate the conflict at Ua Ragallaig's crannóg on Lough Oughter (Co. Cavan), which was to become William de Lacy's headquarters.[125]

The Lacys' stake in Bréifne went back to the time of Walter's father Hugh, who at his death was called 'king of Mide, and Bréifne, and Airgialla' by the Annals of Loch Cé.[126] In 1197, John, lord of Ireland, provided the Lacys with a firmer foothold in the region by granting Walter all of Gilbert de Angulo's lands in Bréifne.[127] Gilbert and Walter were reconciled in 1207,[128] but Walter retained an interest in Bréifne, including the castles of Kilmore and Belturbet (Co. Cavan), both in the vicinity of Ua Ragallaig's crannóg (with Belturbet, which was also on an island, being linked to Ua Ragallaig's crannóg by an inland water network). By 1211/12, the ruling Uí Ruairc dynasty was paying a rent of forty cows to Meath.[129] The Lacys had long exerted their tributary lordship over Bréifne, but from 1220 their lordship was to become specifically based on land tenure.

The immediate precursor to Walter's expedition was a raid in 1219 or 1220 by Domnaill Mór Ua Domnaill, king of Tír Conaill, in which he took hostages from both the Uí Ruairc and Uí Ragallaig.[130] It is unclear whether Walter had exerted a hegemonic overlordship over the Uí Ragallaig as he had over the Uí Ruairc, but in 1221 he decided to change the nature of his lordship in the region. First, he granted the land of Ualgarg Ua Ruairc to Gilbert de Angulo's son, Philip. William de Lacy was to build three castles for Philip to help secure his territory, and, once his lands had been farmed, Philip was to render Walter the service of three knights.[131] Orpen characterises the grant as a speculative one, while Otway-Ruthven states that it must have been confirmatory.[132] They are both probably correct. Philip was in possession of at least some of the territory in 1214,[133] but it is doubtful that he had even loose control over it all, given the light service demanded and the stipulation that Walter (through William) had to provide three castles for its defence. What is more, the Bréifne poem '*Eriu oll oilen aingeal*' (Noble Ireland, isle of angels) characterises Philip's early rule as that of an absentee.[134] The role played by William in securing Philip's lands is also an indication of his vested interest in the success of the grant. It would serve to protect William's flank as he carved out an independent lordship for himself in the lands of the Uí Ragallaig.

William de Lacy embraced this task, earning himself the enmity of the Irish of the region. The king of Connacht, Cathal Crobderg Ua Conchobair, was especially displeased with the encroachment of the Lacys into a region that he had earmarked as an appanage for his son Áed. When William built a castle at Ballyloughloe (bar. Clonlonan, Co. Westmeath) in 1223, the Connachtmen destroyed it.[135] The following year, Cathal Crobderg petitioned for the transference of Uí Briúin, Conmaicne and Caladh na hAnghaile (bar. Rathcline, Co. Longford), which amounted to all of Bréifne, from William to Áed.[136] Although Hugh de Lacy's rebellion (discussed in Chapter 7 below) meant that the king ordered the transference of lordship over Bréifne from William to Áed,[137] William did not give up so easily. The Bréifne poem contains two verses on William which suggest that he was active in Bréifne about 1226. After recording the destruction of the ecclesiastical site of Fenagh by the English, and the slaying of Áed Ua Ruairc (which occurred in 1226),[138] it declares:

> Stoutly will I avenge
> My church upon the Foreigners;
> For 'tis a burning to me this day
> That William Gorm [de Lacy] should profane me.

> I will grant, without deceit,
> And the noble saints of Ireland also.
> That William Gorm shall not obtain, thereafter,
> Power over the Irish (*Gaedhil*), until doom.[139]

The following year, 1227, William successfully rebuilt the castle of Athleague and received a yearly stipend at the Dublin Exchequer for his support in the king's service.[140] Although he had other interests in England and Wales, and served the English king in France,[141] an independent lordship of Bréifne remained his primary ambition. This ambition eventually killed him. Under the year 1233, the annals of Loch Cé report that he was mortally wounded during a raid into the territory of the Uí Ragallaig in Bréifne, and died in his own house.[142] The Clonmacnoise annalist provides this eulogy: 'William Delacy, chiefest champion in these parts of Europe, and the hardiest and strongest hand of any Englishman from the Nicene seas to this place, or Irishman, was hurt in a skirmish in the Brenie [Bréifne], came to his house, and there died of the wounde.'[143]

Conclusion

The regency government set up to rule in the young Henry III's name was one largely composed of the late king's most loyal magnates, who, like Walter de Lacy, were quite familiar with the personal form of royal lordship utilised by Henry II and his sons, Richard and John. As soon as the royalist barons gained power, they began limiting English kingship – as we saw above – through, for instance, their reissues of Magna Carta. More particularly, during the government of the regent, William Marshal, he and his fellow Irish and Welsh marcher lords reaped the benefits of victory. The papal legate Guala placed an interdict on native Wales, the liberties of Leinster and Meath were restored, and lenient overtures of reconciliation were addressed to their closest associates amongst the rebels.

Once the civil war was won, royalist barons remained entrenched in their wartime shrievalties and continued to exploit Crown revenues without reference to the Exchequer. Walter de Lacy's entrenched position as sheriff of Herefordshire made him the dominant force in the region, and, once his comrade-in-arms, William Marshal, had died, Walter forced the new Minority government to negotiate with him in order to obtain any action in his shire. An intriguing episode involving the English justiciar's attempts to secure seisin of the castles granted him in 1201 illustrates Hubert de Burgh's rising star in the Minority government, the Crown's persistent weakness in the localities, and the incessant negotiations which consequently dogged royal initiatives. More particularly, it also brings to the fore the longstanding rivalry between the families of Burgh, Briouze and Lacy, first fostered by King John in 1201, and shows how, during the minority, interbaronial politics could shape (and hamper) royal initiatives.

Walter may have been able to do as he wished in Herefordshire, but a weak royal government was detrimental to his application of lordship in

Ireland, where he and other absentee lords found portions of their lands withheld by the Irish justiciar, Geoffrey de Marisco, who was using their proceeds (and other royal revenue) for personal gain. The power and corruption of the justiciar of Ireland during the minority of Henry III is brought to the fore in this study as never before. It took a personal trip to Ireland in 1220 for Walter to set things right, and even then he met with resistance from the justiciar. During the reign of King John, Walter had helped to secure Ulster for his brother Hugh and sought to consolidate the position of his father-in-law, William de Briouze, in Limerick. In 1220, he set out to establish his half-brother William Gorm de Lacy in Bréifne. Walter de Lacy's positions in Herefordshire and Ireland during this period again highlight the dangers of particularisation of lordship to a transnational magnate. In this period, Walter's power was great, but geographically limited.

Notes

1 Susan Reynolds, 'Secular power and authority in the middle ages', in Huw Pryce and John Watts (eds), *Power and Identity in the Middle Ages: Essays in Memory of Rees Davies* (Oxford, 2007), pp. 11–22, at p. 12.
2 See, for instance, J. C. Holt, 'The barons and the Great Charter', *English Historical Review*, 70 (1955), pp. 1–24; Ralph Turner, 'England in 1215: an authoritarian Angevin dynasty facing multiple threats', in J. S. Loengard (ed.), *Magna Carta and the England of King John* (Woodbridge, 2010), pp. 10–26.
3 Carpenter, *Minority*, pp. 1–2.
4 For Poitou: *ibid.*; Robert Stacey, *Politics, Policy and Finance under Henry III, 1216–1245* (Oxford, 1987); F. M. Powicke, *King Henry III and the Lord Edward* (Oxford, 1947). Ireland will be dealt with below.
5 Carpenter, *Minority*, p. 3.
6 A. A. M. Duncan, *Scotland: The Making of the Kingdom* (Edinburgh, 1975), p. 523; R. R. Davies, *The Age of Conquest, Wales 1063–1415* (Oxford, 2000), p. 243. To place the possible 'election' of the new king in perspective, Henry I's coronation charter claimed that he had been 'elected', when he certainly had not been. Felix Liebermann, 'The text of Henry I's Coronation Charter', *Transactions of the Royal Historical Society* new ser, 8 (1894), pp. 21–48, at pp. 40–6.
7 Carpenter, *Minority*, p. 13.
8 *Rot. Litt. Claus.*, i, p. 293.
9 *Hist. William Marshal*, ii, lines 15347–72; Holden, *Lords*, p. 193.
10 Carpenter, *Minority*, p. 14.
11 *The Statutes of the Realm*, 11 vols (London, 1810–28), i, pp. 108–13.
12 'Annales de Waverleia', p. 286, *s.a.* 1216. For the interdict and reissues of Magna Carta, see *The Letters and Charters of Cardinal Guala Bicchieri, Papal Legate in England, 1216–1218*, ed. Nicholas Vincent (Woodbridge, 1996).

13 *Statutes of the Realm*, i, pp. 108–13.
14 Carpenter, *Minority*, p. 24.
15 *Ibid.*, p. 22.
16 *Foedera*, I, i, p. 145.
17 *Ibid.*, I, i, p. 145; *PR, 1216–25*, p. 4. William Ferrers was Margery de Lacy's cousin. The links between Chester and the Lacys are discussed below, Chapters 7 and 8.
18 Carpenter, *Minority*, p. 25.
19 *Ibid.*, p. 312. They also retained clause 37 on the limitation of prerogative wardship (which became clause 30), *Statutes of the Realm*, i, pp. 108–13.
20 See Holt, *Magna Carta*, pp. 75–122.
21 Carpenter, *Minority*, p. 26.
22 *Rot. Litt. Claus.*, i, p. 335. The second truce was agreed on 13 January, to last until 23 April. Carpenter, *Minority*, p. 25.
23 *PR, 1216–25*, p. 22.
24 *Royal Letters*, i, pp. 527–9; *Mem. Walteri Coventria*, pp. 235–6.
25 *PR, 1216–25*, pp. 108–9.
26 *Hist. William Marshal*, lines 15872–16044.
27 BL MS Lansdowne 229, fo. 143v.
28 Carpenter, *Minority*, pp. 36–40.
29 Norgate, *Minority*, pp. 29–33.
30 *PR, 1216–25*, pp. 109–10.
31 Carpenter, *Minority*, pp. 41–2.
32 *Rot. Litt. Pat.*, pp. 72–5, 112–13; *Rot. Litt. Claus.*, i, p. 312.
33 *PR, 1216–25*, pp. 72–3, 112.
34 Lloyd, *Wales*, ii, pp. 652–3.
35 See, for instance *PR, 1216–25*, pp. 113ff.; *Rot. Litt. Claus.*, i, p. 312ff.
36 *Foedera*, I, i, p. 148.
37 Walter de Lacy was a witness, *The Acts of Welsh Rulers, 1120–1283*, ed. Huw Pryce (Cardiff, 2005), pp. 397–400; *Foedera*, I, i, pp. 150–1; *Rot. Litt. Claus.*, i, 378b–379.
38 Davies, *Age of Conquest*, p. 242.
39 Carpenter, *Minority*, pp. 51, 118.
40 *Royal Letters*, i, p. 535.
41 *Rot. Litt. Pat.*, p. 151–151b.
42 *Ann. Clon.*, p. 228, *s.a.* 1215.
43 Simms, *Gaelic Sources*, pp. 26–7. See also Gearóid Mac Niocaill, *The Medieval Irish Annals* (Dublin, 1975), pp. 21–3.
44 *ALC*, i, p. 250, *s.a.* 1215; See Chapter 5.
45 *Rot. Litt. Claus.*, i, p. 260.
46 *Rot. Litt. Pat.*, p. 188b.
47 *Ibid.*, p. 194; *Rot. Litt. Claus.*, i, p. 282.
48 *PR, 1216–25*, p. 26.
49 *Ibid.*, pp. 25–6.
50 *Ibid.*, p. 26.
51 *Ibid.*, pp. 72, 74.

52 *Ibid.*, pp. 77–8.
53 *Ibid.*, p. 78.
54 *Rot. Litt. Claus.*, i, p. 476b-7.
55 *Ibid.*, i, p. 306.
56 *PR, 1216–25*, p. 57.
57 *Ibid.*, pp. 157–8.
58 Ralph Turner, *Men Raised from the Dust: Administrative Service and Upward Mobility in Angevin England* (Philadelphia, 1988), p. 95.
59 Aubrey Gwynn, 'Henry of London, archbishop of Dublin: a study in Anglo-Norman statecraft', *Studies: An Irish Quarterly Review*, 38 (1949), pp. 295–306, 389–402, at p. 390.
60 Orpen, *Normans*, iii, p. 20.
61 *PR, 1216–25*, pp. 117, 119, 125.
62 *Ibid.*, p. 157.
63 *Rot. Litt. Claus.*, i, p. 369.
64 *PR, 1216–25*, p. 132.
65 *Rot. Litt. Claus.*, i, pp. 392b, 402b; Duffy, 'Lords of Galloway', pp. 43–4.
66 *Rot. Litt. Claus.*, i, p. 362b.
67 See Chapter 5.
68 *Pipe Roll 2 Henry III*, p. 90.
69 *Pipe Roll 3 Henry III*, p. 165.
70 The totals were: 1220: £15 17s 8d (*Pipe Roll 4 Henry III*, p. 194); 1221: £14 8s 6d (*Pipe Roll 5 Henry III*, p. 13); 1222: £16 15s 5d (*Pipe Roll 6 Henry III*, p. 64) 1223: £8 14s 9d (*Pipe Roll 7 Henry III*, p. 185).
71 Davies, *Age of Conquest*, p. 244.
72 Holden, *Lords*, pp. 199–200.
73 *Pipe Roll 2 Henry III*, p. 90; *Pipe Roll 3 Henry III*, p. 165.
74 Hillaby, 'Hereford gold, part 2', pp. 193–5.
75 *Ibid.*, pp. 211–12.
76 Carpenter, *Minority*, pp. 82–3.
77 *PR, 1216–25*, p. 157; S. H. Rigby, *English Society in the Later Middle Ages: Class, Status and Gender* (Basingstoke, 1995), pp. 286–7.
78 See Chapter 7.
79 Carpenter, *Minority*, p. 149.
80 See Chapter 4.
81 *Bracton's Note Book: A Collection of Cases Decided in the King's Courts During the Reign of Henry the Third*, ed. F. W. Maitland, 3 vols (London, 1887), iii, pp. 319–20, no. 1330.
82 *Rot. Litt. Claus.*, i, p. 404.
83 *Ibid.*, i, p. 386b.
84 *Ibid.*, i, p. 394b. The council met at Hereford from 28 June to 3 July.
85 Carpenter, *Minority*, pp. 149–50.
86 *PR, 1216–25*, pp. 211–20; Carpenter, *Minority*, p. 150.
87 TNA SC 1/1/213; *Cal. Ancient Correspondence Wales*, p. 8.
88 *Rot. Litt. Claus.*, i, p. 398.

89 John of Acton and Ralph Musard, sheriff of Gloucester, complained in a similar vein about the actions of the bailiffs of Savaric de Mauléon and Hugh de Vivon in Harewood and Alveston forests, TNA SC 1/1/160.
90 *Royal Letters*, i, pp. 42-3.
91 *CFR, 1218-19*, no. 344.
92 *Rot. Litt. Claus.*, i, p. 400b.
93 TNA SC 1/1/110.
94 TNA SC 1/1/213; *Cal. Ancient Correspondence Wales*, p. 8.
95 *Rot. Litt. Claus.*, i, p. 404.
96 R. F. Walker, 'Hubert de Burgh and Wales, 1218-32', *English Historical Review*, 87 (1972), pp. 465-94, at p. 471.
97 Carpenter, *Minority*, pp. 163-4.
98 *Rot. Litt. Claus.*, i, pp. 433b-4.
99 *Ibid.*, i, p. 435.
100 *PR, 1216-25*, pp. 263-5.
101 Norgate, *Minority*, pp. 129-30, 146-7.
102 *Royal Letters*, i, pp. 121, 535-6; *Cal. Pap. Let.*, p. 72; Norgate, *Minority*, pp. 146-7, 154.
103 *Rot. Litt. Claus.*, i, p. 428.
104 Lloyd, *Wales*, ii, pp. 658-60.
105 *CFR 1219-20*, no. 18.
106 *Rot. Litt. Claus.*, i, p. 495.
107 Holden, *Lords*, p. 205.
108 Crouch, *Beaumont Twins*, pp. 175-6.
109 *Rot. Litt. Claus.*, i, p. 430b; *Pipe Roll 3 Henry III*, p. 165; *Pipe Roll 4 Henry III*, p. 194; *Pipe Roll 5 Henry III*, p. 19. Walter and Thomas were back in England by 1222, *Pipe Roll 6 Henry III*, p. 64.
110 TCD MS 1281, *s.a.* 1220; Orpen, *Normans*, vol ii, p. 249; vol iii, p. 31; Brian Graham, 'Medieval Settlements in County Meath', *Ríocht na Mídhe*, 5/4 (1974), pp. 40-59, at p. 44.
111 Michael Potterton, *Medieval Trim: History and Archaeology* (Dublin, 2005), pp. 213-14; Seán Duffy, *'The Key of the Pale': A History of Trim Castle* (Forthcoming).
112 *PR, 1216-25*, pp. 315-17; *Rot. Litt. Claus.*, i, p. 505b.
113 *Rot. Litt. Claus.*, i, p. 479b.
114 *Ibid.*, i, pp. 501b. Minaluwy might signify Muinter Angaile (Co Longford), or perhaps Móin Alúine, the bog of Allen, which stretched into the lordship of Meath.
115 *Rot. Litt. Claus.*, i, pp. 504.
116 *CFR 1221-22*, nos 213, 217.
117 See Chapter 3.
118 *ALC*, i, p. 262, *s.a.* 1221; *Ann. Clon.*, p. 229, *s.a.* 1220 [*recte* 1221]; *AFM*, iii, pp. 198-200 *s.a.* 1220 [*recte* 1221].
119 Linda Doran, 'Medieval communication routes through Longford and Roscommon and their associated settlements', *Proceedings of the Royal Irish Academy, Section C*, 104 (2004), pp. 57-80, at pp. 63, 68.

120 *ALC*, i, p. 262, s.a. 1221; *Ann. Clon.*, p. 229, s.a. 1220 [*recte* 1221]; *AFM*, iii, pp. 198-200, s.a. 1220 [*recte* 1221].
121 *Ann. Clon.*, p. 233, s.a. 1227.
122 *Rot. Litt. Claus.*, i, pp. 427, 427b.
123 For more on William see Colin Veach and Freya Verstraten Veach, 'William *Gorm* de Lacy, "Chiefest Champion in These Parts of Europe"', in Seán Duffy (ed.) *Princes, Prelates and Poets in Medieval Ireland: Essays in Honour of Katharine Simms* (Dublin, 2013), pp. 63-84. For the Uí Ragallaig see Katharine Simms, 'The O'Reillys and the kingdom of East Breifne', *Bréifne*, 5 (1979), pp. 305-19.
124 Éamonn de hÓir, 'Annála as Bréifne', *Bréifne*, 4 (1970), pp. 59-86, s.a. 1220. My thanks to Dr Freya Verstraten Veach for her help with this source.
125 *ALC*, i, pp. 260-2, s.a. 1220. A crannóg is a fortified artificial island.
126 *ALC*, i, p. 172, s.a. 1186. See also Chapter 2.
127 See Chapter 3.
128 *Rot. Litt. Claus.*, i, p. 98. See Chapter 5.
129 *Rot. Litt. Pat.*, p. 148b; Irish Pipe Roll 14 John, pp. 23, 25, 33, 35-9, 41.
130 *ALC*, i, pp. 260-2, s.a. 1220; *AFM*, iii, pp. 196-8, s.a. 1219 [*recte* 1220?].
131 *Calendar of the Patent and Close Rolls of Chancery in Ireland from the Eighteenth to Forty-Fifth of Queen Elizabeth, volume 2*, ed. James Morrin (Dublin and London, 1862), p. 197. The territories included: Muinter Eolais (bar. Mohill, Co. Leitrim), Magh Nissi (in bar. Leitrim, Co Leitrim), Muinter Cinaith (in Drumahaire, Co. Leitrim), Cenel Luachain (in Carrigallen, Co. Leitrim), and Tellach Dunchadha (Tullyhunco, Co. Cavan).
132 Orpen, *Normans*, iii, 34-5; A. J. Otway-Ruthven, 'The partition of the de Verdon lands in Ireland in 1332', *Proceedings of the Royal Irish Academy, section C*, 66 (1968), pp. 401-55, at p. 412.
133 Otway-Ruthven, 'Verdon lands', p. 412.
134 *Book of Fenagh*, p. 71.
135 *ALC*, i, p. 266, s.a. 1223.
136 *Royal Letters*, i, p. 223.
137 *Cal. Doc. Ireland, 1171-1251*, no. 1195; *Royal Letters*, i, pp. 500-30.
138 *AFM*, iii, p. 240, s.a. 1226.
139 *Book of Fenagh*, p. 73. The nickname 'Gorm' is unique for this period, appearing again only from the fifteenth century in galloglass families. It is usually translated as 'swarthy' or 'dark blue' (perhaps relating to William's hair), but is also used as a descriptive adjective relating to arms and armour. Veach and Verstraten Veach, 'William *Gorm*', p. 81n.
140 *ALC*, i, p. 470, s.a. 1271; *Ann. Clon.*, p. 233, s.a. 1227; *Rot. Litt. Claus.*, ii, p. 186b; *CR, 1227-31*, p. 193.
141 *CR, 1227-31*, pp. 255-6, 412. See Veach and Verstraten, 'William *Gorm*', pp. 77-8.
142 *ALC*, i, pp. 314-16, s.a. 1233.
143 *Ann. Clon.*, p. 234. s.a. 1233.

7

The dangers of transnational lordship: 1222–41

The reign of King John cast a long shadow. His rule provided the context, and his administrative appointees the personnel, for his son's Minority government. It was also in this later period that some of his policies began to bear fruit. As argued in Chapter 4, King John's removal of John de Courcy and promotion of Hugh de Lacy as earl of Ulster in 1205 seem to have been done to counterbalance Earl William Marshal's control of the southern Irish Sea littoral. The elder Marshal's good relations with the Lacys at the time meant that no competition was apparent before Hugh was exiled in 1210. By 1222, however, the elder Marshal was replaced by his energetic son, and Hugh was ready to return. The rebellions that gripped the British Isles from 1223 to 1224 and again from 1233 to 1234 were a direct result of King John's creation of the earldom of Ulster, pitting the Lacys against the Marshals. These conflicts vividly illustrate the interconnectivity of the British Isles, and one of the dangers of transnational landholding: the international reach of conflicts.

This period also saw Walter take a step back from high politics, increasingly associating his son and heir, Gilbert, with the rule of the Lacy inheritance. Gilbert's unexpected death in 1230 threatened to remove large portions of the inheritance from Walter's control, and illustrated the complexities of medieval landholding when heirs could be well into their adulthood before fully entering their inheritance. In 1233, the overlapping and ever fluctuating alignments of power along Britain's Atlantic fringe matched the Lacys with the Marshals in a struggle for dominance of the Irish Sea. The case is less clear in 1233–4 than it had been in 1223–4, but in both instances the Crown backed one faction over another, giving royal support to the most aggressive aspects of aristocratic lordship. Although his faction ultimately reaped the rewards of victory in Ireland,

Walter's prominence quickly faded. But the demands of his lordship were not diminished. No longer conspicuous on the battlefield, Walter now faced opponents in the law courts. His lengthy quarrel with the Knights Hospitaller at the papal curia (one initiated by his wife) is an impressive display of the strength of his brand of aristocratic lordship, but it also cost Walter dearly. Burdened with his great debts to the Crown and Jewish money-lenders, Walter was an invalid by 1237, blind shortly thereafter, and dead by 1241. The great Lacy inheritance, which once extended across four realms of the Plantagenet empire, and had found its strength in the territorial integrity of its honors, was then carved up between his two granddaughters.

The return of Hugh de Lacy: 1222-3

The annals of Dunstable record under 1222 that Hugh de Lacy, having been expelled from Languedoc by the Albigensians, returned to England and petitioned for the restoration of his Irish lands. The king, the annalist continues, denied this request, and instead offered him a pension of 300 marks.[1] Writing before Hugh's subsequent rebellion, knowledge of which might have otherwise instilled Hugh's return with a greater importance, it is significant that this contemporary set of Bedfordshire annals should notice Hugh's return to England. The safe-conduct for Hugh and his retinue to enter England was issued on 17 September 1221 to last until that Christmas,[2] though little progress seems to have been made in negotiations for his reinstatement. As mentioned above, Walter had negotiated the restoration of Ulster as early as 1215, and the Minority government had offered Hugh complete reconciliation one month after King John's death in 1216. Hugh ignored these overtures (perhaps owing to his rewards in Languedoc), but the door to restoration was left open while the elder William Marshal remained regent and head of the Minority government.[3] However, the ascendancy of the Marshal's political circle died with him. Hugh de Lacy may have been a valuable asset worth courting during the civil war, and a member of the protected aristocratic elite for the duration of the Marshal's regency, but, by the time of his return in 1221, those days had passed.

Hugh was no stranger to conflict, and, if he could not walk back into his northern earldom, the experienced conquistador would take it by force. He first secured an alliance with two discontented western British figures, Llywelyn ab Iorwerth and Ranulf, earl of Chester and Lincoln. In 1222, styling himself 'earl of Ulster', Hugh witnessed the marriage of Llywelyn's daughter Helen to Earl Ranulf's nephew and heir, John the Scot.[4] At about the same time, the Lacys sealed their own alliance with Llywelyn through William de Lacy's marriage to another of Llywelyn's daughters, Gwenllian.[5] This new Ulster-Gwynedd-Chester axis harked back to the Ulster-Man-Cumbria axis that John de Courcy had utilised in the late twelfth century,[6] but it had its origin in the longstanding association between the Lacys and the earls of Chester. The elder Hugh de Lacy had held land of Ranulf's father Hugh in the fee of Bisley (Gloucestershire), and Walter de Lacy held one knight's fee of Ranulf in Wiltshire.[7] Walter also cultivated a maritime link between Meath and Chester. In an undated charter, Walter de Lacy remitted to the citizens of Chester the customary duty of twopence paid to him on every cargo of white corn exported from his land of Ireland, and granted them the liberty of entering and leaving his port of Drogheda, and all of his other ports, without paying the customary duty. The charter was witnessed by Ranulf, earl of Chester, 'my kinsman' (*consanguineus meus*), attesting to an otherwise unspecified blood relationship.[8] Before the Lacys' expulsion from Ireland in 1210, Walter's brother, Hugh, had granted lands in Ulster to Earl Ranulf's familiar Henry de Audley, as well as to Henry's brother Adam (d. *c*.1211).[9] Earl Ranulf then helped to secure the offer of full restoration that Hugh ignored in 1216.[10] The Crown's retention of Drogheda from 1220 would have threatened the maritime link between Meath and Chester, and might indicate that Hugh's efforts in 1222 were aimed at re-establishing a strategic alliance that the elder Marshal's successors in government had managed to disrupt.

Hugh's efforts brought the Minority government back to the negotiating table, but also prompted it to fortify Ireland against invasion. Instructions concerning the restoration of Hugh's lands within his brother's fee were sent to Walter on 23 June 1222,[11] and, on 18 July 1222, the council issued instructions for Ireland's defence. Irish ports, including Dublin, Waterford, Drogheda, Cork and Limerick, were ordered to construct galleys for the defence of the king's realm (*regnum*) of Ireland. Thomas of Galloway and Richard Tyrell were ordered to surrender their castles of Antrim (Co. Antrim) and Cnoc (Castleknock, Co. Dublin) to the justiciar, Archbishop Henry of Dublin. In addition, the fidelity of Donnchad Cairprech Ua Briain, king of Thomond, was ensured through a revised charter for his kingdom, and the young Theobald Walter (whose father's death in 1205 had sparked the Irish crisis of 1207) was granted seisin of his inheritance.[12] On 27 December 1222, the Minority government notified Archbishop Henry that it had granted Hugh de Lacy seisin of the lands which he held both of his brother, Walter, and through his marriage to

Lescelina de Verdun, ordering Walter to deliver Hugh seisin of lands in his custody. There was no mention of Ulster. The Crown used another Lacy brother, Gilbert, to convey its offer to Hugh, and assured Hugh that Gilbert's message had been agreed upon by the majority of the council and had been shown to Earl Ranulf.[13] Earl Ranulf was clearly backing Hugh's restoration as he had in 1216.

Hugh declined to take up these terms, and eventually decided to vent his anger on William Marshal the younger. Early in 1223, Hugh's ally Llywelyn attacked and took the Shropshire fortresses of Kinnerley and Whittington. Hubert de Burgh hastened to the Welsh border, and, with Earl Ranulf speaking for Llywelyn, agreed to a peace. However, William Marshal seized this opportunity. The Marshal was at Chepstow on 23 March, but hastened to Ireland to gather an army (where he issued a charter to the burgesses of Kilkenny on 5 April).[14] He then made a hasty return to Wales, landing at St David's (Pembrokeshire) on 15 April, and ensuring that he was prepared to strike once the Crown's peace with Llywelyn expired on 24 April. The Marshal then marched on the royal castles of Cardigan and Carmarthen, both held for the king by Llywelyn, and took them without a fight.[15] Hugh de Lacy played a major role in the ensuing war, being named by Matthew Paris as one who, together with Llywelyn 'united in their hatred of the king', attacked the Marshal.[16]

Hugh's aggression towards the young Marshal was a direct consequence of King John's counterbalancing of the earls of Ulster and Pembroke. Since 1210, the Marshals had been able to control the Irish Sea from its southern littoral. The younger William Marshal had only just inherited this powerful position in 1219, and may have resented any attempt to reinstate the counterpoise in the north. William Marshal was a powerful figure at court, and was allied to the English justiciar, Hubert de Burgh, from at least 1221.[17] What is more, in the wake of the Welsh conflict, Henry III agreed to the marriage between his sister and William Marshal. In 1222, as part of the negotiating process, the Marshal had threatened alternative marriage alliances with the houses of Brabant and Scotland. The latter alliance could have been all the more dangerous, as the king's own brief on the matter states, saying: 'no small danger might arise, for by how much nearer Scotland is to Ireland and the Marshal lands, so much the more dangerous would the marriage be to the king'.[18] Ulster lay within that axis, and the Crown's refusal to restore the earldom of Ulster along with the rest of Hugh's lands in 1222 needs to be seen within this context. With Earl Ranulf of Chester arguing for Hugh de Lacy, and Earl William Marshal against, the royal policy regarding Ulster was infected with factional rivalries. In this light, the wars of 1223 to 1224 were fought over control of the Irish Sea province, and it should come as no surprise that the struggle spanned the region.

The war in Wales caused the Crown to rethink its position. In the summer of 1223, a royal letter explained that after a conference of the king's council held in London the council had offered to commit Hugh's land and castles to Walter de Lacy and the earls of Chester, Salisbury and Gloucester for five years from the previous Easter (23 April 1223), to be restored into the king's hands at the end of that term, provided the custodians agreed to be compelled by their lands and ecclesiastical jurisdiction to make this restoration. However, the named magnates refused to undertake such an obligation and the matter remained unresolved.[19] By offering to place Hugh's lands in commission, the Minority government sought to deny Hugh seisin, while making sure that the magnates kept him out until the king reached his majority. Even if the four potential custodians considered the offer, a letter sent by the pope on 13 April, ten days before the custodial period was to begin, would have given them pause for thought. Pope Honorius III commanded the council and barons of England to give King Henry free and unfettered disposal of his kingdom, including the resignation to him of all Crown lands and castles held in wardship. In a separate letter sent to the vice-chancellor, the pope ordered him to use the great seal only at the king's command.[20] Thus, at about the time of the council's proposed compromise regarding Ulster, the pope attempted to give the king the full powers of legal age with respect to the government of his realm in general, including the custody of royal castles and demesne, and the issue of royal letters under the great seal.[21] Unsurprisingly, the four chose not to step between Hugh de Lacy, a veteran soldier with a history of recalcitrance, and a royal government on the brink of a systematic resumption of authority.

With neither side willing to back down over the issue of Ulster, war seemed inevitable. After informing the Irish justiciar, Archbishop Henry, of the failed diplomacy on 4 June 1223, the royal government wrote that it had heard that Hugh planned to invade Ireland, and ordered the justiciar to fortify the king's castles against Hugh's attack. More particularly, the household knight, William de Serland and his companions were given custody of Hugh's old stronghold of Carrickfergus, with Archbishop Henry ordered to provide them with men and victuals as they saw fit. The government also sent papal letters excommunicating Hugh and his accomplices in the event of an invasion, to be used at the proper time.[22] The council even went so far as to establish a new system of provincial government in Ireland, with a number of local seneschals placed under the Irish justiciar's authority.[23] John Marshal (Earl William's cousin) was given custody of Cork, Decies (Co. Waterford) and Desmond, with their castles; Richard de Burgh was made seneschal of Munster (i.e. colonial Thomond, including the former honor of Limerick) and constable of Limerick castle, and William de Serland was promoted as seneschal of Ulster. On the same day as Serland's appointment, 18 July 1223, Thomas of Galloway, earl of Atholl and one of King John's grantees in Ulster, was ordered to fortify his Castle of Antrim against Hugh's invasion, or to forfeit his custody to the Irish justiciar.[24]

Walter de Lacy's refusal to act as a custodian of Hugh's lands did not sit well with Hubert de Burgh and his fellow royal councillors, who were determined that Walter should play a leading role in the dispute's resolution. Their next step was to choose Walter's castle of Ludlow as the site of a meeting between Llywelyn, William Marshal and the council to discuss a settlement to the ongoing war in Wales.[25] The conference, which ran from 8 to 10 July, was a failure, with the result that the government hardened its stance against Llywelyn and his allies, and threw its support behind the Marshal.[26] From this point, it was determined that Walter should take a more active role in the suppression of his brother's revolt. On 11 July, Walter, as sheriff of Herefordshire, was ordered to prevent supplies from Herefordshire reaching Llywelyn or his adherents.[27] Three days later, he was ordered to fortify Hereford Castle.[28] He was then in the army, led by William Marshal and the earl of Salisbury, that marched south to Pembroke.[29] According to the Welsh *Brut y Tywysogyon*, William Marshal travelled by way of Ewyas Harold,[30] which took his army through the heart of Walter's power base in Herefordshire. The march would have been a clear demonstration to Walter's followers of their lord's adherence to the Crown. On its way to Pembroke, the royal army was caught by Llywelyn's son, Gruffudd, in a pass in the Welsh hills, and only narrowly escaped destruction. The remaining force pressed on to the Marshal's lands and fortified the districts about Caermarthen and Gower.[31] Walter fought for the Marshal against his brother and Llywelyn in Wales that summer, while Ulster was braced for invasion.[32] The full details of the Welsh war need not be rehearsed here. Suffice to record that, after his attention returned to the conflict, Hubert de Burgh hitched his wagon to the Marshal's and played a leading role in the Crown's victory. A settlement with Llywelyn was finally reached on 8 October at Montgomery, and, as one modern authority puts it, 'Hubert could bask in Pembroke's glory'.[33]

The failure of diplomacy: Ireland and England, 1223-4

After Llywelyn came to terms, events gathered pace. Hugh de Lacy took no part in the peace at Montgomery, and, having lost an ally in his struggle against William Marshal, he turned to the recapture of his earldom. The Marshal's heavy recruitment in Ireland for the Welsh war provided Hugh with his opportunity, and the Dunstable annalist records that Hugh sailed for Ireland after the Welsh war.[34] On 16 October 1223, John Marshal was granted the bailiwick (*baillium*) of Ulster, placing William's cousin between Hugh and the former earldom.[35] However, when Hugh arrived in Ireland, he did not immediately march north to wrest Ulster from John Marshal. Instead, he took the time to secure the lordship of Meath for himself.[36] It is not immediately clear whom Hugh was proceeding against in Meath. As in 1210, though the Lacy brothers were ostensibly divided by conflict, what evidence exists suggests that there was no real rift between Walter and Hugh. In both instances, Walter worked to reconcile Hugh to the Crown. What is more, the major tenants of Meath seem to have remained loyal to the king during both conflicts. Perhaps Hugh de Lacy's actions in Meath were directed against its resident knightly community, rather than his brother's demesne. In conjunction with his half-brother William de Lacy, Hugh ravaged the country, even threatening Dublin itself and forcing the Irish justiciar to negotiate a truce to last until the summer of 1224.[37]

With Meath in revolt under his two brothers, it is little wonder that Walter de Lacy found his power curtailed in England. Walter's removal as sheriff of Herefordshire and custodian of Hereford castle, while perhaps owing more to the Crown's (i.e. Hubert de Burgh's) general desire to resume royal lands and castles than is usually admitted, was a direct result of his brothers' war. So too, it seems, was the growing bond between Hubert de Burgh and William Marshal. After their victory in Wales, the annals of Dunstable report that a great council in London decreed that, in accordance with the pope's letters of April 1223, King Henry III should have legal age regarding the free disposition of his castles, lands and wardships, stopping just short of the right of permanent alienation.[38] On 7 November, the benefits of this for Hubert and his party were made plain. Hubert rewarded the Marshal for his services by granting him custody of Cardigan and Carmarthen castles, the royal castles that William had wrested from their royal custodian, Llywelyn, that spring.[39] At about the same time, he made his move against Walter de Lacy. According to the *Querimonia* of Falkes de Bréauté, in which Falkes justified his rebellion the following year (mentioned below), the English justiciar and his accomplices are said to have summoned Walter de Lacy and Ralph Musard (the sheriff of Gloucester) to court, where they forced them to assign their royal castles to the justiciar.[40]

Falkes characterised the sheriffs' removal as an instance of Hubert's 'tyranny', and others have followed suit. For instance, Kate Norgate states that both Lacy and Musard were of 'high standing and approved fidelity to the King', while Powicke calls them 'two English barons of unimpeachable respectability'.[41] This is going too far. Walter de Lacy had a chequered history of sequestration and exile, and had been implicated in a plot to overthrow King John. Walter may have remained nominally loyal since his return from exile in 1213, but he still had abused his power as sheriff of Herefordshire, ignored royal mandates (including those ordering the delivery of seisin of the Three Castles to Hubert de Burgh), and, if Michael the Welshman can be believed, had sent an armed force against a royal official to prevent him from carrying out Hubert's orders.[42] Hubert de Burgh presided at the Exchequer, 'the operations room where the battle for control of the king's manors and sheriffdoms was fought out',[43] and would have been well aware of the meagre sums that Walter's undersheriffs routinely returned there. Walter may have been an aristocrat of high standing, but he was not one of approved fidelity or unimpeachable respectability. More recently, historians have come to view Walter's removal in the context of his brother's rebellion, which is certainly where it belongs.[44] Interestingly, the other man deprived of office, Ralph Musard, was a former retainer of the elder William Marshal, and had obtained Gloucester as a Marshal agent. While Walter's resignation was effected immediately, Musard's was only nominal. He retained possession of Gloucester castle until November 1225, well after the resolution of the conflict.[45]

When Earls Ranulf of Chester, Gilbert of Gloucester and William of Aumale resolved to appeal to the king in person against Walter's forced resignation, Hubert took the king to Musard's castle of Gloucester and forbade the earls to approach.[46] On his way to Gloucester, on 16 November, Hubert retained Walter in the king's service.[47] The Marshal's hand was clearly visible in the English justiciar's actions during his flight from London, with the Marshal's comrade, William earl of Salisbury, in Hubert's company. The choice of Gloucester may even have been due to its proximity to the Marshal's lordship of Netherwent, including its castle of Chepstow.[48] Walter may have been in actual attendance on the king when he was retained, and would have been bundled along to Gloucester under Hubert's surveillance.[49] On the way, on 15 November, Walter was ordered to deliver the castle of Hereford and shrievalty of Herefordshire to his replacement, the king's senior steward, Ralph fitz Nicholas.[50] Ralph's 100 mark allowance largely consumed the profits of the shire until his removal in 1229,[51] which shows that Walter's removal was not aimed at clawing back the royal revenue for the king. In this light, Walter's retention in the king's service the following day appears all the more tactical.

Walter's retention looks sinister when Irish matters are taken into consideration. During the course of two later thirteenth-century inquests into the liberties of the lordship of Meath, it emerged that Walter de Lacy had inherited from his father all of the liberties which the king ought to have enjoyed in Meath, excepting ecclesiastical investiture. These he held until:[52]

> Richard fitz Ranulf appealed in Walter's court of Trim against Robert Ua Máel Ruanaid (*Omalroni*) for the death of his brother. A day was named for the duel, but Walter's wife, in the absence of her lord at Robert's procurement, commanded her seneschal to respite the duel. Richard the appellor, having collected evidence, came to Dublin on the same day, and complained to Henry Archbishop of Dublin, then justiciar, of the injustice done to him in that court. The justiciar, by counsel of Robert Huscarl, then justice of the Common Pleas, Dublin, and of others, took into the king's hand all Walter's liberty, save ... pleas belonging to the baronial court, neither Walter himself nor any person on his behalf having been summoned to hear judgment; and they made Walter sheriff and keeper of pleas of the crown in his own lands, to answer therefore to the king in his court at Dublin.[53]

This action is not dated, but Robert Huscarl, a judge of the English bench, had been sent to Ireland to aid the justiciar only in December 1222.[54] Since Archbishop Henry was replaced as justiciar in May 1224,[55] this action must have been taken during Hugh de Lacy's wars. If Archbishop Henry acted thus during the Welsh war of 1223, then it may have provoked Hugh de Lacy's war against him from Meath that winter. Regardless, the Irish justiciar's conduct in Meath suggests that the issues behind Hugh de Lacy's Irish war were many and complex.

Returning to England, Walter's absence at court meant that he was not among the malcontents, who, seemingly as his allies, led a demonstration to the Tower of London.[56] It is important to note that the degree of Walter's involvement in the ensuing factional feud in England is unclear. Except for the earl of Chester, there is little evidence that any of the barons who aligned themselves against Hubert de Burgh and William Marshal were Walter's allies. Chester's partisans may have used Walter's cause as an excuse, but this was mere opportunism. They had their own reasons for opposing Hubert's circle. The progress of their famous dispute, in which no contemporary authority claims Walter played an active part, need not occupy much space here.[57] The true source of Walter's predicament now lay in Ireland, where Hugh de Lacy's truce with Archbishop Henry did not stay Hugh's hand in Ulster.

The war in Ulster: 1224

Having secured Walter's lordship of Meath and humbled the Irish justiciar, Hugh de Lacy advanced against the men King John had placed in Ulster. Allied with the king of Tír Eógain, Áed Méith Ua Néill (d. 1230), he captured and destroyed Thomas, earl of Atholl's castle of Coleraine.[58] He also seized the Duncan, earl of Carrick's lands in Ulster.[59] These acts against the Gallowegians display the danger of viewing this conflict from a single perspective. Hugh de Lacy was at war with the Marshals, but he also was at war with others who had profited from his downfall. Nor was Hugh's the only war in the region. The Manx chronicle and Icelandic sagas record under 1223 that King Rǫgnvaldr's brother, Óláfr Guðrøðarson (Amlaíb Dub), caught Rǫgnvaldr's son and heir, Guðrøðr after a skirmish between their two forces on the Isle of Skye, blinding and castrating him (thereby disqualifying him from the kingship). Óláfr then used the occasion of Hugh's war in Ulster to invade Man in 1224, forcing a partition of the kingdom.[60] King Rǫgnvaldr was a tenant-in-chief of the English Crown, routinely under the protection of the Irish justiciar. Just four years earlier, in 1220, Rǫgnvaldr had appealed to the Minority government for protection against the king of Norway, who, he claimed, was threatening an invasion of Man due to Rǫgnvaldr's homage to Henry III. Consequently, the Irish justiciar was ordered to provide that protection.[61] It is unlikely to be a coincidence that Óláfr attacked Rǫgnvaldr at the precise time that the Gallowegians were under attack in Ulster, and the Irish justiciar was preoccupied with the war in Ireland.

It is against this backdrop that a letter sent to King Henry III by his sister Joan, wife of King Alexander II of Scotland, should be set. In it, she informed King Henry of a rumoured invasion of Ireland in support of Hugh de Lacy by King Hákon IV of Norway.[62] However, this rumour makes little sense in the context of Anglo-Norwegian relations. England and Norway had been on good terms since the accession of King Hákon Hákonsson in 1217, the Manx protection order of 1220 notwithstanding, with a free trade agreement between the kingdoms proving mutually beneficial.[63] Amidst the gathering clouds of war in Ireland, the Minority government had, in August 1223, taken into protection the men and merchants of its 'beloved and special friend', the king of Norway.[64] Then, in the winter of 1223-4, while Hugh de Lacy pursued his war in Ireland, King Hákon sent a letter to the English king informing him of his desire that the alliance between their two kingdoms should continue.[65] Joan's letter of warning was sent shortly thereafter, about March 1224, but just three months later at least seventeen Norwegian ships were exempted from a general royal arrest order aimed at securing England against its enemies.[66] Hákon had very little to gain, and much to lose, by actively supporting the rebellious Hugh de Lacy against the English Crown. Norwegian intervention in the region makes much more sense viewed in the context of the dynastic dispute over Man and the Isles just mentioned, where the Norwegian king still held a hegemonic claim. Indeed, *Hákon's Saga* claims that at about the same time Jon, jarl (earl) of Orkney and Caithness, and many other men from the isles, were at King Hákon's court in Norway, seeking his aid.[67] Relations between Scotland and Norway were at their nadir, and a Scottish rumour could easily have elided the object of King Hákon IV's expedition with Hugh de Lacy's war in Ulster. As much would have been apparent to King Hákon, explaining his own letter to Henry III and ensuring his absence from the region for the duration of the war.

Returning to the Irish mainland, in about February 1224, Cathal Crobderg Ua Conchobair wrote to the king, informing him of Hugh de Lacy's depredations in Ireland, and complaining of his own mistreatment by certain of the king's barons.[68] This may have been a reference to the seneschal of Munster, Richard de Burgh, who had been thwarted in 1220 in his bid to have his grant of Connacht activated, and whose name Cathal may have been reluctant to invoke in a letter to the king. Hubert de Burgh seems to have thought better of placing his nephew in Connacht just yet, however, for he wrote glowingly of Cathal to the king about this time, asking that the king receive Cathal's messengers.[69] On 9 February 1224, King Henry III proposed to induce Richard to stay out of Connacht by granting him 250 marks a year, if Cathal would augment his service by 200 marks.[70] Whether or not this was taken up, on 5 March, the Crown granted Cathal protection for as long as he remained faithful.[71] This proviso may indicate the government's motive for protecting Cathal's interests. With Meath and Ulster engulfed in war, Connacht had to be kept in line. The conquest of Connacht would soon come to dominate the politics of Ireland in the aftermath of Hugh de Lacy's war,[72] but, had Richard de Burgh been allowed to press his claim before Hugh was brought to heel, the entire island could have descended into warfare. The Crown (under the influence of Hubert de Burgh) sought to do no more than what necessity required to achieve stability in Connacht. It is in this context that the government's grant of William de Lacy's territory in Bréifne to Cathal's son Áed (mentioned above) must be viewed.[73] When Cathal (who was at this point seventy-two)[74] went one step further by asking that his son be granted his own charter for the kingdom of Connacht to secure his succession, the government declined to act.[75] King and council may have been keen to secure an ally in the war against Hugh de Lacy, but it had other plans for Connacht.

With the fidelity of Cathal Crobderg secured, the king and his councillors turned their attention to defeating Hugh de Lacy. The government's view of Walter de Lacy's role in the disturbances in Ireland is evident in an agreement touching Walter's service and the crimes committed by his men in Meath, which was drawn up in March 1224. In it, Walter surrendered his castles of Ludlow and Trim for two years, and undertook to go to Ireland and combat his rebellious vassals, whose possessions the king would hold for a year and a day when seized. As a lord, Walter was responsible for the actions of his tenants, yet in past years he would also have been entitled to custody of their sequestrated lands. However, the council had doubts about Walter's own fidelity, and claimed these profits of lordship for the Crown. The king went even further, adding a rather menacing clause that stated that, once the war was concluded, the king's court would decide what should be done to Walter. Whatever Walter's complicity with his brother's rebellion, by March 1224, royal lordship had quite clearly trumped seigniorial lordship in Meath.

There is no question as to who dictated the terms of the Crown's agreement with Walter, for the only secular witnesses were Hubert de Burgh, William Marshal and the earl of Salisbury (whose name is written twice in the roll).[76] Hubert and his associates seem to have acted with a heavy hand, but Walter's terms may have been deserved. As seen in the Irish crisis of 1207, acting through a proxy was a well-known means of achieving one's aims while retaining an air of respectability, and there is no evidence to suggest that this was not the case from 1223 to 1224. In the wider conflict, Falkes de Bréauté disavowed any foreknowledge of his brother William's actions when the latter seized the royal justice Henry of Braybrook that June. As with Walter, Falkes professed his innocence, while being unable to help bring his brother to justice. David Carpenter asserts that the eight-week-long siege of Bedford castle is 'inexplicable' if Falkes had not told his brother William to surrender neither castle nor Braybrook.[77] As will be seen, Walter de Lacy's castle of Trim, besieged at the exact same time, held out for five weeks with Walter in the army before it.[78] Walter may have steered a safer course than Falkes (he had his experience from 1210 from which to draw), but it would be naive to suppose him a purely innocent victim of circumstance.[79]

That safer course involved Walter ostensibly joining Hubert de Burgh and William Marshal in their fight against his own family. He had campaigned under William Marshal and the earl of Salisbury in Wales in 1223, and, after agreeing to the terms described above, Walter left for Ireland.[80] Before he left, on 29 March, he was granted custody of the castles of Rathwire (Co. Westmeath) and Nobber (Co. Meath), formerly held by Robert and Hugh de Lacy respectively.[81] His tenant and familiar, Richard de Tuit, was granted custody of the strategic royal castle on the Shannon at Clonmacnoise, with a further £20 yearly to sustain him.[82] Although Walter had to surrender his castle of Trim, he was granted its hall, houses and chambers as a lodging place for himself and his retinue while on royal service.[83]

On the face of it, Walter proved his loyalty to the Crown by performing the task assigned him. In the approximately two-and-a-half months between Walter's landing and the arrival of William Marshal in mid-June, the castles of *Rathune* ('Ráth Áed', Rahugh, Co. Westmeath?), Rathfeigh (Co. Meath) and Ratoath (Co. Meath), a castle of Walter Sancmille, and a castle of William fitz John were all taken for the king.[84] That said, Walter's commission should not have been very difficult. He was meant only to punish those disturbers of the peace who held lands in his lordship of Meath, and, as in 1210, Walter's greatest tenants had remained loyal to the king. Only a few of his brother's adherents had to be disciplined. This makes the case of Trim Castle all the more suspicious. William Marshal later reported that, when he had arrived in Ireland, he had found Trim being held against the king by a group of lesser knights, whom he shut up inside and besieged with the help of Walter de Lacy.[85] Trim was the *caput* of the lordship of Meath, and its masonry castle a showpiece of Lacy power in the region (see Figure 7.1).[86] That Walter would have suffered it to be held against him for two-and-a-half months before the Marshal's arrival is incredible. Trim was supposed to have been a staging post for his expedition, his first stop once in Ireland. Even if his surrender of the castle to the Crown precluded him from garrisoning it once taken, his commission included bringing those knights within to justice. How did a small band of knights hold Trim unopposed while the lord of Meath rode the length and breadth of his lordship capturing minor motte-and-bailey castles? Where

Figure 7.1   Trim Castle

were Walter's tenants? Where were all of the barons and citizens of Ireland about whose fidelity to, and willingness to fight for, the Crown William Marshal was to write so glowingly in the coming months?[87] Walter could have done a great deal more to further the king's cause in Ireland had he chosen so to do. This again suggests that Walter was complicit to a degree in Hugh's war, a suspicion which the government seems to have shared.

On 2 May, William Marshal had been appointed justiciar of Ireland.[88] At about the time of his arrival in Ireland on 19 June, the colonial barons held a conference with Áed Ua Conchobair, who, after the death of his father Cathal Crobderg on 25 May 1224, now called himself king of Connacht. The barons then travelled to the Marshal's siege of Trim, where they rendered their service.[89] The conference with Áed was held in Meath, and may have been a result of his burning of the castle of Lisardowlan (Co. Longford) about this time. The annals report that Áed and his forces 'killed every one whom they found in it, both Foreigners and Irish (*Gaedil*)'.[90] Because Lisardowlan is situated along the borders of Bréifne, Áed's attack may have been prompted by the king's grant to him of William de Lacy's lands in Bréifne on 14 June.[91] Unfortunately for Áed, Lisardowlan did not belong to the outlawed William de Lacy, but rather to his brother Walter,[92] who was under the king's protection. Consequently, Áed was in breach of the king's peace, and remained so until reconciled through the efforts of his first cousin, who, ironically, was William de Lacy's mother.[93]

While William Marshal conducted the siege at Trim, he sent two forces after the rebellious Lacy brothers, William and Hugh. One, a detachment of horse, overtook William de Lacy and forced him to flee into an unidentified moor, where he used his local connections to take shelter with the native Irish. The other, under the Marshal's cousin William le Gros, found Hugh de Lacy besieging the castle of Carrickfergus, which still held out for the king. William was able to gain entry to the castle, forcing Hugh to withdraw.[94] Abandoning the siege at Carrickfergus, Hugh de Lacy and Áed Ua Néill fortified the Fews of Armagh, one of the main passages into Ulster, challenging the justiciar to attack. William Marshal and his allies, who included Donnchad Cairbrech Ua Briain, Diarmait Mac Carthaig, and the now reconciled Áed Ua Conchobair went as far as Nicholas de Verdun's town of Dundalk,[95] but refused to proceed against Hugh. The passes could not be forced without much difficulty, and while the army that he led might have been impressive, coming from four of the five provinces of Ireland, the Marshal may have doubted its mettle in a pitched battle. What is more, Alan of Galloway and his kin, whom the Crown expected to launch an amphibious assault upon Hugh's army from the north-east, never came. Alan later explained that he had gone from isle to isle collecting a force to cross to Ireland, but that, on the very day that he was at last prepared to embark, he learned that peace had been agreed between Hugh and the Marshal.[96] The logistical problems facing Alan were real enough. The north-western sea-lords did not maintain standing fleets that could be deployed at short notice, but instead had to collect men and ships in the manner described.[97] What is more, the Manx succession dispute would have made mobilising another fleet in the region particularly difficult. With no help from the sea, William Marshal must have recognised the impasse for what it was. Consequently, the door was left open for a peaceful resolution negotiated by (and as it turned out at the expense of) Walter de Lacy.[98]

Negotiating peace: 1225-6

The war of 1223 to 1224 should not be seen as a defeat for Hugh de Lacy. Although he surrendered and was sent to the king, Hugh lost nothing.[99] Negotiations over the terms of his surrender took some time to complete, and on 10 May 1225 it was ordered, at the instance of William Marshal, that Hugh be given the sum of 200 marks a year to sustain him until their discussions resulted in his better provision.[100] William Marshal was still justiciar of Ireland, and he recognised the danger of leaving Hugh de Lacy destitute while negotiations dragged. Connacht had lately boiled over, with Hugh's ally, Áed Ua Néill, leading a successful coup and installing his preferred candidate, Toirdelbach, William de Lacy's uncle and son of the former high-king Ruaidrí Ua Conchobair, in place of Áed Ua Conchobair. At least two distinct colonial forces had involved themselves in the dynastic struggle, and, to make matters worse, Richard de Burgh was once again eyeing Connacht.[101] At some point before 21 April 1225, Richard had married Walter de Lacy's daughter, Egidia.[102] Egidia's marriage sealed a peace between the families of Lacy and Burgh, giving the Lacys a stronger voice at court and providing the Burghs with local support in Herefordshire, the Welsh march and Ireland. It also potentially reactivated Hugh de Lacy's claim to the ten cantreds in Connacht that Richard's father had granted him. Such an alliance was dangerous for William Marshal's position in Ireland. The Marshal had been one of Áed Ua Conchobair's strongest supporters at court, and was to be one of those most determined to ensure that Richard de Burgh's grant of Connacht went unrealised.[103] Consequently, seven days after Hugh received his maintenance grant, Richard was likewise allowed 250 marks per year to sustain him.[104] As Irish justiciar, William knew that these grants were less expensive than the territorial gold rush that the conquest of Connacht promised to become.

Three days after Hugh was granted his allowance, the king's court finally decided what should be done to Walter de Lacy. He was fined 3,000 marks for having the lands of his knights and free tenants in Ireland who had gone against the Crown in his brother's war. For an additional fine, Walter was allowed seisin of his castles of Trim, Kilmore (taken as part of the Crown's operations in Bréifne) and Ludlow, but, as before, Hugh's sub-tenancies of Ratoath and Nobber, and Walter's strategic castle of Drogheda, were retained for the Crown.[105] These were harsh terms for what amounted to a recognition of Walter's rights of lordship over Meath. Only a decade earlier Walter had agreed to a 4,000 mark fine for seisin of the entire lordship.[106] In 1225, Walter was allowed to keep the fines for seisin that his rebellious tenants made for their lands, which led Orpen to conclude that 'Walter's fine may be in part regarded as a convenient way of collecting these fines for the king'.[107] However, the Crown retained three of the more lucrative fines for itself (although this came to only 330 marks), and, given the limited extent of open rebellion in Meath, Walter's taking may have been relatively paltry.[108] Instead, the 3,000 mark fine was clearly punitive, reflecting the government's suspicions of Walter's complicity in his brother's rebellion.

As negotiations with Hugh de Lacy continued to drag, an interim measure was agreed. On 12 May 1226, the king notified William Marshal that Walter had been granted custody of the lands and castles of the earldom of Ulster, in addition to those which Hugh held within Walter's fee and through his marriage to Lescelina de Verdun. These territories, which amounted to all of Hugh's Irish lands, were to be returned to the king after three years, unless Hugh had negotiated their restoration in the meantime.[109] This was in essence a modified form of that settlement mooted by the government in the spring of 1223, which failed owing to lack of support from the proposed custodians. Now that a war had been fought, Walter was willing (or forced) to take the risk. Hugh's ultimate restoration was not achieved until Henry III assumed his full majority in 1227. On 20 April 1227, King Henry ordered that Hugh be given seisin of all his lands and castles in Walter's custody, and that his knights be attentive to him.[110] Thus, almost four years after Hugh de Lacy began the war to recover his earldom, Ulster was restored to him. This seems not to have been a grant in perpetuity, for upon Hugh's death Ulster reverted to the Crown despite the survival of at least one heiress.[111] However, it was much more than might have been expected. It is one of history's ironies that Walter de Lacy was fined 3,000 marks for the revolt of several of his minor tenants, while Hugh de Lacy, the man who actually led their revolt, walked away with a maintenance grant and was ultimately gifted the earldom of Ulster for no recorded fine.

Gilbert de Lacy: 1226-30

Walter was able to assume responsibility for his brother's Irish lands in 1226, because his family, including his son and heir, Gilbert, was able to assume some of the responsibilities of lordship. The terms of Walter's charter for the custody of Hugh's lands seem to associate Gilbert as security in the event of Walter's death, stating that both bound themselves by oath to the observance of the conditions, and that the sureties listed were to ensure that Walter and his heir (whether Gilbert or otherwise) would surrender the castles and lands.[112] Walter's half-brother, William de Lacy, was given actual custody of Ulster under Walter,[113] but the fact that Gilbert issued a separate charter for Hugh's lands suggests that he was playing an active role in the family administration.[114] Later that year, the family's fortunes were set to increase with the activation of Richard de Burgh's grant of Connacht. Throughout 1225, the recognised king of Connacht, Áed Ua Conchobair, was able to hold on to his kingship only thanks to the diplomatic and military aid of William Marshal. It was abundantly clear, however, that Áed's position was untenable without that support. Hubert de Burgh had restrained his nephew Richard's ambitions for quite some time, but, through his position as seneschal of Munster and marriage alliance with the Lacys, Richard had a firm foundation from which to launch his long-awaited conquest of Connacht.

The first step was taken on 22 June 1226, when William Marshal was replaced as justiciar by Geoffrey de Marisco.[115] One week later, Geoffrey was ordered to summon Áed to appear before him at the king's court in Ireland and surrender the entire land of Connacht. Connacht had been granted to Áed's father Cathal Crobderg only during pleasure, which gave the Crown the legal authority it needed to seize it. The king's court was to decide whether Áed's forfeiture was warranted, thus honouring the stipulation in Cathal Crobderg's 1215 charter that he should not be disseised without judgement of the king's court.[116] Áed's attacks on Walter de Lacy's castles in Bréifne in 1221, 1223 and 1224, though pardoned by the then Irish justiciars, Archbishop Henry and William Marshal, would have provided all of the justification that the king's court needed. As with John de Courcy in Ulster, the outcome was a foregone conclusion, and the royal government issued several mandates shortly thereafter concerning the transferal of Connacht to Richard de Burgh. One ordered the Irish justiciar to deliver seisin of Connacht to Richard de Burgh as soon as the court had declared Connacht forfeit, and detailed the Crown's retention of five cantreds near Athlone.[117] Another halted Richard's 250 mark compensatory rent, while yet another ordered that the feudal host of Ireland be called out for forty days to help Richard fortify Connacht.[118]

Despite the royal position, the outgoing Irish justiciar, William Marshal, was determined to see Áed retain his kingship. He was on his way to Ireland, when, on 10 July 1226, the king expressed his displeasure at his departure. William cancelled his voyage, but this did not stay his hand in Ireland.[119] Some time later, Geoffrey de Marisco wrote to the king about the events that followed.[120] He stated that, upon reaching Waterford, he prepared to travel to Dublin to communicate several of the king's mandates to the barons of Ireland. However, he learned that William Marshal, by the agency of Theobald Walter, was about to oppose his passage with all the force of Leinster. Geoffrey nevertheless made his way through to Dublin, where he held a council and received the oaths of fealty from all present, save several of the Marshal's tenants. Geoffrey claimed that all of the royal castles of Ireland were held against the king (except Limerick, held by Richard de Burgh), and that Theobald Walter even went so far as to fortify Dublin castle against the king.

That Connacht was at the heart of the dispute is suggested both by Geoffrey's special praise for the assistance given him by Richard de Burgh and by his claim that William Marshal's seneschal of Leinster, William le Gros, had instructed Áed Ua Conchobair to ignore the king's mandates and was banding the Irish together against the king. Geoffrey further reports that Walter de Lacy had been appointed the task of conducting Áed from Athlone to Dublin (where the council would have decided whether to strip him of Connacht in keeping with the June mandates), but the Irish king did not come. However, the Irish annals offer an alternate scenario. They claim that Áed went to Dublin, but, facing deceit and treachery at the court, was whisked away in the nick of time by William Marshal, 'his personal friend', and his followers.[121] This seems unlikely given Geoffrey's account, which one would expect to have mentioned the Marshal or his men acting against the king's interests in this way. However, although it is therefore more likely that William le Gros informed Áed of the government's duplicitous plans, and that this convinced Áed to refuse to meet Walter de Lacy at Athlone,[122] the annals should not be written off lightly.

The annals of Clonmacnoise preserve what appears to be an independent account of Áed's trip to Dublin, which states that:

Hugh [Áed] o'Connor king of Connaught went to the English court of Dublin by the compulsary means of the English, they tooke his sonn and daughter as hostages with the hostages of all the principall men of Conaught, upon examining of some criminall causes there objected to the said Hugh [Áed], he was found guiltie in their censure and being to be aprehended for the same, a speciall friend of his then within, and of great favour and power with the king of England, did assist Hugh [Áed], and by the help of his sword, and strength of his hand, he conuayed Hugh [Áed] away from them, and soe departed to Conaught in safety.[123]

Following the failure of the Dublin conference, the justiciar's son, William de Marisco, met Áed at a place just west of Athlone. When William arrived, Áed, who 'remembered the deception and treachery practised against him in Dublin', seized William and two of his men. The Connachtmen then slew the constable of Athlone, plundered the market and burned the town. The Irish annals declare that 'this was a felicitous act for all the Connachtmen, for they obtained their sons and daughters, and the hostages of Connacht, and peace for the Connachtmen afterwards'.[124] This short-sighted appraisal betrays a naivety among some of the native Irish about the current of Irish politics, but, by mentioning the hostages of Connacht, may also lend credence to the testimony of the Clonmacnoise annalist regarding events in Dublin.

Throughout his letter, Geoffrey stressed that the blame for the Irish disturbances should lie with Theobald Walter and his associates in Leinster, not William Marshal. Since Marshal was the king's close friend and was betrothed to his sister, this is hardly surprising. Geoffrey wrote that he did not believe that William was responsible for the Irish conspiracy (despite it being organised by William's cousin and seneschal), or the retention and fortification of royal castles against the Crown (even though they were in the hands of the Marshal's deputies). Geoffrey even ascribed Walter de Lacy's fidelity (and that of his knights) to the confederacy between Walter's son Gilbert and the Marshal.[125] Whatever the Marshal's role in the struggle over Connacht, he finally surrendered Cardigan and Carmarthen to the Crown (probably in return for Caerleon) and had returned to Ireland by 27 August 1226, after which Áed's colonial support collapsed.[126]

If Áed had managed to escape forfeiture at Dublin, his actions at Athlone sealed his fate. On 21 May 1227, one month after Hugh de Lacy had been restored to the earldom of Ulster, Richard de Burgh was granted the entire province of Connacht.[127] The grant was permanent, made possible by King Henry III's coming of age that January. The Lacys were to play a major part in the conquest of Connacht, with an army from Meath being one of the several to invade that year, but a suggestion as to the full measure of their involvement was revealed only in 1228. That year, Áed Ua Conchobair treated for peace. While he was in the justiciar's house, however, 'he was treacherously killed by an Englishman, for which cause the [justiciar] the next day hanged the Englishman'.[128] The annals of Connacht contend that 'this deed of treachery was done on this righteous, excellent prince at the instigation of Hugh de Lacy's sons and of William [de Marisco] son of the justiciar'.[129] Whatever the veracity of the conspiracy theory, the annals' statement shows that, in Connacht at least, the Lacys were blamed for the assassination. With his main barrier to the province removed, Richard de Burgh replaced Geoffrey de Marisco as justiciar on 13 February 1228.[130] His triumph seemed complete. As Brendan Smith writes, 'the restoration of de Lacy to his lands and title in 1227 set the seal on a new chapter in Anglo-Irish relations, and for the next fifteen to twenty years the fortunes of the English in Ireland rested with a small group of magnates of whom the most important were Maurice FitzGerald, Walter de Ridelisford, Hugh de Lacy, Walter de Lacy and Richard de Burgh'.[131] Once again, Ireland was to be controlled by a handful of powerful magnates.

The Lacys were riding high on royal favour during this period, and they showed themselves willing to serve in Henry III's royal armies. In September 1228, Gilbert de Lacy answered the king's call to arms and served in Hubert de Burgh's disastrous campaign in Wales.[132] The following year, on 26 October 1229, Walter, Hugh and William de Lacy were among those prepared to embark on Henry III's continental expedition.[133] Although the army's departure was delayed,[134] when it finally sailed the following year, Gilbert de Lacy had joined its ranks.[135] Gilbert quickly gained the favour of the king, being granted remission of all of the interest on his Jewish debt on 21 May 1230,[136] and being granted the king's portion of the treasure recently discovered at Bordeaux on 12 August 1230.[137] Meanwhile, Walter had returned to England, where, in mid-June 1230, he was among those appointed to hold the assize of arms in Herefordshire.[138] Prestigious though this commission may have been, the real prize was in Ireland, where he and his fellow magnates were in the ascendant. Consequently, Walter was given leave to travel on 26 August to Ireland, where he fought alongside his son-in-law Richard de Burgh in Connacht.[139] Gilbert's administration of much of the Lacy inheritance must have aided the ageing Walter in his Irish endeavours. That was all to change, however, for by that winter Gilbert was dead. His death, and the complex legal proceedings that surrounded it, were eventually to embroil Walter de Lacy in the last great conflict of his life: the rebellion of Richard Marshal.

Resumption of lordship in England: 1230-3

Gilbert de Lacy's death (leaving an infant son and two daughters) was a potentially disastrous event for Walter, for, in addition to his son and heir, he faced the prospect of losing a substantial chunk of the Lacy inheritance to the Crown. Gilbert had been increasingly associated with the lordship of the Lacy lands. Gilbert's involvement in two pleas of mort d'ancestor on 24 April and 6 September 1229, concerning territories in the Lacys' honorial *caput* of Weobley, suggest that he was then in possession of the Lacys' English lands.[140] Gilbert also made two grants from the Lacys' demesne in Shropshire. In the first, Gilbert granted a single knight's fee at the Lacy large demesne manor of Stanton Lacy (Shropshire) to Stephen d'Évreux 'so that he will be in my m*esnie*/household'.[141] Gilbert also obtained custody of Stephen's heir when Stephen died in 1228.[142] In the second grant, Gilbert provided for his illegitimate son, Robert de Lacy, born to Imena, daughter of Stephen of Oakley (*Acley*). Gilbert granted Robert a quarter knight's fee at Downton Hall (Shropshire), a mill on the stream of *Morebroc* (Moorbrook?) in Gilbert's forest of Stanton Lacy and his forest of *Estontleg*' (?).[143]

In a genealogy of the Lacys preserved in the register of St Thomas's, Dublin, Gilbert is listed as having been lord of Meath.[144] What is more, at about the time of Gilbert's death, Walter issued a general confirmation of Llanthony Priory's possessions in Ireland, which suggests that Walter felt the need to reassert his lordship.[145] The Lacys' Welsh marcher lordship of Ewyas Lacy, which was also held by Gilbert, served as dower for his wife, Isabella, daughter of Earl Hugh II Bigod of Norfolk (d. 1225).[146] A wife's dower usually amounted to a third of her husband's possessions, meaning that Gilbert must have held a substantial fee. The vital question was whether Walter had actually demised these lands upon his son. If so, then they would have been taken into the king's hand during the wardship of Gilbert's son and heir, Walter, as lands of a tenant-in-chief. When the younger Walter came of age, the lands then would have gone to him, not his grandfather. It was therefore quite possible that the elder Walter de Lacy could have been left with very little. For one who had once held territories in England, Wales, Ireland and Normandy, this was a daunting possibility. Fortunately for Walter, his recent fidelity to the Crown, and (perhaps more importantly) alliance with Hubert de Burgh, were not forgotten at court. On Christmas Day 1230, the king declared that Walter de Lacy had not demised upon his son Gilbert the lands which the latter held in Herefordshire and Shropshire, but rather that Gilbert had held them of Walter *ad se sustentandum* (for his maintenance).[147] Walter retained his territories. He could not have received a better present.

Walter's resumption of lordship was at once hampered by the death of Hamo of Hereford that same year.[148] Walter had been instrumental in establishing the Jewish community in Hereford in the wake of the Magna Carta civil war, and had formed a close relationship with Hamo, its most prominent member. However, their symbiosis was based on a personal affinity, which did not pass to Hamo's heirs. Part of the blame here lies with Henry III, who made Hamo's son Ursell find 1,000 marks of the enormous 6,000 mark fine for seisin of his inheritance, with 300 marks demanded annually thereafter. Others, such as Walter's son-in-law Walter of Clifford,[149] were pardoned their debts to Ursell, making it even more difficult for Ursell to pay his fine. Neither was Ursell the only one of Walter's creditors so squeezed. Henry III placed more and more pressure on the Jews, and they were forced to pass this on to their clients. For the next two years, while his brothers fought to extend their influence in Ireland and the political storm surrounding the return to court of Peter des Roches and the fall of Hubert de Burgh engulfed England,[150] Walter fought attempts to call in his Jewish debts. Even the Welsh war of 1231 saw him play only a late, diplomatic role: he and several of his fellow marcher lords brokered a truce with Llywelyn to last until 30 November 1231.[151] Walter remained in royal favour throughout this period, with little besides litigation and financial arrangements to mark his actions.[152]

One business transaction is particularly revealing of Walter's financial difficulties. On 11 April 1231, Walter sold twelve sacks of Irish wool to one Richard fitz John, citizen of London. The conditions of their contract reveal Richard's lack of faith in the security of Meath and in Walter's financial wherewithal. Walter was to deliver the sacks to Richard's messenger at Drogheda by 24 June, and then convey them to Bristol at his own expense (though at Richard's risk). For security until the wool could be delivered to Drogheda, Walter was forced to surrender his manor of Britford (Wiltshire).[153] Short of credit, Walter was reduced to mortgaging his inheritance to secure this business deal.

The rebellion of Richard Marshal: 1233-4

While Walter was otherwise occupied, changes in royal policy gathered pace. The failure of the royal military operations of 1228 (Wales), 1230 (Brittany and Poitou) and 1231 (Wales) had reflected poorly on the English justiciar, Hubert de Burgh. The death of Hubert's long-time supporter, William Marshal, in July 1231 was a further blow. The story of Hubert's fall from power need not be repeated here, but, by the end of July 1232, he had been dismissed from court.[154] His dismissal was to have a profound effect on Lacy interests either side of the Irish Sea with the rise to prominence of Peter des Roches's close relation, Peter de Rivallis. King Henry III set out to re-establish royal authority wherever it had been in abeyance as a result of his minority or the actions of his former justiciar, and Peter des Rivallis was to be the instrument of royal control in several areas, including the Welsh march and Ireland. As his father, King John, had done with his own *familiaris*, William de Briouze, Henry III entrusted Rivallis with the custody of a good number of strategic territories in those regions, the difference being that, while Briouze had held them in fee, Peter de Rivallis was only their custodian. Nicholas Vincent and Brock Holden have described Peter's introduction into the Welsh march, where he was granted custody of the lands of John de Briouze in Gower, St Briavel's Castle, the Forest of Dean, the Three Castles, and all of Hubert de Burgh's marcher lands and castles, including the honors of Carmarthen, Ceredigion, and custody of Glamorgan with the castles of Cardiff and Newport. He was also granted the heir of John Marshal, whom he intended to marry to his niece.[155] While Holden is probably correct that patronage to this extent in any one region was always likely to offend those of the region who might have otherwise sought to profit from these custodies, it was not a foregone conclusion that rebellion would foment along the Welsh march as a result of Peter's rise.

The advancement of Peter de Rivallis in the march was reminiscent of King John's generous patronage of William de Briouze, who in 1202 might himself have been viewed as an outsider by his new tenants in Gower and Glamorgan.[156] Just like William, Peter was also promoted within the Burgh ambit in Ireland. As seen above, Richard de Burgh had benefited greatly from his uncle Hubert's rise to power in the preceding decade. According to King Henry III's later testimony, Hubert's dismissal in England led directly to Richard's disseisin in Ireland.[157] Richard was replaced as Irish justiciar and ordered to surrender the royal castles in his charge. When he resisted, his lands were forfeited and the conquest of Connacht halted.[158] On 28 July 1232, Peter de Rivallis was granted offices that gave him complete control of the finances of Ireland. He also was given custody of the cities and castles of Limerick and Cork, the strategic castles of Athlone, Drogheda, Dungarvan (Co. Waterford) and Rinndown (Co. Roscommon), of Decies and Desmond and of the five cantreds of Connacht which had been reserved to the Crown. The removal of Richard de Burgh, and the introduction of an absentee lord in his place, touched off yet more fighting in Connacht. The situation became such that by the middle of July 1233, Henry III was planning a royal expedition to Ireland for the early autumn in order to pacify his lordship.[159] Before that expedition could be mounted, however, Richard Marshal's rebellion flared up on the Welsh march.

The Marshal rebellion was, at its core, a rebellion against the seemingly arbitrary rule which had become more commonplace since the return to court of Peter des Roches.[160] The most galling instance to the Marshal, and the catalyst for his dismissal from court, was the removal *per voluntatem regis* of the Marshal's father's associate Gilbert Basset from the manor of Upavon (Wiltshire) in February 1233. Richard retired by 9 February from court, whence he travelled to Wales (where he launched an unsanctioned offensive against Llywelyn) and then on to Ireland, where he landed by 1 April 1233.[161] The storm clouds gathered, and the king took no chances. On 13 June, Walter de Lacy was one of the Welsh marcher lords from whom Henry III took hostages to ensure their fidelity 'so that there is a firm peace'.[162]

Far from joining the rebellion, Walter was one of its initial targets. In August 1233, forces under the direction of Richard Marshal's chief supporter in the march, Walter's son-in-law Walter of Clifford, attacked and took the castles of Hay and Ewyas Lacy. Ewyas Lacy had belonged to Gilbert de Lacy before his death in 1230, and been assigned as dower to his wife, Isabella Bigod. However, once the king declared that Walter de Lacy should recover all of his son's lands as those held *ad se sustentandum*, Walter failed to provide Isabella with her dower. Isabella's brother, Earl Roger III Bigod, was Richard Marshal's nephew and supporter, and was present at the initial planning meeting (though he did not thereafter join the rebellion). This, as well as the ongoing rivalry between the houses of Lacy and Marshal, may have suggested Walter's castle as a target.[163] Both Hay and Ewyas Lacy were quickly recovered by royal forces,[164] and the rebellion was soon extinguished in the central march. The legitimacy of Isabella Bigod's claim to Ewyas Lacy was confirmed by the Crown, which then granted custody to Peter de Rivallis instead of to Walter de Lacy.[165] Walter de Lacy therefore lost seisin of his Welsh marcher lordship as a result of to the Marshal's rebellion, a fact which probably did not sit well with him.

Walter was prepared to go on the offensive to retaliate against the Marshal in Ireland, where he was dispatched by December 1233.[166] Roger of Wendover claims that Peter des Roches and Peter de Rivallis then sent a letter in the king's name to Walter and Hugh de Lacy, Richard de Burgh, Geoffrey de Marisco and the Irish justiciar, Maurice fitz Gerald, in which they declared that Richard Marshal had been disinherited and banished from England. This letter then ordered its addressees to seize Richard Marshal if he were to travel to Ireland, and bring him to the king, dead or alive. If they did this, they were to divide his Irish lands and possessions amongst themselves to be held of the king in perpetuity.[167] Such an order, if sent, has not survived in any other form. However, although Wendover's account of the dispute is open to criticism, it is corroborated by the Irish annals on several points.[168] At the very least, Henry III may have suspected the bloody outcome of the transference of the war to Ireland.[169] It should be noted that, while the parcelling out of Leinster among those responsible for the Marshal's destruction may seem far-fetched, it was precisely what had happened when the Lacy brothers drove John de Courcy from Ulster in 1204.[170] In that instance there were similarly no direct statements enrolled by the chancery of the king's intent to reward Hugh de Lacy for his attacks, only oblique instructions regarding what was to be carried out should Courcy default in court. However, while Peter des Roches and Peter de Rivallis may well have wished such an outcome, Wendover's account cannot be trusted on this point without further corroboration. As Nicholas Vincent declares, 'the evidence points not to conspiracy but to total confusion'.[171] Whatever the king and his counsellors wanted, the Irish magnates were pursuing their own private interests.

Nevertheless, the Irish government prepared for war against Leinster. Troops were sent from England, and a naval patrol was ordered to guard the Irish Sea.[172] The Irish Pipe Roll 19 Henry III, now lost, contained accounts for horses being bought for use against the Marshal.[173] Richard Marshal was not idle either, and evidence exists which suggests that the Marshal temporised with Richard de Burgh at this point. Richard de Burgh and the Marshals had been at loggerheads ever since the beginning of the conquest of Connacht.[174] Richard Marshal then had sat on the committee that tried and condemned Hubert de Burgh, which led directly to Richard de Burgh's dispossession in Ireland.[175] However, Richard de Burgh plainly blamed Henry III for Hubert's fall, not Richard Marshal. Henry later admitted that a genuine rift had opened between himself and

Richard de Burgh because of Hubert's imprisonment.[176] What is more, at the height of the Marshal's rebellion in Wales, Richard Marshal's knight, Richard Siward, mounted a destructive raid on Devizes, freeing Hubert de Burgh and delivering him to Chepstow, where Richard Marshal welcomed him on 1 November 1233.[177] This, as well as the eventual course of events in Ireland (discussed below), makes it difficult to follow some historians in dismissing the impact of the Marshal's rescue of Hubert de Burgh as mere propaganda.[178] At the very least, the king's testimony proves that that the powerful Irish baron Richard de Burgh was not a staunch royalist throughout the rebellion.

Richard Marshal had sent his brothers, Gilbert and Anselm Marshal, to Ireland at the outbreak of the rebellion, and, according to the annals of Tewkesbury, 'all of Ireland, except for the Lacys and their allies, gave up and subjected themselves to Gilbert Marshal, either by truce or completely'.[179] Whatever the extent of Gilbert's success in recruiting supporters (and this statement reinforces the idea that Richard de Burgh was briefly counted among them), the Lacys and their allies were a powerful faction as well. What is more, whatever his brothers' achievements, Richard Marshal had drawn upon his Irish lands for his rebellion in England and Wales. With those forces still east of the Irish Sea, Leinster was underprepared for an attack.

Richard Marshal sailed to Ireland in late February 1234, after which the exact course of events is difficult to ascertain.[180] The Dunstable annalist claims that Gilbert Marshal had agreed to a truce in Ireland, which all sides had kept till Richard arrived and deliberately broke it.[181] One obvious reason for breaking the peace would have been if Richard de Burgh had broken an oath to the Marshal and defected to the king about this time. Such an oath-breaking, had it occurred, would also explain why the Marshal was said to have reproached Burgh as 'vilest of traitors' (*proditor nequissime*) when they later met at Kildare.[182] On about 7 March 1234, Henry III issued Richard de Burgh a safe-conduct to go to England and speak with the king,[183] proving that Burgh was not at peace with the king around the time of Richard Marshal's arrival in Ireland. Wendover's portrayal of Burgh as a staunch royalist from the beginning of the Marshal's rebellion seems less credible in light of this evidence. Nevertheless, Wendover appears to be more reliable on other aspects of the war in Ireland. He claims that the Irish magnates accepted the king's proposal for the division of Leinster, and launched an attack upon the Marshal's lands once the lines of partition had been agreed. Wendover then goes on to detail Richard Marshal's campaign of conquest and destruction throughout Richard de Burgh's ambit in Munster and Connacht (during which he was aided by the Irish of Thomond), including his successful four-day siege of Limerick city.[184] Orpen had little time for Wendover's testimony, stating categorically that it was 'quite certain that the Marshal never went to Limerick or outside his own fief', and historians have followed his lead by ignoring the Marshal's supposed western campaign.[185] However, Wendover's testimony is corroborated by the (independent) continuations of the annals of Margam, which were composed in the southern Welsh march and are very sympathetic to the Marshals.[186] Those annals state that 'coming to Ireland, the Marshal, earl of Pembroke, besieged the royal city of Limerick, and it was given to him'.[187] What is more, the account for Limerick on the Irish Pipe Roll 19 Henry III mentioned expenditure to guard the county in 'the war of Connacht and Thomond' and to repair the injuries caused at Limerick by Donnchad Cairprech Ua Briain. It also contained a long list of fines for those who either joined with Richard Marshal (thirty-three named) or who failed to heed the royal summons to fight his rebellion (two hundred named).[188]

Such an expedition against Richard de Burgh suggests a personal grievance between the pair, because it would have left the Marshal's own lands in Leinster open to attack from Meath. The Margam continuation states that the Lacys were quick to strike: 'Then Walter de Lacy and his brother Hugh, a notorious traitor to his many lords, and many others, laid siege to the Marshal's castle of Kildare.'[189] Hearing this, Richard Marshal gathered his forces and marched to his castle's relief. On 1 April 1234 the opposing forces attempted a parley on the Curragh of Kildare. By this point, pressure had been mounting on Henry III in England to accept the Marshal's demands and dismiss his current advisers. The new archbishop-elect of Canterbury, Edmund Rich, joined with his suffragan bishops in warning Henry, under threat of ecclesiastical censure, to dismiss the foreign advisers who had led him to estrange his faithful subjects such as Richard Marshal.[190] Perhaps understanding the emerging political situation in England, but underestimating the other magnates' resolve, the Marshal refused to accept the terms demanded of him, despite his numerical disadvantage. The encounter erupted into violence, during which Richard was mortally wounded.[191] Almost all contemporary commentators write of treachery, alleging that the Marshal was abandoned by his own guard at the crucial moment, dying some days later in captivity.[192] Whether or not this was true (Geoffrey de Marisco and his followers certainly remained close enough to have been captured along with the Marshal),[193] the 'murder' sent shockwaves through Ireland and England,

and Richard Marshal was transformed into a martyr. The ultimate removal of Peter des Roches and his associates from power was largely accomplished on the back of the moral outrage at Richard's estrangement and death.[194] In these circumstances, King Henry III had no choice but to grant Richard's brother, Gilbert, seisin of his inheritance, and to try to smooth over the whole conflict. He wrote that, through the grant, he hoped to end the hatred between the Marshal and the other magnates of Ireland and England,[195] which desire was made manifest in a formal peace treaty between the Marshals and the nominally royalist earls, barons and knights of Ireland.[196]

This public desire for reconciliation did not prevent the king from rewarding at least one of the perpetrators of the bloody deed. The main beneficiary was Richard de Burgh, who was restored to Connacht.[197] Although the king explicitly stated that the remission of the king's ire against him was bought because of his service during Richard Marshal's rebellion[198] it must be remembered that Richard de Burgh had lost Connacht when Peter des Roches came to power in 1232. It cannot have been a coincidence that his restoration immediately followed Peter's fall. What is more, the reigning king of Connacht, Feidlim Ua Conchobair, had used the occasion of the Marshal's rebellion to invade Meath, ravaging Ballyloughloe (bar. Clonlonan, Co. Westmeath), Ardnurcher and other places.[199] The time was ripe for Burgh to take power over Connacht once more. 'What 1234 meant for Ireland was that the final conquest of Connacht, which began the following year, would be conducted the de Burgh way.'[200]

A grant to Furness Abbey about 9 April 1234, just eight days after the confrontation with Richard Marshal (while the dying earl still had six days to live), provides a unique glimpse at Walter de Lacy's household. The witness list names four of Walter's retained knights ('*milites mei*'), Richard and John of Copeland, Walter le Petit and Robert of Leyburn. It also names his chaplain, Hugh, canon of Llanthony; his seneschal, Nicholas d'Évreux; his chamberlain, Paul le Cornwalays; his clerks, Richard and William; the steward (*procurator*) of his demesne manor of Donacarney (Co. Meath), Walter le Dispenser; and servants, John of Clifford and Philip de Wichetot, with others. It also mentions, but does not name, his foresters and rabbit warrens (which imply warreners) at Trim.[201] However, Walter soon rearranged his seigniorial administration to allow him to take full advantage of the new situation. Before May 1234, Walter granted another seneschal, Simon of Clifford, a rent of £30 drawn from two manors, one in Meath and one in Herefordshire, in exchange for Simon's English manor of Yarkhill (Herefordshire).[202] This allowed Simon a ready source of revenue as he followed Walter through his ambit. At his seigniorial *caput* of Trim, on 1 August, Walter granted the hereditary stewardship of his English lands and the constableship of Ludlow castle to William de Lucy and his heirs.[203] He then turned to William for help paying off his Jewish debts. William loaned Walter £322 to be paid off at £80 per year, which cleared all except Walter's two largest debts.[204] Those, which amounted to roughly £1,000 to the heirs of Hamo of Hereford and to David of Oxford, Walter carried with him to his grave. Having provided for the administration of his English lands, he turned to imposing lordship upon his Irish territories. That same year, he made grants in Meath to Llanthony Secunda, the abbey of St Mary of Furness (Cumbria) and the monastery of St Mary of Tristernagh (Co. Westmeath).[205]

The underlying enmity between the government's co-conspirators and the Marshals seems not to have dissipated, however, for the following year retribution was taken. Matthew Paris writes that the Irish magnates' messenger, Henry Clement, was killed in London (while the king was staying there) after insulting the memory of Richard Marshal and boasting that he had caused Richard's death.[206] The murder caused a scandal in England and Ireland at the time. Powicke concluded that the murderers were connected to Gilbert Marshal in some way, and, although the king was unable to tie Gilbert to the crime, the implication remains. In 1236, Gilbert was forced to swear on the gospels before the king, the archbishop of Canterbury and assembled magnates of the realm that he would observe his promises, the first of which was not to harbour William de Marisco (son of the former justiciar of Ireland Geoffrey de Marisco) and his companions, who had been outlawed for the crime.[207] William, it should be remembered, had been implicated in the murder of Áed Ua Conchobair in 1228, when he was supposed to have been acting in concert with the Lacys.[208] His family had also been singled out for unique calumny in the wake of Richard Marshal's death, his father Geoffrey being unjustly accused of treacherously leading the Marshal to the slaughter.[209] In 1234, Geoffrey and William de Marisco each had been imprisoned and fined 3,000 marks for joining Richard's rebellion. They had even been constrained after their release, lest they revert to rebellion.[210] Given the circumstances, it is likely that the murder was carried out on Gilbert's behalf. Afterwards, William took flight and became a notorious pirate from his base on Lundy Island in the Bristol Channel.[211] His escape and successful piracy were unthinkable without the complicity of Gilbert Marshal, whose own fleet controlled those waters.[212]

Fighting on all fronts: the end of the Lacy line, 1233-41

While Richard Marshal's rebellion and its aftermath filled Walter's attention, his wife Margery began an even tougher struggle with the Knights Hospitaller in Rome.[213] When King John had granted Margery three carucates of land in the forest of Aconbury to found a house of nuns for the souls of her father, mother and brother in 1216, she had given the foundation to the Hospitallers. Neither the Lacys nor the Briouzes were great patrons of the order of the Hospital, which was at that time preparing for the Fifth Crusade (1217-21). But there were precedents. In the reign of King Richard, Walter de Lacy had founded a Hospitaller preceptory at Kilmainhambeg (Kells, Co. Meath), and his brother Hugh founded another in Ulster at Castleboy (bar. Ardes, Co. Down).[214] Moreover, the Hospitallers of Clerkenwell near London (whose prior presided over all English houses) had acted as intermediaries when Walter negotiated the restoration of his Irish lands the previous year (1215). This highlights the unique freedom of passage between rebel and royalist spheres of influence that the Hospitallers and Templars enjoyed during the period of Margery's foundation, which may also have played a part in her decision. Whatever the case, Margery subsequently became embroiled in disputes with the order over the running of Aconbury to the extent that, by 8 April 1233, she had travelled to Rome to put her case directly to Pope Gregory IX.[215]

According to Margery's testimony in 1233, it was through being 'led by her own simplicity and induced by the exhortations of the brothers of the Hospital of Jerusalem' that she had given them the house in 1216 without first consulting the diocesan bishop, or even her husband Walter.[216] Margery's account was not an admission of female ignorance but a calculated strategy to render her donation invalid. Indeed, the guile with which Margery, or her lawyers, presented their argument to the pope is impressive. Under common law, a married woman required her husband's consent to alienate her lands.[217] By 'playing dumb' and claiming that she had failed to get that consent, Margery hoped to render her donation void. What is more, Margery also claimed that she had thought it permissible for communities of women to be founded under Hospitaller observance. As Helen Nicholson points out, the implication was that the Hospitallers did not permit female houses, which also would have rendered her donation void.[218] Although her claim was not true, Pope Gregory IX believed Margery's insinuation and, taking into account her *simplicitas*, ultimately found in her favour. The pope's final verdict was the product of years of expensive litigation, involving claim and counterclaim by the Lacys and the Hospitallers, in the course of which Margery was at one time excommunicated by the prior of St Albans. It also involved Walter de Lacy, who, in accordance with legal procedure in disputes over land, was brought in as co-appellant with his wife by June 1233.[219] This meant that the aftermath of Richard Marshal's rebellion had a direct impact upon the legal proceedings, because it prevented Walter from attending any hearings in England for some time. The Hospitallers knew this, and used it to their advantage by getting local ecclesiastics to try their case and find against the Lacys for failure to appear.[220]

In the context of lordship, the allegations revolved around the battle between patron and order over control of a religious foundation. The Hospitallers claimed that Margery had assumed the role of prioress, controlling Aconbury's property as her own ever since the death of the previous prioress in 1230. For their part, in addition to resenting the Hospitallers' attempts to impose their own prioress (as was their custom) rather than allowing a free election, Margery and the sisters complained of the harsh financial exactions that the Hospitallers made upon Aconbury to fund their wars in the east. To free herself from the burden of a bankrupt, if very influential, military order, Margery lied about the circumstances of her foundation. Even so, the matter was not resolved until 16 July 1237, by which time Margery and Walter de Lacy had spent in excess of 600 marks.[221]

A month after the Lacys' victory at the papal curia, the pope wrote about the situation in Ireland. On 25 August 1237 he sent a letter to the archbishop of Dublin, ordering him:

> to cause by ecclesiastical censure, to be faithfully observed the peace made between Maurice fitz Gerald, Walter de Lacy, Richard de Burgh, Walter de Riddlesford, and other barons of Ireland of the one part, and Gilbert Marshal, earl of Pembroke, and his brothers Walter and Anselm, of the diocese of Derry [recte Kildare], on the other, by the mediation of the king and prelates and nobles of Ireland.[222]

If fighting between the factions had occurred in Ireland once more, then no record of it survives. By this point Walter would have been at least sixty-nine years old, and was in frail health. On 9 December 1237, the king wrote to the Irish justiciar stating that Walter de Lacy was unable to undertake his proposed voyage to Ireland because of his infirmity.[223] Little more is heard of Walter, except with regard to his two great legacies: his inheritance and his debt. On 15 May 1238, Walter went before the king at Westminster and signified that his grandson, Walter eldest son of Gilbert de Lacy, was his sole heir for the Lacy inheritance in England and Ireland.[224] That same year, the Lacy demesne manors of Weobley and Ludlow, along with Stanton Lacy, were distrained by the elder Walter's creditors. Walter sent his representatives to petition for their restoration, but nothing further is heard of the matter.[225] Two years later, disaster struck on both fronts. Walter, who was probably by now blind,[226] was impleaded by a number of his Jewish creditors, and, after a brief respite, King Henry III ordered his possessions to be distrained on 10 December 1240.[227] Far more seriously, his grandson and heir, Walter the younger, died that same year. This probably explains the entry in the annals of Clonmacnoise under 1240: 'William Delacie lord of Meath, the onely son of Walter Delacie, and his wife died in own week, some say they were poysoned.'[228] These twin tragedies would bring Walter de Lacy's career to an inauspicious end, for he himself died shortly thereafter. His end had come before 24 February 1241, when the sheriffs of Hereford and Shropshire were ordered to take his lands and possessions into the hands of the king.[229] Thereafter Walter's lands, chattels and debt (the Jewish portion of which stood at £955 13s 4d)[230] were divided between his two granddaughters.[231]

Conclusion

During this period, the fortunes of the three Lacy brothers, Walter, Hugh and William, were inextricably tied to one another. Walter's misfortunes, which included his removal from the shrievalty of Herefordshire, and the confiscation of his administrative centres in Ireland and England (Trim and Ludlow castles) and the massive fine demanded of him for his tenants' actions from 1223 to 1224, were directly linked to his brothers' rebellion in Wales and Ireland. Walter's removal from the shrievalty of Herefordshire elevated him to the status of figurehead in the movement against Hubert de Burgh, which factional dispute was the English corollary of the Welsh and Irish rebellions. Hugh de Lacy's attempts to return to Ulster were obfuscated at court by the younger William Marshal, who had no desire to see the restoration of the Irish earldom threaten his dominance of the Irish Sea. Hugh's rebellion was a long delayed product of King John's aristocratic counterbalancing. The conflicting ambitions of both factions led to a war which spanned the region, starting in Wales and concluding in Ireland, showing the wide reach of conflicts in this transnational aristocratic society. In 1223, the influence of William Marshal at the English court convinced Hugh de Lacy that his only option for the restoration of his earldom of Ulster was through military means. He formed a political alliance with those opposing Hubert de Burgh's faction at court, and attacked William Marshal in Wales. He then took advantage of the Marshal's heavy recruitment from Ireland to attack in Ireland while the Marshal and the government were unprepared. The resulting removal of Walter de Lacy from the shrievalty of Hereford was held up as an instance of misrule by an English faction, who marched against Hubert de Burgh in England. In this way, the rebellions from 1223 to 1224 in England, Wales and Ireland were linked. Likewise, while the rebellion of Richard Marshal was sparked by factionalist English court politics, one of its first military strikes was against Walter de Lacy's castle of Ewyas Lacy in Wales. Walter then took advantage of Richard's recruitment in Ireland to attack a poorly defended Leinster. In this instance, Walter and his allies performed the will of the dominant faction at the English court, but the horror of their bloody victory helped to bring about a change in regime. In both rebellions, the Lacys fought the Marshals and deliberately moved hostilities to Ireland, where they were better able to win. Neither of these conflicts could be appreciated fully by concentrating on one realm. Supranational lords had supranational disputes.

Henry III's majority saw a return to the great days of baronial power in Ireland. Richard de Burgh was installed in Connacht, Hugh de Lacy restored to Ulster and Walter de Lacy retained Meath. The marriage between Walter's daughter and Richard de Burgh sealed an alliance which was to provide lasting rewards for both sides. The death of Walter's son Gilbert in 1230 came as a shock, forcing Walter to resume the full burden of transmarine lordship. After a period of success involving the Marshal rebellion and the conquest of Connacht, age and finance finally caught up with him. In addition to growing costs of refortification along the frontier, Walter and his wife Margery were embroiled in a lengthy dispute at the papal curia with the Hospitallers. This was no benign trial based on simple evidence; both sides were underhanded in their pursuit of victory. Husband and wife were ultimately successful, but the cost associated with standing up to the might of the Hospitallers meant that theirs was a pyrrhic victory. As age and infirmity crept up on him, Walter de Lacy was less and less valuable to the king. Consequently, the orders for peace touching fines and loans ceased at about the same time that we hear of his ill-health. In an age when secular power was ultimately imposed by armed force, Walter de Lacy had outlived his usefulness.

Walter's death was not lamented nearly as much as his father's had been over half a century earlier. The most flattering obituary was written in the annals of Clonmacnoise: 'Walter Delacie, the bountifullest Englishman for horses, cloaths, mony & goold, that ever came before his tyme into this kingdome, Died in England of a wound.'[232] The other Irish annals that notice his death all call him (in varying forms) 'Lord of Meath and chief counsellor of the Foreigners of Ireland'.[233] Perhaps Matthew Paris comes closest to the mark when he writes, 'Walter de Lacy, the most eminent of all the nobles of Ireland, after losing his vision and suffering from other bodily afflictions, passed from this life'.[234] Like his father before him, Walter was clearly identified with Ireland. Although he held approximately equivalent fees either side of the Irish Sea, he was first and foremost an Irish magnate in the eyes of those of his contemporaries who marked his passing. Unlike his father, however, who was lauded by the Irish annals and feared by the English commentators, Walter de Lacy seems to have outlived his notoriety. Had he died at the height of his power in 1201, 1206 or 1221, then the obituaries might well have been full of the overblown praise heaped upon his father. By 1241, however, Walter de Lacy was an old and enfeebled man. His death brought an ignoble end to one of the more notable aristocratic families in the Plantagenet empire.

Notes

1 'Annales Dunstapilia', p. 75, *s.a.* 1222.
2 *PR, 1216-25*, p. 301.
3 See Chapters 5 and 6.
4 *The Acts of Welsh Rulers, 1120-1283*, ed. Huw Pryce (Cardiff, 2005), pp. 413-14; *The Charters of the Anglo-Norman Earls of Chester, c.1071-1237*, ed. Geoffrey Barraclough (Chester, 1988), no. 411.
5 Veach and Verstraten Veach, 'William *Gorm*'.
6 Duffy, 'The first Ulster plantation'.
7 Hugh de Lacy's land, which is described as being held '*in capite*' of the earl, was excluded from Earl Hugh's grant of Bisley to Humphrey de Bohun, c.1170. F. M. Stenton, *The First Century of English Feudalism* (Oxford, 1932), pp. 257-8; *CFR 1233-34*, no. 25.
8 Cheshire Archives CHB/2, fo. 31r, printed in: R. H. Morris, *Chester in the Plantagenet and Tudor Reigns* (Chester, 1893), p. 11; *Eighth Report of the Royal Commission on Historical Manuscripts. Appendix - part 1 (section II)* (London, 1881), no. 370a (calendar of lost original).
9 Robin Frame, 'King Henry III and Ireland: the shaping of a peripheral lordship', in Frame (ed.), *Ireland and Britain 1170-1450* (London and Rio Grande, 1998), pp. 31-57, at pp. 44-5.
10 See Chapter 6.
11 *Rot. Litt. Claus.*, i, p. 501.

12 *PR, 1216-25*, pp. 336-7; *Rot. Litt. Claus.*, i, p. 505b.
13 *Rot. Litt. Claus.*, i. p. 527b.
14 *The Acts and Letters of the Marshal Family, 1156-1248*, ed. David Crouch (Camden Series, forthcoming), from which: BL MS Arundel 19, fos 1r-7v (Chepstow); *Liber Primus Kilkenniensis*, ed. Charles McNeill (Dublin, 1931), pp. 10, 74 (Kilkenny).
15 Lloyd, *Wales*, ii, pp. 655-61; Norgate, *Minority*, pp. 191-3.
16 'In odium regis sibi cohaerentes', *Mathaei Parisiensis Chronica Majora*, iii, p. 82.
17 Carpenter, *Minority*, p. 315.
18 *Royal Letters*, i, pp. 244-6.
19 *Rot. Litt. Claus.*, i, p. 549b.
20 *Foedera*, I, i, p. 190; Carpenter, *Minority*, pp. 301-6.
21 Norgate, *Minority*, pp. 202-3.
22 *Rot. Litt. Claus.*, i, p. 549b.
23 *PR, 1216-25*, p. 375.
24 *Ibid.*, pp. 374-5, 378.
25 *Ibid.*, p. 376; *Brut (RBH)*, pp. 225-6, *s.a.* 1223.
26 Lloyd, *Wales*, ii, 661n.
27 *Rot. Litt. Claus.*, i, p. 569b.
28 *Ibid.*, i, p. 554b, 555b.
29 *Rot. Litt. Claus.*, i, p. 571-571b.
30 *Brut (RBH)*, p. 227, *s.a.* 1223.
31 Norgate, *Minority*, p. 195.
32 *PR, 1216-25*, p. 378.
33 Carpenter, *Minority*, pp. 311-15 (quote p. 315).
34 'Annales Dunstapilia', p. 85, *s.a.* 1223.
35 *PR, 1216-25*, p. 387.
36 Orpen, *Normans*, iii, p. 38; Otway-Ruthven, *Medieval Ireland*, p. 91.
37 'Annales Dunstapilia', p. 85; Orpen, *Normans*, iii, p. 38n.
38 Norgate, *Minority*, p. 203.
39 *PR, 1216-25*, pp. 413-14; *Rot. Litt. Claus.*, i, p. 574.
40 *Mem. Walt. Coventria*, ii, p. 261.
41 Norgate, *Minority*, p. 203; Maurice Powicke, *Henry III and Lord Edward: The Community of the Realm in the Thirteenth Century*, 2 vols (Oxford, 1947), i, p. 58.
42 See Chapter 6.
43 Carpenter, *Minority*, p. 144.
44 See, for instance, *ibid.*, p. 316; Stacey, *Henry III*, p. 28.
45 *PR, 1225-32*, p. 71.
46 *Mem. Walt. Coventria*, ii, p. 261. They were at Gloucester from 16 to 22 November. *Rot. Litt. Claus.*, i, pp. 575-6.
47 *Rot. Litt. Claus.*, i, pp. 575-6.
48 Arguments put forward in, Carpenter, *Minority*, p. 319.
49 Norgate, *Minority*, p. 204n.
50 *PR, 1216-1225*, p. 414.

51 David Carpenter, 'The decline of the curial sheriff in England, 1194–1258', *English Historical Review*, 91/358 (1976), pp. 1–32, at p. 11.
52 Cf. Chapters 5 and 6.
53 *Calendar of the Close Rolls, Preserved in the Public Record Office, Edward I, A.D. 1279–1288* (London, 1902), p. 55 (quoted inquest); *Calendar of Documents Relating to Ireland Preserved in Her Majesty's Public Record Office, London, 1252–1284*, ed. H. S. Sweetman (London, 1877), nos 810, 1645 (quoted inquest). These were requested by Theobald de Verdun, TNA SC 8/145/7236.
54 Otway-Ruthven, *Medieval Ireland*, p. 159.
55 See below, p. 205.
56 Norgate, *Minority*, pp. 204–5.
57 The best account is Carpenter, *Minority*, pp. 314–75.
58 *AU*, ii, p. 270, s.a. 1222 [*recte* 1223].
59 TNA SC 1/3/28; *Rot. Litt. Claus.*, i, pp. 587, 615.
60 McDonald, *Manx Kingship*, pp. 80–1, 153.
61 *Rot. Litt. Claus.*, i, p. 439.
62 *Royal Letters*, i, pp. 219–20.
63 Knut Helle, 'Anglo-Norwegian relations in the reign of Håkon Håkonsson (1217–63)', *Mediaeval Scandinavia*, 1 (1968), pp. 101–14, at pp. 101, 104–5.
64 *PR, 1216–25*, p. 384.
65 *Royal Letters*, i, pp. 216–17. A Norwegian messenger was in England in February 1224, *Rot. Litt. Claus.*, i, p. 584.
66 *Rot. Litt. Claus.*, i, p. 607; Helle, 'Anglo-Norwegian relations', p. 103.
67 *Early Sources*, pp. 455, 461.
68 *Royal Letters*, i, pp. 183–4.
69 *Ibid.*, pp. 177–8.
70 *Rot. Litt. Claus.*, i, p. 584.
71 *PR, 1216–25*, p. 433.
72 Brendan Smith, 'Irish politics, 1220–1245', in Michael Prestwich, Richard Britnell and Robin Frame (eds), *Thirteenth Century England, VIII* (Woodbridge, 2001), pp. 13–32, at p. 13.
73 *Royal Letters*, i, p. 223, and see Chapter 6.
74 *AC*, p. 4, s.a. 1224.
75 *Royal Letters*, i, p. 233.
76 *Royal Letters*, i, p. 507; *PR, 1216–1225*, p. 483.
77 Carpenter, *Minority*, p. 361.
78 *Royal Letters*, i, pp. 500–3.
79 At least one Irish source tied Walter to his brother's rebellion, stating 'Aogh Óg [Hugh the younger] and Báitéar [Walter] rebelled against their own king along with the Scots and they were declared traitors; Aogh Óg went to France in disguise and received a pardon and the restoration of his earldom of Ulster afterwards', *Leabhar Mór na nGenealach. The Great Book of Irish Genealogies Compiled (1645–66) by Dubhaltach Mac Fhirbhisigh*, ed. Nollaig Ó Muraíle, 5 vols (Dublin, 2003–5), iii, no. 798E.3. This may be a confusion with the events of 1210.
80 *Rot. Litt. Claus.*, i, p. 590b.

81 *PR, 1216–25*, p. 432. Robert de Lacy died before 1215, *Rot. Litt. Claus.*, i, p. 185b.
82 *PR, 1216–25*, p. 433; *Rot. Litt. Claus.*, i, p. 591.
83 *Rot. Litt. Claus.*, i, p. 591.
84 *Royal Letters*, i, pp. 500–3.
85 *Ibid.*, i, pp. 500–3.
86 T. E. McNeill, 'The great towers of early Irish castles', in Christopher Harper-Bill (ed.), *Anglo-Norman Studies XII* (Woodbridge, 1989), pp. 99–117, at pp. 104–9.
87 *Royal Letters*, i, pp. 500–3.
88 *PR, 1216–25*, pp. 437–8.
89 *Royal Letters*, i, pp. 500–3.
90 *ALC*, i, p. 272, *s.a.* 1224; *AC*, p. 6, *s.a.* 1224.
91 The annals of Loch Cé situate Lisardowlan (*Ard-abhla*) within Bréifne, *ALC*, i, p. 272, *s.a.* 1224.
92 Otway-Ruthven, 'Partition of the de Verdon lands', pp. 414–15.
93 *Royal Letters*, i, pp. 500–3.
94 *Ibid.*, i, pp. 500–3. For the le Gros family see Nicholas Vincent, 'The borough of Chipping Sodbury and the Fat Men of France (1130–1270)', *Transactions of the Bristol & Gloucestershire Archaeological Society*, 116 (1999), pp. 141–59.
95 *Rot. Litt. Claus.*, i, p. 618.
96 *Calendar of Documents Relating to Scotland Preserved in Her Majesty's Public Record Office, London, A.D. 1108–1272*, ed. Joseph Bain (London, 1881), no. 890.
97 Colin Martin, 'Maritime transport on the western seaboard from prehistory to the nineteenth century', in Kenneth Veitch (ed.), *Scottish Life and Society: A Compendium of Scottish Ethnology. Volume 8: Transport and Communication* (Edinburgh, 2009), 137–67, at pp. 147–8.
98 Orpen, *Normans*, iii, pp. 38–48.
99 *ALC*, i, pp. 270–2, *s.a.* 1224; 'Annales Dunstapilia', pp. 91–2, *s.a.* 1225.
100 *Rot. Litt. Claus.*, ii, p. 37b.
101 Otway-Ruthven, *Medieval Ireland*, pp. 92–3.
102 *CFR 1224–25*, no. 171; *Rot. Litt. Claus.*, ii, p. 35b. Being the feminine form of 'Giles', 'Egidia' reveals a strong Briouze family sentiment in Walter and Margery de Lacy's choice of name.
103 Smith, 'Irish politics', p. 18.
104 *PR, 1216–25*, p. 528.
105 *Rot. Litt. Claus.*, ii, p. 39b; *Royal Letters*, i, pp. 500–3.
106 See Chapter 5.
107 Orpen, *Normans*, iii, pp. 46–7.
108 *Rot. Litt. Claus.*, ii, pp. 35b, 39b; *CFR 1224–25*, nos 174–6.
109 *PR, 1225–32*, pp. 31–2, 75–8.
110 *Ibid.*, p. 118. The king sent a separate letter to Walter on the same day, empowering him to retain Hugh's castles if he saw fit. *Rot. Litt. Claus.*, ii, p. 182b.
111 Orpen, *Normans*, iii, pp. 264–5.
112 *PR, 1225–32*, pp. 75–6.
113 *Rot. Litt. Claus.*, ii, p. 140.

114 *PR, 1225–32*, pp. 77–8.
115 Ibid., p. 47.
116 Ibid., p. 48; *Rot. Chart.*, p. 219.
117 *PR, 1225–32*, pp. 48–9.
118 *Rot. Litt. Claus.*, ii, pp. 124, 127.
119 *PR, 1225–32*, pp. 80–1.
120 For what follows see *Royal Letters*, i, pp. 290–3.
121 *ALC*, i, p. 292, *s.a.* 1227 [*recte* 1226]; *AC*, p. 24, *s.a.* 1227 [*recte* 1226]; *AFM*, iii, p. 242, *s.a.* 1227 [*recte* 1226]; *Ann. Clon.*, p. 231, *s.a.* 1226.
122 Orpen, *Normans*, iii, p. 170.
123 *Ann. Clon.*, p. 231, *s.a.* 1226.
124 *ALC*, i, p. 292, *s.a.* 1227 [*recte* 1226]; *AC*, p. 24, *s.a.* 1227 [*recte* 1226]; *AFM*, iii, p. 244, *s.a.* 1227 [*recte* 1226].
125 *Royal Letters*, i, p 292.
126 *PR, 1225–32*, p. 57–9; Orpen, *Normans*, iii, p. 168.
127 *Cal. Chart., 1226–57*, p. 42.
128 *Ann. Clon.*, pp. 232–3, *s.a.* 1227.
129 *AC*, p. 28, *s.a.* 1228.
130 Orpen, *Normans*, iii, pp. 172–3.
131 Smith, 'Irish politics', p. 14.
132 *CR, 1227–31*, p. 115. For the campaign see Walker, 'Hubert de Burgh and Wales', pp. 478–82.
133 *CR, 1227–31*, p. 256.
134 Powicke, *Henry III and Lord Edward*, i, p 72.
135 *PR, 1225–32*, pp. 357–62 (Gilbert and Walter at p. 360). For the campaign see Stacey, *Henry III*, pp. 160–73.
136 *CR, 1227–31*, p. 410.
137 *PR, 1225–32*, p. 391.
138 *Royal Letters*, i, p. 374.
139 *CR, 1227–31*, p. 432; *Flores Historiarum*, iii, pp. 4–5; *Mathaei Parisiensis Chronica Majora*, iii, p. 197.
140 *PR, 1225–32*, pp. 289, 305. Gilbert also confirmed his father's grant of Aylburton (Gloucestershire) to Philip de Coleville, TNA C 115/77, fo. 77.
141 'Pro eo quod sit in familia mea', HCA, no. 3235. And see Chapter 8. Brock Holden misidentifies this manor as Staunton-on-Wye, Herefordshire (Holden, *Lords*, p. 100). Within the charter, the land is identified as '*Hayton*'. Stephen's heir, William, held half a knight's fee at Lower Hayton (Shropshire), within the manor of Stanton Lacy in 1242–3 (*Liber Feodorum*, ii, p. 964; and see Appendix 2).
142 Holden, *Lords*, pp. 100–1.
143 HCA, no 3236.
144 *Reg. St Thomas*, pp. 419–20.
145 *Irish Llanthony*, pp. 83–4.
146 *Calendar of the Patent Rolls preserved in the Public Record Office, Henry III, A.D. 1232–1247* (London, 1906), p. 42. Nicholas Vincent, *Peter des Roches: An Alien*

in *English Politics, 1205-1258* (Cambridge, 1996), pp. 390-1; Marc Morris, *The Bigod Earls of Norfolk in the Thirteenth Century* (Woodbridge, 2005), pp. 10-11.
147 *CR, 1227-31*, pp. 464-5. See S. F. C. Milsom, *The Legal Framework of English Feudalism (Maitland Lectures)* (Cambridge, 1976), pp. 134-8.
148 For Walter's Jewish debt see Joe Hillaby, 'Hereford gold, part 2', pp. 231-9.
149 He married Walter's daughter Katharine, HCA, no. 3241.
150 Vincent, *Peter des Roches*, pp. 273-320; David Carpenter, 'The fall of Hubert de Burgh', *Journal of British Studies*, 9/2 (1980), pp. 1-17.
151 *CR, 1227-31*, pp. 585-6, 601. For the expedition see Walker, 'Hubert de Burgh and Wales', pp. 484-94.
152 *CR, 1227-31*, pp. 535, 565; *CR, 1231-34*, pp. 4, 7, 73, 182, 254.
153 *The Memoranda Roll of the King's Remembrancer for Michaelmas 1230 - Trinity 1231 (E 159.10)*, ed. Chalfant Robinson (Princeton, 1933), pp. 46-7.
154 See Vincent, *Peter des Roches*, pp. 259-309; Carpenter, 'Fall of Hubert de Burgh', pp. 1-17.
155 Vincent, *Peter des Roches*, pp. 372-5; Holden, *Lords*, p. 209.
156 See Chapter 4.
157 *Cal. Pat. Rolls, 1232-1247*, p. 73.
158 Vincent, *Peter des Roches*, pp. 371-5; Crooks, '"Divide and rule"', p. 292.
159 Otway-Ruthven, *Medieval Ireland*, pp. 96-7.
160 For a narrative of the rebellion see Vincent, *Peter des Roches*, pp. 399-428. For the march see Holden, *Lords*, pp. 207-14. For those who rebelled see R. F. Walker, 'The supporters of Richard Marshal, earl of Pembroke, in the rebellion of 1233-1234', *Welsh History Review*, 17 (1994-5), pp. 41-65. For a Marshal-centric account of the rebellion see David Crouch, 'Earl Gilbert Marshal and his mortal enemies', *Historical Research*, 87 (2014), forthcoming.
161 Vincent, *Peter des Roches*, pp. 334-9, 372.
162 'Quod firma pax sit', *CR, 1231-34*, p. 312.
163 Vincent, *Peter des Roches*, pp. 390-1; Morris, *Bigod*, pp. 10-11.
164 *Cal. Pat. Rolls, 1232-47*, p. 25; *CR, 1231-34*, p. 257.
165 *CR, 1231-34*, p. 265.
166 *Ibid.*, p. 352.
167 *Flores Historiarum*, iii, pp. 72-3.
168 Smith, 'Irish politics', p. 17 Cf. Orpen, *Normans*, iii, pp. 60-74.
169 Crooks, '"Divide and rule"', pp. 293-7.
170 *Ibid.*, p. 295, and see Chapter 4.
171 Vincent, *Peter des Roches*, p. 438.
172 *Cal. Pat. Rolls, 1232-1247*, p. 35; *CR, 1231-34*, pp. 351-2, 368, 376.
173 *Thirty-Fifth Report of the Deputy Keeper of the Public Records and Keeper of the State Papers in Ireland* (Dublin, 1903), pp. 35-6.
174 Crooks, '"Divide and rule"', p. 294.
175 Carpenter, 'Fall of Hubert de Burgh', pp. 57-8.
176 *Cal. Pat. Rolls, 1232-1247*, p. 73.
177 David Crouch, 'The last adventure of Richard Siward', *Morgannwg*, 35 (1991), pp. 7-30, at pp. 13-15.

178 Vincent, *Peter des Roches*, pp. 415-16; Walker, 'Supporters of Richard Marshal', p. 64.
179 'Tota Hibernia praeter illos de Lacy et eorum imprisos reddiderunt et subdiderunt [se] Gileberto Mariscallo, tum per treugas, tum de toto.' 'Annales de Theokesberia' in H. R. Luard (ed.), *Annales Monastici*, 5 vols (London, 1864-69), i, pp. 41-180, at p. 91, *s.a.* 1233.
180 Crouch, 'Earl Gilbert Marshal', provides one possible chronology.
181 'Annales de Dunstaplia', pp. 136-7, *s.a.* 1234.
182 *Flores Historiarum*, iii, p. 85.
183 *Cal. Pat. Rolls, 1232-1247*, p. 40.
184 *Flores Historiarum*, iii, pp. 80-1.
185 Orpen, *Normans*, iii, p. 63n.
186 Crouch, 'Earl Gilbert Marshal'.
187 'Marescallus comes de Penbroc ueniens in Hyberniam obsedit Limerick ciuitatem regis et reddita est ei', M. J. Colker, 'The "Margam Chronicle" in a Dublin Manuscript', *Haskins Society Journal*, 4 (1992), pp. 123-48, at pp. 139-40.
188 *Thirty-fifth Rep. Ireland*, p. 35; Orpen, *Normans*, iii, p. 71.
189 'Tunc Walterus de Laci et Hugo frater suus, proditor famosus plurimorum dominorum suorum, et plures alii castrum Marescalli quod dicitur Kildar obsederunt.' Colker, 'The "Margam Chronicle"', p. 140.
190 See Vincent, *Peter des Roches*, pp. 429-65.
191 Smith, 'Irish politics', p. 15.
192 *AC*, p. 234, *s.a.* 1234; *ALC*, i, p. 318, *s.a.* 1234; *AFM*, iii, pp. 270-2, *s.a.* 1234; *AU*, ii, pp. 292-4, *s.a.* 1234; *MCB*, p. 98, *s.a.* 1234; *AI*, p. 350, *s.a.* 1234; *Flores Historiarum*, iii, pp. 82-7; *Mathaei Parisiensis Chronica Majora*, iii, pp. 246-79; *Brut (RBH)*, p. 233, *s.a.* 1234.
193 *CR, 1231-34*, p. 428.
194 David Carpenter, 'Kings, magnates, and society: the personal rule of King Henry III, 1234-1258', *Speculum*, 60 (1985), pp. 39-70.
195 *Cal. Pat. Rolls, 1232-47*, p. 48.
196 Crouch, 'Earl Gilbert Marshal', which details the formal state of 'mortal enmity' Gilbert pursued against Maurice fitz Gerald.
197 *Cal. Pat. Rolls, 1232-47*. p. 73. Burgh granted Hugh de Lacy five cantreds in Connacht (which he received and subinfeudated). Orpen, *Normans*, iii, pp. 193-201.
198 *Cal. Pat. Rolls, 1232-1247*, p. 73.
199 *Ann. Clon.*, p. 234, *s.a.* 1234.
200 Smith, 'Irish politics', p. 19.
201 Also mentioned in his charter of liberties to Trim. *Chartae, Privilegia et Imunitates* (Dublin, 1829), p. 10.
202 HCA, no. 483; Bodleian Library MS Rawlinson B 329, fos 175r-v. Walter had previously granted the Lacy demesne manor of Yarkhill to Simon, see Chapter 8.
203 He had already granted William the manor of Wyck Rissington (Gloucestershire) for an annual rent of 20s and the service of two knights. Nicholas Vincent, *The Lucys of Charlecote: The Invention of a Warwickshire Family, 1170-1302* (Dugdale

Society Occasional Papers, 42, 2002), nos 13, 15 (pp.40-3). William had accompanied Walter to Ireland in December 1233. *Cal. Pat. Rolls, 1232-1247*, p.34.
204 Hillaby, 'Hereford gold: part 2', p.231.
205 *Irish Llanthony*, pp.214-15; *Gormanston Register*, 180-1; *The Coucher Book of Furness Abbey*, ed. J. C. Atkinson, 3 vols (Manchester, 1886-7), i, pp.18-20; *Registrum Cartarum Monasterii B. V. Mariae de Tristernagh in Commitatu Occidentalis Midiae*, eds M. V. Clarke, J. S. A. Macaulay and K M. E. Murray (Dublin, 1941), pp.67-8.
206 *Mathaei Parisiensis Chronica Majora*, iii, p.327.
207 Powicke, *Henry III and Lord Edward*, ii, pp.740-59.
208 See above, p.211.
209 Smith, 'Irish politics', p.16.
210 *Thirty-fifth Rep. Ireland*, pp.30-6; Orpen, *Normans*, iii, p.71.
211 Powicke, *Henry III and Lord Edward*, ii, pp.747-54.
212 Crouch, 'Earl Gilbert Marshal'.
213 An excellent account is Helen Nicholson, 'Margaret de Lacy and the Hospital of St John at Aconbury, Herefordshire', *Journal of Ecclesiastical History*, 50/4 (1999), pp.629-51.
214 James Ware, *De Hibernia & Antiquitatibus Ejus, Disquisitiones* (2nd edn, London, 1658) pp.194, 210; Aubrey Gwynn, and R. N. Hadcock, *Medieval religious Houses: Ireland* (London, 1970), pp.335, 337.
215 The entire dispute may be followed in the letters of Pope Gregory IX, *Les Registres de Grégoire IX*, ed. Lucien Auvray, 4 vols (Paris, 1896-1955), i, nos 1330, 1422, 2038; ii, nos 3103, 3123, 3780. Kathryn Hurlock suggests that Margery may have feared that the military order would become embroiled in warfare along the Welsh march. Kathryn Hurlock, *Britain, Ireland & the Crusades, c.1000-1300* (Basingstoke, 2013), p.157; Hurlock, *Wales and the Crusades, c.1095-1291* (Cardiff, 2011), pp.162-3.
216 'Ducta simplicitate ac exhortationibus fratrum Jerosolimitanorum Hospitalis inducta', *Registres Grégoire IX*, i, no. 1330.
217 Nicholson, 'Margaret de Lacy', pp.636-7.
218 *Ibid.*, p.637.
219 *Registres Grégoire IX*, i, no. 1422; Helen Nicholson, 'Margaret de Lacy', p.645.
220 *Registres Grégoire IX*, i, no. 2038; ii, no. 3103.
221 *Ibid.*, ii, nos 3103, 3780.
222 *Cal. Pap. Let.*, pp.165-6.
223 *CR 1237-42*, p.11.
224 *Cal. Pat. Rolls, 1232-47*.
225 *CR, 1237-42*, pp.122-3.
226 *Mathaei Parisiensis Chronica Majora*, iv, p.93.
227 *CR, 1237-42*, pp.226, 258.
228 *Ann. Clon.*, p.237, *s.a.* 1240.
229 *CFR 1240-41*, no. 230.
230 *CFR 1245-46*, nos 86-7.
231 See Otway-Ruthven, 'Partition of the de Verdon lands', pp.409-11.

232 *Ann. Clon.*, p. 237, s.a. 1241.
233 *ALC*, i, p. 354, s.a. 1241; *AC*, p. 74, s.a. 1241; *AFM*, iii, p. 302, s.a. 1241.
234 'Walterus de Lascey, vir inter omnes nobiles Hyberniae eminentissimus, post visus sui privationem et multas alias corporis sui afflictiones, ex hujus saeculi transiit incolatu.' *Mathaei Parisiensis Chronica Majora*, iv, p. 93.

III

Lordship

8

Lordship in four realms

The period covered by this book belongs to a formative age in the shaping of aristocratic lordship in north-western Europe. In the world of transnational landholding, the territorial portfolios of the greater barons could span any number of categories of lordship, from the long-established tenurial holdings in Normandy and lowland England to the colonial outposts of Ireland and Wales. Settled aristocrats could become colonial aristocrats, just by crossing a stretch of water. The Plantagenet empire of the late twelfth and early thirteenth centuries was a miscellany of varied realms with varying lordship structures. The king-centred hierarchy of authority in England contrasted with the pattern of lordship in other provinces, posing unique challenges to transnational aristocrats, not to mention those who study them. Hugh and Walter de Lacy did not deal with their lands in Herefordshire as they did those in Meath, where 'English' lordship had to be grafted on to pre-existing Celtic conditions, or even in Normandy, which had a pattern of lordship all its own. The preceding chapters have told the story of the Lacy family's experience of lordship as it unfolded over time, as both lords and vassals. The individual strands of their experience have been placed in their temporal and political contexts to better appreciate their place in the overall history of the period. But such a view risks obscuring the more subtle aspects of lordship amidst the pace of the narrative. Consequently, this chapter takes a broader view of Hugh and Walter de Lacy's exercise of lordship, examining its aspects thematically and comparatively.

The Lacys had a number of ways by which to control their surroundings, both intensively (through tenure and the control of courts) and by tribute (receiving acknowledgements of superior status from their neighbours); all of these can be characterised as dimensions of 'lordship'.

The methods used depended on the pre-existing social structures within each realm. Thus, while focusing on lordship in general, this chapter still remains sensitive to local variations. As aristocrats, one of the Lacys' means to enforce lordship was war. Whether as captains in royal armies, or through the conquest and defence of their own territories along the frontier, their military acumen was a key determinant of their wider success or failure. The growth of seigniorial households and affinities was in part a result of the increasing demands of medieval warfare, made more necessary for the Lacys by the collateral administration of their transmarine interests. The necessary personnel was supplied by the emerging knightly class whose members were also courted by the king of England. No study of aristocratic lordship in this period can ignore the impact of expanding royal lordship, the way that lords were themselves subject to a greater lordship than their own. Although the relationship with the king has been a recurrent theme in the preceding narrative, this chapter includes a more focused look at the competition between royal and aristocratic lordship for support from below. As has been seen, the Lacys often turned to each other for security. The place of the family in lordship, including marriage, filial piety and inheritance, rounds off this study. By anatomising the Lacys' experience, it is hoped that a better understanding of the nature of transnational lordship is achieved.

Local lordship

One of the essential aspects, perhaps *the* essential aspect, of medieval lordship was the ability of a lord to dominate his immediate surroundings. This was not limited to the acquisition of a compact group of tenurial holdings; pre-existing political geography could confound this ambition. Local lordship could also include, for instance, the effective control of local justice through the courts, an economy through rents, mills and markets, and defence through the custody of strategic castles and maintenance of a military household. An analysis of the Lacys' conduct across their scattered holdings reveals that the trajectory of power was moving away from armed intimidation towards more formalised mechanisms of dominance. None the less, it was still lordship. There is no evidence to suggest that Walter de Lacy was any less ruthless in exerting his power in 1234 than his father Hugh had been in 1166, or that Hugh had been less concerned for the common weal than his son. Great strides had been made towards formalising mechanisms of command, but lordship's overall character remained the same. What also emerges is that the basis of change was not time, cultural mores or political philosophy, but rather the particular imperatives of the region in question. Conquest was by its very nature based on violence and intimidation, and the speculative grant of the lordship of Meath in 1172 demanded that Hugh de Lacy forcibly subjugate or eject the native population before he could control the region. At the same time, Hugh worked to extend his authority in England and Normandy, but within the framework of local conditions. In England, for instance, where new land was in short supply and obligation was all-important, he attempted to deny the full service he owed the bishop of Hereford for land at Holme Lacy (Herefordshire).[1] In Normandy, where the revolt of 1173-4 had left its mark, Hugh was able to profit from the depressed finances of one of the main combatants, Count Robert II of Meulan, to purchase the honor of Le Pin-au-Haras for 200 *livres* Angevin.[2]

Recent research into English aristocratic endeavour has shown that it was evolving in this period, with an emphasis on overt intimidation slowly giving way to the exploitation of the legal system.[3] This was given added impetus for aristocratic lordship by the legal reforms of Henry II, and for royal lordship by the constraints of Magna Carta and its several reissues. The shift was evolutionary, not revolutionary. The grip of lordship simply adapted to new and altogether more efficient mechanisms of control and exploitation. Powerful lords retained the ability to dominate the localities, but this was increasingly achieved through control of the judicial process. That is not to say that English lordship was as inherently peaceful as the concise records of royal justice might lead us to believe. The legal process itself could be aggressive, and did not necessarily entice the king and aristocracy away from violence.

The use of distraint, or forcible dispossession of goods, remained a legally acceptable way for Anglo-Norman lords to coerce their non-compliant tenants.[4] Distraint was used to compel the performance of a service, with whatever had been seized always available for restoration, either by 'repleivin' (giving security) or by the performance of the disputed service. The act could be relatively violent, threatening the very livelihood of the tenant in question. One need only view the king's use of distraint against Walter de Lacy's father-in-law, William de Briouze, in 1208, or against Walter himself in the final years of his life, to get a clear indication of its devastating potential.[5] There is no explicit evidence for the Lacys' own use of distraint, but the potential was certainly there. In the 1166 *cartae baronum* returns, Hugh de Lacy reported three tenants whose service was in dispute. Elias de Sai acknowledged that he owed the service of three knights, while Hugh claimed he owed five. William de

Fourches admitted owing two knights, but disputed a third. Finally, Philip of Sarnesfield acknowledged owing half a fee, while Hugh demanded a full fee.[6] The normal venue for these disputes would have been Hugh's seigniorial court, with distraint not unlikely, and disseisin (to be discussed below) Hugh's prerogative should he win the case. Unfortunately, records of the Lacys' seigniorial courts do not exist, but Hugh's conflict with the bishop of Hereford listed in the *cartae baronum* return of 1166 involved similar themes.[7] That case was drawn out for over a decade until 3 June 1177, when its result was recorded on the final leaf of a psalter at Hereford Cathedral. As examined in Chapter 2, Hugh was brought in front of a great assembly as a recalcitrant tenant, and forced to acquiesce to the bishop's demands.[8]

More visible at the seigniorial level are acts of disseisin, or forced dispossession of lands. As with distraint, disseisin was a recognised step in medieval dispute resolution. It would have been the ultimate guarantor of decisions handed down by the lord in his honorial court. One of King Henry II's legal reforms was the stipulation that disseisin should only follow legal judgement, with the production of a swift legal remedy to unlawful disseisin, known as the assize of *nouvel disseisin*, supplying victims with recourse to royal courts.[9] Evidence for only three explicit cases of *nouvel disseisin* survives for the Lacys. The first and second were those brought in 1201 by Aubrey of Curtun, and in 1204 by Robert fitz Jordan for land in Meath, both of which were discussed in Chapter 4.[10] From 1172 to 1208 and 1216 to 1224, pleas of the Crown theoretically were tried by the Lacys in Meath,[11] but, as seen in Chapters 4 and 5, King John went to great lengths to detach the royal prerogatives from the great Irish lordships. Robert lost his suit, but his widow, Christiana, raised the matter again in 1225 – just after the Crown pleas were taken from the Lacys by the Irish justiciar.[12] In a third instance, William de Angulo took advantage of a period of Meath's sequestration (1210–15) to bring a claim against Walter. William fined 300 marks for seisin on two separate occasions, the first in 1213, just as Walter began negotiations for restoration of Meath, and the second in 1215, just as terms for that restoration were finally agreed.[13] In fact, every known plea over land involving the Lacys, excepting three cases of *mort d'ancestor*, concerned lands in Ireland.[14] The surviving evidence suggests that, as one might assume, the Lacys' lordship was more unsettled in Ireland than in England or Normandy. Such coercive actions may have been impracticable in the more peaceful and socially stable regions of the Lacys' patrimony. Conversely, in the late twelfth and early thirteenth centuries, Ireland was – for its conquerors – a new land, where a free-booting spirit still prevailed and where unifying social structures akin to those in England and Normandy had yet to be formed. More acts of disseisin no doubt were contested in the seigniorial court of Meath, especially as the first generation died out and Walter de Lacy was faced with tenants whom he and his father did not enfeoff. Much attention must be paid to the conditions on the periphery of the Lacys' lordship of Meath, but it also should be kept in mind that Meath's internal configuration required quite a bit of organisation.

Structures of lordship: Normandy and England

The ways in which a lord dominated – and expressed his dominance – depended on the structure of lordship in which they worked. For those possessing lands in more than one region, different approaches were often required. For instance, the character of Norman lordship was a far cry from that in Ireland in this period; nor was it of the English model. The duchy lacked the socio-political unity of England, and was consequently a land of fractional and in many cases localised lordship. While a mingling of landholdings was not uncommon in certain regions, lords generally possessed territorially compact fees, which allowed them to dominate their localities in ways which were rarer in England. This is not to say that Hugh and Walter de Lacy were all-powerful in their Norman lands. As in England and Ireland, aristocratic power in Normandy reached its apogee on the frontier, where it served as a protective buffer against neighbouring princes. In contrast to their positions in England, Wales and Ireland, the Lacys possessed no marcher component to their Norman holdings. The Lacys' lands fell roughly into areas of relatively strong ducal (and consequently weak aristocratic) lordship.[15] The Lacys' control of their immediate neighbourhoods would not have been as attenuated as in England, but neither were they as unrestrained as they were in Wales or Ireland.

The formation of the Lacys' English inheritance was handled ably by W. E. Wightman in his monograph on the family, but, owing to a relative paucity of evidence, the story in Normandy has been somewhat neglected. The discovery of a substantial Lacy estate in the Évreçin allows for a better, if not altogether complete, picture of their Norman interests to emerge.[16] As Gilbert de Lacy (d. c.1163) prepared to depart on crusade as a Knight Templar, he divided his inheritance among his three sons, giving Robert the larger English honor (held *in capite*), Amaury the fee in the Évreçin and Hugh the Welsh marcher lordship and (perhaps) the ancestral fee at Lassy and Campeaux. Such a division would have been in keeping with the Norman practice of partible inheritance, and was paralleled by the situation following the death of Hugh de Lacy in 1186. Hugh succeeded his brother Robert in England and Wales by about 1166, reuniting the family's English, Welsh and Norman patrimonies. However, the survival of Amaury's heir Gilbert meant that the Évreux interest was permanently alienated from the main line. The loss of the Évreux inheritance may have prompted Hugh de Lacy to purchase the honor of Le Pin-au-Haras from Count Simon's nephew, Count Robert of Meulan, before the end of 1175. In addition, the Lacys also acquired two knights' fees in Count Robert's honor of Pont-Audemer (Eure). Although the timing of their entry into Pont-Audemer is difficult to ascertain, a circuit of the Lacys' fees at Lassy and Campeaux, Le Pin-au-Haras (including the satellite fees at Azeville and Beuzeville) and Pont Audemer would have involved travelling over 250 miles and passing the important towns of Falaise (Calvados), Argentan (Orne), Sées (Orne), Orbec (Calvados), Lisieux (Calvados), Saint-Lô (Manche) and Caen (Calvados).

The chief mechanism for Norman magnate control of their territories was financial, with customary rents and milling ensuring the tenants' adherence to their lord.[17] Evidence for contemporary seigniorial taxation exists in an 1196 act of Roger Payne, one lord of the village of Le Bois-Gencelin (Eure) near Évreux. In it, Roger mentions '*his* new tallage', a significant development in this period.[18] Evidence of a different sort survives for the Lacys' financial lordship. As seen in Chapter 1, after acquiring the honor of Le Pin-au-Haras for 200 *livres*, Hugh de Lacy granted Durand du Pin the fee of Neauphe-sur-Dive (Orne).[19] The financial arrangements involved in the grant, which included rent and milling rights, ensured that Hugh would have a quick return on his financial outlay for Le Pin-au-Haras. The lucrativeness of the Norman system is further displayed in the yearly issues of (at least a portion of) Walter de Lacy's Norman territories, returned by a ducal custodian during a period of sequestration in 1198, which came to (in *livres* Angevin) 759l 8s 5d.[20] In English currency (worth roughly four times the Angevin) this would have been £189 17s 1d: a significant sum. Unfortunately, no direct comparison is possible for the Lacy lands in England, Wales or Ireland, because, although accounts exists for different periods of royal custodianship (quite detailed in the case of Ireland),[21] the amounts rendered were generally for the farm (which was a set, and not necessarily representative, sum), rather than the issues (which were the actual profits) of the honors.

Only one lay grant in England survives for Hugh de Lacy, that of lands in Wootton and Onibury (Shropshire) to William of Wootton, which, though based on knight's service, also addresses the financial aspect of contemporary lordship. William was to hold both manors by the service of half a knight in the army or castle guard, but was to pay the equivalent of three-quarters of a knight if Hugh levied an aid on his knights.[22] This is likely the 'knight William' mentioned in the 1177 Hereford dispute discussed above, who Hugh claimed should pay the 20s rent for Onibury at Hereford each year. Many of the new lay enfeoffments made by Walter de Lacy and his son Gilbert were small, for fixed rents.[23] Only three surviving grants utilised knights' service, though more may have been made.[24] The largest, Walter's grant of Wyck Rissington (Gloucestershire) c.1227 to William de Lucy, was for two knights' fees and 20s.[25] This is the only such surviving grant by Walter. As discussed in Chapter 7, Walter's son, Gilbert, made two grants involving knights' service after taking over a large proportion of the Lacy inheritance before 1230, but both were in special circumstances. Gilbert's grant of a single knight's fee at Stanton Lacy to Stephen d'Évreux was in order to entice Stephen to his affinity. This will be discussed in further detail below, but Stephen's service was clearly worth having.[26] Gilbert's second grant, for the service of a quarter knight, provided for his illegitimate son, Robert de Lacy, born to Imena, daughter of Stephen of Oakley (*Acley*).[27] Also pertinent is Walter's designation of the manor of Mansel Lacy (Herefordshire) as the *maritagium* of his daughter Katharine upon her marriage to Walter of Clifford. Even though no service was due from a *maritagium* until the third generation, Walter stipulated the terms on which the manor would eventually be held.[28] This reinforces the importance of military tenure in English lordship, which, whatever its increasingly financial character, still revolved around the knight's fee. In Ireland, existing evidence for lay grants indicates that they were almost exclusively based on knight's service.[29]

The geographically concentrated fees in Normandy helped increase the power of aristocratic lordship in the localities, which partly explains the magnates' desire to export the model to their new lands in England, but they also constrained that power geographically. What is more, 'in contrast to England, Maine, Anjou, and Aquitaine, the greatest landed power in Normandy belonged to dynasties whose main interests lay outside the province; amongst the Plantagenet dominions, only in Ireland and Brittany did the leading noble families have comparable external interests'.[30] Transnational though they may have been, Anglo-Norman lords such as Hugh de Lacy still tended to identify strongly with Normandy, their homeland. The importance of Normandy is highlighted for the Lacys, as with others, in their active interest in acquiring further estates in the duchy. By acquiring lands across the duchy, Hugh was able to buck the regionalised trend in Norman lordship, allowing him greater freedom of action within Normandy and a stronger voice at the ducal court. His actions in the duchy also ran counter to the trend of regionalisation in the Anglo-Norman nobility, which had begun in the wars of succession which divided England and Normandy following the death of William the Conqueror (1087), but which gained new impetus in the unification of the Anglo-Norman realm under Henry II.[31] Instead of divesting his Norman interests in order to focus on England and the Welsh march, or vice versa, Hugh expanded on all fronts. His purchase of Le Pin-au-Haras came shortly after he had been given a speculative grant of the vast lordship of Meath in Ireland. His promotion of the abbey of Saint-Taurin d'Évreux in Ireland (continued by his son, Walter) preserved the Lacys' connection with Normandy even after King John lost the duchy to King Philip in 1204.[32] Despite his new western acquisition, or perhaps because of it, Hugh de Lacy reasserted his status as a *Norman* aristocrat.

Yet upon Hugh's death in 1186, much of his work was undone by the Norman custom of partible inheritance. In contrast to his holdings in Ireland and Britain, which descended intact to his eldest son Walter, Hugh's Norman lands appear to have been divided among three of his sons. Walter held the Pont Audemer sub-tenancy in 1204, but this may have been his only stake in the duchy once each of his brothers came of age. From Walter's 1189 grant to Durand du Pin, it appears that the honor of Le Pin-au-Haras may have been held by Walter's elder brother Robert before Walter's succession. Le Pin-au-Haras was not long in Walter's hands, however, because it was used to provide for his younger brother Hugh.[33] Hugh the younger's marriage between 1194 and 1199 to Lescelina de Verdon is particularly interesting in this light. Although the Verdons held lands neighbouring the Lacys in Ireland, Hugh's in-laws were also active in the Évreçin, with Lescelina's brother Thomas enjoying money fief in the honor of Évreux.[34] Hugh's marriage formed a link between the family's ancestral association with Évreux and its newest endeavour in Ireland. The family's patrimony at Lassy and Campeaux was passed on to a third brother, Gilbert de Lacy, who contested lands there in the ducal court.[35] Although it is possible that Walter, Hugh and Gilbert de Lacy fostered a close political identity across their separate Norman holdings (as Walter, Hugh and their half-brother William were to do in Ireland), the partition of the Lacys' Norman lands would have circumscribed Walter's political power there. Nevertheless, Walter utilised his transnational holdings to reinforce a connection with Normandy. Just as the elder Hugh de

Lacy had patronised the abbey of Saint-Taurin d'Évreux in Ireland, so in the reign of King John Walter de Lacy granted the Norman abbey of Beaubec (Seine-Maritime) land just south of Drogheda at Kilkieran (Co. Meath).[36] Such religious patronage was a clear manifestation of transnational lordship.

Structure of lordship: Ireland

If the Lacys' lordship was constrained in England and Normandy, it found room for rapid expansion in Ireland. Being one of the most important socio-political units in Plantagenet Ireland, Meath is also extremely well documented when compared to the other Lacy interests east of the Irish Sea. Because the Lacy lordship of Meath was founded by Hugh de Lacy in 1172 and dismantled after the death of his son Walter in 1241, it presents an opportunity to witness the entire life-cycle of a seigniorial lordship.

The territorial boundaries of Meath were at least loosely derived from an Irish exemplar, the ancient kingdom of Mide, and historians have debated whether more than mere geography was meant when Henry II granted the territory to Hugh de Lacy 'as Murchad Ua Máel Sechlainn had held it' (*sicuti Murcardus Ha Mulachlyn melius eam tenuit*).[37] Current opinion has moved away from the idea of Hugh de Lacy inheriting the powers of Irish kingship through the grant, due mostly to the disparity between the contemporary weakness of the Uí Máel Sechlainn (who long since had been sidelined in their own province) and the far greater power wielded by the Lacys in their new lordship.[38] This opinion notwithstanding, there is evidence to suggest that the Lacys played the part of Irish provincial kings to the Irish in their lordship and on the frontiers of colonisation.

The role and nature of Irish provincial kingship had evolved in the years preceding the English invasion.[39] While initially confined in their direct rule to their own *tuatha*, or petty kingdoms, the strong provincial kings who emerged in the years following the battle of Clontarf (1014) exercised increasingly intrusive powers over their sub-kingdoms. By the late eleventh century, tactics such as the partition of kingdoms, expulsion of ruling dynasties and setting up of puppet kings were being utilised by powerful provincial kings to extend their influence throughout Ireland. That said, the Irish model of power was still largely dependent upon dynastic overlordship; expressions of direct lordship beyond one's own *tuath* remained the exception rather than the rule. This highlights the basic distinction to be drawn between intensive lordship, involving a lord and his tenants, and tributary lordship, which bound together large swathes of society in the 'Celtic' regions of Britain and Ireland. Ireland may have been heading towards lordship on the European model, but it still had far to go in 1172. Famously, the attempts by Diarmait Mac Murchada, king of Leinster, to institute a more European system on the provincial scale were disastrous.[40]

A Lacy 'kingdom' of Mide in the Irish sense, had one been possible, would have been a less powerful entity than the lordship of Meath proved to be. It was for this reason that Robin Frame described as 'implausible' any attempt to view Murchad Ua Máel Sechlainn as Hugh's legal *antecessor*. It could be added that the Uí Máel Sechlainn continued to view themselves as kings of Meath, in theory if not in practice.[41] However, Frame allowed that, whatever was meant by the grant, Henry's use of Murchad's lordship over Mide as the exemplar for Hugh's lordship symbolised Hugh's engagement with native Irish leaders.[42] The Irish model of lordship (based on tribute) was born of the particular circumstances in Ireland, and, as such, it recommended itself for the extension of the Lacys' authority beyond Meath's settled core. It allowed the lord of Meath to impose his will upon his neighbours in regions that lacked an advanced agrarian socio-economic structure. The Lacys formed a marriage alliance with the powerful king of Connacht, exacted tribute in cattle, and played kingmakers in their neighbouring territories. In this way, their 'Irish' lordship was the embodiment of aggressive French lordship as expressed in Chrétien de Troyes's contemporary *Erec et Enide*: 'I'm very rich and powerful, for in this land there's no lord whose lands border mine who goes against my authority and does not do everything I wish. I have no neighbour who does not fear me, however proud and confident he may be.'[43] But there was more to the use of Murchad Ua Máel Sechlainn in the grant of Meath than Hugh's relations with neighbouring kings. In 1175, the Treaty of Windsor stipulated that those Irish returning to their lands were to hold as they had under their former (i.e. Irish) lords, or pay tribute. No mention was made of conforming to a new model of imported lordship. Hugh's marriage to Murchad's (likely) granddaughter in about 1180 even established a direct family connection between Hugh and his Ua Máel Sechlainn predecessor. In this light, it is increasingly difficult to see Murchad Ua Máel Sechlainn as anything other than Hugh de Lacy's legal *antecessor* in Meath, at least with regard to the Irish.

At his death, Murchad Ua Máel Sechlainn was said to have been 'King of Tara (*Teamhair*) and Meath, with its dependent districts, of Airgialla, and, for a time, of the greater part of Leinster'. Whether or not this was obituarial flattery (and the title 'king of Tara', evoking the high kingship, certainly was), Murchad at least exerted some influence over the north Leinster kingdoms of Uí Fáeláin and Uí Failge. Moreover, a later king of Meath, Diarmait Ua Máel Sechlainn, was also called king of Dublin, Uí Fáeláin and Uí Failge at his death in 1169.[44] The status of these territories at the time of Hugh de Lacy's grant of Meath is unclear, though their separate character seems to have been acknowledged by the English king. It therefore may not be a coincidence that Uí Fáeláin and Uí Failge were among the territories whose custody was given to Hugh de Lacy in 1177 after Strongbow's death.[45] While royal patronage thus extended Hugh's influence beyond Meath's southern frontier, his own endeavour took it north and west. At his death in 1186, the annals of Loch Cé describe Hugh as 'king of Meath, and Bréifne, and Airgialla',[46] an indication of the extent of his hegemony. By 1210, Walter de Lacy was receiving a tribute in cattle from the Ua Ruairc king of Bréifne, and had imprisoned the neighbouring Irish king, Ua Ragallaig.[47] This tributary arrangement suited Walter until 1219, when Domnall Mór Ua Domnaill, king of Tír Conaill, forced the two main families of Bréifne to renounce their allegiance to the Lacys.[48] Walter immediately abandoned tributary lordship in Bréifne, which, as this proved, could be transitory, in favour of intensive lordship. Walter made two speculative grants in Bréifne, displacing its native dynasties just as the he and his father had displaced the Ua Máel Sechlainn in Meath.[49]

Hugh de Lacy's systematic approach to realising his grant of Meath included an aggressive mix of subinfeudation and encastellation, which in the process by which he did it made him one of the most effective agents of English conquest in Ireland. However, extra-judicial compulsion was merely one of the means by which Hugh sought to establish his lordship in Meath; it was not the defining characteristic of that lordship. The Lacys' move from violent coercion to peaceful coexistence in Ireland was reminiscent of the process in England, but on a drastically truncated timeline. The picture that emerges is one of overt violence between native and newcomer on the frontier and (relatively) peaceful coexistence in the settled core. The Lacys already addressed their faithful men 'whether French, English or Welsh'[50] in charters granted in their marcher lordship of Ewyas Lacy, and soon brought the practice to Ireland, a common form being to all their faithful men, 'French, English or Irish'.[51] This distinctive form of address made an early appearance among the settlers in Ireland, but had disappeared by the end of the thirteenth century, when the Irish were increasingly classed as 'the enemy'.[52] The native Irish loyal to the Lacys were recognised as participants in the lordship of Meath. None the less, the distinction between the natives and colonists within Meath was emphasised through the application of two separate strains of judicial lordship, necessitated by the denial of English law to the vast majority of the native Irish. However, while separate was not equal, neither was it necessarily discriminatory in the modern sense. Hugh de Lacy's marriage to the daughter of the king of Connacht, and the prominent role later played in Meath's administration by the issue of that marriage, William 'Gorm' de Lacy, is testament to the fact that notions of English cultural superiority expressed by writers such as Gerald of Wales and William of Newburgh were not necessarily universally held, or applicable.[53]

It would be naive to suggest that this comparatively inclusive environment in terms of culture was the product of altruism or of some modern notion of ethnic equality; it, like so many other frontier arrangements, was based on pragmatism. The violent progress of conquest had forced many of the Irish to flee the disputed territories. However, the English barons' new lordships were useless without the hands to work them, and, lacking an imported labour force commensurate with the displaced population, they were faced with the task of repopulating their lands locally. The Treaty of Windsor, which in 1175 sought to achieve a *modus vivendi* between Henry II and the Irish high king, Ruaidrí Ua Conchobair, addressed this problem directly. As mentioned above, it stated that the Irish who had fled were to be allowed to return to the lands of the English barons, either paying tribute or performing to the barons the service that they had previously performed for their lands (whichever their new lords preferred). More to the point, if any baron requested that his lands be repopulated in this way, and any of the Irish refused his invitation, then Ruaidrí was to compel the Irish to return so that they might live there in peace.[54] Hugh de Lacy was particularly successful in establishing bonds of lordship with the native Irish in Meath and, from 1177, was able to apply his policy more broadly as royal representative in Ireland.

Meath presented the Lacys with opportunity to monopolise the legitimate use of physical force within their borders. Henry II's grant of Meath stipulated that Hugh and his heirs were to control the judicial process within Meath, including pleas of the Crown.[55] With secular authority concentrated in their hands, they moved to wed it to the ecclesiastical authority of a single bishop within their lordship.[56] When the Irish kingdom of Mide was granted to Hugh de Lacy in 1172, its territory was covered by at least three bishops, those of Clonard, Kells and Duleek. Some pre-conquest bishops, such as Ua Dúnáin, styled 'bishop of Mide' in a 1096 letter to Archbishop Anselm of Canterbury, had been able to exert superior ecclesiastical authority over their rival bishops in the territory of the kings of Mide, but there was no 'diocese of Mide'.[57] Once Hugh de Lacy established his lordship of Meath, Eugenius, bishop of Clonard, quickly began a process of actually suppressing the other sees, and establishing his own diocese as being co-terminous with the Lacy lordship. In 1177, he appears in the foundation charter of St Thomas's Dublin as 'bishop of Meath', his first use of title. This was also the year in which Hugh de Lacy took a renewed interest in Meath, and began a period of long residency in the lordship. By 1190, both Kells and Duleek had been absorbed by Clonard, and the following year an 'archdeacon of Meath' appeared. The process of unification was completed in 1204, when the new colonial bishop of Meath, Simon de Rochfort, moved his episcopal seat from Clonard to the Lacys' *caput*, Trim. Henceforth secular and ecclesiastical power were concentrated in, and radiated from, the same location.[58]

The Lacys created boroughs to promote trade and encourage settlement on the frontier. A list of these creations survives in Walter's grant to his Grandmontine foundation of St Mary's Priory, Craswall (Herefordshire), issued when he was sheriff of Herefordshire (see Figure 8.1 and Appendix 3).[59] By that point, the Lacys' Irish boroughs included Trim, Kells, Duleek, Fore, *Loxmethi* (?), Lough Sewdy, Ardnurcher, Incheleffer (Co. Longford) and *Adlech* (?). The same source also lists the Lacys' demesne manors: *Lohleythi* (Loch Ennell: Dysart, Co. Westmeath?), Coolock (Co. Dublin), Ardmulchan (bar. Skreen, Co. Meath), Donacarney, (bar. Duleek Lower, Co. Meath), *Moygarthan* (Muinter Gearadain, east of Loch Gowna, Co. Longford?), and *Fachlet* (?). The rest of Meath was subinfeudated, a process which is recorded in the near-contemporary *Song of Dermot and the Earl*.[60] The pattern that emerges indicates Hugh de Lacy's strategy for the conquest of Meath. Hugh divided the endowments of his more powerful tenants, giving them lands in the relatively peaceful east from which they could draw almost immediate revenue and lands in the unsettled west into which they sought to push the boundaries of colonial rule.

One instance of a geographically divided grant involved William le Petit. As discussed in Chapter 2, Hugh granted William Dunboyne and Rathkenny, and lands in the baronies of Magheradernon and Shrule to provide for his service. Dunboyne and Rathkenny were both situated in the east of the lordship of Meath, while Magheradernon and the lands in Shrule were in the west. William's service (one knight for every thirty carucates) was to be performed at Hugh de Lacy's seigniorial castle of Killare, which was at the westernmost frontier of Hugh's effective lordship.[61] Similarly, Hugh granted Thomas de Craville Emlagh (bar. Lower Kells,

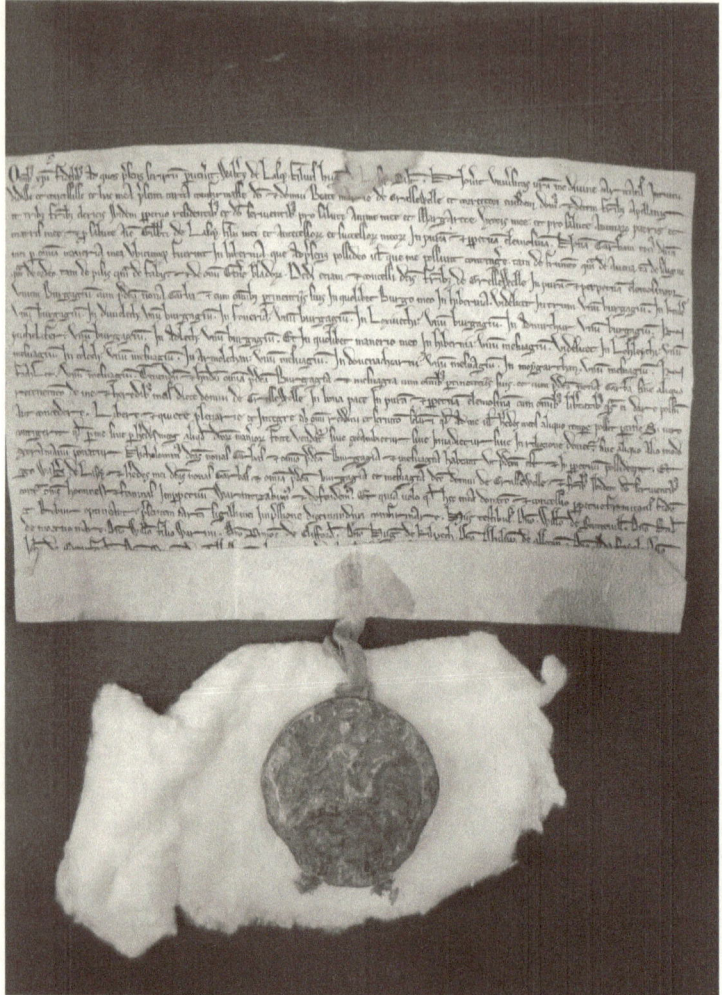

Figure 8.1 Walter de Lacy's charter to Craswall Priory (Herefordshire)

Co. Meath) in the east, and Laragh and Shanonagh (bar. Moygoish, Co. Westmeath) in the west. The division of grants made Hugh's principal feudatories as anxious as Hugh himself to gain effective control of the whole lordship of Meath. It also kept their power relative to his own constant. They could efficiently exploit their western lands only when the frontier of his control was pushed past them, and stood to lose their peaceful eastern lands if they overstepped their authority on the western frontier. This corresponds well with emerging English royal practice, which tended to make speculative grants on the frontier to men, such as Hugh, who already held of the king in more settled regions. In addition to providing the resources for conquest, the Lacys' lands in England and Normandy maintained their connection to the English king, who could call upon their service (or take action against them) in four of his own dominions.

Lordship and war

The subjugation of Meath satisfied the Lacys' aristocratic drive for war and conquest. From its seventh-century origins, the western European aristocracy cultivated the self-image of a warrior caste, manifested by this time, for instance, in its equestrian seals and imposing castles.[62] In the late twelfth and early thirteenth centuries this conception was closer to the reality of their lifestyle than it was later to become, yet the warrior identity was (and remained) even more appropriate for those on the frontier. This disjunction between image and reality was recognised by contemporaries. By the late twelfth century there was a belief amongst continental aristocrats and their commentators that the English aristocracy had grown ineffectual at arms through relative peace and stability, a perception clearly seen in the works of Jordan Fantosme and the biography of William Marshal. For instance, in 1174, Fantosme has the Norman countess of Leicester, Petronilla de Grandmesnil, say: 'the English are great boasters, but poor fighters; they are better at quaffing great tankards and guzzling'.[63] Whether or not this was true for the English aristocracy in general, it was certainly not the case for the marcher lords, whose very existence depended on their military acumen. In England and Normandy, the Lacys adorned themselves with the same symbolic trappings of military might as their fellow aristocrats, yet, in Ireland and (to a lesser extent) Wales, the Lacys *were* warlords. They parleyed with native kings, exacted tribute in cattle, mounted hostings and punitive raids, and took hostages. Just as significantly, they also suffered reversals in their campaigns, and were forced to retreat to the safety of their castles. The challenges of frontier lordship were a far cry from those of more settled regions, and the Lacys had to adapt their approach to suit each circumstance.

The difference between waging war in the Anglo-French 'core' and the Celtic 'periphery' was down to more than mere topography, though this played its part. More than anything else, the socio-economic structure of these regions dictated the nature of warfare.[64] Immediately preceding this period, England, Normandy and much of Western Europe witnessed the formation of a self-conscious knightly class, which developed a '*notitia contuuernii*' (fellowship of arms) and adhered to an unwritten body of custom regulating the conduct of war based on mutual respect.[65] One of the reasons that this was possible was the primacy of land in the socio-economic, and therefore military, life of western Europe. To a society based on the cultivation of crops, the holding or destruction of an enemy's lands was a viable means to achieve victory. Ravaging and burning the countryside were the essential ingredients of 'chivalrous' warfare, which allowed it to safeguard the lives of knights and non-combatants (if not their livelihoods).

Such preservation of life was not a luxury enjoyed by the Celtic societies of Britain and Ireland. Although the quaint image of the Irish and Welsh as pure pastoralists was dispelled long ago,[66] wealth was still based largely on movable commodities: livestock and men. Therefore, while the English and French attacked land and tried to limit deaths in battle to common foot soldiers and (especially) archers,[67] the Irish and Welsh engaged in hostings, part cattle raids, part slave hunts. As in England and France, this asserted the dominance of one king or lord over another by depriving the target of their most important economic assets. In Ireland and Wales, most battles were fought on the return trip, as the raiders were weighed down with booty. The slowest of the captives, the old, young and infirm could consequently be slaughtered to aid escape. Gerald of Wales observes:

> In France men choose the open plains for their battles, but in Ireland and Wales rough, wooded country; there heavy armour is a mark of distinction, here it is only a burden; there victory is won by standing firm, here by mobility; there knights are taken prisoner, here they are beheaded; there they are ransomed, here they are butchered.[68]

This level of violence was an abomination to European commentators, but was predicated upon the socio-economic base of Celtic society. It was even observed by William of Newburgh to have paralleled that of the similarly fragmented Anglo-Saxon England.[69] So it transpired that when the English won their famous victory in Ireland at Baginbun (Co. Waterford), they eschewed chivalry and slaughtered their captives.[70] When entering Ireland, the English decided to fight on Celtic terms, because those were the only terms on which they could win.

Having adapted to a philosophy of warfare based on the Celtic model, the English colonists were quick to import their own military technology. Castle-based lordship was imported from England and Normandy, where it had become fiscal, and proved to be devastatingly effective in the Celtic context. *Castellaria*, in which land was granted out for military service provided at specific castles, survived along England's border with Wales in this period, where the threat of attack demanded a swift and local response.[71] In Ireland, they were introduced from the initial invasion, as is clear from Hugh de Lacy's stipulation (mentioned above) that William le Petit perform his knights' service at Hugh's castle of Killare.[72] Hugh de Lacy was a renowned castle builder who so changed the topography of his lordship of Meath that upon his death an Irish annalist remarked, 'Mide, from the Shannon to the sea, was full of [his] castles and of [his] Foreigners'.[73] Castles were too strong to be quickly reduced by raiding parties, and provided useful vantage points from which to observe and launch counterattacks on the attackers' retreat. By this period, the Lacys' castles on the Welsh border and in the March were largely defensive.[74] In Ireland, castles had an offensive character, dominating the landscape and carrying the constant threat of a rapid strike from the English forces within.

Those colonial forces were (initially) much better equipped than their Welsh and Irish opponents, carrying state-of-the-art arms and armament. The ability to produce large quantities of metal armour for their troops, and arrowheads for their archers, gave the colonists the advantage.[75] So did the longbow, which meant that English archers could rain down salvo after salvo upon the Welsh or Irish, without being touched by opposing missiles. Although the Welsh and Irish were inevitably able to acquire the trappings of the English war machine, from the battlefield or otherwise,[76] this gap remained at the production end. So it was that, in 1260, an Irish poet could still depict (perhaps a bit too figuratively) the 'uneven combat' between the Irish in their 'shirts of thin satin' and the English who were 'a single phalanx of iron'.[77] If this is unlikely to be a wholly accurate description of the mid-thirteenth-century combatants, it is at least testament to the accustomed disparity between the two military traditions on the island.

The Lacys may have had the advantage of superior military supply, but they still had to get everything to the battlefield. It is important to remember that the logistical difficulties in mounting different types of campaign, whether simple issues of armament or larger concerns regarding supply chains and tactical deployment, had to be handled by the Lacys and their administrators. This was not simply the generic 'Anglo-Norman aristocracy' fighting on so many fronts: this was one family. Mobilising seigniorial resources for war included recruiting men, finding horses, assembling arms and arranging supplies. Even war's aftermath required a high level of organisation, including the payment of compensation in the form of money for wages, horses lost, commandeered goods and ransoms.[78] Unfortunately, detailed accounts do not survive for Hugh and Walter de Lacy, though some evidence sheds light on their operations. In a grant to Ralph de Tosny made between 1233 and 1236, Walter mentioned that his knights and free tenants of the honor of Weobley were summoned for service by one Simon of Weston.[79] He also mentioned the summons pertaining to the castle of Weobley in a charter to Craswall Priory.[80] In addition to mechanisms for the mobilisation of troops, there were arrangements for their provision. According to a 1285 inquisition held before one of Walter's successors, Geoffrey de Geneville, at Trim:

> Walter de Lacy, every time he needed corn, or was in the marches or elsewhere, was accustomed to take corn of abbots, priors, and other religious persons, priests, clerks, and sellers of tithes, saving their reasonable sustenance, at all time of the year when it pleased him and he needed it, and to value that corn by oath of good men, according to what it was worth on the day when he took it, and to pay the price at a set day to him from whom he took the corn. So he was accustomed to take from them, great horses, palfreys, and other horses, oxen and cows, by price aforesaid.[81]

Another judgement before Geoffrey *c.*1290 detailed the customs in Meath for the aftermath of war, which gives some indication of the arrangements the Lacys may have made:

> [The jurors] ... say that they who are maintained in all things upon the cost of the lord, if they take horses or other animals, that the lord ought to have half, and they who are upon his cost have the other half, unless it shall be that they overthrow anyone from his horse by stroke of lance. And if they overthrow anyone by stroke of lance, then he shall have all those horses from which they shall have thrown the knights. And if they take prisoners, all prisoners shall remain to the lord. And if the lord or his seneschal shall be there present, then they shall have nothing, unless the lord will to give it of grace.

A list of services, including the required armament according to the value of a man's holding, then followed.[82] The ability quickly to adapt and redeploy their resources, often across the sea, was a vital component of the success or failure of the Lacys' military endeavours.

Success in war was important for more than the immediate cause of strife, it was also a way to forge an effective relationship with the king. The

Lacys' military service was their main connection to the king, and successful service ameliorated all manner of trouble. The most obvious manifestation of this relationship was the grant of Meath, which was prompted by Henry II's appreciation of Hugh de Lacy's military endeavour. Although Gerald of Wales claims that Hugh 'was not a success as a general, for he often suffered heavy losses on his expeditions',[83] what successes he had prompted Henry to make Hugh a royal representative on a number of occasions. His worth was proved in the revolt of 1173-4 through his vital defence of the Norman town of Verneuil-sur-Avre, besieged by King Louis of France.[84] Hugh's value to the conquest of Ireland was widely recognised – one Irish annalist claimed that 'it was he who won all Ireland for the Foreigners'[85] – and this made him too important to be disciplined seriously as he increasingly overstepped the bounds of lordship.

Walter de Lacy's military activities were even more important to his relationship with the Crown.[86] His service on behalf of King Richard from 1194 to 1195 led Richard to secure Walter's position in Ireland against the aggression of John, lord of Ireland. Following a period of sequestration and exile brought on by an attempted conspiracy with King Philip Augustus of France, Walter was forced to prove his loyalty on the Poitevin campaign of 1214 before his inheritance was returned. His efforts during the Magna Carta civil war 1215-17 were then rewarded with a grant of the shrievalty and castle of Hereford, which made him virtual military governor of his home county. Walter's service on Henry III's 1230 continental expedition likely influenced the king's decision to return to Walter the lands demised to his son Gilbert upon Gilbert's death that same year (rather than hold them in wardship with Gilbert's underage son, Walter). Four years later, in 1234, Walter and his allies were rewarded for their part in the bloody end of Richard Marshal's rebellion with a free hand in Ireland. Hugh and Walter de Lacy fought for the English Crown in France, England, Wales and Ireland, facing opponents who included local Celtic rulers, English rebel barons, and the king of France himself. War was their business, and business was good.

Lordship, affinity and household

The conduct of war in multiple theatres was just one of a number of logistical headaches faced by transnational aristocrats, all of which strained their administrations. It is no coincidence that the only lords to maintain lands successfully in more than one region were those wealthy enough to employ regional administrations set up to govern in their absence.[87]

This period also witnessed the growth and increased specialisation of the seigniorial household, which travelled with the lord and provided, among other things, a standing military force and ready source of counsel. This was the heart of the aristocratic enterprise, and the basis of a magnate's power. By this period, a magnate's household might be drawn largely from men outside his tenurial base. This involved the construction of affinities, or households knights attracted to a lord, not so much by traditional bonds of tenure, but by office, salaries, money-fiefs or the hope of future patronage. The knights thus retained were an expensive luxury, because their bed, board, equipment and wages all had to be met by their lord. A lord's tenants still played their part, but, increasingly, were more important for the money that could be squeezed from them through scutage, fines or aids than for their personal military service.

In 1166, Hugh de Lacy provided a list of his retinue in his *cartae baronum* return: Richard le Bret, Ralph de Riqueot, Adam de Feipo, Anketil and William de Escotot, the son of Gerard de Macgne, Roger de Escorchebeuf and one Bartholomaeus. Of the eight men, who held for no fixed service, Hugh reported 'some reside with me and I find their necessities. And some are in my castles (*domus*) in Wales and I find their necessities.'[88] No such statement exists for Walter de Lacy, though Walter's grant to Furness Abbey about 9 April 1234, comes close.[89] As explained in Chapter 7, the witness list names four of Walter's retained knights ('*milites mei*'), Richard and John of Copeland, Walter le Petit and Robert of Leyburn; his chaplain, Hugh, canon of Llanthony; his seneschal, Nicholas d'Évreux; his chamberlain, Paul le Cornwalays; his clerks, Richard and William; the steward (*procurator*) of his demesne manor of Donacarney (Co. Meath), Walter le Dispenser; and his servants, John of Clifford and Philip de Wichetot. It also mentions, but does not name, his foresters and rabbit warrens (which imply warreners) at Trim.[90] Such a find is exceptional. Four months later, several of these men, without their titles or descriptions, joined Walter's chancellor (*cancellarius mei*), Brother Hugh of Stanton, in the witness list of another of Walter's grants at Trim.[91] That Walter de Lacy employed a chancellor in his household is exceptional. In this period, only the greatest earls and bishops employed chancellors. It has been suggested that lay magnates attached chancellors to their households as 'an expression of comital prestige'.[92] Walter de Lacy's employment of a chancellor highlights the sophistication of his transnational administration. The Lacys employed officials to ease the administrative burden from an early point and, while those identifiable are listed in Table 4 (Appendix 2), there were surely many more. However, these two grants show the increased specialisation of the seigniorial household which was a characteristic of the second quarter of the thirteenth century.

Several appointments are worth further elaboration, because they reveal something of the texture of the Lacys' lordship. From the late 1220s, Walter de Lacy began to step back from public life. As discussed in Chapter 7, he demised the majority (if not all) of his lands in England, Wales and Ireland to his son Gilbert. In this, he followed the example of his father-in-law, William de Briouze, who had done the same for his son William in the early 1200s.[93] Gilbert's death in 1230 forced Walter to shoulder the full burden of lordship once more, a burden he sought to ease by appointing stewards to oversee his vast inheritance. The case of Walter's seneschal *c*.1231, Simon of Clifford,[94] is particularly interesting. Simon was a junior member of a marcher family whose principal allegiance was to the great Anglo-Norman house of Tosny, lords of Clifford and Flamstead in England. Walter de Lacy actively courted the family, and was successful in forging strong ties with several of its members. Simon's brother, Walter of Clifford (d. 1263), worked closely with Walter de Lacy in Herefordshire and the Welsh march, sharing a number of royal commissions and eventually marrying Walter's daughter Katharine.[95] One Giles of Clifford was also prior of Walter de Lacy's monastic foundation at Craswall.[96] Just as interesting are the arrangements made between Simon of Clifford and Walter de Lacy, discussed in Chapter 7, which aided Simon's commission as Walter's seneschal. Before May 1234, Simon exchanged his manor of Yarkhill for an annual rent of £30, still owing the service of one and a half knights. The rent was split, with £15 drawn from the manor of Holme Lacy (Herefordshire) and £15 from Hayestown (Co. Meath).[97] Yarkhill likely had been granted to Simon by Walter previously, because it was one of the Lacy demesne manors confirmed to Walter's father Hugh in a lost charter of Henry II,[98] so this was in part a way of returning the manor to demesne. However, this exchange also freed Simon from the burden of managing such a large estate, and allowed him to carry out his duties in Walter's itinerant household, whether in England, Wales or Ireland.

Walter's arrangements for the administration of his English lands are also worth mentioning. Philip de Colleville was Walter's 'steward in England' on 12 June 1234.[99] As steward, Philip seems to have been based at Ludlow, where he received and imprisoned a royal hostage. Ludlow was an obvious choice, because, besides being the centre of a large cluster of Lacy lands and a significant castle in its own right, it was also on the road between the Lacys' English *caput* of Weobley and the port of Chester, which had a thriving trade with the Lacys' Irish port of Drogheda, and was the preferred point of embarkation for Meath.[100] Walter de Lacy maintained his own fleet, which would have greatly increased his economic as well as political power in the Irish Sea region, facilitating swift, independent movement and communication between his territories.[101] Any letter from his Irish court at Trim would have travelled down the river Boyne to Drogheda and from there across the Irish Sea to Chester. Ludlow was therefore the fulcrum of the Lacy inheritance, a fact which made its confiscation the English king's remedy of first resort when dealing with Hugh and Walter de Lacy's occasional truculence. It is little wonder that when Walter granted the hereditary stewardship of his English lands to William de Lucy two months later (1 September 1234), the terms included two carucates at Ludlow and the hereditary constableship of Ludlow castle.[102]

Apart from such explicit statements of relationship, it can be quite difficult to establish the composition of the Lacys' affinities. Charter witness lists provide the best hope, and of these a surprising number survive, at least for Walter de Lacy. David Crouch was able to provide a convincing sketch of William Marshal's affinity (the fullest analysis of a working aristocratic affinity to date) based on sixty-eight charters (fifty with witness lists).[103] For the present purpose, Hugh de Lacy provides at least twenty grants, including ten with their witness lists. An impressive seventy-seven grants from Walter de Lacy have been identified, including forty-nine with their witness lists. The essential problem with witness lists, however, is that it is very difficult to know why a person acted as a witness. If the grant was made to a religious house, those attesting could have been benefactors of that house. If the grant was made at the honorial or hundred court (as they often were), then the witness could have been one of the knights of the shire, important locally, but unattached to either grantor or grantee. What is more, the denial of English law to the vast majority of Irishmen meant that any of the Lacys' native Irish adherents would be invisible in their charters, which were instruments of English law requiring attestation by those of good legal standing.

At first glance, the statistical breakdown of the Lacys' witness lists is discouraging. Hugh de Lacy's ten charters with witness lists were spread out over at least twenty-three years (1163–86), or fewer than one every two years. Walter de Lacy lived in an age of improved record keeping, but his forty-nine charters with witness lists cover a period of fifty-two years, still not quite one every year. Approximately 340 distinct witnesses appear in the combined fifty-nine witness lists, with only thirty-one laymen appearing more than twice.[104] None of the men listed as Hugh de Lacy's household knights in 1166 witnessed any of his surviving charters. Even their families make only sporadic appearances in the charters of Hugh's sons Walter and Hugh the younger. In fact, just two of Hugh de Lacy's tenants from 1166 make an appearance in any of his witness lists, and these were both in the same list.[105] Clearly, witness list data must be corroborated by other sources.[106] When working with William Marshal, Crouch had the advantage of the near-contemporary *History of William Marshal*, which he used to great effect. The Lacys (and those studying them) are not blessed with a similar resource, though enough external evidence survives for Walter de Lacy to allow a tentative sketch of his affinity.

Table 5 (Appendix 2) provides a list of the most frequent witnesses of Lacy acta. The highest number of attestations came from their constable of Meath, William le Petit, who witnessed one of Hugh's charters and ten of Walter's.[107] He even witnessed four of Hugh the younger's charters, making him one of Walter's brother's most frequent witnesses as well.[108] If William was a member of the Herefordshire 'Parvus' family, as suggested in Chapter 2, this would show that Hugh de Lacy actively recruited from the former Hereford affinity after its extinction in 1165. The appearance of Walter of Caldicot (whose toponym points to the Herefords' Welsh marcher lordship of Caldicot in Gwent) as Walter de Lacy's seneschal might indicate the same.[109] Hugh's father-in-law, Baderon of Monmouth, had been a retainer of Roger earl of Hereford, as had Walter of Clifford, whose family also entered Walter de Lacy's service. Strongbow had used the break-up of the earldom of Hereford to expand his lordship in Gwent and to recruit colonists for his Irish lordship.[110] It would have made sense for Hugh and Walter to do likewise.

Having been attracted to Ireland, William le Petit was not a retained knight. His commission as constable was tied to Meath, and all of his attestations were within Ireland. He was also a first-generation tenant in Meath, and would have been in attendance at the Lacys' court at Trim on the grand occasions when grants were made. His eldest son, Nicholas, succeeded to the family lands, and appears in only two of Walter's charters.[111] A younger son, Walter le Petit, was certainly a member of Walter de Lacy's affinity. He is specifically named as one of Walter de Lacy's retained knights in 1234, and attested ten of Walter's charters.[112] The original le Petit feoffee was close to his Lacy lords; his eldest son inherited and drifted away from court, and a younger son was employed by the lord of Meath as a household knight. The family populated the higher echelons of Meath's colonial society. Another brother, Ralph le Petit, was made archdeacon of Meath (based at Trim),[113] while yet another, Adam le Petit, became archdeacon of Kells.[114] Archdeacons were senior members of the clergy, under the diocesan bishop. They were very powerful locally, tasked with enforcing the moral and religious conformity of the churches and lay population within their territories. In aid of this, they were granted wide judicial and administrative authority, and allowed to maintain large households.[115] This knightly family's relationship with the Lacys was mutually beneficial.

Walter also drew from the Welsh border for his affinity. Simon of Clifford, Walter's seneschal c.1231, has been mentioned above. He, like William and Walter le Petit, attested ten of Walter de Lacy's charters.[116] Simon's successor as seneschal, Nicholas d'Évreux, witnessed seven. His elder brother, Stephen d'Évreux, is well known to historians owing to the tug-of-war which the Marshal's son William the younger and Walter de Lacy's son Gilbert waged over his service.[117] Like the le Petits in Meath, the Évreux were a useful family to have on one's side; the Marshal earls were happy to acknowledge them as cousins.[118] They were major landholders in the Lacys' English honor, possessing a castle about five miles from Weobley at Lyonshall (Herefordshire). What is more, Stephen also held lands in the Évreçin at Bosnormand (Eure),[119] which would have helped the Lacys maintain their links to the region. Also like the le Petits (whose case in this regard will be discussed shortly), they were courted by King John when his relations with Walter de Lacy turned sour.[120] Gilbert de Lacy eventually won Stephen's service through a grant of land at Stanton Lacy (Shropshire) 'so that he will be in my *mesnie*/household',[121] and had custody of his heir upon Stephen's death in 1228.

Of the other prominent members of Walter's affinity, Walter of Caldicot, who appears five times, was Walter's seneschal at some point after 1216. Also with five attestations was Richard de la Corner, bishop of Meath (1231–52). One of Richard's appearances came before his elevation, which suggests that, having moved the episcopal seat from Clonard to Trim, Walter was able to influence the bishop's election within Meath as late as 1231. As one might expect, several Lacys also appear. Walter's brother Hugh (four attestations) and half-brother William (six attestations) have been prominent throughout this book. They were closely involved in Walter's political career, and carved out lordships for themselves in Ireland. Amaury de Lacy (four attestations) was likely a son of Gilbert fitz Amaury de Lacy, of the Évreux branch.[122] The Tuit family was also prominent, with a Richard (there was a father and son) attesting eight times, and Matthew four. The geographical origins of the discernible members of Walter's affinity are also telling. William Marshal used the land of his childhood, the English West Country, in recruitment to his household.[123]

Likewise, Walter de Lacy drew men from the heartland of Lacy power in England, Herefordshire and south Shropshire, and recruited indiscriminately from among tenant families of other lords. As with the Marshal, Walter's affinity was made up almost exclusively (apart from Évreux) of English (as opposed to Norman) knights, a bias which reflected the family's increasingly westward orientation.

Lordship and the king

A baron's need to maintain an affinity was not only the result of competition for the service of his tenants by his fellow aristocrats; the Crown played its part. The 'Angevin leap forward' aimed to make royal lordship available to all, and the existence of a more pervasive and illustrious mechanism of lordship superior to and more potent than their own was a particular problem for aggrieved barons, who could not depend upon the unequivocal support of their feudal tenants against the king, even if the paid retainers of their affinity were loyal.[124] The recognised dispute structure of medieval England had always included a degree of brinksmanship, in which a display of aggression and overt violence could be used to signal displeasure and (possibly) achieve redress.[125] However, as Henry II and his sons progressively undercut their magnates' tenurial power bases, they also jeopardised the barons' capacity to resist the encroachment of royal lordship. The threat to aristocratic power provoked a violent response from several members of the baronage, which contributed to the crises of 1173-4 in Normandy and England, 1207-8 in Ireland and 1215-17 in England and Wales.[126] Thereafter, the narrative of the later Middle Ages is one of ever-weakening royal lordship in England, Ireland and the Welsh march.

The Lacys' first brush with such 'royal' intrusion actually came from the king's brother in 1192. In that year, John, as lord of Ireland, ignored Walter de Lacy's rights in Meath and permanently alienated portions of Walter's lordship.[127] John then sought to mollify any local opposition by appointing Walter's constable, William le Petit, as justiciar of Ireland.[128] Where William went, the colonial community of Meath followed, and (although evidence is patchy) there is no suggestion of any resistance to John in Meath. The rough and tumble of frontier life encouraged resident barons and knights, such as the Welsh marchers or the 'Foreigners of Meath' ('*Gaill na Mide*', as they are called in the Irish annals) to bind themselves together in exclusive associations for security. These communities could became strong and coherent political entities in their own right, which could act

261

independently of, and even against, their baronial lords. The 'Foreigners of Meath' can be found raiding territories under the generalship of a rival colonial lord, and even in the service of a native Irish dynast. For instance, in 1187, the 'Foreigners of Meath' journeyed to the west coast of Ireland to join Áed Ua Ruairc, son of the king of Bréifne, in plundering Drumcliff (Co. Sligo);[129] in 1203 they fought alongside the 'Foreigners of Munster' under William de Burgh in Connacht.[130] It was this corporate character of the colonial community of Meath that made it especially dangerous. As seen in Chapter 5, when a dispute flared up between the Irish justiciar and the magnates in 1207, King John wrote directly to the 'barons and knights of Meath', thanking them for their fidelity and for trying to 'avert evil' from their lord (Walter). He also enjoined them to aid the Irish justiciar in fortifying the royal position against the magnates (including their immediate lord) in Ireland.[131] A similar letter was sent to the barons and knights of Leinster, but most of the settler community sided with the magnates in the ensuing warfare, and were victorious over the Irish justiciar.

Of course, this particular dispute between royal and aristocratic lordship did not end there, and its entire progress, which included John's destruction of William de Briouze in 1208 and victory over the Lacys in 1210, displays the vital part played by the local colonial communities in these power struggles. In 1208, when William de Briouze sought to defend himself and his family against what he considered their persecution at the hands of King John, he looked to his tenants for support. This was not an unrealistic expectation as marcher society had a tradition of standing together in rebellion. However, in 1208, few if any of William's tenants followed him. The near contemporary *History of William Marshal* cites this as his reason for fleeing to the company of his fellow magnates in Ireland.[132] Similarly, when Walter de Lacy and his brother Hugh were implicated in a conspiracy with King Philip Augustus of France, which was to include a co-ordinated rising 'with friends and allies' in England and Ireland, King John gathered an army comprising men likely to be those 'friends and allies', sailed to Ireland, and crushed them. In the event, Walter gave up without a fight, submitting his lands to the king and taking flight to Normandy. Thereafter, Walter's greatest tenants in Meath were among King John's entourage as the king continued his tour of eastern Ireland, and were granted high office upon John's departure. One, Richard de Tuit, was made Irish justiciar. Walter's constable of Meath, William le Petit, was made seneschal of Meath, and, when Richard was killed in office, William replaced him as justiciar.[133] There are many other examples of the growing disconnection between magnates and their tenurial followings. For instance, during the far better known dispute between royal and aristocratic lordship in 1215, the sheriffs of England were asked to determine who in their shires were rebelling and who remained loyal. The sheriff of Hereford reported that 'the whole county of Hereford, besides the barons and their men, was with the bishop of Hereford against the king, and bore arms against the king or sent armed men'.[134] Clearly, even on the frontier, tenurial loyalty was not a foregone conclusion.

Lordship and family

Just as external aggression forged bonds among the colonial communities on the frontier, so social and political pressures from above and below forced the aristocracy to turn inward for security. In a world of near-constant conflict and violence, overt or systemic, the family could constitute a stable core from which the web of lordship might radiate. This was to find later expression in the rise of the great lineages in Ireland, but the earliest stages of its development may have begun at the point of invasion. The focus on family was tied to a lord's identity. Under increasing social and political pressure from vocal knightly communities, the upper aristocracy had to assert its separateness.[135] Heraldry – as it was later understood – had been a recognisable phenomenon since the mid twelfth century, and, although it had not reached the ostentatious levels of display it was to achieve in the later Middle Ages, the existence of the king's 'herald of arms' in this period suggests that heraldry was beginning to take off as the preferred way for a status-conscious elite to parade their identity.[136] The Lacys possessed a simple device (*or, a fess gules*), which was displayed proudly on Walter's seals,[137] documented by Mathew Paris[138] and depicted vividly in the pages of the *Romance of Fulk fitz Warin* (in which Walter de Lacy is an opponent).[139]

Heraldry was a means of flaunting a family's history, 'the validating charter of its identity and power'.[140] Filial piety in religious patronage was another common method, one highly visible in the extant sources. Walter de Lacy dedicated many of his donations to the souls of his ancestors, named and unnamed, including his father, Hugh, mother, Rose, and the former heir-apparent of the Lacy inheritance, his predeceased elder brother, Robert.[141] Interestingly, there is no record of his father, Hugh, having done the same for his own father, mother or predeceased elder brother (also Robert). Churches so patronised often felt the necessity of perpetuating the historical memory of a donor family. The chronicle of Llanthony Secunda preserved a flawed genealogy of the Lacys, from the founder of Llanthony Prima, Hugh de Lacy (d. *c*.1115), to Edmund Mortimer earl of March (d. 1381).[142] The register of the abbey of St Thomas Dublin also preserved such a record for the Lacys, but only from the point of the family's entry to Ireland.[143] St Thomas's was heavily patronised by the Lacys and their followers, and seems to have been used as an ancestral tomb for the Lacys in Ireland. When Walter de Lacy recovered the body of his father Hugh in 1195, Hugh's head was sent to St Thomas's, and his body to the Lacy foundation of Bective Abbey, near Trim. This initiated a decade-long quarrel between the two religious houses, which ended only in 1205, when Hugh's body was translated from Bective to St Thomas's.[144]

A lord's need to justify his privileged position through the cultivation of his family's history was a luxury largely confined to the more settled regions of the Plantagenet empire. In a frontier zone such as Ireland or the Welsh march, a lord's personal reputation was even more important than his family history. As seen above, lordship was as much about the actual control of men as it was about theoretical ties of hereditary obligation. In this, Hugh de Lacy was spectacularly successful. In his account of the conquest of Ireland, Gerald of Wales provides a detailed description of Hugh (modelled on Suetonius),[145] which includes a marginal illustration in an early thirteenth-century copy (see Figure 8.2):

> If you wish to know what Hugh's complexion and features were like, he was dark, with dark, sunken eyes and flattened nostrils. His face was grossly disfigured down the right side as far as the chin by a burn, the result of an accident. His neck was short, his body hairy and sinewy. If you further enquire about his height, he was a short man; if you want a description of his build, he was misshapen, and as to his character, resolute and reliable, restrained from excess by French sobriety. He paid much attention to his own private affairs, and was most careful in the administration of the office entrusted to him and in his conduct of public affairs. Although extremely well versed in the business of war, he was not a success as a general, for he often suffered heavy losses on his expeditions. After the death of his wife he was a womaniser and enslaved by lust, not just for one woman, but for many. He was avaricious and greedy for gold, and more ambitious for his own advancement and pre-eminence than was proper.[146]

Hugh's exploits are immortalised in the *Song of Dermot and the Earl*, in Gerald of Wales's *Expugnatio Hibernica*, and in various English chronicles and Irish annals (both Gaelic and Latin). Hugh was able to cut

Figure 8.2   Hugh de Lacy from Gerald of Wales's *Expugnatio Hibernica*

a grand figure for himself on the Irish scene, which was enough to validate his family's identity and power in Meath.

Following Hugh's great successes (which gained him enemies in Ireland and at court) his sons, Walter, Hugh and William were almost inseparable politically. Witness list data suggest not only that they attended one another but that Hugh at least shared some of Walter's household personnel.[147] Together, the brothers were able to preserve their status in England and, for a time, Normandy, and to make their family a dominant force in Ireland. Their conduct suggests that the early thirteenth-century aristocratic family could be quite cohesive. The general strategy that they adopted (if it may be so characterised) was one in which Walter pursued their advancement through official channels, attending the king, sitting on commissions and serving as royal representative, while Hugh and William used the blunt (if effective) method of martial conquest. This saw the

Lacys attack, unseat and replace John de Courcy in Ulster from 1203 to 1205, help to preserve magnate power in Ireland in 1207, harbour fugitives and negotiate rebellion with the king of France in 1209, save themselves from permanent disinheritance as a result in 1210, wrestle Meath from the Irish justiciar 1215-17, create a lordship in Bréifne for William in the 1220s and secure the restoration of the earldom of Ulster in 1223-27.[148] In each instance, Walter professed his loyalty to the Crown while Hugh and William took on the part of quasi-independent aggressors, before the younger brothers' efforts were excused (or rewarded) through Walter's diplomacy. It was only when Walter was forced to prove his loyalty to the Crown in 1223 and 1224 by fighting against his brothers in Wales and Ireland, that the strategy threatened to come undone. However, Walter escaped with a heavy fine for his lukewarm efforts, and Ulster was restored. When political success could promote jealousy in their rivals, family loyalty was of paramount importance.

Such loyalty could extend beyond blood ties to alliances formed through marriage. This is one of the reasons that frontier families tended to intermarry, to buttress themselves against outside aggression. However, while the Lacy family stood together on the peripheries of effective lordship, it chose increasingly to eschew the traditional closed frontier identity by fashioning marriage alliances that were truly ecumenical. Hugh and Walter de Lacy contracted marriages for themselves or their children with members of every region they touched: English, Norman, Irish (colonist and native), Welsh (marcher and native), and, of course, with families who held in several realms. The extension of the family unit through marriage is one way to uncover how medieval aristocrats viewed themselves. Marriages were often arranged in order to cement alliances, or to seal a peace, and the bonds formed could prove strong in the face of adversity. They are consequently important indicators of a baron's priorities at the time of their formation.

Hugh de Lacy took a very localised view of marriage politics at the beginning of his career. His first marriage, to Rose of Monmouth, was a reflection of his immediate concerns. She was the daughter of the neighbouring Welsh marcher lord, Baderon of Monmouth, and his wife, Rose de Clare, which linked Hugh to two of the more prominent families of the southern Welsh march. Hugh's connection to this region, from which so many of the earliest adventurers in Ireland were drawn (including his wife's cousin Strongbow), may have recommended him for his task in Meath. At the very least, it would have eased his entry into Ireland.[149] Just as his own marriage was designed to consolidate his influence locally, so too were his daughters'. As seen above, once in Meath, Hugh was quick to make marriage alliances to attract men such as Gilbert de Nugent and Meiler fitz Henry to his direct service in Meath. He also sought to preserve his authority in Normandy, where he married his daughter, Elayne, to the local Norman baron Richard de Beaufour (d. pre-1204), who held two knights' fees at Beaufour-Druval (Calvados, cant. Cambremer).[150] Yet another of Hugh's daughters was married to the prominent Shropshire baron William fitz Alan (d. 1210), whose family were traditionally sheriffs of Shropshire.[151]

Hugh's second marriage c.1180 to the daughter of Ruaidrí Ua Conchobair was very different in character. His previous marriage alliances had involved strengthening ties with families of equal or lower prestige than the Lacys, and all had been to Anglo-Normans. By contrast, Ruaidrí was the king of Connacht, and high king of Ireland. He was also Hugh's greatest rival in Ireland. Hugh's marriage had the potential to be as significant for Irish politics as Strongbow's marriage to the daughter of the king of Leinster. As mentioned above, Hugh's bride was probably Ruaidrí's daughter by Dub Coblaid, daughter of Tigernán Ua Ruairc, king of Bréifne, and granddaughter of Hugh's legal *antecessor* in Meath, Murchad Ua Máel Sechlainn, king of Mide. Hugh thus married into the native ruling dynasties of Meath and Bréifne, two territories over which he sought to extend his lordship.[152] Intermarriage was not an essential ingredient to colonial lordship, but was none the less employed by some of the most powerful colonial barons in the early days of the conquest of Ireland, including Strongbow, Hugh de Lacy and William de Burgh.[153] Walter de Lacy later earmarked Bréifne as an appanage for the issue of Hugh's second marriage, William 'Gorm' de Lacy. William's birth meant that the marriage alliance remained strong, ensuring peace between Connacht and Meath, and determining that the Lacys favoured William's branch of the Uí Conchobair (the Meic Ruaidrí) throughout the dynastic struggles that plagued Connacht for much of this period.[154] Hugh and his sons were well aware of the political topography of their western frontier, and Hugh plainly considered success there to be worth the risk he took at court. Strongbow's marriage and succession to Leinster were in the minds of those who cited Hugh's second marriage as a betrayal of his ambitions to rule Ireland himself. Hugh would have known the implications, and the likely whisperings of jealous *lozengiers* at court, but he proceeded. This marriage alliance made Hugh the most powerful man in Ireland for a time, and that was worth the risk.

Walter de Lacy was unmarried at the time he inherited, and remained so for over a decade. When he eventually married Margery, daughter of

King John's (then) favourite, William de Briouze, in 1201, he fashioned one of the tightest bonds discernible between two families in this period. The families' holdings complemented each other, allowing a high level of co-operation and co-ordination across the different realms of England, Wales, Ireland and Normandy. The importance of the territorial aspect of the marriage is clear from the marriage treaty, in which Walter stated that he would not alienate any of his English or Norman territories without his father-in-law's consent.[155] Apart from being mutually beneficial, the marriage was also highly symbolic. Hugh de Lacy's two marriages betrayed his outlook and ambitions at two points in his career. In both instances, they were confined to strengthening his position in one realm. This meshes well with what is known of Hugh, in that he focused on each component of the Lacy inheritance in turn, to the possible detriment of his position in the others. Walter, however, was consciously transnational in his policies. This was to lead him into difficulty, but it was an ambition that was mirrored in the marriages he chose for himself and his children.

Walter's son and heir, Gilbert, married Isabella, daughter of Hugh Bigod earl of Norfolk (d. 1225) and Matilda Marshal (d. 1248).[156] Through this marriage, the Lacys gained links to two of the more powerful families in England, Wales and Ireland, links which were eventually to embroil them in the violence of Richard Marshal's rebellion, 1233-4.[157] Walter's daughters were distributed far and wide. Two were married to lords of the Welsh march, Katharine to Walter of Clifford (d. 1263), and Petronilla to Ralph de Tosny (d. 1239).[158] Another, Egidia, was married in 1225 to the Irish baron Richard de Burgh. This alliance was a peace treaty of sorts between the Lacys and Burghs (including the powerful English justiciar Hubert), who had a long-standing rivalry in Ireland and the Welsh march. If it did not form as strong a bond between the two families as Walter's marriage had formed between the families of Lacy and Briouze, the Burghs and Lacys nevertheless enjoyed better relations after 1225. Yet another of Walter's daughters, Juliana, was married (between 1205 and 1220) to the native Welsh chieftain Maredudd ap Rhobert (d. 1244), whose strategic positioning as ruler of Cedewain (Powys) led to him being acclaimed 'chief counsellor of Wales'.[159]

Walter's half-brother, William 'Gorm' de Lacy married Gwenllian, daughter of Llywelyn ab Iorwerth, prince of Gwynedd, in about 1222.[160] While the marriage of Egidia was to seal a peace following the rebellion of 1223-4, William's was to cement an alliance in preparation for that rebellion. It was made around the same time as the Lacys' ally (and relation) Earl Ranulf of Chester formed his own marriage alliance with

Llywelyn. In its immediate martial applications, the alliance was a failure. Llywelyn temporised with King Henry in the middle of their rebellion, forcing Hugh and William de Lacy to face a royal army alone. However, the marriage had more lasting implications, as it brought the Lacys a stake in north Wales and allowed William to serve as a royal representative to Llywelyn in the 1230s. Another of Walter's sisters may have been married to the Welsh chieftain Madog ap Gruffudd of Powys. In a letter to the justiciar Hubert de Burgh in 1227, Walter asked him to forward the marriage of his niece (*neptis*), Angharad, daughter of Madog ap Gruffudd, to Fulk fitz Warin.[161] Walter also likely was responsible for the marriage of his sister, Alice, to the Irish baron Roger Pipard (d. 1225).[162] Once Roger died, Alice married the Irish justiciar and powerful Munster baron Geoffrey de Marisco.[163] Geoffrey had been a thorn in Walter's side for some time, encroaching upon Walter's rights in Meath and seizing the lordship's proceeds in the period from about 1215 to 1220. However, from the marriage, which perhaps occurred around the time of Egidia de Lacy's marriage to Richard de Burgh, the families of Lacy, Marisco and Burgh formed a substantial faction in Ireland, which, among other things, was able to dispose of its rivals Áed Ua Conchobair king of Connacht (d. 1228), and Richard Marshal earl of Pembroke (d. 1234).[164] Walter's grandson, namesake and eventual heir was married to a daughter of the powerful Munster baron Theobald Walter (d. 1230).[165] Theobald already had a marriage alliance with the Lacys, having married his son and heir Theobald (d. 1248) to Margery de Burgh, the daughter of Richard de Burgh and Walter's daughter Egidia de Lacy. This second marriage brought the families even closer.

These marriage alliances form just one small skein of a great prosopographical web that spreads out to link vast swathes of aristocratic society. However, one final connection is perhaps sufficient to display the way in which marriage, land and local politics were often inseparable. This is the interesting case of Walter's other grandson, Gilbert's bastard son Robert de Lacy (mentioned above). Having been granted a quarter knight's fee at Downton Hall (Shropshire), Robert de Lacy was then married to Amicia, daughter of Robert of Wootton. Robert of Wootton was the son of the William of Wootton to whom Gilbert's grandfather Hugh de Lacy had granted Wootton and Onibury (Shropshire) before 1177 (and who Hugh thought should pay the rent due to the bishop of Hereford for Onibury).[166] He was also appointed as his father's attorney in Michaelmas 1207, when Walter de Lacy impleaded William of Wootton for having made waste of Moketree (*Moketr'*) Forest while *custos* there as appointed by Hugh de Lacy.[167] Through Robert de Lacy's marriage to Amicia, he came into possession of the half knight's fee at Wootton, the 20*s* rent at Onibury and Walton (over which Hugh de Lacy had fought the bishop of Hereford) and a further third of a knight's fee at Colemere (Shropshire). He owed service at Ludlow for all but Colemere, which was on the northern Shropshire border with Powys.[168] Colemere was an interesting fief. As seen in Chapter 1, Hugh de Lacy had been enfeoffed at Colemere well before his entry into the Lacy inheritance.[169] On 25 July 1155, Hugh de Lacy appears with the territorial identifier 'of Colemere' in the witness list of a grant by William fitz Alan to Haughmond Abbey (Shropshire).[170] Because Hugh was not the eldest son, it is likely that he was granted Colemere so that it might descend through a cadet branch. Hugh's succession to the main inheritance threatened that plan, but the marriage patterns of the Shropshire aristocracy ensured that through Robert de Lacy of Colemere (as he was thereafter called) it eventually did.[171] Walter de Lacy may have promoted a transnational identity through his marriage alliances, but they were at once broad in outlook and intimately tied to the politics of each locality.

Conclusion

Medieval lordship was a many-faceted structure founded upon ties of dependence and obligation. One of its most basic functions was local control. This was not limited to a lord's acquisition of compact tenurial holdings, but could also include, for instance, the effective control of local justice through the courts, an economy through rents, mills and markets, and defence through the custody of strategic castles and maintenance of a military household. An analysis of the Lacys' conduct across their scattered holdings in Ireland, Britain and Normandy reveals that the trajectory of power was moving away from overt hostility towards more formalised mechanisms of dominance,[172] though on different timescales in each region. The precise application of lordship also depended on its socio-political setting. For those possessing lands in more than one region, dissimilar approaches were often required. Perhaps unsurprisingly, the Lacys' experience displays the spectrum of lordship models, from the almost purely financial lordship of their Norman sub-tenancies to the military frontier lordship in Wales and Ireland, with England in between. Each of these structures involved a degree of coercion, covert or overt, yet none appears to conform to Thomas Bisson's vision of unremittingly violent 'private' lordship.[173] Throughout this period – the period of Bisson's crisis and transformation of European society – aristocratic aggression was tempered by a concern for the preservation of order. This should not come as a surprise. Warfare was aimed at the destruction of an enemy's economic base. While war (especially foreign war) could be lucrative, incessant local warfare was bad for business. So, once Hugh de Lacy had driven the native lords from Meath, he invited the Irish peasants back to their former lands, where his lordship over them was characterised by its mildness. Conversely, almost sixty years later, Walter de Lacy used his influence at the English court to retain the lands of his son, Gilbert, with the net result that Gilbert's widow, Isabella Bigod, was denied her dower. This (highly suspect) court decision was as much an instance of coercion as any of Hugh's activities in the conquest of Meath.

This period also witnessed the growth and increased specialisation of the seigniorial household, which travelled with the lord and provided, among other things, a standing military force and ready source of counsel. This was the heart of the aristocratic enterprise, and the basis of a magnate's power. There was a concomitant rise in the independence of local knightly communities, whose uncertain loyalty necessitated (and was in part caused by) the recruitment of affinities. For instance, although firmly bound to the Lacys through intensive lordship, the settler community of Meath comprised a strong and coherent political entity in its own right, one which could act independently of, and even against, its Lacy lords. This was a tendency that the English Crown sought to exploit, and the interplay of royal and aristocratic lordship often revolved around the constructing of a stable power base from below.

With the loyalty of a lord's tenantry increasingly uncertain, his family could constitute a stable centre from which their lordship could spread. The question of family coherence in this period is especially pertinent in the career of Walter de Lacy, whose political fortunes were inextricably linked to those of his brothers. The intriguing possibility that Walter and Hugh de Lacy consciously operated a joint, two-pronged strategy in the frontier regions of Ireland and Wales would suggest a strong family bond in this thirteenth-century aristocratic family. While the Lacy family stood together on the peripheries of effective lordship, they displayed their evolving identities by fashioning multicultural marriage alliances. Hugh and Walter de Lacy contracted marriages for themselves or their children with members of every region they touched: with the English, Normans, Irish (colonists and natives), Welsh (marchers and natives) and, of course, those who were also transnational.

Notes

1. See Chapter 2.
2. BM Rouen, Y201, fo. 61v.
3. David Crouch, *The English Aristocracy, 1070–1272: A Social Transformation* (New Haven, 2011), part 3, 'Imposing hegemony'.
4. Paul Brand, 'Lordship and distraint in thirteenth-century England', in (ed.), Brand *The Making of the Common Law* (London, 1992), 301–24; Crouch, *English Aristocracy*, pp. 101–2, 108.
5. For William see Crouch, 'Baronial paranoia', pp. 45–62. For Walter see Chapter 7.
6. *RBE*, i, pp. 281–3.
7. *Ibid.*, i, p. 279.
8. Colvin, 'Holme Lacy', pp. 36–7. And see Chapter 2.
9. Warren, *Henry II*, pp. 335–41; Donald Sutherland, *The Assize of Novel Disseisin* (Oxford, 1973).
10. See Chapter 4.
11. *Gormanston Register*, p. 177.
12. *Rot. Litt. Claus.*, ii, 64.
13. *Rot. Obl. et Fin.*, pp. 479, 551.
14. Irish cases: *Curia Regis Rolls of the Reigns of Richard I and John Preserved in the Public Record Office, vol. iv, 7–8 John* (London, 1929), p. 195; *Rot. Litt. Claus.*, i, p. 590b, ii, pp. 64, 103b–4; *CR, 1227–31*, pp. 453, 597–8; *CR, 1231–34*, p. 26. English cases: *Curia Regis Rolls of the Reigns of Richard I and John Preserved in the Public Record Office, vol. ii, 3–5 John* (London, 1925), p. 33; *PR, 1225–32*, pp. 289, 305.
15. Daniel Power, 'Henry, duke of the Normans (1149/50 – 1189)', in Christopher Harper-Bill and Nicholas Vincent (eds), *Henry II: New Interpretations* (Woodbridge, 2007), pp. 85–128, at pp. 102–9 (map p. 108).
16. See Chapter 1.
17. Power, 'Henry, duke of the Normans', pp. 96–7.
18. Power, 'Revolt at Alençon', p. 451n; Power, *Norman Frontier*, p. 212n.
19. BM Rouen Y201, fo. 61r–v; and see Chapter 1.
20. *Mag. Rot. Normanniae*, ii, pp. lxx, 368–9.
21. Irish Pipe Roll 14 John, pp. 21–3.
22. BL MS Additional 6041, fo. 37r.
23. Walter de Lacy: HCA, nos 3226 (Robert Wychecote), 3227 (William son of Odo of Stanton), 3228 (Adam son of Alured), 3232 (freemen of Staunton, Shropshire), 3237 and 3246 (Walter of Caldicot), 3243 (Walter of Wormsley, for a pound of cinnamon annually); TNA C115/77/6683, fos 77r (Philip de Colleville), 90r (Walter Kutel); BL Additional Charter 8055 (Henry the feltmaker of Hereford). Gilbert de Lacy: HCA, nos 3229 (William the harper), 3230 (William de Fen'es), 3234 (Roger son of William Pire).
24. Holden, *Lords*, pp. 105–6.
25. Vincent, 'Lucys', no. 13, p. 40.
26. HCA, no. 3235. And see below, p. 260.

27 HCA, no. 3236. And see Chapter 7.
28 HCA, no. 3241. Explored in Holden, *Lords*, p. 57.
29 For instance, Hugh de Lacy: *Chart. St Mary's*, ii, p. 21 (Adam de Feipo); *Song*, p. 310 (William le Petit). Walter de Lacy: *Cal. Pat. and Close Ire.*, p. 197 (Philip de Angulo); Nicholls, 'Charter of William de Burgo', p. 121 (William and Hubert de Burgh); BL MS Cotton Titus B XI, fo. 72r (Geoffrey de Costentin); *Gormanston Register*, pp. 142, 190 (Hugh de Lacy); *Ormond Deeds*, no. 852 (Roger Pipard).
30 Power, 'Henry, Duke of the Normans', pp. 90–3 (quote p. 93).
31 *Ibid.*, pp. 94–5.
32 See Chapters 1 and 5.
33 See the grant of Le Pin-au-Haras 'which had been Hugh de Lacy's' to William de Briouze in 1203, Rot. Norm., p. 74.
34 See Chapter 3.
35 *Cartulaire Normand.*, no. 72.
36 *Monasticon Anglicanum*, vi, part 2, p. 1129. The name 'Kilkieran' suggests an earlier religious foundation dedicated to St Ciarán of Clonmacnoise (d. c.546). The place name was soon changed to Beaubec.
37 *Gormanston Register*, p. 177.
38 For instance, Robin Frame, 'Lordship and liberties in Ireland and Wales, c.1170-c.1360', in Huw Pryce and J. L. Watts (eds), *Power and Identity in the Middle Ages: Essays in Memory of Rees Davies* (Oxford, 2007), pp. 125–38; Frame, *Political Development*, pp. 69–70; Bartlett, 'Colonial aristocracies', pp. 31–2.
39 For what follows see Donnchadh Ó Corráin, *Ireland Before the Normans* (Dublin, 1972), esp. chapter 4; Dáibhí Ó Cróinín, *Early Medieval Ireland, 400–1200* (Harlow, 1995), chapters 3 and 10; Duffy, 'Irishmen and Islesmen'; Byrne, *Irish Kings*.
40 See Donnchadh Ó Corráin, 'Diarmait MacMurrough (1126–71) and the coming of the Anglo-French', in Ciaran Brady (ed.), *Worsted in the Game, Losers in Irish History* (Dublin, 1989), 21–36; F. X. Martin, *No Hero in the House, Diarmait Mac Murchada and the Coming of the Normans* (O'Donnell Lecture, Dublin, 1975).
41 See, for instance, the change in the kingship of Mide in 1184 from one Ua Máel Sechlainn dynast to another, *ALC* i, p. 166, *s.a.* 1184.
42 Frame, 'Lordship and Liberties', pp. 128, 133–4.
43 The translation is from Crouch, *English Aristocracy*, p. 125 (quoting *Erec et Enide*, ed. M. Roquez (Paris, 1952), lines 3848–55).
44 *AFM*, ii, p. 1104, *s.a.* 1153 (quote), p. 1174, *s.a.* 1169; Flanagan, *Irish Royal Charters: Texts and Contexts* (Oxford, 2005), pp. 217–18.
45 See Chapter 2.
46 *ALC*, i, p. 172, *s.a.* 1186. See also Chapter 3.
47 Irish Pipe Roll 14 John, pp. 37, 45.
48 *AFM*, iii, pp. 196–8, *s.a.* 1219; *ALC*, i, pp. 260–3, *s.a.* 1220.
49 Veach and Verstraten Veach, 'William *Gorm*'.
50 Hugh: A. T. Bannister, *The History of Ewias Harold Its Castle, Priory and Church* (Hereford, 1902), p. 54. Walter: HCA, no. 3239.
51 For instance, *Reg. St Thomas*, pp. 11–12; *Na Buirgéisí*, p. 172. These addresses

referred to linguistic groups (a major component of ethnic identity); Richard Sharpe, 'Peoples and languages in eleventh- and twelfth-century Britain and Ireland: reading the charter evidence', in Dauvit Broun (ed.), *The Reality behind Charter Diplomatic in Anglo-Norman Britain* (Glasgow, 2011), pp. 1–119.

52 James Lydon, 'The middle nation', in Lydon (ed.), *The English in Medieval Ireland* (Dublin, 1984), 1–26, at pp. 12–13.

53 See the essays in John Gillingham (ed.), *The English in the Twelfth Century: Imperialism, National Identity and Political Values* (Woodbridge, 2000).

54 Howden, *Gesta*, i, p. 103.

55 See Chapter 1.

56 For what follows see Veach, 'Question of timing', pp. 178–80.

57 *The Letters of St Anselm of Canterbury*, 3 vols (Kalamazoo, MI, 1990–94), ii, no. 201; M. T. Flanagan, *The Transformation of the Irish Church in the Twelfth and Thirteenth Centuries* (Woodbridge, 2010), p. 39.

58 David Crouch has noticed a similar concentration of ecclesiastical and political power by William Marshal at Kilkenny in Leinster (D. Crouch, pers. comm.).

59 HCA, no. 402.

60 *Song*, lines 3129–82; *Deeds*, lines 3127–80; and see Chapter 1 and Appendix 2.

61 *Song*, p. 310.

62 For Trim see Figure 7.1. For Walter's seal see Figure 8.1.

63 'Li Engleis sunt bon vantur, ne sevent ostëer; Mielz sevent as gros hanaps beivre e gueisseillier', *Jordan Fantosme's Chronicle*, ed. and trans. R. C. Johnston (Oxford, 1981), pp. 72, 73; Crouch, *English Aristocracy*, pp. 110–11. The stereotype of the drunk Englishman was relatively popular in contemporary French writing, and seems to have been taken on by the English themselves. David Crouch, 'The Roman des Franceis of Andrew de Coutances: text, translation and significance', in David Crouch and Kathleen Thompson (eds), *Normandy and Its Neighbours, 900–1250: Essays for David Bates* (Turnhout, 2011), pp. 175–98, at pp. 180, 185.

64 John Gillingham, 'Conquering the barbarians: war and chivalry in twelfth-century Britain', in Gillingham (ed.), *The English in the Twelfth Century: Imperialism, National Identity and Political Values* (Woodbridge, 2000), pp. 41–58.

65 Crouch, *English Aristocracy*, part 1 'Knights and their consequences'; *The Ecclesiastical History of Orderic Vitalis*, ed. Marjorie Chibnall, 6 vols (Oxford, 1968–1980), vi, pp. 240–1 (quote).

66 See, for instance, Fergus Kelly, *Early Irish Farming* (Dublin, 2000).

67 Matthew Strickland, *War and Chivalry: The Conduct and Perception of War in England and Normandy, 1066–1217* (Cambridge, 1996), pp. 180–1, 223.

68 *Expugnatio Hibernica*, p. 246; *Giraldi Cambrensis Opera*, vi, pp. 179–82, 209–11.

69 *Chronicles of the Reigns of Stephen, Henry II and Richard I*, ed. Richard Howlett, 4 vols (London, 1884–89), i, p. 167.

70 *Song*, lines 1474–87; *Deeds*, lines 1474–87; *Expugnatio Hibernica*, pp. 58–64.

71 Holden, *Lords*, pp. 54–5.

72 See above, p. 249.

73 ALC, i, p. 172, s.a. 1186; AFM, iii, p. 70, s.a. 1186.

74 See Holden, *Lords*, p. 53.
75 Gillingham, 'Conquering the barbarians', p. 49.
76 See *Giraldi Cambrensis Opera*, i, pp. 217–18; Verstraten [Veach], 'Anglicisation of the Irish nobility', chapter 4, 'Warfare and settlement'.
77 *The Poems of Giolla Brighde Mac Con Midhe*, ed. N. J. A. Williams (Dublin 1980), poem no. xiii, pp. 136–61 at pp. 140–1 (verse 20).
78 Rees Davies has detailed the process in the later Middle Ages. Davies, *Lords and Lordship*, p. 123.
79 Somerset Record Office DD/SAS/H/348, fo. 59r. My thanks to Professor Nicholas Vincent for drawing my attention to this charter.
80 Bodleian Library MS Rawlinson B 329, fos 172v–173r.
81 *Gormanston Register*, pp. 13–14.
82 *Ibid.*, pp. 10, 182.
83 *Expugnatio Hibernica*, p. 192.
84 Warren, *Henry II*, pp. 127–8
85 *ALC*, i, p. 172, *s.a.* 1186.
86 For the following, see Chapters 3, 5–7 above.
87 Bartlett, 'Colonial aristocracies', pp. 38–41; Veach and Verstraten Veach, 'William Gorm'. For a glimpse of the correspondence of an administration spanning three realms see Crouch, 'Between three realms', pp. 75–90.
88 *RBE*, i, p. 283.
89 *Coucher Book of Furness*, i, pp. 18–20.
90 Also mentioned in his charter of liberties to Trim. *Chartae, Privilegia et Imunitates* (Dublin, 1829), p. 10.
91 Vincent, 'Lucys', no. 15, p. 43.
92 David Crouch, 'The administration of the Norman earldom' in A. T. Thacker (ed.), *The Earldom of Chester and Its Charters: A Tribute to Geoffrey Barraclough*, *Journal of the Chester Archaeological Society*, 71 (1991), pp. 69–95, at pp. 85–8 (quote p. 87).
93 See Chapter 4.
94 *Memoranda Roll 1230–31*, p. 46.
95 HCA, no. 3241.
96 TNA E 315/55, fo. 34r.
97 HCA, no. 483; Bodleian Library MS Rawlinson B 329, fos 175r–v.
98 Wightman, *Lacy*, pp. 201–5.
99 *Cal. Pat. Rolls*, 1232–47, p. 56.
100 See Chapter 7.
101 Frame, 'Aristocracies', p. 155.
102 During a period of royal sequestration, from 1177 to 1191, the constableship of Ludlow had been held by Thurstan Dispenser, one of William's ancestors. Vincent, 'Lucys', no. 15, pp. 41–3, and analysis, pp. 15–16.
103 Crouch, *William Marshal*, p. 144.
104 Six clerical names appear more than twice.
105 They were Richard de Escotot (three knights' fees) and Herbert de Castello (two knights' fees). *RBE*, i, p. 282; Balliol College, Oxford MS 271, fo. 47v.

106 See David Bates, 'The prosopographical study of Anglo-Norman royal charters', in K. S. B. Keats-Rohan (ed.), *Family Trees and the Roots of Politics: The Prosopography of Britain and France from the Tenth to the Twelfth Century* (Woodbridge, 1997), pp. 89–102; M. T. Flanagan and Judith Green (eds), *Charters and Charter Scholarship in Britain and Ireland* (Basingstoke, 2005).

107 Hugh de Lacy: *Cal. Doc. France*, p. 105. Walter de Lacy: BL MS Cotton Titus B XI, fo. 72r; TNA E 210/7221; Hereford Record Office [HRO], Hopton Collection, no 107; *Cal. Doc. France*, pp. 105–6; *Irish Llanthony*, p. 84; *Gormanston Register*, pp. 190, 142; *Chartae, Privilegia et Immunitates*, pp. 10, 17–18; *Na Buirgéisí*, pp. 124–5, 172–3.

108 BL MS Additional 4797, fo. 43r; *Reg. St Thomas*, pp. 9, 13–14; *Irish Llanthony*, p. 81.

109 See Tables 4 and 5 in Appendix 2.

110 David Crouch, 'The transformation of medieval Gwent', in R. A. Griffiths, Tony Hopkins and Ray Howell (eds), *The Gwent County History, Volume 2, The Age of the Marcher Lords, c.1070–1536* (Cardiff, 2008), pp. 1–45, at pp. 29–30.

111 HRO, Hopton Collection, no. 93; *Gormanston Register*, pp. 161–2. He is in two of Hugh the younger's: *Irish Llanthony*, p. 81; *Gormanston Register*, pp. 161–2.

112 TNA E315/55, fo. 34r; BL Additional Charter 19803; Bodleian Library MS Rawlinson B 329, fos 149v–150r; HRO, Hopton Collection, no. 93; *Reg. Tristernagh*, pp. 67–8, 70; *Coucher Book of Furness*, i, pp. 18–20; *Reg. St Thomas*, pp. 12–13; *Monasticon Anglicanum*, vi, part 1, pp. 138–9; Vincent, 'Lucys', no. 15, pp. 41–3.

113 He attested three of Walter de Lacy's charters. *Cal. Doc. France*, nos 314–15; *Irish Llanthony*, p. 84.

114 *Irish Llanthony*, pp. 22–3, 268–9. He attested one of Hugh the younger's charters, *Reg. St Thomas*, pp. 9–11.

115 Jane Sayers, 'Monastic archdeacons', in C. N. Brooke (ed.), *Church and Government in the Middle-Ages: Essays Presented to C. R. Cheney* (Cambridge, 1976), pp. 177–203.

116 BL Additional Charter 19803; TNA E315/55, fos 34r-v; HCA, no. 482; Bodleian Library MS Rawlinson B 329, fo. 172v; *Monasticon Anglicanum*, vi, part 1, pp. 138–9; *Na Buirgéisí*, pp. 74–5; *Reg. Tristernagh*, p. 70; *Reg. St Thomas*, pp. 12–13; *Memoranda Roll, 1230–31*, p. 46; Gearóid Mac Niocaill, 'Cairt le Walter de Lacy', *Galvia*, 11 (1977), pp. 54–56.

117 Crouch, *William Marshal*, pp. 107, 109–11, 113, 148, 151, 173, 175, 225; Holden, *Lords*, pp. 100–1.

118 Holden, *Lords*, pp. 97–102.

119 Archives Nationales de France, S 5202A, nos 64, 65. My thanks to Professor Daniel Power for drawing my attention to this.

120 Holden, *Lords*, p. 99.

121 'Pro eo quod sit in familia mea', HCA, no. 3235.

122 See Chapter 1.

123 Crouch, *William Marshal*, pp. 150–1.

124 See Crouch, 'Baronial paranoia', esp. p. 54.

125 Crouch, *English Aristocracy*, pp. 117–20, 130–2. The situation in Normandy was different, Power, *Norman Frontier*, p. 181.
126 See Chapter 5. Magna Carta protected the authority of a lord within his honor. Carpenter, 'Second Century of English Feudalism', pp. 36–7.
127 See Chapter 3.
128 Otway-Ruthven, *Medieval Ireland*, p. 72.
129 *ALC*, i, p. 176, s.a. 1187; *AU*, ii, p. 210, s.a. 1187.
130 *ALC*, i, p. 228, s.a. 1203; *AI*, pp. 330–2, s.a. 1203.
131 *Rot. Litt. Pat.*, p. 69. See Chapter 5.
132 *Hist. William Marshal*, ii, lines 14161–8; Crouch, 'Baronial paranoia', p. 54.
133 See Chapter 6.
134 *Cal. Ancient Correspondence Wales*, p. 1.
135 David Crouch has written widely on this topic. His latest is Crouch, *English Aristocracy*, esp. chapter 3, 'The shifting borders of nobility'.
136 David Crouch, 'The Court of Henry II of England in the 1180s and the Office of King of Arms', *The Coat of Arms*, 3rd ser. 6/220 (2010), pp. 47–55.
137 Two separate seal designs survive for Walter de Lacy: his great seal featured a mounted knight on the obverse and the Lacy device on the reverse (TNA DL 25/532; TNA DL 25/533; TNA DL 27/296; BL Additional Charter 19803; HCA, no. 402). His private 'secret' seal had the Lacy arms as its obverse and a winged creature on the reverse (HRO, Hopton Collection no. 93; BL MS Lansdowne 229, fo. 143v). Hugh de Lacy is said to have had a seal (now lost) depicting a mounted knight, Butler, *Trim*, p. 54.
138 *Matthaei Parisiensis, Chronica Majora*, vi, p. 474.
139 *Fouke Le Fitz Waryn*.
140 Davies, *Lords and Lordship*, p. 33.
141 *Coucher Book of Furness*, i, pp. 18–20.
142 *Monasticon Anglicanum*, vi, part 1, pp. 135–6.
143 *Reg. St Thomas*, pp. 419–20.
144 *Reg. St Thomas*, pp. 348–50 and see Chapter 2.
145 For Gerald's knowledge of Suetonius see Nicholas Vincent, 'The strange case of the missing biographies: the lives of the Plantagenet kings of England 1154–1272', in David Bates (ed.), *Writing Medieval Biography 750–1250: Essays in Honour of Frank Barlow* (Woodbridge, 2012), pp. 237–58.
146 *Expugnatio Hibernica*, p. 193.
147 See Table 5 (Appendix 2).
148 See Chapters 4–7 above.
149 See Chapter 1.
150 *RBE*, ii, p. 630. The Norman lands were held by their son Henry in 1204. Powicke, *Loss of Normandy*, pp. 332–3. Hugh granted Richard the manor of Stoke Lacy (Herefordshire) with the marriage, *Calendar of Inquisitions Post Mortem, Volume 1: Henry III* (London, 1904), pp. 10–14.
151 *Rot. Hundred.*, ii, pp. 69, 76, 80. Hugh de Lacy's earliest appearance is attesting a 1155 charter of William's father, William fitz Alan (d. 1160). *Cart. Haughmond*, p. 137.

152 Veach and Verstraten Veach, 'William *Gorm* de Lacy'.
153 Frame, '"Les Engleys nées en Irlande"', pp. 84–5.
154 Veach and Verstraten Veach, 'William *Gorm*'. Also see Chapters 6 and 7.
155 *Rot. Obl. et Fin.*, p. 81; *Rot. Chart.*, p. 80; *Pipe Roll 3 John*, p. 87.
156 *Cal. Pat. Rolls, 1232–47*, p. 42; Morris, *Bigod*, pp. 10–11.
157 See Chapter 7.
158 HCA, no. 3241; Holden, *Lords*, p. 85; *Hungerford Cartulary*, pp. 12–13 no. 999.
159 TNA SC 1/1/111; *Acts of Welsh Rulers*, pp. 6, 157–8; *Brut (RBH)*, p. 239, s.a. 1244.
160 For what follows see Chapter 7.
161 *Royal Letters*, i, pp. 306–7.
162 *Ormond Deeds*, i, nos 98, 852.
163 E. St J. Brooks, 'The Family of Marisco', *Journal of the Royal Society of Antiquaries of Ireland*, 61 (1931), pp. 22–38, 89–112, and 62 (1932), pp. 50–74, at p. 57.
164 See Chapter 8.
165 *Reg. St Thomas*, p. 420.
166 See Chapter 2 and p. 243.
167 *Curia Regis Rolls, 8–10 John*, p. 63.
168 *Rot. Hundred*, ii, p. 69b, 80; Eyton, *Shropshire*, v, p. 17, x, p. 195.
169 Eyton, *Shropshire*, x, p. 194. And Chapter 1.
170 *Cart. Haughmond Abbey*, p. 137.
171 *Ibid.*, p. 57, no. 199.
172 A process identified even by historians as different as Thomas Bisson and David Crouch: Bisson, *Crisis*, p. ix and *passim* (esp. chapters 5 and 6); Crouch, *English Aristocracy*, part 3, 'Imposing hegemony'.
173 Bisson, *Crisis*, pp. 6ff.

Conclusion

This study of the careers of Hugh and Walter de Lacy has involved a fresh look at transnational lordship and the interplay between aristocracy and crown from 1166 to 1241. One of the major conclusions that has emerged is that the extent and achievements of the Lacys' lordship was often enhanced by the inability of the English Crown to exercise its own authority effectively without them and their like. A number of the Lacys' greatest triumphs occurred while they were ostensibly instruments of the royal will. This is precisely the way in which Hugh de Lacy built his relationship with King Henry II, through his position as *custos* of Dublin in 1172 and defender of Verneuil in 1173, and the way he extended his profile in Ireland following his royal commission in 1177. Because his perceived fidelity to Henry II was the basis for his advancement, it was also the link that his rivals sought to challenge. Contemporaries report that Hugh de Lacy was recalled from Ireland several times owing to King Henry's anxiety at his growing stature. However, none of these eclipses lasted longer than a few (winter) months, and Hugh always resurfaced with a royal commission the following year. Whispers at court were one thing, but the need for Hugh de Lacy's strong personal lordship in Ireland silenced them.

Similarly, when King Richard sought to assert his authority in Ireland following his return from crusade in 1194, Walter de Lacy was empowered by him to extend his influence within the island. So too in 1234, when the rebellion of Richard Marshal allowed Walter and his allies to settle their grievances against the lord of Leinster in the name of the king. Whether or not one accepts the authenticity of the supposed royal mandate promising the division of Leinster among its conquerors, the king and his advisers authorised the Irish magnates to make war on the Marshal. Such

CONCLUSION

devolution of authority was not unique to Ireland. During the civil war from 1215 to 1217, Walter de Lacy was elevated by King John to a position of great power in Herefordshire and the central Welsh march in order to secure the region for the Crown. The minority of Henry III saw Walter's commission extended, and forced the royal government to negotiate with him for actions within his bailiwick.

The Lacys were thus able to profit from the English Crown's weakness in more than one realm, but they also had to adapt to the varying circumstances of these realms. The degree to which they were able to habituate themselves to different local customs often determined their relationship with their immediate lord, whether king of England, duke of Normandy or lord of Ireland. Hugh de Lacy appears to have been able to balance his concerns. Because Hugh was a regular in royal armies, and trusted by Henry II despite his critics, any complaint against his growing power in Ireland resulted in only minor sanctions. On the balance sheet of royal favour Hugh remained in the black. However, his premature death at the height of his power deprives us of a full insight into how his relationship would have developed with both King Henry II and the new lord of Ireland, John.

Hugh's death, which denied Henry and John the chance to reclaim publicly their authority over him, also had far-reaching consequences for his son and heir, Walter. As a result of his father's troublesome dominance in Ireland, Walter may have been denied seisin of his inheritance by Henry II, and certainly felt the force of John's predatory lordship in Ireland in 1192 (if not before). John's decision to ignore Walter's rights in Meath and permanently alienate portions of Walter's demesne was a legacy of Hugh de Lacy's independent conduct in 1185. However, Walter's divided allegiance may also have played a part in his initial problems. Walter was John's man for his Irish holdings, and might have been expected to support John in 1192. No evidence of Walter's political positioning exists for this period, but he was certainly a Ricardian by the king's return in 1194. From John's succession to the English throne in 1199, the matter of allegiance became much simpler as Ireland was brought under the direct lordship of the head of the Plantagenet empire. But Walter still had to remain adaptable. Ireland was home to a rugged frontier society, and Walter was determined to use this fact to further his family's interests there. He worked together with his younger brother Hugh, pursuing their advancement through official channels, while Hugh would used the blunt (if effective) method of martial conquest. In Ireland, Walter de Lacy could contemplate extending his lordship through whatever means were necessary, as long as his brother Hugh was able to do the dirty work. In England, Wales and Normandy, Walter remained steadfastly loyal (at least on the surface), acting as royal warden of the march and sheriff of Herefordshire. He even joined the royal army against the rebellion of his brother and Llywelyn in 1222.

Balancing these concerns was a difficult task, and when Walter failed to ensure such balance in 1196, he incurred the wrath of King Richard. This episode also illustrates the international reach of conflicts arising from the complexities of transnational landholding. From 1195 to 1196, Walter went from being an instrument of King Richard's rule in Ireland to the object of his ire, apparently for his failure to answer the king's call to arms in Normandy. Preoccupied with his Irish interests, Walter forgot his duty as a Norman baron. This provoked Richard to confiscate Walter's Norman fees and demand a 1,000 mark fine. The transferability of the largely Norman dispute was further demonstrated by the confiscation of Walter's English lands in 1197, and the increased fine for Walter's restoration in Normandy and England. Walter learned from his mistake and, at the outset of John's reign, took measures to ensure that his in-laws, the Briouzes, looked after his English and Norman interests while he concentrated on Ireland. King John's destruction of Walter's father-in-law, William de Briouze, a few years later, was a truly definitive transnational incident. Perhaps deriving from issues in Normandy, it included court action in the Welsh march and administrative restructuring in Ireland in 1206. It flashed into open conflict between Crown and baronage in the Irish crisis of 1207, and afterwards into open rebellion on the Welsh march in 1208. It involved flight through Ireland and Scotland, and ended with William's death in Capetian France, and the deaths of his imprisoned wife and son in England.

The factionalist rebellions of Hugh de Lacy (1223-4) and Richard Marshal (1233-4) both involved actions in England, Wales and Ireland. In 1223, the influence of William Marshal at the English court convinced Hugh de Lacy that his only option for the restoration of his earldom of Ulster was through military means. He formed a political alliance with those opposing Hubert de Burgh's faction at court, and attacked William Marshal in Wales. He then took advantage of the Marshal's heavy recruitment from Ireland to attack in Ireland while the Marshal and the government were unprepared. The resulting removal of Walter de Lacy from the shrievalty of Hereford was held up as an instance of misrule by an English faction, who marched against Hubert de Burgh in England. In this way, the rebellions from 1223 to 1224 in England, Wales, and Ireland were linked.

CONCLUSION

Likewise, while the rebellion of Richard Marshal was sparked by factionalist English court politics, one of its first military strikes was against Walter de Lacy's castle of Ewyas Lacy in Wales. Walter retaliated against the Marshal lordship of Leinster in Ireland. In this instance, Walter and his allies performed the will of the dominant faction at the English court, but the horror of their bloody victory helped to bring about a change in regime. Neither of these conflicts could be appreciated fully by concentrating on one realm. Transnational lords had transnational disputes.

The manner in which the English Crown related to the aristocracy has also been an important component of this book. At the heart of the matter lies the very nature of English kingship over four reigns. The ways in which each successive king (or those ruling in his name) exerted their influence and allowed themselves to be guided by their greatest magnates provide welcome insight into their individual reigns. Although the nature of the sources fluctuated over time, it has been possible to develop a general impression of each reign that transcends the particular characteristics of the sources at hand. In the reign of Henry II, Hugh de Lacy was utilised as a soldier and military governor in Ireland, Wales and Normandy. The council of Oxford should be remembered first and foremost for Henry's declaration that he wished his youngest son, John, to be crowned king of Ireland. However, Henry's decision to empower Hugh de Lacy with extensive authority in Ireland at that same conference shows his policy regarding the security of his westernmost realm. Indeed, it is significant that the strongest measures Henry ever used against the growing power of Hugh de Lacy were several brief and feeble recalls. The pipe rolls record no fine for Hugh's misdeeds in Ireland (though one could have been paid in by other means). It is significant that the first evidence of real retribution arises with the possibility that Henry withheld seisin of the Lacy inheritance from Hugh's son Walter. There was no threat of confiscation while Hugh lived. This is consistent with what is known of Henry II's restrained use of reliefs and other fines, and stands in stark contrast to his sons' practices.

The reign of King Richard has been especially fascinating, owing to a relative lack of historiographical insight into the political configuration of Ireland at this time. The interaction between the king of England and lord of Ireland regarding Ireland is invaluable to our understanding of the island's history before John's reign in England. It appears that King Richard was able to exert his influence over John regarding purely Irish matters, but recognised John's position as immediate lord of Ireland. In 1194, William Marshal was applauded (at least by his biographer) for his refusal to perform homage to Richard for his Irish lands, a ritual submission which belonged to John. In 1195, Walter was forced to pay the enormous sum of 2,500 marks to secure a charter for Meath from John, even though he had received just such a charter from King Richard the previous year. This was a reminder (if one was needed) that adherence to one lord did not guarantee immunity from another. Indeed, the converse happened the following year, when Walter ignored Richard while expanding upon his reconciliation with John in Ireland. Richard may have been willing to admit John's rights over Walter *vis-à-vis* Ireland, but he issued a firm reminder through a heavy fine and sequestration that *he* was Walter's lord in England and Normandy.

John's resumption of direct lordship over Ireland in 1195 marked the end of the powerful magnate-justiciars. Having been overshadowed by Hugh de Lacy in 1185 and seen his interests eroded by Walter de Lacy and John de Courcy from 1194 to 1195, John chose to promote his loyal advisers, or barons of the second rank to head the Irish administration. These appointments required more investment in the colony's defences, but the recipients were that much more reliant upon John for their positions. This trend lasted well into the minority of Henry III, until William Marshal the younger was eventually granted the position in 1224 and took aim at Hugh de Lacy in Ulster. John's reign thus involved a much more guarded relationship with the baronage. While his promotion of William de Briouze in Wales and Ireland might seem to contradict this point, the reasons behind that promotion involved counterbalancing the barons against one another. Likewise Hugh de Lacy was established in Ulster as a counterpoise to William Marshal in Leinster, at the same time that the fate of William de Burgh's claim to Connacht hung in the balance. When Walter de Lacy was elevated to a role as veritable military governor of Herefordshire at the height of the civil war in 1216, it was to counteract the activities of Llywelyn, the Bohun earls of Hereford, and the Briouzes in the region.

John was quick to seize any opportunity to expand his royal lordship, as when he authorised the taking of Limerick city, Uí Failge and possibly Fircal in Ireland, but he also was prepared to admit tactical defeat and regroup if he had to. The aborted Irish expedition of early 1208 is a case in point. John was prepared to intervene personally in Ireland to assert his authority over its barons, yet reversed course once his Irish justiciar had been irretrievably worsted. John's method of backing down involved his removal from the lords of Meath and Leinster of the right to try Crown pleas in their lordships, a significant concession bought by his renunciation of prerogative wardship there. The importance of John's compromise in 1208 was made clear when the liberties' restoration was one of the first acts of William Marshal's regency in 1216. Having been forced to compromise in 1208, John waited two years before returning to his unfinished business in Ireland. In 1210, he launched a grand expedition against the increasingly intractable Lacys, driving them into exile in France.

The minority of King Henry III was a complicated period in which the English Crown was controlled by successive regimes with differing priorities. The first, that of the regent William Marshal, placed the promotion of aristocratic interests alongside the security of the Plantagenet dominions. While it could be argued that this was an inevitable consequence of the weakened state of the English Crown in the period immediately following the civil war, it is still worth noting that several of the baronial concessions, such as the restoration of the royal liberties to Meath and Leinster mentioned above, were decidedly self-interested. Of course, the nature of English kingship in this period may have been inherently self-interested, and any expectation that the regency might display an unprecedented altruism in its rule may be an unfortunate by-product of the romanticised testimony of the *History of William Marshal*. The men in charge of the king had won the war for him, and, if they were generous to the barons against whom they had just fought, they still sought rewards for their own good service, none more so than the Marshal and his son.

After the death of the regent in 1219, the situation was further complicated. A handful of non-baronial ministers, including the papal legate Pandulf, the English justiciar, Hubert de Burgh, and Bishop Peter des Roches, exerted control of the royal administration for the remainder of the minority. A general theme for this period (though by no means universally constant) was the gradual clawing back of royal power from the baronage. This book has shown how the edicts of the government could be ignored, or even openly opposed, by its powerful local officials. From 1216 to 1223, Walter de Lacy governed Herefordshire as he saw fit. Geoffrey de Marisco did the same (to Walter's detriment) in Ireland. Whereas royally supported factionalism had been a characteristic of earlier reigns, a situation soon developed in which factionalism imposed itself upon royal policy. Partisan politics lay behind the failure of the government's negotiations with Hugh de Lacy from 1221 to 1222, and ultimately led to his war with William Marshal the younger. Once begun, the government (controlled by Hubert de Burgh) threw its support behind William Marshal, turning Hugh de Lacy's war into a rebellion. Just as it shows the interconnections between the realms of England, Ireland and Wales, the rebellion of 1223-4 is an ideal illustration of the politics behind Henry III's Minority government.

Henry III's majority in 1227 marked a break with the politics of King John's reign, which had persisted throughout his son's minority. The restoration of magnate power in Ireland harked back to the early days of the colony under Henry II and Richard. Connacht was thrown open to conquest by Richard de Burgh, who was given royal backing for that purpose. The displacement of the Uí Conchobair kings of Connacht gave support to William de Lacy's conquest of Bréifne, which province had been granted to the now beleaguered Áed Ua Conchobair by the Minority government in 1224. Hugh de Lacy was also restored to Ulster, where he once again could extend his influence in the Irish Sea region. The marriage alliance between the Lacys and Burghs in 1225 only reinforced the feeling that Ireland was ruled by its powerful magnate families. However, Hubert de Burgh's dismissal in 1232 saw all of that change. The return to court of Peter des Roches ushered in a period akin to the reign of King John. Checks and balances were once again deemed necessary, with Peter de Rivallis installed as a counterbalance to the Lacy/Burgh alliance in Ireland and Wales (where he replaced Hubert de Burgh). As in John's reign, this policy had dire consequences. Just as King John used the Lacys against John de Courcy in Ulster, so the government of Peter de Roches used the Lacys and their allies against Richard Marshal in Leinster. Had Henry III not utilised Richard's death to rid himself of his alien advisers, his reign might have come to mirror his father's even more closely.

By the time of Henry III's accession to personal rule in 1234, Walter de Lacy was an ageing, and in some ways irrelevant, magnate. The fact that Henry III oversaw the period in which Walter was eventually crushed under the weight of his massive debts to the Crown and Jewish moneylenders might remind one of Matthew Paris's unflattering depiction of Henry III as a new Crassus, in constant pursuit of money.[1] This would be unfair. Walter was the recipient of numerous pardons until the king ultimately allowed his creditors to foreclose. Walter's debts were not even the product of Henry III's personal rule, but the consequence of a long and eventful career as a transnational lord in an age of aristocratic conquest and royal centralisation. His massive debts to the Crown, resulting from grants and misdeeds long past, hung like a weight around his neck. But this was rarely a practical problem, since royal debts were open to negotiation. The real issue was his inescapable private debt to Jewish money-lenders accrued to keep up with the increasingly expensive demands of encastellation and litigation. In the end, the Lacys' international inheritance needed a strong figure at its head, and when Walter de Lacy's last remaining male heir, his grandson, Walter the younger, died in 1240, the family's fate was sealed. When Walter the elder died in 1241, his transnational interests, which had brought the Lacy family renown when he and his father, Hugh, were young and active politically, were distrained to pay off his sizeable debts. The once proud Lacy inheritance was then carved into a patchwork of financial units and divided equally between two co-heiresses. The Lacy family, and many of its structures of lordship, had died out.

Note

1 *Mathaei Parisiensis Chronica Majora*, v, p.274.

APPENDIX 1: FAMILY TREES

The Lacy family

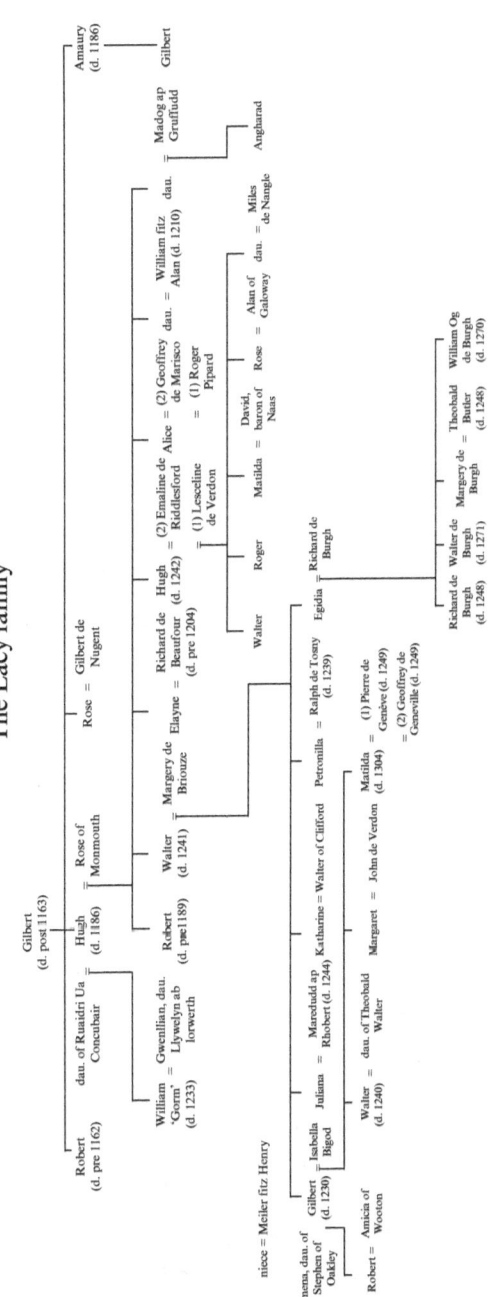

Some notable connections

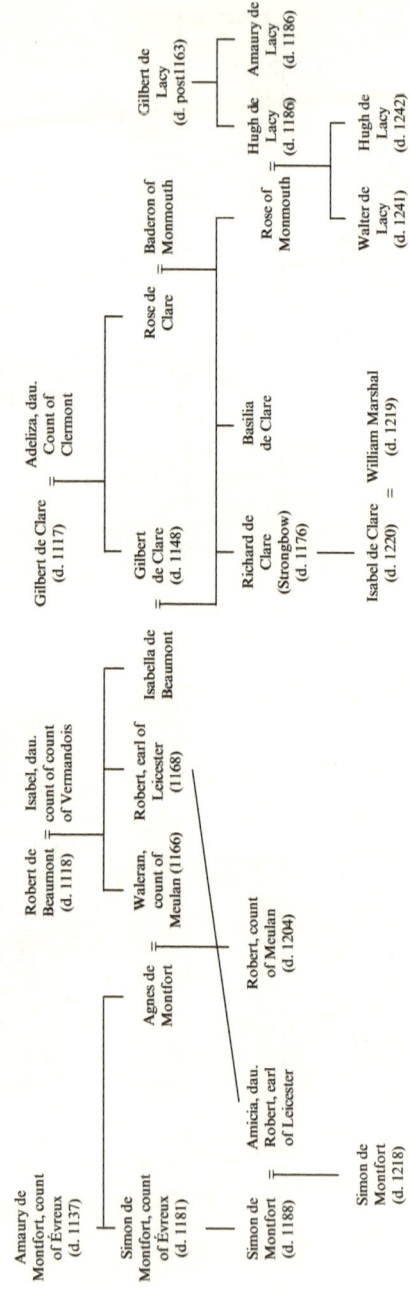

APPENDIX 2: TABLES

Table 1: Tenants of Hugh de Lacy in England
From *Cartae Baronum* and *Herefordshire Domesday*, 1165–6[1]

Combined holdings

Tenant	Territory	Service (new or old feoffment)
Bacton (Bakington), William of	Bacton (5 hides) Hampton [Court] (2 hides) Ledicot (1 hide) Letton (3 hides; *HDB*: Adam) *Wadetune* (1 hide; *HDB*: Gilbert)	4 knights' fees (old)
Bartholomaeus	6 librates of land	No fixed service
*Baskerville, Robert de	Brobury[2] (2 hides) Eardisley; Staunton-on-Wye (4 hides) Stretton Sugwas (2½ hides) Yarsop (1½ hides) Yazor (5 hides)	5 knights' fees (old)[3]
Bret, Richard le		No fixed service
Briouze, W. de	King's Pyon (½ hide)	(Not in *cartae baronum*)
Burford, Roland de		3 knights' fees (old)
*Castello, Herbert de		2 knights' fees (new)
Caulton (*Cauledone*), fee of		½ knight's fee (new)
+Cormeilles, Richard de		2 knights' fees (old)
*Cuillardville, fee of Criquetot fam.	Wolferlow (6½ hides) Webton (2½ hides)	3 knights' fees (old) (Not in *cartae baronum*)
Escorchebeuf, Roger de		No fixed service

APPENDIX 2

Table 1: (continued)

Combined holdings

Tenant	Territory	Service (new or old feoffment)
Escotot, Anketil de	Arkston (1 hide) Cobhall (1 hide)	No fixed service
*Escotot, Richard de	King's Pyon (5 hides) Wormsley (1 virgate)	3 knight's fees (old)
+Escotot, Roger de		1 knight's fee (new)
+Escotot, William de		No fixed service
*+d'Évreux, fee of Walter	Elston (*Elnodestone*) (3 hides) Lyonshall (5 hides)	3 knights' fees (old)
+d'Évreux, Roger		4 knights' fees (old)
+Ewyas, Roger of		1 knight's fee (old)
Feipo, Adam de		No fixed service
Fresne (*Fraxino*), Alvredus du	1 virgate	No service listed
+Fourches, William de		2 knights' fees (old) (Denies another 1 fee)
Gamaches, Godfrey de	Mansel Gamage (8 hides)	2 knights' fees (old)
Gilh (?)	Marston (½ hide)	
Hopton, William of		1 knight's fee (new)
Hungerford, Nicholas of		4 knights' fees (old)
Ley (*Lega*), William of	Almeley (4 hides) Upcott (1 hide) Woonton (1 hide)	3 knights' fees (old)
*Longchamp, Hugh de	Marden (1 hide)	1 knight's fee (old) Fee of William de Burhope, held in *maritagium*
Macgne, son of Gerard de		No fixed service
Malgeri (?)	Grendon (4 hides) Or Stanford (1 hide)[4]	
Mans, Walter del		1 knight's fee (old)

290

APPENDIX 2

Table 1: (continued)

Combined holdings		
Tenant	Territory	Service (new or old feoffment)
Map, Walter	Wormsley (1 hide, 1 virgate)	(Not in *cartae baronum*)
Munsley, Rodland of	Lyde [Mucegros?] (1 hide) Munsley (3 hides, 1 virgate)	3 knights' fees (old)
Odo (?)	Stoke Lacy (10 hides)	(Not in *cartae baronum*)
Poer, R. le	Lawton (in Kingswood) (1 hide)	(Not in *cartae baronum*)
Ralph (?)	Byford (5 hides)	(Not in *cartae baronum*)
Richard fitz Roger	Monkhide (*Hid'*) (1 hide)	(Not in *cartae baronum*)
Riquetot, Ralph de		No fixed service
Roger fitz Odo		1 knight's fee (new)
Sai, Elias de		3 knights' fees (old) (Denies another 1 fee)
Sarnesfield, Philip de	Sarnesfield (1½ hides) (*HDB*: Geoffrey)	½ knight's fee (old) (Denies another ½ fee)
Saussey fam.	Lyde Saucey (2 hides)	(Not in *cartae baronum* – socage in 1242–3)
Staunton, O. de	Staunton-on-Wye (2 hides)	(Not in *cartae baronum*)
Tyrell, son of Rocelin	Evesbatch (1 hide) (*HDB*: H. de Tyrell) Little Marcle (5 hides) (*HDB* O. de Tyrell)	2 knights' fees (old)
Underly, Adam of	Underly (in Wolferlow) (½ hide)	(Not in *cartae baronum*)
William fitz Michael		¼ knight's fee (old)
Wimund	Street (Lestret in Kingsland	(Not in *cartae baronum*)

APPENDIX 2

Table 1: (continued)

Combined holdings		
Tenant	*Territory*	*Service (new or old feoffment)*
Total in Herefordshire (*Herefordshire Domesday*)		23⅓ knights' fees and ⅙ knight's fee
		52 knights' fees from all English lands
Total listed under fee of Hugh de Lacy (*Cartae Baronum*)		57¾ knights' fees (52¼ old and 5½ new)[5]

* Witnessed Walter de Lacy charter.
+ Family witnessed Walter de Lacy charter.

APPENDIX 2

Table 2: Tenants of Walter de Lacy in England
From list of fees, 1242-3[6]

Herefordshire

Tenant	Territory	Service (new or old feoffment)	Sub-tenant(s)
*Baskerville, Walter de	Bodenham *Rogeri* (½ hide)	⅒ knight's fee	+Bodenham, Roger of
	Brobury	⅓ knight's fee (old)	Brobury, Walter of
	Letton (3 hides)	1 knight's fee (old)	Horkesley (*Hurteslege*), Richard of
	Stretton Sugwas (1 hide)	⅓ knight's fee	
	Yazor (2 hides)	⅔ knight's fee (old)	
	Wacton (2 hides)	½ knight's fee (old)	Cardiff, William of
Beaufour, Richard de	Stoke Lacy (2½ hides)	No service (old)	
Bickerton, John of	Bickerton (1 hide)	½ knight's fee (old)	
+Bodenham, Walter of	Byford	1 knight's fee (old) (with John de *Kenell'* and Matilda de Tregoz)	
Caple, William of	Wormsley (1 hide)	⅓ knight's fee (old)	
*+Criquetot, Michael de (heirs of)	Webton, Cobhall, La Mare	1 knight's fee (old) (Not in final list of Lacy fees)	
Englishman, Roger the	Wolferlow	1 knight's fee	
+Escotot (*Scotot*), Walter de (heirs of)	Howton	1 knight's fee	
+d'Évreux, Cecilia	Putley	⅓ knight's fee	

293

APPENDIX 2

Table 2: (continued)

Herefordshire

Tenant	Territory	Service (new or old feoffment)	Sub-tenant(s)
	Street (Lestret in Kingsland)	⅓ knight's fee (old)	Street, Thomas of (*de la Strete*)
+d'Évreux, Isabella (held in dower)	Halmond's Frome (4 hides)	½ knight's fee (old) (1 knight's fee, relaxed by half a fee by writ of Walter de Lacy to Stephen d'Évreux)	
*+d'Évreux, Nicholas (*Colinus* in original hundred return)	Chanston (near Vowchurch)	1 knight's fee (old)	
+d'Évreux, William	Holme Lacy	Moiety of ½ knight's fee (old) (other moiety held by heirs of Walter de Lacy) (Not in final list of Lacy fees)	
	Lyonshall, Upcott	1 knight's fee (old)	
	Stoke Lacy (6½ hides)	¼ knight's fee (old)	
Eynsford, Walter de	Pyon (Moiety of 5 hides)	1 knight's fee (with Hugh de Verlai)	
*+Feipo, Richard de	Lyde Mucegros (½ hide)	⅒ knight's fee (old)	
+Feipo, Thomas de	Munsley (1 moiety of 3 hides)	½ knight's fee (old) (with Henry of Woodhall)	

APPENDIX 2

Table 2: (continued)

Herefordshire

Tenant	Territory	Service (new or old feoffment)	Sub-tenant(s)
*+Fourches, William de	Bodenham (1 hide)	¼ knight's fee (old)	+Fourches, Isabella de (held in dower of William)
Gamaches, Godfrey de	Mansel Gamage	1 knight's fee (old)	
Gloucester, St Peter's Abbey	Monkhide (1 hide)	Alms	
	Lyde Saucy	½ knight's fee (Bought from Ralph de Saussey)	
Grendon, John of	Grendon (1 hide)	¼ knight's fee	
*Hampton, Richard of	Bacton	1 knight's fee (old)	
	Hampton [Court](2 hides)	¾ knight's fee (old)	
	Lawton (in Kingswood) (1 hide)	⅓ knight's fee (old)	+d'Évreux, William
	Ledicot (1 hide)	⅓ knight's fee (old)	Offerton (*Aufertun'*), Robert of and Adam fitz Maelis
	Mintridge (1 hide)	¼ knight's fee (old) (original hundred return lists service as ⅓ knight's fee)	Mintridge, Walter
Hereford, Canons of Hereford Cathedral	Holme Lacy	1½ knight's fee (new) (Lacy held of the bishop of Hereford, so not in final list of fees)	

295

APPENDIX 2

Table 2: (continued)

Herefordshire

Tenant	Territory	Service (new or old feoffment)	Sub-tenant(s)
Hereford, St Guthlac's Priory	Leadon (near Bishop's Frome) (½ hide)	No service (old)	
Hurstley, Richard of	Whitwick (1 moiety)	⅓ knight's fee (old)	Hide, Richard of
Kaerdin	Villa Ricardi[7] (1 moiety of 1 hide)	⅓ knight's fee (old)	Hide, Richard of
+*Kenell'*, John de	Byford	1 knight's fee (old) (with Matilda de Tregoz and Walter of Bodenham)	
+Lacy, Gilbert de	Castle Frome (4 hides)	1 knight's fee (old)	
*+Lacy, Margery de	Weobley[8] (5 hides)	1 knight's fee	
Landa, Henry (heirs of)	Wyle (2 hides)	¼ knight's fee (Original hundred return records that this service is owed to the honor of Castle Richard)	
Llanthony Priory	Yarsop (1 hide)	Socage	
	Canon Frome (3 hides)	No service (*elemosina*)	
Malory (*Malhore*), Robert	Lyde Saucey (1 hide)	Socage	
*Monmouth, John of	Whitwick (2 hides)	½ knight's fee (old)	Hurstley, Richard of
+Muscegros, Amabilia and Juliana de	Lyde Mucegros (½ hide)	¹⁄₁₀ knight's fee (old)	

APPENDIX 2

Table 2: (continued)

Herefordshire			
Tenant	Territory	Service (new or old feoffment)	Sub-tenant(s)
*+Pichard, Roger	Almeley (4 hides)	1 knight's fee (old)	
	Ocle Pychard (4 hides)	¾ knight's fee (old) (original hundred return lists ⅔ knight's fee)	
	Stanford (1 hide)	⅙ knight's fee	Stanford, Walter of
	Staunton-on-Wye (4 hides)	1 knight's fee	*+Pichard, Miles
	Whitechurch Maun (2 hides)	¼ knight's fee (old)	+d'Évreux, Isabella
*+Pichard, Miles	Marston (2 hides)	½ knight's fee (old)	+Pichard, William
Ragun, John son of Hugh	Chanston (near Vowchurch)	⅙ knight's fee (old)	
Sarnesfield, Philip de	Marston (1 moiety of 1 hide)	¼ knight's fee (old) (with heirs of Walter of Traneley)	Grendon, John of Subinfeudated to: +Bradley, Andreas of
	Sarnesfield	½ knight's fee (old)	
	Swanston (1 hide)	⅓ knight's fee (old)	
*+Saussey, Ralph de	Wormeton (in Kilpeck)	½ knight's fee (old)	
Tosny, Petronilla de (née de Lacy)	Yarkhill (4 hides)	1 knight's fee (old)	
Traneley, Walter of (heirs of)	Marston (1 moiety of 1 hide)	¼ knight's fee (old) (with Sarnesfield, Philip de)	Wintercott, John of

APPENDIX 2

Table 2: (continued)

Herefordshire

Tenant	Territory	Service (new or old feoffment)	Sub-tenant(s)
+Tregoz, Matilda de	Byford	1 knight's fee (old) (with John de *Kenell'* and Walter of Bodenham)	
+Tyrell, Roger	Evesbatch (1 hide)	⅓ knight's fee (old)	Evesbatch, Stephen of
	Little Marcle	1 knight's fee (old)	
	Maund (*Magheme*) (½ hide)	⅒ knight's fee (old)	Hammond, Walter
	Wormeton (in Kilpeck)	½ knight's fee (old)	
Verlai, Hugh de	Pyon (Moiety of 5 hides)	1 knight's fee (with Walter of Eynsford)	
Weston, Robert of	Weston Beggard (1 hide)	⅓ knight's fee (old)	
Woodhall, Henry of	Munsley (Moiety of 3 hides)	½ knight's fee (old) (with Thomas de Feipo)	
*Wormsley, Walter of	Staunton-on-Wye (2 hides)	½ knight's fee (old)	
*Elias the clerk, Richard the cook, Richard Caperun and William le Bel	Whyle (Moiety of 1 hide)	¼ knight's fee (old)	
Total listed under fee of Walter de Lacy		27½ knights fees and ⅓ knight's fee and ¹⁄₂₄ knight's fee	

298

Table 2: (continued)

Shropshire

Tenant	Territory	Service (new or old feoffment)	Sub-tenant(s)
Bitterley, Stephen of	Bitterley	1 knight's fee	
	Rushbury	1 knight's fee (with Petronilla de Kenley)	
Clinton, Philip of	Henley	½ knight's fee	
*+Criquetot, Michael de (heirs of)	Upper Hayton	½ knight's fee	
+d'Évreux, William	Lower Hayton	½ knight's fee	
*+Fourches, William de	Corfton	1 knight's fee	
Hopton, Nicholas of	Hopton Waffers	1 knight's fee	
Kenley, Petronilla de (dau. of Roger fitz Odo)	Rushbury	1 knight's fee (with Stephen de Bitterley)	
Mauduit, Thomas	Great Sutton, Witchcot	1 knight's fee	
+Piron, John	Pole	¼ knight's fee	
*+Poer, Roger le and his associates	Aldon	½ knight's fee	
Sai, Walter de	Stokesay, Stoke-upon-Tern, Wheathill	3 knights' fees	
Wootton, Robert of	Wootton	½ knight's fee	
Total		10¾ knights' fees	

299

APPENDIX 2

Table 2: (continued)

Oxfordshire

Tenant	Territory	Service (new or old enfeoffment)	Sub-tenant(s)
Pirneho, Robert de	Barford (*Bereford Olof*)	½ knight's fee	
*+Saussey, Ralph de	Begbroke	1 knight's fee	Leuns, Matilda de and Studley, Prioress of
	Sandford, Cornwell	½ knight's fee	
+Saussey, Leticia de	Nethercote (*Nethercudinton*)	½ knight's fee	
Total		2½ knights' fees	

Gloucestershire, Bailiwick of Cirencester (from 1242 Scutage for Gascony)

Tenant	Territory	Service (new or old enfeoffment)	Sub-tenant(s)
+d'Évreux, Cecilia	Eastleach Turville	2 knights' fees (with Galliana de Tourville)	
Coates, Ranulf of	Coates	1 knight's fee	
*Hampton, Richard of	Stratton	1 knight's fee	
Langley, Geoffrey de	Siddington	½ knight's fee	
Tourville, Galliana de	Eastleach Turville	2 knights' fees (with Cecilia d'Évreux)	
Total		4½ knights' fees	

* Witnessed Walter de Lacy charter.
+ Family witnessed Walter de Lacy charter.

APPENDIX 2

Table 3: The subinfeudation of Meath
From *The Song of Dermot and the Earl*[9]

Tenant	Territory	Service (if known)
Angulo, Jocelin de	Ardbraccan (bar. Lower Navan, Co. Meath) Navan (Co. Meath)	
Angulo, Gilbert de	Morgallion (Co. Meath)	
*+Capella, Richard de	Unspecified 'rich fief'	
Costentin, Geoffrey de	Kilbixy (Co. Westmeath)	
Craville, Thomas de[10]	Emlagh (bar. Lower Kells, Co. Meath) Laragh and Shanonagh (bar. Moygoish, Co. Westmeath)	
Dullard, Adam	Rathconarty (incl. Dollardstown and Painestown, bar. Duleek, Co. Meath)	
*+Feipo, Adam de	Skreen (Co. Meath) Santry and Clontarf (Co. Dublin)	20 knights' fees; 1 knight's fee
+Fleming, Richard le	Slane (Co. Meath)	20 knights' fees
*+Hose, Hugh de	Deece (Co. Meath)	
*+Lacy, Robert de	Rathwire (Co. Meath)	
*Meiler fitz Henry	Ardnurcher (Co. Westmeath)	
*Meset, William de	Lune (Co. Meath)	
*Nugent, Gilbert de	Delvin (Co. Westmeath)	5 knights' fees
*+Petit, William vle	*Chastelbrec* (Castle Bret?) Magheradernon (Co. Westmeath) Rathkenny (Co. Meath) *Leulkeil* and *Kleonkelli* (bar. Shrule, Co. Longford)	1 knight for every 30 carucates, performed at Lacy castle of Killare (Co. Westmeath)
*+Tuit, Richard de	Granard (Co. Longford)	
*+Tyrell, Hugh	Castleknock (Co. Dublin)	

* Witnessed Hugh or Walter de Lacy charter.
+ Family witnessed Hugh or Walter de Lacy charter.

301

APPENDIX 2

Table 4: Assorted Lacy knights and officials

Hugh de Lacy

Name	Position	Dates
Richard le Bret[11]	Retainer	1166
Ralph de Riqueot	Retainer	1166
Adam de Feipo	Retainer	1166
Anketil de Escotot	Retainer	1166
William de Escotot	Retainer	1166
Son of Gerard de Macgne	Retainer	1166
Roger de Escorchebeuf	Retainer	1166
Bartholomaeus	Retainer	1166
Hugh Tyrell[12]	Castellan of Trim and Duleek	1172 – 1173
Richard of Stottesdon[13]	Chamberlain	c.1186

Walter de Lacy

Name	Position	Dates
William de Briouze[14]	Seneschal in England and Normandy	1202 – c.1207
Milo Pichard[15]	Bailiff	1208
William le Petit[16]	Constable of Meath	c.1202 × 1210
William 'Gorm' de Lacy[17]	Seneschal of Meath	1215–post 1217
Thomas d'Anisy[18]	Shrieval Deputy	1218–1219, 1222–1223
Richard de Fay[19]	Knight	1219 × 1220
	Chancellor	1202 x 1231
Warin de Grentemesnil (*Grendon*)[20]	Shrieval Deputy	1220–1221
Walter of Caldicot[21]	Seneschal	Post 1216
Nicholas fitz Leo[22]	Seneschal of Meath	c.1219–c.1221
Simon of Clifford[23]	Seneschal	c.1231
Richard of Copeland[24]	Retained Knight (*milite mei*)	c.9 April 1234
John of Copeland	Retained Knight (*milite mei*)	c.9 April 1234
Walter le Petit	Retained Knight (*milite mei*)	c.9 April 1234
Robert of Leyburn	Retained Knight (*milite mei*)	c.9 April 1234

Table 4: (continued)

Walter de Lacy

Name	Position	Dates
Hugh, conon of Llanthony	Chaplain	c.9 April 1234
Nicholas d'Èvreux	Seneschal	c.9 April 1234
Paul le Cornwalays	Chamberlain	c.9 April 1234
Walter le Dispenser	Procurator of Donacarney	c.9 April 1234
John of Clifford	Servant	c.9 April 1234
Philip de Wichetot	Servant	c.9 April 1234
Brother Hugh of Stanton[25]	Chancellor	1 Aug 1234
Philip de Colleville[26]	Seneschal; Steward in England	1233 × 1236 12 June 1234
William de Lucy[27]	Steward in England; constable of Ludlow castle	1 September 1234

APPENDIX 2

Table 5: Most frequent witnesses to Lacy acta

Walter de Lacy – More than two attestations

Number	Witness	Other Lacy attestations
11	William le Petit	1 – Hugh de Lacy
		4 – Hugh de Lacy the younger
10	Simon of Clifford	1 – Hugh de Lacy the younger
10	Walter le Petit	
8	Richard de Tuit	6 – Hugh de Lacy the younger
7	Nicholas d'Évreux	1 – Katharine de Lacy
6	William 'Gorm' de Lacy	4 – Hugh de Lacy the younger
5	Richard de la Corner, bp Meath	2 – Hugh de Lacy the younger
5	Walter of Caldicot	1 – Margery de Lacy
		1 – Gilbert de Lacy
5	Simon of Tyleshope	
4	Robert de Lacy	5 – Hugh de Lacy the younger
		1 – Katharine de Lacy
4	Hugh de Lacy the younger	1 – Gilbert de Lacy
4	Richard de Feipo	1 – Margery de Lacy
4	Matthew de Tuit	1 – Hugh de Lacy the younger
4	Adam Fayel	
4	Amaury de Lacy	
4	Milo Pichard	
4	Philip de Wichetot	
3	Philip de Colleville	1 – Margery de Lacy
3	Peter des Roches, bp. Winchester	1 – Gilbert de Lacy
3	William de Fourches	1 – Gilbert de Lacy
3	Ralph le Petit, adn. Meath	1 – Hugh de Lacy the younger
3	William Talbot	
3	Hugh Hose	
3	John of Cranford	
3	William Hachet	
3	Robert of Fenhampton	
3	William of Tregoyd	
3	Ralph de Saussey	

APPENDIX 2

Table 5: (continued)

Hugh de Lacy – More than one attestation

Number	Witness	Other Lacy attestations
3	William de Meset	
3	Miles de Muscegros	
2	Gilbert de Nugent	1 – Walter de Lacy
2	William, son of William fitz Alan	
2	Robert de Hautvilliers (*Alto Villari*)	
2	Robert de Baskerville	
2	Robert de Bigarz	
2	John d'Évreux	
2	Nicholas de Dignon	
2	Robert Marshal	
2	William de Mineres	

Notes

1 *Liber Niger*, i, pp. 153–5; *RBE*, i, pp. 281–3; *Herefordshire Domesday, circa 1160–1170*, eds V. H. Galbraith and James Tait (London, 1950).
2 *Hereford Domesday*, p. 48, simply lists 'Robert' as the tenant. This is most likely either Robert de Baskerville or Robert, ancestor of the Walter of Brobury who held Brobury of Walter de Baskerville in 1242–3 (see below).
3 *Liber Niger*, i, p. 153. *RBE*, i, p. 281, incorrectly lists the service as eight fees.
4 It is unclear from the marginal notation which manor is intended, *Hereford Domesday*, p. 51.
5 The service of 3½ knights (old feoffment) was denied by tenants.
6 *Liber Feodorum*, ii, pp. 797–840, 954.
7 Gailbraith and Tait identify this with Monkhide, *Herefordshire Domesday*, p. 99.
8 Newly held by Margery by command of the archbishop of York and the justiciar.
9 *Song*, lines 3132–77; *Deeds*, lines 3130–75. See also, Orpen, *Normans*, ii, chapter 15, 'The sub-infeudation of Meath'.
10 He witnessed a charter of Hugh the younger to Maurice fitz Gerald. *The Red Book of the Earls of Kildare*, ed. Gearóid Mac Niocaill (Dublin, 1964), no. 21.
11 For all of these 1166 retainers, *Liber Niger*, i, p. 155; *RBE*, i, p. 283.
12 *Expugnatio Hibernica*, p. 140.
13 *Register of the Hospital of S. John the Baptist without the New Gate, Dublin*, ed. E. St J. Brooks (Dublin, 1936), no. 191.
14 See Chapters 4 and 5.

APPENDIX 2

15 *Rot. Litt. Pat.*, p.91.
16 *Irish Llanthony*, pp.74, 215-16.
17 See Chapters 5 and 6.
18 *Pipe Roll 2 Henry III*, p.90; *Pipe Roll 3 Henry III*, p.165; *Pipe Roll 6 Hen III*, p.64; *Pipe Roll 7 Hen III*, p.185.
19 Morris, *Chester*, p.11; *Cal. Doc. Ireland, 1171-1251*, no. 934.
20 *Pipe Roll 4 Henry III*, p.194; *Pipe Roll 5 Henry III*, p.13.
21 TNA E315/55, fos 34r-v.
22 *Rot. Litt. Claus.*, i, p.390b; *Cal. Pat. and Close, Ireland*, p.197.
23 *Memoranda Roll 1230-1*, p.46.
24 For all of Walter's officials *c.*9 April 1234, *Coucher Book of Furness*, i, pp.18-20.
25 Vincent, 'Lucys', no 15, p.43.
26 'Pilippo de Ecleuill' tunc senescallo meo', Somerset Record Office DD\SAS\H/438, fo. 59r; *Cal. Pat. Rolls, 1232-47*, p.56.
27 Vincent, 'Lucys', no. 15, pp.41-3.

APPENDIX 3: CHARTER OF WALTER DE LACY TO CRASWALL PRIORY

Grant by Walter de Lacy in pure and perpetual alms for the salvation of his soul, as well as those of his wife, Margery, mother, father and son, Gilbert, to the head of Craswall Priory, (Herefordshire) and his ten brother chaplains and three brother clerks of the ninth sheaf of wheat, oats, rye, barley, peas, beans and other types of crop throughout Walter's demesne manors in Ireland, as well as one burgage in each of his boroughs in Ireland. Namely: one burgage each in Trim (Co. Meath), Kells (Co. Meath), Duleek (Co. Meath), Fore (Co. Meath), Loch Sewdy (Ballymore, bar. Rathconrath, Co. Westmeath), Ardnurcher (Co. Westmeath), Incheleffer (Co. Longford), and Adlech (?Áth Liag: Athleague, Cos Longford and Roscommon). In addition he grants one messuage in each demesne manor in Ireland, namely: in Lohleythi (Loch Ennell: Dysart, Co. Westmeath?), Coolock (Co. Dublin), Ardmulchan (bar. Skreen, Co. Meath), Donacarney, (bar. Duleek Lower, Co. Meath), Moygarthan (Muintir Gearadain, east of Loch Gowna, Co. Longford?), and Fachlet(?). If any of the aforesaid manors should be alienated by Walter or his heirs by sale, by exchange, by pledge for a loan or by grant to a religious house, the brothers of Craswall may still have all of these in perpetuity. Walter and his heirs will warrant and shall defend these gifts against all men and women.

Witnessed by Sir William de Stuteville, Sir Ralph de Mortimer, Sir William fitz Warin, Sir Simon of Clifford, Sir Hugh of Kilpeck, Sir Phillip of Alton, Sir Adam Fayel, Sir John of Cranford, Sir Simon of Tyleshope, Henry of Bradley, clerk.

A: Hereford Cathedral Archives 402 (13c original with seal, see figure 8.1).

24.5cm (across) × 16 cm (down). Turn up of 2.7cm at base, containing a double central slit, through which a yellow cord exits.

Seal: round 6.5 cm green wax attached to cord.

B: Bodleian Library Rawlinson B 329, fos 139v-140r (Hereford Cartulary) (13c).

APPENDIX 3

B printed in: Gearóid Mac Niocaill, 'Cairt le Walter de Lacy', *Galvia*, 11, (1977), pp. 54-6.

A

Omnibus Christi fidelibus ad quos presens scriptum pervenerit. Walterus de Lascy. filius Hugonis de Lascy salutem. Noverit universitas vestra me divine caritatis intuitu dedisse et concessisse et hac mea presenti carta confirmasse deo et domui beate Marie de Crassewelle et correctori eiusdem domus et decem fratribus capellanis et tribus fratribus clericis ibidem perpetuo residentibus et deo servientibus pro salute anime mee et Margarete uxoris mee. et pro salute animarum patris et matris mee et pro salute anime Gilberti de Lascy filii mei et antecessorum et successorum meorum in puram et perpetuam elemosinam. Nonam garbam tocius dominici mei per omnia maneria mea ubicumque fuerint in Hibernia. que ad presens possideo vel que me possunt contingere. tam de frumento quam de auena tam de siligine quam de ordeo. tam de pisis quam de fabis. et de omni genere bladorum. Dedi etiam[1] et concessi dictis fratribus de Cressewelle in puram et perpetuam elemosinam unum burgagium cum predicta nona garba et cum omnibus pertinenciis suis in quolibet burgo meo in Hibernia. videlicet in Trum. unum burgagium. in Kenles unum burgagium. in Duuelech. unum[2] burgagium in Foueria unum burgagium. in Loxiuethi. unum burgagium. in Adnurchur. unum burgagium. in Ynchelefer.[3] unum burgagium. in Adlech.[4] unum burgagium. Et in quolibet manerio meo in Hibernia unum mesuagium. videlicet. in Lohleythi.[5] unum mesuagium. in Coloch. unum mesuagium. in Armolethan.[6] unum mesuagium. in Douenathcarni.[7] unum mesuagium. in Moygarthan unum mesuagium. in Fachlet. unum mesuagium. Tenenda et habbenda omnia predicta burgagia et mesuagia cum omnibus pertinentiis suis et cum predicta nona garba. sine aliquo retenemento de me et heredibus meis dicte domui de Cressewelle in bona pace in puram et perpetuam elemosinam cum omnibus libertatibus quas ei dare possum aut concedere. libere et quiete plenarie et integre ab omni redditu et servitio seculari quod ad me vel heredes meos aliquo tempore possit pertinere. Si vero contigerit quod per me sive per heredes meos aliquod dictorum maneriorum forte vendatur sive excambietur. sive invadietur. sive in religione donetur. sive aliquo alio modo extramanum ponatur. nichilomnius dictas nonas garbas et omnia predicta burgagia et mesuagia habeant ut predictum est et in perpetuum possideant. Et ego Walterus de Lascy et heredes mei dictas nonas garbas et omnia predicta burgagia et mesuagia dicte domui de Crassewelle et fratribus ibidem deo servientibus contra omnes homines et feminas imperpetuum warantizabimus et defendemus. Et quia volo quod hec mea donatio et concessio perpetue firmitatis fidem et robur optineant. presentem cartam sigilli mei impressione dignum duxi confirmare. Hiis testibus domino Will(elm)o de Stuttevill'. domino Rad(ulfo) de Mortuo mari. domino Will(elmo) filio Warini. domino Simo(n)e de Clifford. domino Hug(one) de Kilpech.[8] domino Phillip(o) de Alleton(a). domino Ada Fayel.[9] domino Joh(ann)e de Cranford. domino Simone de Tilleshopp'. Henrico de Bradeleg' clerico.

Notes

1 Mac Niocaill, p. 55: 'eciam'.
2 B: 'unum unum'.
3 Mac Niocaill, p. 55: 'Yncheleser'.
4 'Adleth'?
5 B: 'Lochleyti' or 'Lothleyti'.
6 'Ardmolechan'?
7 'Douenachcarni'?
8 B: 'Kylepek'.
9 B: 'Fael'.

SELECT BIBLIOGRAPHY

Manuscript sources

Cheshire Archives
CHB/2 (Pentice Cartulary).

Dublin, National Library of Ireland
MS 1646 (Gormanston Register).

Dublin, Trinity College
MS 1281 (Dublin Annals of Inisfallen).

Évreux, Archives Départementales de l'Eure
G 122 (Cartulaire du Chapitre Cathédral Notre-Dame d'Évreux).
H 793 (Petit Cartulaire de St-Taurin d'Évreux).

Gloucester Cathedral Library
Register A (Gloucester Register).

Hereford Cathedral Archives
No. 482.
No. 483.
Nos 3226–49 (Charter Roll of Lacy Deeds).

Hereford Record Office
Hopton Collection, nos 93, 107.

London, British Library
Additional Charter 19803.
Additional Charter 33658.
MS Additional 4792.
MS Additional 6041 (Mortimer Cartulary).
MS Cotton Titus B XI.
MS Cotton Vitellius F VIII.
MS Hargrave 313.
MS Harley 1087.
MS Harley 1240.
MS Lansdowne 229.

SELECT BIBLIOGRAPHY

National Archives (PRO), Kew
C 115/75, 77 (Cartulary of Llanthony Priory).
DL 25/532.
DL 25/533.
DL 27/296.
E 40/5924.
E 210/7221.
E 315/55.
SC 1 (Ancient Correspondence).
SC 8 (Ancient Petitions).

Oxford, Balliol College
MS 271 (Cartulary of St Guthlac, Hereford).

Oxford, Bodleian Library
MS Ashmole 833.
MS Rawlinson B 329 (Hereford Cartulary).
MS Rawlinson B 498 (Cartulary of St John the Baptist, Dublin).
MS Rawlinson B 499 (Extract of Deeds of St Thomas, Dublin).

Paris, Archives Nationales de France
S 5202A.

Rouen, Bibliothèque municipale
Y201, (Cartulaire Normand).

Taunton, Somerset Record Office
DD\SAS\H/348, (Hungerford Cartulary).

Troyes, Bibliothèque municipale
MS 1316 (Marleburgh's Chronicle).

Printed primary sources

Acta of Henry II and Richard I, eds J. C. Holt and Richard Mortimer (List & Index Society, Special Series, 21, Gateshead, 1986).
Acta of Henry II and Richard I, part II, ed. Nicholas Vincent (List & Index Society, Special Series, 27, Gateshead, 1996).
The Acts of Welsh Rulers, 1120–1283, ed. Huw Pryce (Cardiff, 2005).
Annála Connacht. The Annals of Connacht (A.D. 1224–1544), ed. A. Martin Freeman (Dublin, 1944).
Annála Ríoghachta Éireann: Annals of the Kingdom of Ireland by the Four Masters, from the Earliest Period to the Year 1616, ed. and trans. John O' Donovan, 7 vols (Dublin, 1848–51).

SELECT BIBLIOGRAPHY

Annála Uladh. Annals of Ulster, Otherwise Annála Senait, Annals of Senat; a Chronicle of Irish Affairs A.D. 431-1131: 1155-1541, ed. and trans. Bartholomew Mac Carthy, 4 vols (Dublin, 1893).
Annales Cambriae, ed. John Williams ab Ithel (London, 1860).
Annales Cestrienses; or, Chronicle of the Abbey of St. Werburg at Chester, ed. and trans. Richard Copley Christie (London, 1887).
Annales Monastici, ed. H. R. Luard, 5 vols (London, 1864-69).
The Annals of Clonmacnoise: Being the Annals of Ireland from the Earliest Period to A.D. 1408, ed. Denis Murphy (Dublin, 1896).
The Annals of Inisfallen (MS, Rawlinson B. 503), ed. Seán Mac Airt (Dublin, 1951).
The Annals of Loch Cé. A Chronicle of Irish affairs from A.D. 1014 to A.D. 1590, ed. W. M. Hennessy, 2 vols (Oxford, 1871).
Bower, Walter, *Scotichronicon: in Latin and English, Vol. iv: Books vii and viii*, eds D. J. Corner, et al. (Aberdeen, 1994).
Brut y Tywysogyon or the Chronicle of the Princes, Red Book of Hergest Version, ed. Thomas Jones (Cardiff, 1955).
Calendar of Documents Preserved in France, Illustrative of the History of Great Britain and Ireland, A.D. 918-1206, ed. J. H. Round (London, 1889).
Calendar of Documents Relating to Ireland Preserved in Her Majesty's Public Record Office, London, 1171-1251, ed. H. S. Sweetman (London, 1875).
Calendar of Entries in the Papal Registers Relating to Great Britain and Ireland: Papal Letters, vol. i, A.D. 1198-1304, ed. W. H. Bliss (London, 1893).
Calendar of Ormond Deeds, ed. Edmund Curtis, 2 vols (Dublin, 1932-34).
Calendar of the Charter Rolls Preserved in the Public Record Office, vol I., Henry III, A.D. 1226-1257 (London, 1903).
Calendar of the Fine Rolls of the Reign of Henry III [1216-1242], eds Paul Dryburgh and Beth Hartland (Woodbridge, 2007-9).
Calendar of the Gormanston Register, eds James Mills and M. J. McEnery (Dublin, 1916).
Calendar of the Patent Rolls Preserved in the Public Record Office, [Henry III - Richard II, 1232-1392] (London, 1893-1905).
Cartulaire Normand de Philippe-Auguste, Louis VIII, Saint-Louis et Philippe-le-Hardi, ed. Léopold Delisle (Paris, 1882).
The Cartulary of Haughmond Abbey, ed. Una Rees (Cardiff, 1985).
Catalogue des actes de Philippe-Auguste, ed. Léopold Delisle (Paris, 1856).
Chartularies of St Mary's Abbey, Dublin: With the Register of Its House at Dunbrody, and Annals of Ireland, ed. J. T. Gilbert, 2 vols (London, 1884).
Chronica Magistri Rogeri de Hovedene, ed. William Stubbs, 4 vols (London, 1868-71).
Close Rolls of the Reign of Henry III, Preserved in the Public Record Office, [1227-1242] (London, 1902-11).
Cronica Regum Mannie & Insularum, ed. George Broderick (Belfast, 1979).
Curia Regis Rolls [1199-1242] (London, 1922-79).
DAVIES, OLIVER and QUINN, DAVID B., 'The Irish pipe roll of 14 John, 1211-1212', *Ulster Journal of Archaeology*, 4, Supplement (1941).

SELECT BIBLIOGRAPHY

The Deeds of the Normans in Ireland. La Geste des Engleis en Yrlande, ed. Evelyn Mullally (Dublin, 2002).
Dialogus de Scaccario, and Constitutio Domus Regis: The Dialogue of the Exchequer, and the Disposition of the Royal Household, eds Amt Emilie and S. D. Church (Oxford, 2007).
Early Sources of Scottish History A.D. 500 to 1286, ed. A. O. Anderson, 2 vols (Edinburgh, 1922).
Expugnatio Hibernica: The Conquest of Ireland by Giraldus Cambrensis, eds A. B. Scott and F. X. Martin (Dublin, 1978).
Freeman, M. A., 'The annals in Cotton MS Titus A. XXV', *Revue Celtique*, 41 (1924), pp. 301–30; 42 (1925), pp. 281–305; 43 (1926), pp. 358–84; 44 (1927), pp. 336–61.
Foedera, Conventiones, Litterae, et Cujuscunque Generis Acta Publica, inter Reges Angliae et Alios Quosvis Imperatores, Reges, Pontifices, Principes, vel Communitates, ed. Thomas Rymer, 4 vols (London, 1816–25).
Gesta Regis Henrici Secundi Bendicti Abbatis, ed. William Stubbs, 2 vols (London, 1867).
Giraldi Cambrensis Opera, eds J. S. Brewer, J. F. Dimock, and G. F. Warner, 8 vols (London, 1861–91).
The Great Rolls of the Pipe for the Second, Third, and Fourth Years of Reign of King Henry the Second (London, 1844).
The Great Rolls of the Pipe, [5 Henry II - 8 Henry III] (London, 1884–2007).
Histoire des ducs de Normandie et des rois d'Angleterre, ed. Francisque Michel (Paris, 1840).
History of William Marshal, eds Anthony J. Holden and David Crouch, trans. Stewart Gregory, 3 vols, Anglo-Norman Text Society, Occasional Series, 4–6 (London, 2002–7).
The Irish Cartularies of Llanthony Prima & Secunda, ed. E. St J. Brooks (Dublin, 1953).
The Letters and Charters of Cardinal Guala Bicchieri, Papal Legate in England, 1216–1218, ed. Nicholas Vincent (Woodbridge, 1996).
Liber Feodorum: The Book of Fees Commonly Called Testa de Nevill Reformed from the Earliest MSS by the Deputy Keeper of the Records, 3 vols (London, 1920).
Magni Rotuli Scaccarii Normanniae sub Regibus Angliae, ed. Thomas Stapleton, 2 vols (London, 1840–44).
Matthaei Parisiensis, Monachi Sancti Albani, Chronica Majora, ed. H. R. Luard, 7 vols (London, 1872–83).
Matthaei Parisiensis, Monachi Sancti Albani, Historia Anglorum, ed. Frederic Madden, 3 vols (London, 1866–69).
Memoriale Fratris Walteri de Coventria: The Historical Collections of Walter of Coventry, ed. William Stubbs, 2 vols (London, 1872–73).
Miscellaneous Irish Annals, AD 1114–1437, ed. Séamus Ó hInnse (Dublin, 1947).
Monasticon Anglicanum: A History of the Abbies and other Monasteries, Hospitals, Frieries, and Cathedral and Collegiate Churches, with their Dependencies, in England and Wales, eds William Dugdale, et al. (New edn, London, 1823).
Na Burgéisí, xii–xv aois, ed. Gearoid Mac Niocaill, 2 vols (Dublin, 1964).

Patent Rolls of the Reign of Henry III Preserved in the Public Record Office, [A.D. 1216-1225, 1225-1232] (London, 1901, 1903).
Recueil des actes de Henri II, roi d'Angleterre et duc de Normandie, concernant les provinces françaises et les affaires de France, eds Léopold Delisle and Élie Berger, 4 vols (Paris, 1906-27).
Recueil des actes de Philippe Auguste Roi de France, ed. H. Delaborde, et al., 4 vols (Paris, 1916-79).
Recueil des historiens des Gaules et de la France, eds M. Bouquet, et al., 24 vols (Paris, 1864-1904).
The Red Book of the Exchequer, ed. Hubert Hall, 3 vols (London, 1896).
Register of the Abbey of St Thomas, Dublin, ed. J. T. Gilbert (London, 1889).
Les registres de Grégoire IX, ed. Lucien Auvray, 4 vols (Paris, 1896-1955).
Rogeri de Wendover Liber Qui Dictur Flores Historiarum ab Anno Domini MCLIV annoque Henrici Anglorum Regis Secundi Primo, ed. H. G. Hewlett, 3 vols (London, 1886-89).
Rotuli Chartarum in Turri Londinensi Asservati, ed. T. D. Hardy (London, 1837).
Rotuli de Liberate ac de Misis et Praestitis, Regnante Johanne, ed. T. D. Hardy (London, 1844).
Rotuli de Oblatis et Finibus in Turri Londinensi asservati, ed. T. D. Hardy (London, 1835).
Rotuli Hundredorum Temp. Hen. III et Edw. I in Turr. Lond. et in Curia Receptae Scaccarii Westm. asservati, eds W. Illingworth and J. Caley, 2 vols (London, 1812-18).
Rotuli Litterarum Clausarum in Turri Londinensi Asservati, ed. T. D. Hardy, 2 vols (London, 1833-44).
Rotuli Litterarum Patentium in Turri Londinensi Asservati, ed. T. D. Hardy (London, 1835).
Rotuli Normanniae in Turri Londinensi Asservati, ed. T. D. Hardy (London, 1835).
Royal and Other Historical Letters Illustrative of the Reign of Henry III from the Originals in the Public Record Office, ed. W. W. Shirley, 2 vols. (London, 1862-88).
The Song of Dermot and the Earl: An Old French Poem. From the Carew Manuscript no.596 in the Archiepiscopal Library at Lambeth Palace, ed. G. H. Orpen (Oxford, 1892).

Secondary sources

AURELL, MARTIN, *The Plantagenet Empire, 1154-1224*, trans. David Crouch (Harlow, 2007).
——, and BOUTOULLE, FRÉDÉRIC (eds), *Les seigneuries dans l'espace Plantagenêt (c. 1150-c. 1250)* (Bordeaux, 2009).
BARLOW, FRANK, *Thomas Becket* (London, 1986).
BARRY, T. B., FRAME, ROBIN, and SIMMS, KATHARINE (eds), *Colony and Frontier in Medieval Ireland. Essays Presented to J. F. Lydon* (London and Rio Grande, 1995).
BARTHÉLEMY, DOMINIQUE, *The Serf, the Knight, and the Historian*, trans. G. R. Edwards (Ithaca, 2009).

BARTLETT, ROBERT, 'Colonial aristocracies of the high middle ages', in Robert Bartlett and A. MacKay (eds), *Medieval Frontier Societies* (Oxford, 1989), pp. 23-47. *Gerald of Wales: A Voice of the Middle Ages* (Stroud, 2006).
——, *The Making of Europe: Conquest, Colonization, and Cultural Change, 950-1350* (London, 1993).
——, 'Medieval and modern concepts of race and ethnicity', *Journal of Medieval and Early Modern Studies*, 31 (2001), pp. 39-56.
——, and MACKAY, A. (eds), *Medieval Frontier Societies* (Oxford, 1989).
BATES, DAVID, 'Normandy and England after 1066', *English Historical Review*, 104 (1989), pp. 851-80.
——, and CURRY, ANNE (eds), *England and Normandy in the Middle Ages* (London, 1994).
BISSON, THOMAS, *The Crisis of the Twelfth Century: Power, Lordship, and the Origins of European Government* (Princeton, 2008).
——, 'The "feudal revolution"', *Past & Present*, 142 (Feb. 1994), pp. 6-42.
——, 'Medieval lordship', *Speculum*, 70/4 (Oct. 1995), pp. 743-59.
BLOCH, MARC, *Feudal Society*, trans. L. A. Manyon, 2 vols (2nd edn, London, 1965).
BOUTRUCHE, ROBERT, *Seigneurie et feodalité*, 2 vols (Paris, 1959-70).
BRADLEY, JOHN (ed.), *Settlement and Society in Medieval Ireland: Studies Presented to F. X. Martin, O.S.A.* (Kilkenny, 1988).
BRAND, PAUL, *Kings, Barons and Justices: The Making and Enforcement of Legislation in Thirteenth-century England* (Cambridge, 2003).
BYRNE, F. J., *Irish Kings and High-kings* (Dublin, 2001).
CARPENTER, DAVID, 'The decline of the curial sheriff in England, 1194-1258', *English Historical Review*, 91/358 (1976), pp. 1-32.
——, 'The English royal Chancery in the thirteenth century', in Adrian Jobson (ed.), *English Government in the Thirteenth Century* (Woodbridge, 2004), pp. 49-69.
——, 'The fall of Hubert de Burgh', *Journal of British Studies*, 9/2 (1980), pp. 1-17.
——, 'Kings, magnates, and society: the personal rule of King Henry III, 1234-1258', *Speculum*, 60 (1985), pp. 39-70.
——, *The Minority of Henry III* (London, 1990).
——, 'The second century of English feudalism', *Past & Present*, 168 (2000), pp. 30-71.
——, *The Struggle for Mastery: Britain 1066-1284* (London, 2003).
CHENEY, C. R., 'King John's reaction to the Interdict on England', *Transactions of the Royal Historical Society*, 4th Ser., 31 (1949), pp. 129-50.
CHURCH, S. D., 'The 1210 campaign in Ireland: evidence for a military revolution?', in Christopher Harper-Bill (ed.), *Anglo-Norman Studies XX* (Woodbridge, 1997), pp. 45-57.
——, *The Household Knights of King John* (Cambridge, 1999).
——, 'King John's testament and the last days of his reign', *English Historical Review*, 125 (2010), pp. 505-28.
——, (ed.), *King John: New Interpretations* (Woodbridge, 1999).
CLANCHY, MICHAEL, *From Memory to Written Record. England 1066-1307* (3rd edn., Oxford, 2012).
COLVIN, H. M., 'Holme Lacy: an episcopal manor and its tenants in the 12th and 13th

SELECT BIBLIOGRAPHY

centuries', in V. Ruffer and A. J. Taylor (eds), *Medieval Studies Presented to Rose Graham* (Oxford, 1950), pp. 15-40.

Cosgrove, Art (ed.), *A New History of Ireland, ii, Medieval Ireland 1169-1534* (Oxford, 1987).

Coss, Peter, *The Knight in Medieval England* (Sutton, 1993).

——, *Lordship, Knighthood and Locality: A Study in English Society c.1180–c.1280* (Cambridge, 1991).

Crooks, Peter, '"Divide and rule": factionalism as royal policy in the Lordship of Ireland, 1171-1265', *Peritia*, 19 (2005), pp. 263-307.

Crouch, David, *The Beaumont Twins: The Roots and Branches of Power in the Twelfth Century* (Cambridge, 1986).

——, 'Biography as propaganda in the "History of William Marshall"', in Martin Aurell (ed.), *Convaincre et persuader: communication et propagande aux XII et XIIIe siècles* (Poitiers, 2007), pp. 503-12.

——, *The Birth of Nobility: Constructing Aristocracy in England and France, 950-1300* (Harlow, 2005).

——, *The English Aristocracy, 1070 - 1272: A Social Transformation* (New Haven, 2011).

——, *The Image of Aristocracy in Britain, 1000-1300* (London, 1992).

——, 'The local influence of the earls of Warwick, 1088-1241: a study in decline and resourcefulness', *Midland History*, 21 (1996), pp. 1-22.

——. 'Robert of Beaumont, Count of Meulan and Leicester: his lands, his acts, and his self-image', *Haskins Society Journal*, 17 (2006), pp. 91-116.

——, *William Marshal: Knighthood, War and Chivalry, 1147-1219* (2nd edn, London, 2002).

Curtis, Edmund, *A History of Medieval Ireland from 1086 to 1513* (2nd edn, London, 1938).

Davies, R. R., *The Age of Conquest, Wales 1063-1415* (Oxford, 2000).

——, *Domination and Conquest: The Experience of Ireland, Scotland and Wales, 1100-1300* (Cambridge, 1990).

——, *The First English Empire: Power and Identities in the British Isles, 1093-1343* (Oxford, 2000).

——, 'Kings, lords and liberties in the march of Wales, 1066-1272', *Transactions of the Royal Historical Society*, 5th Ser., 29 (1979), pp. 41-61.

——, *Lords & Lordship in the British Isles in the Late Middle Ages*, ed. Brendan Smith (Oxford, 2009).

——, 'The medieval state: the tyranny of a concept?', *Journal of Historical Sociology*, 16/2 (June 2003), pp. 280-300.

——, 'The peoples of Britain and Ireland 1100-1400', *Transactions of the Royal Historical Society*, 6th series, 4 (1994), pp. 1-20; 5 (1995), pp. 1-20; 6 (1996), pp. 1-23; 7 (1997), pp. 1-24.

Doran, Linda, and Lyttleton, James (eds), *Lordship in Medieval Ireland: Image and Reality* (Dublin, 2008).

Duffy, Seán, 'The Bruce brothers and the Irish Sea world, 1306-29', *Cambridge Medieval Celtic Studies*, 21 (1991), pp. 55-86.

——, *Ireland in the Middle Ages* (New York, 1997).
——, 'Ireland's Hastings: the Anglo-Norman conquest of Dublin', in Christopher Harper-Bill (ed.), *Anglo-Norman Studies XX* (Woodbridge, 1997), pp. 69–86.
——, 'Irishmen and Islesmen in the kingdoms of Dublin and Man, 1052–1171', *Ériu*, 43 (1992), pp. 93–133.
——, 'King John's expedition to Ireland, 1210: the evidence reconsidered', *Irish Historical Studies*, 30 (1996), pp. 1–24.
——, 'The lords of Galloway, earls of Carrick, and the Bissetts of the Glens: Scottish settlement in thirteenth century Ulster', in David Edwards (ed.), *Regions and Rulers in Ireland, 1100–1650: Essays for Kenneth Nicholls* (Dublin, 2004), pp. 37–50.
——, 'Town and crown: the kings of England and their city of Dublin', in Michael Prestwich, Robin Frame, and Richard Britnell (eds), *Thirteenth Century England X* (Woodbridge, 2005), pp. 95–117.
——, (ed.), *The World of the Galloglass: Kings, Warlords and Warriors in Ireland and Scotland, 1200–1600* (Dublin, 2007).
DUGGAN, ANNE, *Thomas Becket* (London, 2004).
EMPEY, C. A., 'Conquest and settlement: patterns of Anglo-Norman settlement in North Munster and South Leinster', *Irish Economic and Social History*, 13 (1986), pp. 5–31.
EYTON, R. W., *Antiquities of Shropshire*, 12 vols (London, 1854–60).
FLANAGAN, M. T., 'Defining lordships in Angevin Ireland: William Marshal and the king's justiciar' in Martin Aurell and Frédéric Boutoulle (eds), *Les seigneuries dans l'espace Plantagenêt (c. 1150–c. 1250)* (Bordeaux, 2009), pp. 41–59.
——, 'Household favourites: Angevin royal agents in Ireland under Henry II and John', *Seanchas: Studies in Early and Medieval Archaeology, History, and Literature in Honour of Francis J. Byrne* (Dublin, 2000), pp. 357–80.
——, *Irish Royal Charters. Texts and Contexts* (Oxford, 2005).
——, *Irish Society, Anglo-Norman Settlers, Angevin Kingship: Interactions in Ireland in the Late Twelfth Century* (Oxford, 1989).
——, 'Strategies of lordship in pre-Norman and post-Norman Leinster', in Christopher Harper-Bill (ed.), *Anglo-Norman Studies XX* (Woodbridge, 1997), pp. 107–26.
——, 'Strongbow, Henry II and Anglo-Norman intervention in Ireland', in John Gillingham and J. C. Holt (eds), *War and Government in the Middle Ages: Essays in Honour of J. O. Prestwich* (Woodbridge, 1984), pp. 62–77.
FRAME, ROBIN, *Colonial Ireland 1169–1369* (Dublin, 2012).
——, 'Historians, Aristocrats and Plantagenet Ireland, 1200–1360', in Christopher Given-Wilson, Ann J. Kettle, and Len Scales (eds), *War, Government and Aristocracy in the British Isles, c.1150–1500: Essays in Honour of Michael Prestwich* (Woodbridge, 2008), pp. 131–47.
——, *The Political Development of the British Isles, 1100–1400* (Oxford, 1995).
—— (ed.), *Ireland and Britain, 1170–1450* (London and Rio Grande, 1998).
GILLINGHAM, JOHN, *Richard I* (New Haven, 1999).
—— (ed.), *The English in the Twelfth Century: Imperialism, National Identity and Political Values* (Woodbridge, 2000).
——, 'The travels of Roger of Howden and his views of the Irish, Scots and Welsh',

SELECT BIBLIOGRAPHY

in Christopher Herper-Bill (ed.), *Anglo-Norman Studies XX* (Woodbridge, 1997), pp. 151-69.

GRAHAM, B. J., 'Anglo-Norman settlement in County Meath', *Proceedings of the Royal Irish Academy, section C*, 75/11 (1975), pp. 223-48.

——, 'Medieval settlements in County Meath', *Ríocht na Mídhe*, 5/4 (1974), pp. 40-59.

——, 'The Mottes of the Norman Liberty of Meath', in Harman Murtagh (ed.), *Irish Midland Studies: Essays in Commemoration of N. W. English* (Athlone, 1980), pp. 39-56.

GWYNN, AUBREY, and HADCOCK, R. N., *Medieval Religious Houses: Ireland* (London, 1970).

HAGGER, MARK, *The Fortunes of a Norman Family: The de Verduns in England Ireland and Wales, 1066-1316* (Dublin, 2001).

HARPER-BILL, CHRISTOPHER, and VINCENT, NICHOLAS (eds), *Henry II: New Interpretations* (Woodbridge, 2007).

HILLABY, JOE, 'Colonisation, crisis-management and debt: Walter de Lacy and the lordship of Meath, 1189-1241', *Ríocht na Mídhe*, 8/4 (1992-3), pp. 1-50.

——, 'Hereford gold: Irish, Welsh and English land, part 2: The clients of the Jewish community at Hereford, 1179-1253: four case studies', *Transactions of the Woolhope Naturalists' Field Club*, 41/1 (1985), pp. 192-270.

HOGAN, ARLENE, *The Priory of Llanthony Prima and Secunda in Ireland, 1172-1541: Lands, Patronage and Politics* (Dublin, 2008).

HOLDEN, BROCK, 'King John, the Braoses, and the Celtic fringe, 1207-1216', *Albion*, 33/1 (2001), pp. 1-23.

——, *Lords of the Central Marches: English Aristocracy and Frontier Society 1087-1265* (Oxford, 2008).

HOLT, J. C., *Magna Carta* (2nd edn, Cambridge, 1992).

——, *The Northerners: A Study in the Reign of King John* (Oxford, 1992).

—— (ed.), *Colonial England, 1066-1215* (London, 1997).

JOBSON, ADRIAN (ed.), *English Government in the Thirteenth Century* (Woodbridge, 2004).

KEEFE, THOMAS, *Feudal Assessments and the Political Community Under Henry II and His Sons* (Berkeley, 1983).

LATIMER, PAUL, 'Henry II's campaign against the Welsh in 1165', *Welsh History Review*, 14/4 (1989), pp. 523-52.

——, 'Rebellion in south-western England and the Welsh marches, 1215-17', *Historical Research*, 80/208 (2007), pp. 185-224.

LLOYD, JOHN, *History of Wales*, 2 vols (London, 1939).

——, 'Who was Gwenllian de Lacy?', *Archaeologia Cambrensis*, 19 (1919), pp. 292-8.

LOENGARD, J. S. (ed.), *Magna Carta and the England of King John* (Woodbridge, 2010).

LYDON, JAMES, 'The defence of Dublin in the middle ages', in Seán Duffy (ed.), *Medieval Dublin*, iv (Dublin, 2003), pp. 63-78.

——, *The Lordship of Ireland in the Middle Ages* (2nd edn, Dublin, 2003).

——, (ed.), *England and Ireland in the Later Middle Ages: Essays in Honour of Jocelyn Otway-Ruthven* (Blackrock, 1981).

——, (ed.), *The English in Medieval Ireland* (Dublin, 1984).

McDonald, R. A., *The Kingdom of the Isles: Scotland's Western Seaboard, c.1100 - c.1336* (East Linton, 1997).
——, *Manx Kingship in Its Irish Sea Setting: King Rǫgnvaldr and the Crovan Dynasty* (Dublin, 2007).
Milsom, S. F. C., *The Legal Framework of English Feudalism (Maitland Lectures)* (Cambridge, 1976).
Morris, Marc, *The Bigod Earls of Norfolk in the Thirteenth Century* (Woodbridge, 2005).
Nicholson, Helen, 'Margaret de Lacy and the Hospital of St John at Aconbury, Herefordshire', *Journal of Ecclesiastical History*, 50/4 (1999), pp. 629–51.
Norgate, Kate, *England Under the Angevin Kings*, 2 vols (London, 1887).
——, *John Lackland* (London, 1902).
——, *The Minority of Henry the Third* (London, 1912).
Oram, Richard, *Domination and Lordship: Scotland, 1070–1230* (Edinburgh, 2011).
——, *The Lordship of Galloway* (Edinburgh, 2000).
Orpen, G. H., *Ireland Under the Normans*, 4 vols (Oxford, 1912–20).
——, 'Motes and Norman castles in Ireland', *English Historical Review*, 22 (1907), pp. 228–54, 440–67.
Otway-Ruthven, A. J., *A History of Medieval Ireland* (2nd edn, New York, 1993).
——, 'The native Irish and English law in medieval Ireland', *Irish Historical Studies*, 7 (1950), pp. 1–16.
——, 'The partition of the de Verdon lands in Ireland in 1332', *Proceedings of the Royal Irish Academy, Section C*, 66 (1968), pp. 401–55.
Painter, Sidney, *The Reign of King John* (Baltimore, 1949).
——, *William Marshal: Knight-Errant, Baron, and Regent of England* (Baltimore, 1933).
Peros [Walton], Helen, 'Crossing the Shannon frontier: Connaught and the Anglo-Normans, 1170–1224', in T.B. Barry, Robin Frame and Katharine Simms (eds), *Colony and Frontier in Medieval Ireland: Essays Presented to J. F. Lydon* (London and Rio Grande, 1995), pp. 117–38.
Pollock, Melissa, 'Rebels of the West, 1209–1216', *Cambrian Medieval Celtic Studies*, 50 (2005), pp. 1–30.
Poly, Jean-Pierre, and Bournazel, Eric, *The Feudal Transformation, 900–1200*, trans. Caroline Higgitt (New York, 1983).
Potterton, Michael, *Medieval Trim: History and Archaeology* (Dublin, 2005).
Power, Daniel, 'The end of Angevin Normandy: the revolt at Alençon (1203)', *Historical Research*, 74/186 (Nov. 2001), pp. 444–64.
——, 'The French Interests of the Marshal Earls of Striguil and Pembroke, 1189–1234', *Anglo-Norman Studies*, XXV (2003), pp. 63–85.
——, *The Norman Frontier in the Twelfth and Early Thirteenth Centuries* (Cambridge, 2004).
Powicke, Maurice, *King Henry III and the Lord Edward: The Community of the Realm in the Thirteenth Century*, 2 vols (Oxford, 1947).
——, *The Loss of Normandy, 1189–1204: Studies in the History of the Angevin Empire* (Manchester, 1961).

PRYCE, HUW, and WATTS, J. L. (eds), *Power and Identity in the Middle Ages: Essays in Memory of Rees Davies* (Oxford, 2007).
REYNOLDS, SUSAN, *Fiefs and Vassals: The Medieval Evidence Reinterpreted* (Oxford, 1994).
ROWLANDS, IFOR, 'William de Braose and the lordship of Brecon', *Bulletin of the Board of Celtic Studies*, 30 (1982), pp. 123-33.
SIMMS, KATHARINE, *From Kings to Warlords: The Changing Political Structure of Gaelic Ireland in the Later Middle Ages* (Woodbridge, 1987).
——, 'The O'Hanlons, the O'Neills, and the Anglo-Normans in thirteenth-century Armagh', *Seanchas Ardmhacha: Journal of the Armagh Diocesan Historical Society*, 9/1 (1978), pp. 70-94.
——, 'The O'Reillys and the kingdom of East Breifne', *Bréifne*, 5 (1979), pp. 305-19.
SMITH, BRENDAN, *Colonisation and Conquest in Medieval Ireland. The English in Louth, 1170-1330* (Cambridge, 1999).
——, 'The concept of the march in medieval Ireland: the case of Uriel', *Proceedings of the Royal Irish Academy, Section C*, 88 (1988), pp. 257-69
——, 'Irish politics, 1220-1245', in Michael Prestwich, Richard Britnell and Robin Frame (eds), *Thirteenth Century England, VIII* (Woodbridge, 2001), pp. 13-32.
——, (ed.), *Britain and Ireland 900-1300: Insular Responses to Medieval European Change* (Cambridge, 1999).
STACEY, ROBERT, *Politics, Policy and Finance under Henry III, 1216-1245* (Oxford, 1987).
SYNOTT, N. J., 'Notes on the family of de Lacy in Ireland', *Journal of the Royal Society of Antiquaries of Ireland*, 4th ser., 49 (1919), pp. 113-31.
TURNER, RALPH, *King John* (London, 1994).
——, *Men Raised from the Dust: Administrative Service and Upward Mobility in Angevin England* (Philadelphia, 1988).
VEACH, COLIN, 'Henry II's grant of Meath to Hugh de Lacy in 1172: a reassessment', *Ríocht na Mídhe*, 18 (2007), pp. 67-94.
——, 'King and magnate in medieval Ireland: Walter de Lacy, King Richard and King John', *Irish Historical Studies*, 37/146 (2010), pp. 179-202.
——, 'A question of timing: Walter de Lacy's seisin of Meath 1189-94', *Proceedings of the Royal Irish Academy, Section C*, 109 (2009), pp. 165-94.
——, and Verstraten Veach, Freya, 'William *Gorm* de Lacy, "Chiefest Champion in These Parts of Europe"', in Seán Duffy (ed.), *Princes, Prelates and Poets in Medieval Ireland: Essays in Honour of Katharine Simms* (Dublin, 2013), pp. 63-84.
VINCENT, NICHOLAS, 'The Lucys of Charlecote: the invention of a Warwickshire family, 1170-1302' (Dugdale Society Occasional Papers, 42, 2002).
——, *Peter des Roches: An Alien in English Politics, 1205-1238* (Cambridge, 1996).
——, (ed.) *Records, Administration and Aristocratic Society in the Anglo-Norman Realm* (Woodbridge, 2009).
WALKER, R. F., 'Hubert de Burgh and Wales, 1218-32', *English Historical Review*, 87 (1972), pp. 465-94.
——, 'The supporters of Richard Marshall, earl of Pembroke, in the rebellion of 1233-1234', *Welsh History Review*, 17 (1994-5), pp. 41-65.

WARREN, W. L., *Henry II* (2nd edn, London, 1991).
——, 'The historian as "private eye"', in J. G. Barry (ed.), *Historical Studies IX* (Belfast, 1974).
——, 'John in Ireland, 1185', in John Bossy and Peter Jupp (eds), *Essays Presented to Michael Roberts, Sometime Professor of Modern History in the Queen's University of Belfast* (Belfast, 1976), pp. 11–23.
——, *King John* (London, 1961).
WEBER, MAX, *Economy and Society*, ed. Guenther Roth and Claus Wittich, 2 vols (Berkeley, 1979).
WEILER, BJÖRN and ROWLANDS, IFOR (eds), *England and Europe in the Reign of Henry III (1216–1272)* (Aldershot and Bushington, 2002).
WIGHTMAN, W.E., *The Lacy Family in England and Normandy 1066–119* (Oxford, 1966).

Unpublished theses

DUFFY, SEÁN, 'Ireland and the Irish Sea region, 1014–1318', PhD (University of Dublin, 1993).
HOLDEN, BROCK, 'The aristocracy of western Herefordshire and the middle march 1166–1246', DPhil (University of Oxford, 2000).
POLLOCK, MELISSA, 'Franco-Scottish politics: crown and nobility, 1160–1296', PhD (University of St Andrews, 2005).
VERSTRATEN [VEACH], FREYA, 'The anglicisation of the Irish nobility *c.*1169 – *c.*1366', PhD (University of Dublin, 2008).
WALTON, HELEN, 'The English in Connacht 1171–1333', PhD (University of Dublin, 1980).

INDEX

Abergavenny (Monmouthshire) 103, 107
Aconbury (Herefordshire) 157, 178–9, 221–2
Affrica Guðrøðardóttír 57
Aífe, dau. Diarmait Mac Murchada 26, 57
Airgialla 53, 57, 63–4, 66, 72n.90, 183, 246–7
Albigensian Crusade 139, 150–1, 192
Alexander III, king of Scotland (1214–49) 168, 200
Alwin, earl of Lennox 121, 144
Anesy, Thomas de 176, 181
Angaile (Co. Longford) 35, 45n.95
Angharad, dau. Madog ap Gruffudd 269, 287
Angoulême, Isabella de 155
Angulo, Gilbert de 30, 90, 108, 183–4
Angulo, Jocelin de 30
Angulo, Philip de 184, 273n.29
Angulo, William de 240
Antrim (Co. Antrim) 193, 196
Ara (Co. Tipperary) 132
Ardbraccan (bar. Lower Navan, Co. Meath) 30, 143
Ardmayle, cantred of (Co. Tipperary) 136, 160n.36, 173, 175, 182
Ardmulchan (bar. Skreen, Co. Meath) 110, 249
Ardnurcher (bar. Moycashel, Co. Westmeath) 30, 61, 84, 97n.48, 108, 132, 182, 219, 249
Ardree (bar. Kinkea and Moone, Co. Kildare) 61
Argentan (Orne) 103, 242
Arthur of Brittany 102, 111, 117
Áskell Ragavalsson (Ascall mac Ragnaill mic Turcaill) 32
Athboy (Co. Meath) 31, 145
Athleague (now Ballyleague, Co. Roscommon) 182, 184
Athlone (Co. Westmeath) 38, 39, 87–8, 90, 108, 122, 145, 209–10, 215
Athlumney (Co. Meath) 29
Audley, Adam de 193
Audley, Henry de 193
Azeville (Manche) 37–8, 242

Baginbun (Co. Waterford) 252
Ballybin (bar. Ratoath, Co. Meath) 83
Ballyloughloe (bar. Clonlonan, Co. Westmeath) 184, 219
Barry, Philip of 62
Basset, Alan 92
Basset, Gilbert 215
Beaubec (Seine-Maritime), abbey of 245, 273n.36
Beauchamp, Hugh de 34
Beauchamp, Walter de 171
Beauchamp, William de 111, 170
Beaufour, Richard de 267
Beaufour-Druval (Calvados, cant. Cambremer) 267
Becket, Thomas, archbishop of Canterbury (1162–1170) 27, 34, 40, 42n.16, 43n.40
Bective Abbey (Co. Meath) 67, 87, 264
Bedford (Bedfordshire) 170, 202–3
Belturbet (Co. Cavan) 145, 183
Béthune, Baldwin de, count of Aumale 105
Beuzeville (Manche) 37, 242
Bigarz, Robert de 61
Bigod, Isabella, dau. Hugh II Bigod, earl of Norfolk, 212, 215, 268, 271
Bigod, Roger III, earl of Norfolk 215
Bishop's Castle (Shropshire) 104
Bisley (Gloucestershire) 193, 225n.7
Blathach, castle of, near Limerick 175
Blund, Henry le see London, Henry of
Bohun, Henry de, earl of Hereford 103, 154, 156–7, 283
Bosnormand (Eure) 260
Bramber (Sussex) 103
Braose see Briouze
Bréauté, Falkes de 169, 197–8, 202–3
Brecon (Powys), lordship of 103, 105, 124n.26, 131
Bréifne 4, 27, 31, 57, 60, 64, 66, 90–1, 182, 183–6, 202, 205, 207–8, 228n.91, 247, 262, 266–7, 285
Bret, Richard le 23, 256
Brewer, William 97n.40, 170

INDEX

Briouze, family 13, 101, 104-5, 138, 140, 142-4, 158, 221, 228n.102, 283
Briouze, Giles de, bishop of Hereford 104, 107, 140, 148, 154, 156
Briouze, Margery de *see* Lacy, Margery de
Briouze, Matilda de *see* St Valery, Matilda de
Briouze, Philip de 49, 69n.7, 105
Briouze, Reginald de 144, 148, 154, 156, 168, 170-1, 174, 176, 178-81
Briouze, William de (d. 1211) 112, 257
   alliance with Walter de Lacy 101, 105, 107, 122, 130, 183, 185, 186, 268.
   and Burgh family 106-7, 110, 122-3, 178, 185, 214
   destruction by King John 131-42, 157, 160n.20, 239, 262, 281
   grants by King John 103-6, 113, 115, 116, 122, 178, 214, 283
   honor of Limerick 105-6, 111, 118, 126n.67, 130-5, 142-3, 183, 186
   and Lacy inheritance 96n.19, 111-14, 123, 134, 273n.33, 281
Briouze, William de the younger (d. 1210) 137, 143
Bristol 27, 80, 104, 132, 135, 155, 168-9, 213
Britford (Wiltshire) 181, 213
Burgh, Hubert de 86, 106-7, 122, 179, 180-1, 185, 194, 196-8, 201-2, 208, 211, 213-14, 216-17, 223-4, 269, 273n.29, 281, 284-5
   ally of William Marshal (d. 1231) 194, 196-7, 199, 202-3, 281, 284-5
   and the Three Castles 106, 178-80, 198.
Burgh, Margery de 269
Burgh, Richard de 120, 122, 196, 201-2, 206, 208-11, 214-19, 222, 224, 231n.197, 285
Burgh, William de 60, 86-7, 89, 105-6, 108-10, 113-16, 120-3, 131, 262, 268-9, 273n.29, 283
Butler, Theobald (d. 1230) *see* Walter, Theobald
Butler, Theobald (d. 1248) 269

Caen (Calvados) 93, 103, 242
Caerleon (Gwent) 210
Caldicot, Walter of 259-60, 272
Campeaux (Calvados, cant. Condé-sur-Noireau) 24-5, 80, 241-2, 244
Cantelupe, William de, 122, 169
Canterbury (Kent) 34
Capella, Richard de 44n.67, 135
Cardigan (Ceredigion) 171, 194, 197, 210
Carlingford (Co. Louth) 142, 173-4

Carmarthen (Carmarthenshire) 171, 194, 197, 210, 214
Carrickfergus (Co. Antrim) 143, 195, 205
Cashel (Co. Tipperary) 35, 126n.65
Castello, Herbert de 275n.105
Castelnaudary (Aude), lordship of 139, 150
Castle Frome (Herefordshire) 24, 42n.23, 80, 85, 97n.54
Castleboy (bar. Ardes, Co. Down) 221
Castleknock (Co. Dublin) 30
   castle of *see* Cnoc
Castletown Delvin (bar. Delvin, Co. Westmeath) 61
Cenél Láegaire, land of (bar Upper and Lower Navan, Co. Meath?) 96n.27
Cenél n-Enda, land of (Kinalea, Co. Westmeath?) 96n.27
Chepstow (Monmouthshire) 194, 198, 217, 226n.14
Chester (Cheshire) 72n.95, 78
   earldom of 104-5, 193
   links with Meath 193-4, 257-8
Chinon (Indre-et-Loire) 102, 122
Cigogné, Engelard de 156
Cirencester (Gloucestershire) 23, 154
Clahull, John de 59, 133
Clare, Gilbert de, earl of Gloucester 195, 198
Clare, Isabel de, dau. Strongbow 79-81
Clare, Richard fitz Gilbert de *see* Strongbow
Clare, Rose de 26, 266
Clatere, Norman 134
Claville (Eure, cant. Évreux-Ouest) 24, 39, 90
Clement, Henry 220
Clifford, Giles of 257
Clifford, John of 219, 256
Clifford, Roger of 170, 178
Clifford, Simon of 219-20, 257, 260
Clifford, Walter of (d. 1190) 259
Clifford, Walter of (d. 1263) 154, 156, 170-1, 178, 213, 215, 243, 257, 268
Clonard (bar. Upper Moyfenrath, Co. Meath) 38, 61-2, 249, 260
   bishop of *see* Echthigern mac Máel Chiaráin
Clonfane (bar. Navan Upper, Co. Meath) 89
Clonmacnoise (Co. Offaly) 54-5, 108, 203
Clonmore (bar. Lune, Co. Meath) 89
Clontarf (Co. Dublin) 29, 245
Cnoc (Castleknock, Co. Dublin), castle of 193
Cogan, Miles de 48
Colemere (Shropshire) 22, 24, 270
Coleraine (Co. Londonderry) 200
Colleville, Philip de 257, 272n.23
Conmaicne 89, 183-4

INDEX

Connacht 27, 35-7, 39-40, 48, 54-5,
  57-8, 66, 86, 108, 110, 113-16,
  118, 120-3, 145, 182, 201-2, 206,
  208-10, 262
  kingship of 56, 60-1, 63, 82, 96n.31,
  108-10, 113, 206, 208, 267, 285
  lordship of *see* Burgh, Richard de
Coolock (Co. Dublin) 249
Copeland, John of 219, 256
Copeland, Richard of 219, 256
Cornwalays, Paul le 219, 256
Costentin, Geoffrey de 84, 89, 110, 273n.29
Courcy, John de 48, 52-3, 57, 84, 86-9, 93-4,
  108-10, 114, 116-21, 123, 125n.53,
  126n.56, 135, 143, 191, 193, 208,
  216, 266, 283, 285
Coutances, Walter de, archbishop of Rouen
  84
Craswall (Herefordshire), St Mary's priory of
  165n.149, 249-50, 254, 257
Craville, Thomas de 249-50
Cumin, John, archbishop of Dublin
  (1181-1212) 59, 65, 87
Curragh of Kildare (Co. Kildare) 218
Curtun, Aubrey of 110, 240
Cusack, Geoffrey de 29

Danestown (Co. Meath) 29
David, baron of Naas 119
Decies (Co. Waterford) 196, 215
Delbna Ethra (bar. Garrycastle, Co. Offaly)
  38-9, 54, 146
Delvin (Co. Westmeath) 30, 61
Derbforgaill, dau. Murchad Ua Máel
  Sechlainn 60
Derry (Co. Londonderry) 146
Desmond 131, 134, 196, 215
Devizes (Wiltshire) 217
Diarmait mac Máel na mBó 49-50
Dinan, Joce de (d. 1166) 107
Dispenser, Walter le 219, 256
Donacarney (bar. Duleek Lower, Co. Meath)
  219, 249, 256
Donaghmore (bar. Ratoath, Co. Meath) 30
Dore (Herefordshire), monks of 179
Dowdstown (Co. Meath) 29
Downpatrick (Co. Down) 116, 119
Downton Hall (Shropshire) 212, 269
Drogheda (Co. Louth – then in Meath) 30,
  38-9, 53-4, 83, 86, 89, 145, 155,
  173, 175-6, 183, 193, 207, 213, 215,
  257-8
Drumcliff (bar. Carbury, Co. Sligo) 82, 262
Dub Coblaid (d.1181), dau. Tigernán Ua
  Ruairc 60, 267

Dublin 22, 26-9, 31-9, 48-50 53-9, 64-5,
  72n.93, 84, 96n.24, 108-10, 116,
  132, 134-5, 142-3, 148, 158,
  161n.50, 176, 184-5, 193, 197, 199,
  209-10, 247, 279
  Norse of 28, 32, 35, 50
  strategic importance of 28, 36-7, 40,
  43n.47, 49-50
Dublin, St Thomas's abbey 10, 67, 83, 87-8,
  212, 249, 264
Duleek (Co. Meath) 83, 145, 248-9
Dullard, Adam 163n.86
Dunboyne (Co. Meath) 63, 249
Duncan, earl of Carrick 121, 128n.140, 144,
  146, 163n.110, 176
Dundalk (Co. Louth) 89, 205
Dundrum (Co. Down), castle of 173-4
Dunshaughlin (Co. Meath) 83
Durrow (Co. Offaly) 38, 66, 84

Echtigern mac Máel Chiaráin (Eugenius),
  bishop of Clonard/Meath
  (pre1177-1191) 29, 61, 249
Éile Uí Cearbaill (Co. Offaly) 132
Éile Uí Fogartaig (Co. Tipperary) 132,
  160n.33
Elmley (Worcestershire) 111, 157
Emlagh (bar. Lower Kells, Co. Meath)
  249-50
Escorchebeuf, Roger de 256
Escotot, Anketil de 256
Escotot, Richard de 30, 275n.105
Escotot, William de 256
Essarts, Roger des 139, 150
Évreçin 24-5, 40, 90, 241, 244, 260
d'Évreux, Nicholas 219, 256, 260
d'Évreux, Saint-Taurin 40, 140, 144, 147-8,
  150, 244-5
d'Évreux, Stephen 212, 243, 260
Ewyas Lacy, lordship of 21, 23-5, 43n.49, 81,
  107, 212, 215, 224, 247, 282

Fachlet, manor of 249
Falaise (Calvados) 81, 103, 242
Feckenham (Worcestershire) 39, 46n.118
Feipo, Adam de 29, 44n.55, 61, 256, 273n.29
Feipo, Richard de 143
Fenagh (Co. Leitrim) 184
Ferrers, William, earl of Derby 169, 170,
  187n.17
Fews of Armagh (Co. Armagh) 205
Fir Cell (bars Ballycowan, Ballyboy and
  Eglish, Co. Offaly) 38, 132, 146
Fithdwinterwod, tuath of 96n.27
Fitz Alan, family of 22

325

INDEX

Fitz Alan, William (d. 1160) 22, 270, 277n.151
Fitz Alan, William (d. 1210) 107, 267
Fitz Alexander, John 176
Fitz Alured, John 140
Fitz Nicholas, Ralph 199
Fitz Peter, Geoffrey earl of Essex 97n.40, 124n.22
Fitz Walter, Robert 148
Fitz Warin, Fulk (d. 1258) 107, 154, 263
Fitz Warin, Fulk (d. 1264) 269
Flanders, Thomas of 61
Flipou (Eure) 44n.58
Foliot, Gilbert, bishop of London (1163–87) 23, 25
Follistown (Co. Meath) 30
Fore (Co. Westmeath) 31, 35, 40, 140, 145, 249
Fors, William de, count of Aumale 157, 198
Fotharta Uí Núalláin (bar. Rathvilly, Co. Carlow) 59
Fourches, William de 105, 239–40
Furness (Cumbria), abbey of St Mary of 219–20, 256

Galloway, Alan of 121, 145–6, 163n.110, 205
Galloway, family of 121, 128n.138, 205
Galloway, Thomas of, earl of Atholl 121, 163n.110, 176, 193, 196
Galtrim (Co. Meath) 132, 145
Garbestown (Co. Meath) 30
Geneville, Geoffrey de 254
Geoffrey, duke of Brittany 78
Geraldine family 30, 48, 51
Glamorgan, lordship of 80, 111, 214
Gloucester (Gloucestershire) 154, 168, 174, 226n.46
castle of 104, 198
Gloucester, Miles of, earl of Hereford 103
Gloucester, monks of 24
Gofraid, son of Domnall mac William 145
Goodrich (Herefordshire) 168
Gray, John de, bishop of Norwich (1200–14) 138, 145–6
Gregory IX, pope (1227–41) 221–2, 232n.215
Gros, William le 205, 209, 228n.94
Grosmont (Monmouthshire) *see* Three Castles
Gruffudd ap Llywelyn 196
Guala, papal legate 168, 170, 185
Guðrøðr Óláfsson (Gofraid mac Amlaíb), king of Man and the Isles 57, 83
Guðrøðr Rǫgnvaldsson (Gofraid Donn) 200

Gwenllian, dau. Llywelyn ab Iorwerth 193, 268
Gwenwynwyn of Powys 171

Hákon IV, king of Norway (1217–63) 200–1
Haughmond abbey (Shropshire) 10, 22, 270
Hay (Powys) 156, 215
Hayestown (Co. Meath) 257
Henry I, king of England (1100–35) 22, 30, 186n.6
Henry II, king of England (1154–89) 5, 14, 24–5, 30, 34, 38, 45n.106, 81, 111, 140, 150, 185, 239–40, 244, 257, 261, 279, 282
Grant of Meath 12, 21, 26–8, 31–3, 36–7, 158, 245, 248, 255
and Ireland 14 21–2, 26–8, 31–4, 36–7, 39–41, 43n.40, 48–53, 55–60, 63, 65, 68, 69n.18, 81, 105–6, 157–8, 248, 280, 285
and Walter de Lacy 78–9, 282
Henry III, king of England (1216–72) 155, 166n.191, 175, 197, 200–1, 207, 211, 213–20, 223–4, 255, 285
Minority government of 5, 11, 158, 167–72, 174–5, 179–80, 185–6, 194–5, 201, 269, 280, 283–5.
Hereford (Herefordshire) 137, 177–9, 188n.84, 213, 243
castle of 99, 157, 177, 196–7, 199, 255
Hereford Domesday 23
Hereford, Adam of 69, 133
Hereford, earls of 63, 103, 259, 283
see also Bohun, Henry de; Gloucester, Miles of; Roger
Hereford, Hamo of 213, 220
Hereford, St Guthlac, priory of 10, 79
Hereford, Ursell, son of Hamo of 213
Holme Lacy (Herefordshire) 25, 47, 239, 257
Honorius III, pope (1216–27) 170, 172, 180, 195, 197
Hugh, canon of Llanthony 219, 256

Incheleffer (Co. Longford) 145, 249
Inge, king of Norway (1185–1217) 144
Innocent III, pope (1198–1216) 14, 118, 147–50, 152, 156

Joan, dau. King John, married King Alexander II of Scotland 200–1
Joan, dau. King John, married Llywelyn ab Iorwerth 118

INDEX

John, lord of Ireland (1185-1216), later king of England (1199-1216) 14, 80, 83-5, 91, 94-5, 101-4, 107, 110, 112, 118-19, 122, 139, 144, 147-9, 152, 172, 177-8, 185, 191, 194, 198, 221, 223, 280
 French wars 102-3, 107, 112, 114, 149-52, 244
 and Ireland 2, 5, 10-12, 14, 17n.49, 49, 55, 64-5, 68, 72n.95, 77-8, 81, 84-6, 88-94, 101, 109-11, 113-17, 119-23, 130, 137, 146-7, 155-6, 158, 176, 180, 182-3, 191, 200, 280, 282-3, 285
 1185 Irish expedition 12, 57-8, 64-5, 68, 95n.2, 130
 1207 crisis 130-7, 158-9, 169, 283
 1210 Irish expedition 14, 136, 141-4, 159, 284
 and community of Meath 110, 142-3, 145, 260-2
 grants in Munster 65, 86-7, 90, 106, 111, 158
 and lordship of Meath 78, 81-4, 88-9, 94-5, 110, 137-8, 142-3, 145, 153, 155, 169, 172-3, 181-2, 240, 255, 261, 280, 283
 and Magna Carta civil war, 1215-17 130, 153-8, 167-9
 and William de Briouze 103-6, 111, 131, 134-41, 214, 262, 281
John the Scot, earl of Huntingdon 193

Kells (Co. Meath) 84, 143, 145, 248-9, 259
Kilbixy (bar. Moygoish, Co. Westmeath) 84, 89, 145
Kilclare, wood of (Co. Offaly) 66
Kildare (Co. Kildare) 49, 217-18, 222
Kilkea (Co. Kildare) 59
Kilkenny (Co. Kilkenny) 194, 226n.14, 274n.58
Kilkieran (Co. Meath) 245, 273n.36
Killare (bar. Rathconrath, Co. Westmeath) 29, 61-3, 82, 249, 253
Killeen (Co. Meath) 29, 44n.55
Kilmainhambeg (Kells, Co. Meath) 221
Kilmore (Co. Cavan) 145, 183, 207
Kinnerley (Shropshire) 194
Knights Hospitaller 192, 221-2, 224
Knocktopher (Co. Kilkenny) 59

La Corner, Richard de, bishop of Meath (1231-52) 260
La Marche (Haute-Vienne, cant. Ambazac) 151

La Réole (Gironde) 151
La Rochelle (Charente-Maritime) 151
Lacy, Agnes de 44n.56
Lacy, Alice de 269
Lacy, Amaury de (d. 1186) (Claville) 24-5, 39, 42n.24, 80, 139, 241-2
Lacy, Amaury de, son of Gilbert de Lacy (Claville) 260
Lacy, Egidia de 206, 228n.102, 268-9
Lacy, Elayne de 267
Lacy, Gilbert de (d. c.1163) 22-5, 39, 44, 80, 103, 107, 139, 241
Lacy, Gilbert de (d. 1230) 115, 166n.183, 181, 191, 208, 210-13, 215, 224, 229n.140, 243, 255, 257, 260, 268-9, 271, 272n.23
Lacy, Gilbert de, son of Amaury de Lacy (Claville) 24, 42n.23, 242, 260
Lacy, Gilbert de, son of Hugh de Lacy (d. 1186) 80-1, 112, 194, 244
Lacy, Hugh de (d. c.1115) 23, 264
Lacy, Hugh de (d. 1186) 21-2, 26, 33, 79-80, 238, 263-4, 266, 277n.137
 and the Church 28, 66, 83, 244, 248-9
 bishop of Hereford 25, 42n.27, 47
 death 25, 66-7, 77-8, 81-2, 87-8, 244, 280
 and England 22-5, 34, 39, 47, 51, 193, 225n.7, 239-40, 242-3, 267, 269-70, 277n.150, 277n.151
 household and affinity 29-30, 63, 256, 258-9, 267
 and Ireland 26, 34-5, 38-9, 40, 47-8, 52, 54, 63, 68, 72n.90, 82, 86, 94, 110, 183, 255, 264, 266, 271, 280
 castle building 29, 35, 53, 59, 61-3, 247, 253
 grant of Meath 4, 21-2, 26-8, 31, 36-7, 40, 49, 51, 60, 72n.93, 110, 158, 161, 239, 245-8, 255
 and John, lord of Ireland 65, 68, 78, 95, 106, 123, 130
 as royal administrator 27-8, 35, 48, 51, 53-6, 58-61, 64-5, 68, 247, 255, 279, 282
 and Ruaidrí Ua Conchobair 33, 37, 53-60, 63, 68, 248, 267
 stature in Ireland 57, 59-61, 63-4, 68, 77-8, 123, 130, 247, 264-5, 267
 subinfeudation of Meath 28-30, 43n.52, 62-3, 162, 247, 249-50, 273
 and Tigernán Ua Ruairc 31-3, 35, 40, 60, 267
 and King Henry II 5, 39-40, 48, 58-61, 64, 67-8, 258, 279, 282

327

Lacy, Hugh de (d. 1186) (*cont.*)
    and Normandy 24, 34–5, 37–40, 80, 139–40, 239, 241–5, 279
    transnationality 3–4, 9, 14, 21, 25, 29–30, 39–40, 60, 237, 239, 242, 244, 251, 253–5, 268, 279–80, 286
    and Wales 24–6, 241, 247, 266
Lacy, Hugh de, earl of Ulster (d. 1242) 89, 102, 108, 115, 122, 131–3, 135–6, 138–44, 206–7, 211, 223, 244, 259–60, 262, 265–6, 271, 276n.111, 276n. 114, 280
    1223–4 rebellion 184, 192–207, 223–4, 269, 281, 284
    Albigensian Crusade 139, 150–1, 192
    and Connacht 86, 89, 98n.87, 108–10, 118, 120–2, 206, 231n.197
    and Irish Sea region 119, 121, 200–1, 205, 223, 285
    and Le Pin-au-Haras (Orne) 80–1, 96n.19, 112, 244, 273n.33
    and the Marshals 119, 191–4, 197, 200, 216, 218, 223, 279, 281, 283–4
    and Meath 30, 82–3, 92, 96n.27, 143, 147, 193–4, 203, 207
    and Ulster 109, 116–23, 126n.56, 142–3, 146, 151, 153, 169, 174, 183, 186, 191–4, 206–7, 210, 216, 221, 223–4, 281, 285
Lacy, Ilbert de (d. 1093) 21
Lacy, John de, constable of Chester 58–9, 61
Lacy, John de, later earl of Lincoln (d. 1240) 139
Lacy, Juliana de 268
Lacy, Katharine de 230n.149, 243, 257, 268
Lacy, Margery de (nee Briouze) 101, 105, 122, 157, 178–9, 187n.17, 221–2, 224, 228n.102, 232n.215, 267–8
Lacy, Petronilla de 268
Lacy, Robert de (d. pre 1166) 23–5, 41n.12, 80–1, 241–2, 263
Lacy, Robert de (d. pre 1189) son of Hugh de Lacy (d.1186) 79–80, 244, 263
Lacy, Robert de, son of Hugh de Lacy (d. 1186) 115, 131, 133, 161n.48
Lacy, Robert de, of Colemere, son of Gilbert de Lacy (d. 1230) 212, 243, 269–70
Lacy, Robert de, of Rathwire (d. pre 1215) 30, 203
Lacy, Roger de 81
Lacy, Rose de, dau. Gilbert de Lacy (d. *c*.1163) 30
Lacy, Walter de (d. 1085) 21
Lacy, Walter de (d. 1241) 12, 77–9, 238, 263, 277n.137

    and Briouze family 101–2, 105–6, 111–14, 116, 122–3, 130, 137–8, 140–1, 147, 156, 171, 178–80, 185, 228n.102, 267–8, 281
    and Burgh family 86–7, 89, 106, 110, 113, 115–16, 122–3, 178–80, 185, 202, 206, 208, 211, 213, 222, 224, 249, 268–9, 285
    and the Church 140, 144, 147, 165n.149, 192, 212, 219–22, 224, 244–5, 260, 263–4
    confiscation and fines 88, 90–2, 107, 132, 142–3, 146, 148–9, 152–3, 155, 159, 173, 198, 202, 206–7, 221, 223, 242, 255, 258, 266, 281, 283–5
    debt 177–8, 192, 213, 220, 222–4, 230n.148, 285–6
    and England 79, 80, 85, 91–3, 103–5, 107, 139, 152, 154, 156, 166n.194, 167–72, 174, 176–8, 181–2, 189n.109, 193, 197, 207, 211, 213, 219–20, 229n.140, 231n.202, 231n.203, 243, 254, 257, 261, 269
    household and affinity 143, 163n.86, 176, 181, 219, 203, 210, 219–20, 231n.202, 231n.203, 254, 256–62
    and Hugh de Lacy's 1223–4 rebellion 196–200, 202–4, 206–7, 227n.79, 266, 281
    and Ireland 67, 77–8, 84, 90, 92, 102, 107–9, 113–14, 120–3, 136, 139, 175, 182–4, 207–11, 216–18, 222, 225, 247, 267, 269
    1207 Irish crisis 130–4, 266
    1210 Irish expedition 130, 141–3, 227n.79, 266
    and John de Courcy 109–10 , 116–19, 266
    and lordship of Meath 30, 81–4, 86, 88–9, 94–5, 110, 119, 137–8, 140, 142, 152–3, 155, 169, 172–6, 181–3, 186, 193, 199, 202–4, 206–7, 213, 220, 240–1, 248–9, 254, 258, 261–2, 266, 280
    and King Henry III 213, 215–16, 224, 271, 285
    Minority government 168–70, 172, 177–9, 195–8, 202–3, 280, 284
    and King John 84–6, 88–95, 101–3, 110, 112, 130, 134–8, 141–3, 147–8, 151–2, 157–9, 173, 262, 280, 283–4
    and King Richard 79, 80, 82, 85–8, 90–5, 279–81, 283
    and Normandy 38, 80–2, 90–3, 102–3,

108, 111–13, 139–40, 144, 147, 241–2, 244
relationship with brothers 80–3, 109, 116–19, 121–3, 136, 142, 144, 151, 155, 173–4, 182–4, 192–3, 197, 202–4, 206–8, 223, 228n.110, 244, 248, 260, 265, 267, 271, 280–1
and Richard Marshal's 1233–4 rebellion 215–18, 268, 279, 282, 285
royal service
England and Wales 154, 156–7, 168–71, 180, 185, 196, 198–9, 211, 213
sheriff of Herefordshire 157, 168–9, 171–2, 174, 176–81, 185, 196–9, 223, 255, 280–1, 284
France 151, 211, 255
Ireland 86–8, 90, 94, 114–18, 120, 203–4, 209, 216–17, 228n.110, 255, 279
transnationality 3–5, 9, 14, 77–8, 81–2, 90–5, 105, 113–14, 119, 121, 123, 136, 149, 152–3, 181–2, 186, 191, 199, 202–3, 212–13, 219, 223–4, 237, 244–5, 251, 253–4, 256–8, 268, 270–1, 279–86
and Wales 80–1, 91, 102–3, 105, 123, 148–9, 152, 168–9, 171, 178–81, 187n.37, 213, 215, 247, 269
Lacy, Walter de the younger (d. 1240) 212, 223, 286
Lacy, William 'Gorm' de 60, 81, 131, 153, 155, 173–4, 181–6, 190n.139, 193, 197, 202, 205–6, 208, 211, 223, 244, 248, 260, 265–9, 285
Laigis (Co. Laois) 59, 61
Laragh (bar. Moygoish, Co. Westmeath) 250
Lassy (Calvados, cant. Condé-sur-Noireau) 13, 21, 24–5, 80, 112, 241–2, 244
Laurac (Aude, cant. Fanjeaux) 139, 150
Le Pin-au-Haras (Orne) 37–40, 80, 96n.19, 112, 239, 242, 244, 273n.33
Leighlin (Ballyknockan, Co. Laois) 49, 53, 59
Leinster 22, 26, 32, 49–50, 60, 69n.10, 246–7, 267
lordship of 12, 26, 39–40, 48–51, 55, 58–9, 61, 79, 81–4, 87, 108, 119–20, 133–5, 137, 142, 159, 185, 209, 216–18, 224, 274n.58, 279, 282–4
Leyburn, Robert of 219, 256
Limerick (Co. Limerick)
city of 87, 90–1, 105, 111, 113–16, 120, 122–3, 131–2, 134–5, 145, 175, 193, 196, 209, 215, 218, 231n.187, 283
honor of 69n.7, 105–7, 111, 113–14, 122–3, 126n.65, 131–2, 135–7, 142, 145, 158, 160n.36, 176, 183, 186, 196

Lincoln (Lincolnshire) 105, 157, 171
Lisardowlan (Co. Longford) 205, 228n.91
Lisieux (Calvados) 112, 242
Llanthony Priory 10, 16n.30, 23, 28, 43n.49, 43n.53, 44n.55, 83, 212, 219–20, 256, 263–4
Llantilio (Whitecastle, Monmouthshire) *see* Three Castles
Llywelyn ab Iorwerth, prince of Gwynedd 118, 121, 154, 156, 168, 170–1, 176–7, 181, 192–4, 196–7, 213, 215, 268–9, 281, 283
Lohleythi (Loch Ennell: Dysart, Co. Westmeath?) 249
London, Henry of, archdeacon of Stafford, later archbishop of Dublin (1213–28) 114–15, 174–6, 182, 193, 195, 199–200, 208
London, Maurice of 133
Longchamp, Henry 80
Longchamp, Stephen 80
Longchamp, William 80–1, 83–4, 95
Longespée, William, earl of Salisbury 149, 152, 169, 170, 195–6, 198, 202–3
Lough Sewdy (Co. Westmeath) 145, 249
Louis VII, king of France (1137–1180) 34, 150, 255
Louis VIII, son of King Philip II of France, later king of France (1223–26) 150–1, 155, 156–7, 168–70
Loxmethi, borough of 249
Lucy, William de 220, 231n.203, 243, 258
Ludlow (Shropshire) 4, 25, 51, 69n.20, 85, 91, 104, 107, 132, 134, 148, 152–3, 161n.58, 196, 202, 207, 220, 223, 257–8, 270, 275n.102
Luterel, Geoffrey 114
Lyonshall (Herefordshire) 260

Mac Carthaig, Diarmait, king of Desmond 205
Mac Cochláin, Ruaidrí mac Conchobair 38
Mac Murchada, Diarmait, king of Leinster 12, 26, 32–3, 49–50, 60, 66, 246
Macgne, son of Gerard de 256
Machaire Gaileang (bar. Morgallion, Co. Meath) 96n.27
Madog ap Gruffudd of Powys 269
Mag Cuillinn (Cooksborough, bar. Moycashel, Co. Westmeath?) 84
Magheradernon (Co. Westmeath) 63, 249
Magna Carta 155, 158, 167–9, 185, 239, 277n.126

INDEX

Man, Isle of 117–19, 143–4, 193, 200–1
Mandeville, Martin de 163n.86
Mansel Lacy (Herefordshire) 243
Marden (Herefordshire) 85, 97n.54, 182
Maredudd ap Rhobert of Cedewain 268
Marisco, Geoffrey de 134–5, 172–6, 180,
    182, 186, 208–9, 211, 216, 218, 220,
    269, 284
Marisco, William de 175, 210–11, 220
Marlborough (Wiltshire) 171
Marshal, Anselm 217, 222
Marshal, Gilbert 217, 220, 222
Marshal, John 115, 143, 196–7, 214
Marshal, Matilda 268
Marshal, Richard 119, 212, 214–20, 222,
    224, 255, 268–9, 279, 281–2, 285
Marshal, Walter 222
Marshal, William (d. 1219), earl of Pembroke
    2–3, 79–86, 89, 94–5, 97n.40, 104,
    114–15, 119, 121–3, 132–8, 141–5,
    154, 156, 159, 166n.191, 168–71,
    185, 191–3, 198, 215, 251, 258–61,
    274n.58, 282–4
Marshal, William (d. 1231) earl of Pembroke
    169–70, 181, 191, 194, 196–200,
    202–10, 214, 223–4, 260, 281, 283–4
Mauléon, Savaric de 155, 189n.89
Maurice fitz Gerald (d. 1176) 51
Maurice fitz Gerald (d. 1257) 211, 216, 222,
    231n.196, 305n.10
Mauvoisin, William, bishop of St Andrews
    140, 144, 163n.98
Meath, lordship of 4, 9–12, 21–2, 26–33,
    35–40, 48–9, 51–5, 59–64, 68, 78,
    81–4, 86–9, 93–5, 108, 110, 113–15,
    119–20, 132, 135, 137–8, 140–3,
    145–8, 152–3, 155, 158–9, 164n.122,
    172–4, 176, 181, 183, 185, 193, 197,
    200–3, 205, 207, 211–13, 218–20,
    224, 237, 239–41, 244–51, 253–4,
    258–61, 265–7, 269, 271, 280, 283
    community ('Foreigners') of 28–31, 38, 82,
        84, 96n.31, 110, 113, 131–4, 142,
        145, 155, 172, 197, 199, 248, 250–1,
        259, 261–2, 271
    Irish kingdom of Mide 21, 26–7, 31–3,
        43n.38, 50, 60–2, 64, 66, 72n.93,
        146, 183, 245–6, 248–9, 267,
        273n.41
Meiler fitz Henry 30, 59, 61, 93, 97n.48,
    108, 110–11, 113–16, 120, 131–7,
    158, 267
Meiler, son of Meiler fiz Henry 131–2
Meset, Peter de 163n.86
Mide *see* Meath

Minaluwy, land of 182, 189n.114
Moketree (Shropshire), forest of 269
Monktown (Co. Meath) 29
Monmouth, Baderon of 26, 33, 259, 266
Monmouth, Geoffrey of 62
Monmouth, John of 154, 157, 170–1, 178
Monmouth, Rose of 26, 67, 87, 266
Monmouth, St Mary's priory of 79
Montfort, Simon III de, count of Évreux
    (d. 1181) 24–5, 42n.24, 139
Montfort, Simon de (d. 1218) 11, 139, 150–1,
    161n.58
Montfort, Simon de (d. 1265) 140
Montgomery (Powys) 196–7
Mont-Ormel (Orne) 37
Morgallion (Co. Meath) 30
Mortimer, Hugh de (d. *c*.1181) 22
Mortimer, Hugh de (d. 1227) 154, 170–1
Mortimer, Robert de 178
Mortimer, Roger de 170
Mountsorrel (Leicestershire) 171
Moygarthan (Muinter Gearadain, east of Loch
    Gowna, Co. Longford?) 249
Moymet (Co. Meath) 89
Muinter Mailshinna (bar. Kilkenny West, Co.
    Westmeath) 38
Muinter Sercacháin (Co. Westmeath?) 38
Mullingar (Co. Westmeath) 135
Murchad mac Diarmada mic Maíl na mBó 50
Musard, Ralph 189n.89, 198

Narbonne (Aude) 151
Navan (Co. Meath) 30
Neauphe-sur-Dive (Orne) 37–8, 242
Netherwent (Monmouthshire), lordship of
    198
Netterville, Luke de, archbishop of Armagh
    (1218–27) 175
Newport (Gwent) 214
Nobber (Co. Meath) 109, 145, 203, 207
Norrach (now Narraghmore, bar. Narrach and
    Reban, Co. Kildare) 61
Northampton (Northamptonshire) 154
Nottingham (Nottinghamshire) 85
Nugent, Gilbert de 30, 61, 267

Oakley (*Acley*), Stephen of 212, 243
Óláfr Guðrøðarson (Amlaíb Dub), king of
    Man and the Isles 200
Onibury (Shropshire) 47, 242–3, 269–70
Oswestry (Shropshire) 156
Oxford (Oxfordshire) 180
    Council of (1177) 48–9, 51, 55–6, 65,
        69n.7, 95, 282
Oxford, David of 220

INDEX

Pandulf, papal legate 147-8, 284
Payne, Roger 242
Pec, Richard de 58-9, 61
Pembroke (Pembrokeshire) 26, 104, 119, 123, 181, 196
Petit, Adam le, archdeacon of Kells 259
Petit, Nicholas le 259
Petit, Ralph le, archdeacon of Meath 259
Petit, Walter le 219, 256, 259-60
Petit, William le 29-30, 62-3, 65, 114-16, 121, 133, 135, 143, 145, 162n.64, 249, 253, 259-62, 273n.29
Philip Augustus, king of France (1180-1223) 38, 78-81, 84-5, 102-3, 112, 114, 117, 119, 122, 135, 138-41, 147-52, 162n.71, 244, 255, 262, 266
Pin, Durand du 38, 80-1, 96n.24, 242, 244
Pipard, Peter 84, 86
Pipard, Roger 269
Poer, Robert le 49, 51, 53, 83
Pont-Audemer (Eure) 38, 242
Prendergast, Philip de 133
Propensée, André, mayor of Falaise 81

Radnor (Powys) 103, 156
Rahugh (bar. Moycashel, Co. Westmeath) 84, 203
Ranulf, earl of Chester and Lincoln 154, 169, 192-4, 198-9, 268-9
Rathbeggan (bar. Ratoath, Co. Meath) 131
Rathconrath (Co. Westmeath) 84
Rathfeigh (Co. Meath) 84
Rathkenny (Co. Meath) 63, 249
Rathwire (Co. Westmeath) 30, 203
Ratoath (Co. Meath) 83, 96n.27, 143, 147, 203, 207
Raymond le Gros 51, 59-61
Raymond, count of Toulouse 150-1
Rhodri ab Owain 118
Rhys ap Gruffudd of Deheubarth ('Lord' Rhys) 56, 91
Rich, Edmund, archbishop of Canterbury (1234-40) 218, 220
Richard fitz John, citizen of London 213
Richard fitz Ranulf 199
Richard, king of England (1189-99) 59, 77-80, 83, 85, 90-5, 102, 104, 110, 144, 152-3, 158, 167, 185, 281, 283
  and Ireland 81-3, 84-8, 95, 106, 110, 255, 279, 281-3, 285
Ridelesford, Walter de 59
Riqueot, Ralph de 256
Rivallis, Peter de 214-16, 285
Robert fitz Jordan 110, 240

Robert fitz Richard 61
Robert fitz Stephen 30, 50-1
Robert II, count of Meulan 2, 37-8, 40, 112, 181, 239, 242
Robert II, earl of Leicester 2, 112, 181
Roches, Peter des, bishop of Winchester (1205-38) 179, 213-16, 219, 284-5
Roger fitz Miles, earl of Hereford 23
Rǫgnvaldr Guðrøðarson (Ragnall mac Gofraid), king of Man and the Isles 83, 117-18, 121, 143, 144, 146, 163n.110, 200
Rye (Sussex) 170-1

Sai, Elias de 239
St Andrews (Fife) 121, 140, 144
St Valery, Matilda de 105-6, 143-4, 147
Saithne (bar. Balrothery West, Co. Dublin) 64, 72n.93, 83
Sancmille, Walter, castle of 203
Santry (Co. Dublin) 29
Sarnesfield, Philip of 240
Serland, William de 195-6
Shanonagh (bar. Moygoish, Co. Westmeath) 250
Shrewsbury (Shropshire) 154
Shrewsbury, Robert of 61
Shrule (Co. Longford) 63, 249
Silvain, Richard 93
Siward, Richard 217
Skenfrith (Monmouthshire) *see* Three Castles
Skreen (Co. Meath) 29, 61
Slane (Co. Meath) 43n.52, 52
Stanford (Worcestershire) 85, 97n.54
Stanton Lacy (Shropshire) 4, 23, 25, 85, 97n.54, 212, 223, 229n.141, 243, 260
Stanton, Hugh of 256
Staunton-on-Wye (Herefordshire) 229n.141
Stephen, king of England (1135-54) 5, 22, 40, 44, 103
Stoke Lacy (Herefordshire) 277n.150
Strange, John le 154
Strongbow (Richard fitz Gilbert de Clare) 22, 26, 30, 32-6, 39-41, 43n.52, 48-51, 57, 57, 60-1, 63, 68, 69n.18, 79, 119, 158, 247, 259, 266-7

Talbot, Geoffrey 44n.56
Talbotstown (Co. Meath) 30
Tara (Co. Meath) 62, 71n.80, 246-7
Tethba (Cos Longford and Westmeath) 54, 66
Thomond 87, 105-6, 113, 115, 131, 196, 218

331

INDEX

Three Castles, the 106, 122, 178–80, 198, 214
Thurles (Co. Tipperary) 35, 39, 135, 160n.33
Timahoe (bar. Cullenagh, Co. Laois) 30, 61
Tír Eógain 65, 117, 119, 145
Tlachtgha (Hill of Ward, Co. Westmeath) 31, 71n.80
Tosny, Ralph de 254, 268
Totnes (Devon) 103
Treóit (Trevet, bar. Skreen, Co. Meath) 96n.27
Trim (Co. Meath) 35–6, 38–9, 67, 143, 145, 182, 199, 202–3, 204–5, 207, 219–20, 223, 231, 249, 254, 256, 258–60, 264, 274n.62, 275n.90.
Tristernagh abbey (Co. Westmeath) 220
Troyes, Chrétien de 246
Tuit, Matthew de 260
Tuit, Richard de (d. 1211) 133, 143, 145, 173, 260, 262
Tuit, Richard de the younger 203, 260
Tullach Chiaráin (Co. Kilkenny) 84
Tullach Ua Felmeda (Co. Carlow) 84
Tyrell, Henry 84, 94, 161n.51
Tyrell, Hugh 30, 36
Tyrell, Richard 134, 161n.51, 163n.86, 193

Ua Brain, Fergal 39
Ua Brain, Murchad, king of Uí Fáeláin 31
Ua Braoin of Lune (Co. Meath) 66
Ua Briain, Diarmait 63
Ua Briain, Domnall Mór, king of Thomond 86–7
Ua Briain, Donnchad Cairprech, king of Thomond 142, 146, 193, 205, 218
Ua Briain, Muirchertach, king of Thomond 113
Ua Catharnaig, In Sinnach ('the fox') 54, 66
Ua Cerbaill, Máel Ísu, archbishop of Armagh (1184–5) 63–4
Ua Cerbaill, Murchad, king of Airgialla 63–4
Ua Conchobair, Áed (d.1067), king of Connacht 54
Ua Conchobair, Áed (d. 1228), king of Connacht 184, 202, 205–6, 208–11, 220, 269, 285
Ua Conchobair, Cathal Carrach, king of Connacht 108–10
Ua Conchobair, Cathal Crobderg, king of Connacht 87, 108–10, 113, 115–16, 120–1, 125n.53, 143, 145, 182, 184, 201–2, 205, 208
Ua Conchobair, Conchobar Máenmaige, king of Connacht 62–3, 82

Ua Conchobair, Feidlim, king of Connacht 219
Ua Conchobair, Murchad mac Ruaidrí 48
Ua Conchobair, Ruaidrí, king of Connacht 26–7, 32–3, 35 7, 39, 48–50, 52–60, 63, 68, 77, 82, 96n.31, 246, 248, 267
Ua Conchobair, Toirdelbach (d.1156), king of Connacht 54
Ua Conchobair, Toirdelbach mac Ruaidrí 113, 206
Ua Conchobair, Tomaltach, archbishop of Armagh (c.1179–84; 1185–1201) 57, 64
Ua Domnaill, Domnall Mór, king of Tír Conaill 183, 247
Ua Dubthaig, Cadla, archbishop of Tuam (pre1167–1201) 55
Ua Dúnáin, Máel Muire, bishop of Mide (pre1096–1117) 248
Ua hÉanna, Muirgeas (Matthew), archbishop of Cashel (pre1186–1206) 67, 87
Ua Máel Muaid, Gilla Colum 38
Ua Máel Ruanaid, Robert 199
Ua Máel Sechlainn, Art 54, 63
Ua Máel Sechlainn, Cormac mac Art 146, 173
Ua Máel Sechlainn, Diarmait, king of Mide 31–2, 50, 247
Ua Máel Sechlainn, Máel Sechlainn Beg 54
Ua Máel Sechlainn, Máel Sechlainn mac Cormac mac Art 146
Ua Máel Sechlainn, Magnus 38
Ua Máel Sechlainn, Murchad, king of Mide 33, 60, 245–7, 267
Ua Miadaigh, Gilla gan-inathair 66–7
Ua Néill, Áed Méith, king of Tír Eógain 117, 145–6, 200, 205–6
Ua Ragallaig's crannóg (Co. Cavan) 183
Ua Ruairc, Áed 184, 262
Ua Ruairc, Domnall 35
Ua Ruairc, Tigernán, king of Bréifne 27, 31–3, 35, 40, 50, 60, 71n.80, 267
Ua Ruairc, Ualgarg 183
Ua Tuathail, Lorcán, archbishop of Dublin (1162–80) 55, 57–8, 60
Uí Buide (bar. Mallyadams, Co. Laois) 61
Uí Chennselaig 32, 49–51.
Uí Dúnchada 49–50
Uí Dúnlainge 49–50
Uí Fáeláin 32, 39, 49–51, 59, 61, 247
Uí Failge 49–50, 54, 132–3, 137, 159n.13, 247, 283
Uí Felmeda 50, 84
Uí Muiredaig 43n.52, 49–50, 61
Uí Ragallaig 183–5, 247

INDEX

Uisnech, hill of (Killare, Co. Westmeath) 62, 71n.80
Ulaid 48, 52
Ulster 53, 63, 89, 108-9, 114, 117-20, 123, 135, 145-6, 176, 186, 196, 216, 266
   earldom of 118-23, 136, 142-3, 151, 153, 183, 191-7, 200-1, 205, 207-8, 210, 221, 223-4, 227n.79, 266, 281, 283, 285
Upavon (Wiltshire) 215

Valognes, Hamo de 88, 90
Vaudreuil (Eure, cant. Val-de-Reuil) 90, 92
Vaudreuil, Stephen de 92
Verdon, Bertram de 89
Verdon, Lescelina de 89, 244
Verdon, Nicholas de 89
Verdon, Thomas de 89
Verneuil-sur-Avre (Eure) 34-5, 39, 255, 279
Vesci, Eustace de 148

Waleran, count of Meulan 2, 40, 112, 181
Walter, Hubert, archbishop of Canterbury (1193-1205) 104
Walter, Theobald (d. 1205) 83-4, 89, 126n.67, 131-3, 160n.33, 193
Walter, Theobald (d. 1230) 193, 209-10, 269
Walton (Shropshire) 270
Waterford (Co. Waterford) 32, 35, 49, 53, 88, 142, 193, 209

Weobley (Herefordshire) 4, 21, 23, 25, 212, 223, 254, 257, 260
Westminster (London) 161n.51, 177, 222-3
Weston, Simon of 254
Wexford (Co. Wexford) 27, 32, 49, 51
Whittington (Shropshire) 194
Wichetot, Philip de 219, 254
Wicklow (Co. Wicklow) 49, 51, 138
William fitz Audelin 34, 37, 39, 41, 48-9, 51, 53, 55-6, 59
William the Lion, king of Scotland (1165-1214) 58, 105, 140
William, baron of Naas 102, 133
Windsor (Berkshire) 135, 147, 157
Windsor, Treaty of (1175) 37, 39, 48, 52, 54-7, 63, 246, 248
Wolvesey (Winchester, Hampshire) 171
Woodstock (Oxfordshire) 39, 42n.16, 141
Woodstock, council of (1207) 135-6
Wootton (Shropshire) 242, 270
Wootton, Amicia of, dau. Robert of Wootton 269
Wootton, Robert of 269
Wootton, William of 242-3, 269
Worcester (Worcestershire) 135, 171
Worcester, Philip of 64-5, 72n.95, 78, 88, 111, 137, 143
Wyck Rissington (Gloucestershire) 231n.203, 243

Yarkhill (Herefordshire) 25, 220, 231n.202, 257

333

EU authorised representative for GPSR:
Easy Access System Europe, Mustamäe tee 50,
10621 Tallinn, Estonia
gpsr.requests@easproject.com

www.ingramcontent.com/pod-product-compliance
Lightning Source LLC
Chambersburg PA
CBHW030324240426
43673CB00040B/1269